SHARING JESUS
with the CULTS

How to handle the most common
conversations Christians
get into with cult members

JASON OAKES

ISBN-13: 978-0692967959
ISBN-10: 0692967958

This book is dedicated to my wife Amy and three amazing children: Noah, Elijah and Jude. Thank you for all your love and encouragement these many years.

Thank you to the many others who contributed to the completion of this book. Proofreaders: Kevin Olivarez; Bill Fowler; Abigail McCoy; Eric Johnson; Michael Boehm. Editor: Margaret Lekse. Cover art and formatting: JOSEP Book Designs (*joseworkwork@gmail.com*).

CONTENTS

INTRODUCTION

The Meaning Behind the Title

The title "Sharing Jesus with the Cults" has a double meaning for me. The primary and obvious purpose of this book is to equip Christians to reach out to members of cults and pseudo-Christian groups. The second meaning has to do with the claim of most of the cults in this book to be "Christian." Many of the awkward conversations we have with members of these groups have to do with their insistence they follow Jesus, either in the same way we do or in a "better" way than we do.

The Focus of this Book

There are many great ministries, books, websites and resources dealing with Mormonism, Jehovah's Witnesses, and the other groups mentioned in this book. So why another ministry? Why write another book?

Most of the books, seminars, websites, podcasts and ministries dealing with these groups focus on the differences between these groups and Christianity. Most of the time, after listening to a podcast focused on this topic, or attending an entire day seminar focused on this topic, I personally feel most Christians are left thinking, "Wow, they're weird. I better stay away from those people. Glad I'm not one of them." While that's not the heart or the intended goal of so many great ministries, that seems to be the end result. Rather than creating a heart that desires to reach out with the gospel to members of these groups, it results in Christians either not wanting to have anything to do with these groups, or when they do speak with members of these groups, they focus on attacking the character of their leaders, contradictions in their history, or their unusual doctrines in a polarizing way. Even when individuals are effective in getting people to leave these false groups, they have left them with nothing to replace it with, and many tend toward atheism, agnosticism, another controlling group, or legalistic Christian groups.

I hope to focus on the basic essentials one needs to know when ministering to these groups. Following that, we will consider several tactics which will concentrate on sharing the "good news" with them. The desired result is to counteract a polarizing "us vs. them" mentality and to create more of a heart for those misguided and burdened souls. Because they have been given false information, they are erroneously trying to earn salvation and to please an inaccurately conceived version of God.

This book will focus on the most effective tactics I have used in my interactions with members of cults. My tactics have changed dramatically over time through much trial and error. The tactics I have landed on and will spend the bulk of this book focusing on how to deal with the most common conversations that naturally come up when a Christian talks with members of a cult. Most of these conversations tend to be awkward and polarizing. But I feel the Lord has given me insight into tactful ways to steer these dialogues toward conversations that will help others to experience the biblical Jesus, as well as introduce them to the reality of grace, the reliability and inspiration of the Bible, and understanding the doctrine of the Trinity.

Breakdown of the sections

Section #1 - What is a cult?

In this section, we ask what a group needs to believe and/or practice to be considered a cult. We identify the common traits of cults and cult leaders: the use of mind control, scripture twisting, and the connection to ancient heresies and American history. We also ask the question what a person/group needs to believe and/or practice to be considered Christian.

Section #2 - Overview of the cults

In this section, we cover the basic beliefs, history and terminology of the most predominant American cults. The cults we cover in this book are Mormons, Jehovah's Witnesses, Scientology, Christian Science, International Church of Christ, Seventh

Day Adventists, Twelve Tribes, New Apostolic Reformation, United Pentecostal Church International and Great Commission Churches.

Section #3 - Tactics

In this section, we discuss the different strategies Christians can use in sharing the gospel with members of cults. These tactics are based on the six most common conversations Christians get into with cult members. They include using Jesus as our "common ground," using the group's own scriptures and writings, communicating grace to the religious mind, the reliability of the Bible, explaining the Trinity and the Hebrews approach to reaching the cults.

What are the Six Conversations?

1. The moment the cult member says, "I'm a Christian too!" or "You don't think I'm a Christian, do you?"
2. The moment the cult member asks, "Have you read or prayed about our Scripture?"
3. Conversations with the cult member about grace in reference to salvation or rewards
4. Conversations about the cult member's claims the Christian church needed to be restored due to a complete apostasy, or the Bible being corrupted through truths being removed, changed or added.
5. Conversations about the Trinity
6. Conversations regarding the claims of cults to know more about Jesus, have a restored priesthood authority, have better or more Scripture, have a living prophet or their group better represents true Christianity or the early Christian church.

Who Am I?

Let me introduce myself a little bit. In 2002, I received a Bachelors degree in Church Ministry with an emphasis on preaching from Hope International University. I received a Master of Divinity degree from Bethel Seminary San Diego in 2006. I was called into ministry at the age of 17, and have been serving in ministry in various capacities for the last 20 years. I have served as Youth Pastor, College Pastor, Associate Pastor, Interim Pastor, Senior Pastor, as well as a couple of years as missionary In Central Utah to members of The Church of Jesus Christ of Latter-day Saints.

I have also served as an Adjunct Professor at Bethel Seminary San Diego, teaching the online class "Understanding the Cults." This book was written as a textbook for seminary level students with the wider purpose of being a resource that can be put in the hand of every Christian in an effort to equip them to reach out to members of these groups effectively. Beyond this is the more significant goal of seeing many come out of these groups and into a relationship with the biblical Jesus, who is able to save them to the uttermost.[1] I hope this book will help equip pastors to communicate the differences between these groups and biblical Christianity effectively. When this is done, perhaps many younger, ungrounded Christians can be prevented from being lured into one of these groups. It is a fact Christians are being intentionally targeted and even being swept away because they are seen as a primary audience and are likely to join these churches.

Why Am I So Passionate about Reaching Cult Members?

Reaching out to members of cults has been a primary focus of my life ever since I was in high school. My best friend growing up was part of The Church of Jesus Christ of Latter-day Saints, as was his family, and this was at a time when I was getting committed to my Christian faith. I was going to youth group, and my small group leader gave me a video called "The God Makers," and I went home watching it thinking I should learn a little bit about what my friend believes in helping me to relate to him better. About five minutes into the film, my jaw had hit the floor, and I couldn't believe what I was hearing. I knew I needed to talk to my friend. What I found was he was defensive. He often said, "We don't believe any of that stuff." There was a lot of denial and defensiveness from him.

I had a tactic in engaging my friend. If his response to my concern was, "We don't believe that," the two of us would go together to another LDS member and inquire about that matter. Quite often the person we sought out would affirm belief

---

[1] Hebrews 7:25

in what I had brought up as a problem. Over time, enough embarrassing doctrines were building up that my friend began to be confused. Soon he was saying he was having problems affirming certain LDS beliefs. One conversation we had brought things to a head. I became obvious I might risk our friendship if the discussion went any further, but I knew God wanted me to pursue him anyway. Suddenly, in anger and defensiveness, he blurted out something revealing when he said, "It doesn't matter whether I believe any of this or not. I was baptized as an LDS, so I am on their records. I will always be LDS, and there is nothing I can ever do about that." His statement to me is an example which helps illustrate the hold some of these groups have on their people. Even when they come to a place where they don't believe the doctrines, they feel like they will never escape the group.

That was the case with my friend, and once we hit that point, we were able to talk about that. I was able to help him understand that wasn't true. That he could leave the church, and in fact, he could embrace what he was coming to understand and believe about Jesus. The real, biblical Jesus. He started coming to Christian Club with me. He took baby steps, and eventually, he did give his life over to the biblical Jesus. When he went off to college, he got involved with a solid Christian group, and things have taken off from there. He is still my best friend and was the best man at my wedding.

Tongue-in-cheek, I often say after Steve came out of the LDS church, I was drawn into the LDS church. I didn't become a member or anything like that, but in my mind and my heart was a curiosity and interest which grew into a strong heart for these people. In addition, I had a friend who could tell me where all the Mormon bookstores were in town, so we would get equipped and get resources. Any time I see a missionary, even to this day, I'm the one who stops my car and goes out on foot, and tracks them down, introduces myself and wants to start a conversation. I've been friends with several Mormons. I've been able to challenge them to read the Bible while I read their Scriptures. They would go to church with me if I went to church with them, and then we would talk about the differences. As I went into the ministry and went through the ranks of Youth Pastor, Associate Pastor, College Pastor, Interim Pastor and Senior Pastor, I kept on studying these things. I kept on meeting with Mormon missionaries.

In 2012, the Lord put on my heart that he wanted to do something more with my strong interests. I went through a church planting assessment with the thought

I was going to go out to Utah and plant a church that would plant churches. What ended up happening was I got the go ahead, but as we went out to Utah, what I found was I resonated more with the missionaries in Utah than the pastors. One primary reason was the pastors felt pressure not to be vocal or intentional about reaching LDS people out of fear the LDS would have their church shut down. We decided to move to Utah in January 2013 as missionaries. We moved to a town called Manti, which has a population of 3,000 people: Ninety percent LDS, and five-tenths percent Christian. We jokingly would say my family doubled the size of the Christian population in Manti at the time. Manti is where they have the Mormon Miracle Pageant every year at the temple. They hold a play there annually that thousands upon thousands of people have attended. They re-enact the history of the LDS church and the history of the Book of Mormon. It's a huge evangelistic thing.

We lived there for about a year and a half before God called me back to California temporarily, and then on to where I am now. I'm currently Senior Pastor of Emmanuel Baptist Church in Roundup, Montana. I'm thankful the Lord has me where I am. And interestingly enough, most of the people who visit our church have an intersection with the cults somewhere in their own past, or they have people close to them who are a part of one of these groups.

In 2012, before we moved to Utah, I started offering seminars on how to reach out to Mormons to the churches within my region. I was having a conversation with Dr. John Lillis, who was the Dean of Bethel Seminary at the time, about possibly coming and doing a special equipping seminar at one of the events where they reach out to the community. We had lunch, and all of the sudden, the conversation shifted to, "Maybe there's a possibility of you doing a class with us, doing something online." Then I met with Dr. Arnell Motz, who is now the acting Dean of Bethel Seminary. He happened to be the head of the department with which I needed to interact. We both felt this was something the Lord had for us to do. I'm grateful for the opportunity.

Other Voices

What may have come across so far is most of my experience has been talking with LDS people. That is absolutely and unapologetically true. I have had interactions with Jehovah's Witnesses, and I have studied the groups discussed in this book, but since my knowledge is limited, I'm enlisting the help of others who are in ministry to the groups discussed in this book. They have given me full permission to use their materials. Several voices have contributed to this book.

One of the contributing voices is Michael Boehm from Youth Apologetics Training. He lives in Colorado and has a podcast.[2] His podcast covers different worldviews, and he interviews many different great scholars. Next is Nathan Young, who specializes in witnessing to Jehovah's Witnesses.[3] He lives in Europe, has written a couple of books, and has a YouTube channel. His material will be covered on the topics covering the New World Translation and the Trinity.

How to Get in Contact with Me

So there you have it … me in a nutshell, and that's the book in a nutshell. Thank you for taking the time to read this book, especially if you are leading a small group equipping others. If you have any questions that you want to direct to me personally, please don't hesitate to get in touch with me. I would enjoy sharing more with you, and I would be willing to schedule a speaking engagement with your group. You can get in contact with me for all of these purposes at the following:

Facebook - www.facebook.com/peopleofthefreegift
Youtube - www.youtube.com/c/JasonOakesPeopleOfTheFreeGift

---

[2] www.youthapologeticstraining.com

[3] http://www.jwanswers.co.uk/

SECTION 1

WHAT IS A CULT?

Beloved, believe not every spirit, but test the spirits to see whether they are from God, because many false prophets have gone out into the world. (1 John 4:1)

CHAPTER 1

Common Traits of a Cult

What is a cult? There are many well-intentioned churches out there with some of these traits. There are so many definitions. Cults are most often religious groups using teachings and social structures to exhibit a strong and/or controlling influence over its members financial, material and social circles.[4] A single cult leader mainly drives their beliefs and a specific set of religious beliefs unique to that group. A cult is a group that has split off an orthodox type group with a set line of teachings. Most of the groups discussed in this book are Christian cults, so they split from orthodox Christianity, and then they start denying the essential doctrines of the Christian faith, and even the secondary doctrines of the Christian faith.

They might accept one or two of the core doctrines, but for the most part, they will deny the essential doctrines, and then they will go after the secondary doctrines, which aren't essential, but if one is a Christian, they probably should be believing these things.

There's usually a single leader everybody gathers around. They split from orthodox Christianity and create what is usually referred to as a sect. A sect is a little splinter

---

[4] Shelley, Marshall, What's a Cult? http://www.christianitytoday.com/iyf/advice/faithqa/what-is-cult.html

group that splits off and doesn't have a huge influence.[5] They don't have one single leader, although sometimes they do. They're not as far out as cults.

Cults will often start coming up with their own special revelations, and they'll start taking their group off on a whole new trail, a trail nobody has gone down for thousands of years, yet this group has special revelation. Sometimes they'll claim the original apostles believed this, but somehow corruption came down the line. There was a significant falling away or something like that. Now, everything is corrupted, Christianity is of the devil, and salvation is through this little cult group.

One will find in many cult groups the cult will become the mediator between them and God. So one can't get to God except through this cult. A cult is then a group of people polarized around someone's interpretation of the Bible and is characterized by major deviations from orthodox Christianity relative to the essential doctrines of the Christian faith.

Notably, God became man in Jesus Christ.

These groups are all lead by false teachers and false prophets. We are warned about false teachers throughout the Bible.

Every cult has a single, influential, human leader. This group leader is always right. Group leaders are often the exclusive means of knowing truth or receiving validation. No other process of discovery is acceptable or credible.

Questioning doctrines, especially doctrines coming from the leader, is discouraged. Often there is no tolerance for questions or critical inquiry of the cult leaders words or teachings of the cult. They are to become absolute truth, overshadowing the Word of God.

The convenient answer is the Bible is corrupt. If what the group teaches is a match, they will use the Bible as a proof text. If it doesn't match, the Bible is corrupt.

They claim to have found secrets not revealed in Scripture. These groups are often guilty of adding to the Bible with other publications or revelation. Each cult uses pressure tactics to coerce its members into submission. Some cult leaders will teach a Jesus not found in the Scriptures.

The cults often ask their converts to leave their families. One is urged to pull away from worldly influences all together.

---

[5] Sect http://www.dictionary.com/browse/sect

When leaving a cult, there is no legitimate reason to leave. Former followers are always wrong for leaving, harmful or even evil.

Cults will have an unclear doctrinal statement, or they will have radical changes in their doctrine.

One will find these teachings in many cult movements. The repetitive phrases, meditation, speaking in tongues. Another trait of cults is the cult leader, and its leadership will dictate all the major, and even minor, decisions in one's life. The leader is not accountable to any authorities. Some cult groups will encourage their members to take part in things considered unethical or flat-out sinful, but they'll justify it because "the ends justify the means." Often they'll couch that in Christian language.[6]

---

[6] Boehm, Michael, What is a Cult? Common Traits of Cults, Youth Apologetics Training podcast http://w w w.sermonaudio.com/sermoninfo.asp?SID=52132250162

CHAPTER 2

Common Traits of a Cult Leader

Just as there are basic commonalities regarding characteristics of cults as groups, there are some basic commonalities when it comes to the leaders of these cults. There will be some overlap from the previous chapter covering common traits of cults themselves, but also some unique characteristics found in cult leaders and the process they use in forming a cult.

The first thing a leader of a group that will soon become a cult needs to establish is the Bible is not valid. It has been corrupted, or has taught false things, or has been misunderstood over the course of Jewish and Christian history. But anyway they can, the cult leader will take their followers or potential follower's eyes off of the Bible as an authority for doctrine or practice.

The second way the cult leader will establish dependence of the group upon them is by redefining otherwise familiar terms or coming up with their own set of terms and definitions. This further creates the feeling within the group they are not able to understand the Bible by themselves, but need the interpretation of the group and its leader. This also allows the leader to create new doctrines or new ways of looking at historic doctrines.

Third, the cult leader will shift their focus from taking people's eyes off of the Bible to putting their eyes, attention, devotion, upon them. Many cult leaders have done this through special revelation or the finding or creating of new Scripture. Since they have established the Bible to be untrustworthy, when they release the new Scripture, it will be seen as having more authority than the Bible right out of the gate.

When new Scripture disagrees with the Bible, the group and cult leader will favor more modern revelation, which will further put the Bible in the distant background.

One doctrine cult leaders will almost always change will be to move away from Orthodox Christian teachings about Jesus. Jesus will have a different identity, origin, death, resurrection, purpose, etc... In doing so, it allows the leader to establish his move away from grace toward works and complete dependence on the group and the group for salvation.

The cult leader will further the dependence upon the group by creating a unique culture controlling the cult member's behavior, information, thoughts and emotions. Over time, the cult members begin looking the same, acting the same, believing the same, and only having relationships with members of the cult.

The last move completes the circle. With new definitions, new Scripture and new doctrines, the cult leader will point back to the Bible to show their beliefs were taught in the Bible, maybe even prophesied, all along. This is a robust method of attracting new converts. This step may also at times include the re-translation of the Bible using special revelation.[7]

---

[7] Heart of the Matter Episode 342, Nemelka, part 2 https://youtu.be/TVTqFB1M78Y

CHAPTER 3

Mind Control and the Cults

In the 1950's Robert J Lifton conducted a groundbreaking study of techniques used to successfully brainwash captured American pilots to convert to the Communist ideology.[8]

Following these discoveries, others, such as Steven Hassan, who had come out of the Moonie cult, started connecting the dots between mind control practiced by totalitarian government structures and religious cults.[9]

Mind Control vs. Brain Washing

Many people confuse the terms brain washing and mind control. Both the person performing the brain washing, as well as the person who is being brain washed, know deception is taking place. They are usually physically abused or tortured, and the person brain washing them is the enemy. They have their life threatened, or family member's life threatened. The result is known as thought reform. They willingly change their way of thinking to save their life or protect someone they love. This binds them to the organization's leader.

---

[8] Lifton, Robert, Thought Reform and the Psychology of Totalism: A Study of "Brainwashing" in China

[9] Hassan, Steven, Combatting Cult Mind Control: The #1 Best-selling Guide to Protection, Rescue, and Recovery from Destructive Cults

When mind control is taking place, neither the person performing the mind control, nor the person it is being performed on, need to know what is occurring. The person it's being perpetrated on has no way of knowing they are being deceived. It's usually done by a friend or peer, or somebody seen as an authoritative figure. The person under mind control does not feel any threat or danger. They usually see it as a positive outcome. Still, it results in thought reform and binds them to an organization's leader.

Many people are prone to mind control simply because we have a desire to fit in and belong. Many people even desire to be told what to do. The IQ of people in these groups can be over 130 according to studies.

B.I.T.E. Model

Steven Hassan was recruited in the 70's by the Moonies. After a couple of years, he was able to get out and be reprogrammed. He did the research himself, went through schooling, and became an expert in this field.

He came up with one of the most important research items, the B.I.T.E. model, which is a pneumonic showing the four areas a group takes control of an individual, making them dependent on the group leader. The B in the B.I.T.E. model stands for behavior control. I - information control. T - thought control. E - emotional control. The theory of cognitive dissonance states if one of these areas can be affected, the others will shift over time. As soon as one can change all four of those areas in an individual, they will be under mind control.[10] A snapping point is when everything starts to unravel when somebody is in one of these organizations.

Behavior Control

First is B, for behavior control. Cults will perform behavior modifications to control their members. They will tell people what to wear, how to wear their clothes, hair, earrings and tattoos. They will tell them what to eat. They will regulate their time. They will regulate their interactions with people. They will demand perfection

---

[10] McLeod, Saul, Cognitive Dissonance, Simply Psychology, published 2008, updated 2014 http://www.simplypsychology.org/cognitive-dissonance.html

and strict obedience. At times they will have bizarre rituals and ordinances. They will have financial obligation or commitments on the group. Individualism is discouraged and "group think" prevails.

For example, the LDS church will have their members wear their temple garments 24/7. When they go to church, they must dress in business attire and be cleanly groomed. They only allow one piercing. No tattoos. They regulate what a person eats and drinks with the Word of Wisdom. Many LDS people will spend up to 22 hours a week doing church related activities between family home evenings, home teaching, scripture study, prayer, Wednesday night mutual, campouts, temple trips and three-hour blocks of meetings. They regulate who one interacts with, especially apostates. The purpose of all these requirements is to keep their members from having time to stop and think about what they believe and why.

An example of strict obedience would be the following quote. "Always keep your eye on the President of the Church, and if he ever tells you to do anything, and it is wrong, and you do it, the Lord will bless you for it... But you don't need to worry. The Lord will never let his mouthpiece lead the people astray."[11]

Information Control

Next in the B.I.T.E. acronym is I, which stands for information control. Cults withhold information, lie, or do truth bending, or change history altogether. They will tell people what they can and cannot read, and of course no critical information or material is ever okay. They label it anti-material.

These organizations will always teach the Bible is not trustworthy. Only the group's leaders can interpret it correctly, and all other interpretations are wrong. They will have pyramid style doctrines. They will not teach anything up front. They will distort information to make it more acceptable.[12] They will encourage members to spy on each other. They will encourage extensive use of group materials, such as church magazines, church newspapers, church photos, church books, etc. New revelations trump old ones, so members are only to pay attention to the new revelations. Lastly,

---

[11] Heber J. Grant, quoted by Marion G. Romney in Conference Report, Oct. 1960, p. 78

[12] Fear and Mind Control http://www.jwfacts.com/watchtower/fear-cult-mind-control.php

these organizations will hide their leader's false prophecies or criminal and immoral behaviors and downplay them.

Examples of information control:

Boyd K. Packer said, "There is a temptation for the writer or the teacher of Church history to want to tell everything, whether it is worthy or faith promoting or not. Some things that are true are not very useful."[13]

"False religious propaganda from any source should be avoided like poison! Really, since our Lord has used "the faithful and discreet slave" to convey to us "sayings of everlasting life," why should we ever want to look anywhere else?"[14]

"Employers have a right to expect that their Christian employees will 'exhibit good fidelity to the full,' including observing rules on confidentiality. There may be occasions when a faithful servant of God is motivated by his personal convictions, based on his knowledge of God's Word, to strain or even breach the requirements of confidentiality because of the superior demands of divine law. Courage and discretion would be needed. The objective would not be to spy on another's freedom but to help erring ones and to keep the Christian congregation clean."[15]

"From time to time, there have arisen from among the ranks of Jehovah's people those, who, like the original Satan, have adopted an independent, faultfinding attitude...They say that it is sufficient to read the Bible exclusively, either alone or in small groups at home. But, strangely, through such 'Bible reading,' they have reverted right back to the apostate doctrines that commentaries by Christendom's clergy were teaching ..."[16]

Other examples of information control in Mormonism is Joseph Smith burning down the printing press and missionaries not teaching the deep doctrines until one is inside because it's a need to know basis, and one must be indoctrinated in a pyramid type scale. Home teaching is a means of encouraging members to spy on one another by coming into a person's home to find out if they are reading the Scriptures, praying, obeying the Word of Wisdom, and then they report to their superiors.

---

[13] Packer, Boyd K.,"Do not spread disease germs!" Brigham Young University Studies, Summer 1981

[14] *Watchtower* 1987 Nov 1 p. 20 http://www.jwfacts.com/watchtower/fear-cult-mind-control.php

[15] *Watchtower* 1987 Sep 1 p.15 http://www.jwfacts.com/watchtower/fear-cult-mind-control.php

[16] *Watchtower* 1981 Aug 15 p. 29 http://www.jwfacts.com/watchtower/fear-cult-mind-control.php

They will instill in their members that everything is taken out of context, everybody is a liar, the internet is evil, and there is always some worldwide conspiracy against their organization.

Thought Control

The T in the B.I.T.E. acronym stands for thought control. These groups will always instill in their members they have the only truth, and they are the only way to salvation. They teach their members what are called thought stopping techniques. This allows them to stop critical thinking and shuts down their ability to think for themselves. When they are in a confrontation, they're getting upset, somebody's making a good point, cult members are taught to fall back on these thought stopping techniques.

For the LDS, they bear their testimony, they sing a song, they pray to get out the evil spirits, or they say contention is of the devil and shut down the conversation. When this happens, they no longer have a normal, rational conversation about the good and bad of the point being discussed.

If there are any questions, they are always to go to their superiors or the apologists to answer them. They are never to figure it out on their own. They will instill in their followers there is no legitimate concern about a leader or a doctrine. And there is never a legitimate reason to leave the organization. It's always the person's fault, never the organization.

They teach apostates left the group because they did something wrong or somebody hurt them. They are untrustworthy liars, so don't listen to them. Don't talk to them.

Black and white thinking exists. Members think in terms of good vs. evil, us vs. them, inside vs. outside.[17] They attack the person. They don't attack the information because that is what they've been trained to do.

An example of thought control:

"Enlightenment proceeds from Jehovah... and is given to the faithful anointed.... the remnant are instructed by the angels of the Lord. The remnant do not hear audible

---

[17] Fear and Mind Control http://www.jwfacts.com/watchtower/fear-cult-mind-control.php

sounds, because such is not necessary. Jehovah has provided his own good way to convey thoughts to the minds of his anointed ones."[18]

Emotion Control

Last in the B.I.T.E. acronym is E for emotion. Cults will all use guilt and fear heavily. They will make one afraid ever to leave or question the group. They will use their family and their peers to manipulate their emotions and to keep them from leaving or to keep them in line behaviorally. They will teach all feelings are not from God. Good feelings are from God and bad feelings are from Satan. They will teach feelings are the ultimate source of truth.

Irrational fears of leaving or questioning the group or authority figures within the group are planted subconsciously through phobia indoctrination. This is in addition to fears of thinking independently, fear of the "outside" world, fear of enemies and fear of disapproval.[19] They will encourage the belief that happiness only exists inside the group, or there will be terrible consequences if one leaves the group. There might even be real threats of losing family, either in this life, or for eternity. God won't hear their prayers. They will be a failure if they leave. They will be Satan's for eternity.[20]

An example of guilt use within the LDS would be the unethical use of confession, such as a Court of Love, where a member will have to tell all of their sins, including all of the details.

Cults will use one's past sins to manipulate them. There will never be forgiveness or absolution of sins without complete obedience. Examples within the LDS church would be "Those who receive forgiveness and then repeat the sin are held accountable for their former sins."[21] "To remain forgiven, we must never commit the sin again."[22]

Another technique cults use is called the double bind.[23] This is when it is believed there is more than one possible answer to a question or situation when in fact there

---

[18] Preparation p.64 http://www.jwfacts.com/watchtower/fear-cult-mind-control.php

[19] Fear and Mind Control http://www.jwfacts.com/watchtower/fear-cult-mind-control.php

[20] Alma 34:35

[21] Gospel Principles, 1997, p. 253

[22] Mormon Missionary Discussion F, Uniform System for Teaching Families. 1981, p. 36

[23] Gibney, Paul, The Double Bind Theory: Still Crazy-Making After All These Years http://www.psychotherapy.com.au/fileadmin/site files/pdfs/TheDoubleBindTheory.pdf

is only one answer that is acceptable. This is precisely what the Book of Mormon Challenge is. Missionaries encourage a prospective member to read and pray about the Book of Mormon and the LDS church based on little information the LDS person has given them. One is forbidden to read any critical information because if one reads that they're not going to get the right answer. Then they tell the prospective member how to interpret the answer to their prayer, which is, of course, going to be an emotion. The person feels like they have three options, but in reality, they only have one option. They feel like they can say yes, no or I don't have an answer yet. If they say yes, they get baptized. If they say no, the missionary is already conditioned and preprogrammed to tell them how it's their fault. Then the LDS member will modify the prospective member's behavior by having them stop drinking tea or coffee, going to church or reading Scripture. They will continue modifying their behaviors until they begin thinking there is something wrong with them, they give the response the LDS person wants, or they tell them to go away. There is in fact only one right answer.

Top 10 Signs of Mind Control

10. The organization does not allow scrutiny.

9. One runs to the organization's leaders and apologists to explain away all of their concerns.

8. One is unhappy in their organization, but can't see leaving as an option.

7. One dismisses facts because they are scary.

6. One believes there is no happiness ever outside of the group and their life will crumble.

5. One had to change their behavior to become worthy to receive the correct answer to prayer.

4. One fears anti-material because they think the devil will deceive them.

3. One thinks emotions decipher truth.

2. One doesn't think anyone could ever have a legitimate reason to leave their organization.

1. One thinks there is a worldwide conspiracy against their group.[24]

---

[24] Heart of the Matter Episode 348: Mormonism and Mind Control http://hotm.tv/ep-348/

All mind control organizations use the B.I.T.E. model and the double bind to get people to listen to their message and be bound to their group leader. They're going to alter one's behavior. They're going to limit their information. They're going to control their thoughts and emotions. They're going to destroy their ability to think critically. There is only one way to defend this, and it's not to give up one's ability to do critical thinking. Don't give up the ability to look at the good and bad about what the organization is teaching. Don't trust emotions to decipher truth. This is why the Bible teaches time and time again the heart is deceitful, it bears false witness and it cannot be trusted.[25]

"Before he reaches adulthood your child should be so imbued with true knowledge that he will be able to stand up to crucial tests of his faith applied by a hostile world. You have no time to lose. Recent history provided the spectacle of grown men being brainwashed and transformed into putty in the hands of their captors simply because they had never been given any real foundation for faith. A few years of teaching, therefore, will not suffice. A progressive program of training is called for, one that will mold your child's life from infancy right through to adulthood."[26]

---

[25] Proverbs 28:26; Jeremiah 17:9; Matthew 15:19

[26] *Watchtower* 1964 Mar 1 p. 138

CHAPTER 4

Scripture Twisting and the Cults

In this chapter, we will focus on the ways the cults twist the Scriptures.[27] If one wanted to explore this topic in-depth, I would recommend a book by James Sire called Scripture Twisting and the Cults.[28]

The term "scripture twisting" can be found in a statement the Apostle Peter made concerning what some false teachers were doing with the letters written by the Apostle Paul.

> **And account [that] the longsuffering of our Lord [is] salvation; even as our beloved brother Paul also according to the wisdom given unto him hath written unto you; As also in all [his] epistles, speaking in them of these things; in which are some things hard to be understood, which they that are unlearned and unstable wrest, as [they do] also the other scriptures, unto their own destruction. (2 Peter 3:15-16)[29] [30]**

A couple of things I want to point out. First off, Peter referred to Paul's writings as Scripture or being on the same level as Scripture. That's huge for our discussion of

---

[27] Scripture Twisting: Read me First! https://bible.org/article/scripture-twisting-read-me-first

[28] Sire, James, Scripture Twisting: 20 Ways the Cults Misread the Bible

[29] 10 Bible Verses about Twisting https://bible.knowing-jesus.com/topics/Twisting

[30] Twisting God's Word https://www.openbible.info/topics/twisting_gods_word

Why Should We Trust the Bible in Tactic #4. Here's a contemporary of Paul saying there are some things in Paul's writings hard to understand and some people are twisting them. The second thing is some people are twisting the Scriptures.

Inaccurate Quotation

The Biblical text is quoted, but either misquoted or wrongly attributed to another source.

Example: The Maharishi Mahesh Yogi said, "Christ said, 'Be still and know that I am God.'"[31]

Twisted Translation

The biblical text is retranslated without consulting any of the Hebrew, Aramaic or Greek manuscripts. The purpose of the re-translation is to fit a preconceived teaching of the group.[32]

If cults do not redefine words within accepted biblical translations, they will create their own, such as the New World Translation of the Jehovah's Witnesses, the Joseph Smith Translation of the LDS, the Clear Word Translation of the Seventh Day Adventists, the Passion Translation of the NAR, etc.

Example: the Jehovah's Witnesses translate John 1:1 as "In [the] beginning the Word was, and the Word was with God, and the word was a God."

This translation creates a polytheistic structure within the Godhead, or at best a henotheistic structure,[33] which has become the new terminology used by the LDS.

Biblical Hook

The biblical text is quoted to gain the attention of the hearer or give authority to the speaker, then followed up non-biblical teaching by the speaker or by pointing to a non-biblical source.

---

[31] Yogi, Maharishi Mahesh, Meditations of Maharishi Mahesh Yogi, p. 178
[32] Scripture Twisting Methods of the Cults http://www.apologeticsindex.org/5849-scripture-twisting
[33] http://www.merriam-webster.com/dictionary/henotheism

Example: Mormon missionaries quote James 1:5 which promises God's wisdom to those who ask him and, then, follow this by explaining when Joseph Smith did this he was given a revelation from which he concluded God the Father has a body.[34]

This application is asking God for specific knowledge, not wisdom, and it has nothing to do with the context of the statement in the book of James.

Ignoring the Immediate Context

A verse of scripture is quoted, and meaning is drawn from it, that ignores or contradicts, either the verses immediately surrounding the verse or the whole counsel of God.

Example:[35] ("You search the Scriptures, because you think in them you have eternal life"), claiming Jesus was challenging his listeners' overemphasis of the Old Testament, but the remainder of the immediate context reads, "and it is they that bear witness to me; yet you refuse to come to me that you may have life" (verses 39-40), which shows Jesus was upholding the value of the Old Testament as a testimony to Himself.

Collapsing Contexts

Individual biblical verses are paired together with others to build a doctrine that could never be found if studying those same verses in their original context.

Example: The Mormons associate Jeremiah 1:5 with John 1:2,14 and thus imply both verses talk about the pre-mortal existence of all human beings. Jeremiah 1:5, however, speaks of God's foreknowledge of Jeremiah (Not his pre-mortal existence) and John 1:2 refers to the pre-existence of God the Son and not to human beings in general.

Over-specification

A more detailed or specific conclusion than is legitimate is drawn from a biblical text.

Example: The Mormon missionary manual quotes the parable of the virgins from Matthew 25:1-13 to document the concept that "mortality is a probationary period

---

[34] Pearl of Great Price, Joseph Smith - History 1

[35] Romney, Marion G., "Labor Today," Conference Report, April 1954, p. 131-135

during which we prepare to meet God." But the parable of the virgins could, and most probably does, mean something far less specific, for example, human beings should be prepared at any time to meet God or to witness the Second Coming of Jesus Christ.

Word Play

Reading a translation of the original Hebrew, Aramaic or Greek and drawing too much out of the origin of the "translated" word or phrase, causing one to interpret the verse or passage in a way that was never intended.

Example: Mary Baker Eddy said the name Adam consists of two syllables, A DAM, which means an obstruction, in which case, Adam signifies "the obstacle which the serpent, sin, would impose between man and his Creator."[36]

The Figurative Fallacy

Mistaking figurative language for literal language or vice versa.

Examples:

Mary Baker Eddy interprets evening as "mistiness of mortal thought; weariness of mortal mind; obscured views; peace and rest."[37]

The Mormon theologian James Talmage interprets the prophecy "thou shalt be brought down and speak out of the ground" to mean God's Word would come to people from the Book of Mormon which was taken out of the ground at the hill of Cumorah.[38]

That's one of my favorite prophecies in the Book of Mormon, and it will become obvious why when we talk about using the Book of Mormon to teach biblical doctrine when talking with LDS in Tactic #2.

Speculative Readings of Predictive Prophecy

Interpreting prophetic passages in the Bible in a way that applies them to events that no other scholar agrees with and goes outside the bounds of sound interpretation.

---

[36] Milmine, Georgine, The Life of Mary Baker Eddy and the History of Christian Science, p. 191

[37] Eddy, Mary Baker, Science and Health with Key to The Scriptures, Chapter XVII - Glossary

[38] Talmage, James E., The Articles of Faith

Example: The stick of Judah and the Stick of Joseph in Ezekiel 37:15-23 are interpreted by the Mormons to mean the Bible and the Book of Mormon.[39] This is in spite of the fact the passage states the imagery of the two sticks is speaking of the uniting of the Northern and Southern kingdoms of Israel.

Saying but Not Citing

Referring to a verse or teaching within the Bible without citing where that verse or teaching may be found in the Bible. Often the verse or teaching is not found in the Bible.

Example: A common phrase "God helps those who help themselves" or "give a man a fish, and he'll eat for a day. Teach a man to fish and he'll eat for a lifetime" is not found in the Bible.[40]

Selective Citing

Citing part of a verse to make a point when citing the entirety of the verse or examining the entirety of biblical teaching on that topic would lead to a different conclusion.

Example: The Jehovah's Witnesses critique the traditional Christian notion of the Trinity without considering the full text which scholars use to substantiate the concept.

I find this is classic stuff atheists bring out when they're talking about biblical "contradictions." Most of the people have not done their homework, and they're trying to make us look bad.

Inadequate Evidence

A hasty generalization is drawn from too little evidence.

Example: The Jehovah's Witnesses teach blood transfusion is non-biblical, but the biblical data they cite fails either to speak directly to the issue or to substantiate their teaching adequately.

---

[39] Richards, LeGrand, A Marvelous Work and A Wonder, p. 67-68

[40] Sayings Not Found in Scripture https://www.blueletterbible.org/faq/sayings.cfm

Confused Definition

Redefining or reinterpreting a biblical term, causing the meaning of a passage or doctrine to be distorted or rejected.

Example: One of Edgar Cayce's followers confuses the eastern doctrine of reincarnation with the biblical doctrine of being born again.[41]

Oprah stating she rejected the Bible when she read God is a jealous God and interpreted that as God being jealous of her, which is a misrepresentation of that text.[42] As a result, Oprah has started publicizing many new and strange doctrines on her show.

Ignoring Alternative Explanations

Interpreting a biblical text differently than it has been traditionally interpreted, and then pretending this interpretation is the only one that is possible.

Example: Erich von Daniken asks why in Genesis 1:26 God speaks in the plural ("us"), suggesting this is an oblique reference to God's being one of many astronauts and failing to consider alternative explanations that either God was speaking as "Heaven's king accompanied by His heavenly host" or the plural prefigures the doctrine of the Trinity expressed more explicitly in the New Testament.[43]

The Obvious Fallacy

Using words like obviously, undoubtedly, certainly, all reasonable people hold that, etc... as a substitute for a logical argument to make a valid point. Words like this assume or hint that the other person is a fool or not using logic.

Example: Erich von Daniken said, "Undoubtedly the Ark [of the Covenant] was electrically charged!"[44]

---

[41] Van Auken, John, Born Again & Again: How Reincarnation Occurs and What It Means to You

[42] OprahReallyBelievesthatGodisJealousofHerhttps://www.youtube.com/watch?v=Oxao4LmTMfU

[43] Von Daniken, Erich, Chariots of the Gods? p. 18

[44] Von Daniken, Erich, Chariots of the Gods? Chapter 11

Virtue by Association

A cult writer associates his or her teaching with those of figures accepted as authoritative by traditional Christians, or cult writings are likened to the Bible, or cult literature imitates the form of the Bible writing such that it sounds like the Bible.

Examples:

Rick Chapman list 21 gurus, including Jesus Christ, St. Francis and St. Theresa, "you can't go wrong with."[45]

Juan Mascaro in his introduction to the Upanishads cites the New Testament, the Gospels, Ecclesiastes and the Psalms, from which he quotes passages supposedly paralleling the Upanishads.[46]

The Mormon Doctrine & Covenants interweaves phrases from the Gospel of John and maintains a superficial similarity to the Gospel such that it seems to be like the Bible.[47]

The Book of Mormon plagiarizes the King James Version, even when there are grammatical, spelling and other errors during the process of translation that has since been corrected in the updated versions of the King James Version.[48] The Book of Mormon was written in Elizabethan English which wasn't spoken at the time of the people in the Book of Mormon, or in Joseph Smith's day. But the LDS say the Book of Mormon has a familiar spirit, which we will get into later in this book in Tactic #2.

Esoteric Interpretation

The belief that the Bible can only be properly understood by a limited few because its real meaning is hidden, esoteric, or only open to those initiated into its secrets.

Examples:

---

[45] Sire, James, Scripture Twisting: 20 Ways the Cults Misread the Bible, p. 101

[46] Mascaro, Juan, The Upanishads. Translations from the Sanskrit, with an Introduction by Juan Mascaró

[47] Frederick, Nicholas J., Illuminating the Text of the Doctrine & Covenants through the Gospel of John https://rsc.byu.edu/archived/you-shall-have-my-word/illuminating-text-doctrine-and-covenants- through-gospel-john

[48] Plagiarism http://www.mormonismdisproved.org/plagiarism.html

Kabbalah and many New Age and occult-based religion, which go all the way back to Gnosticism in the late 1st and 2nd centuries, and emphasize secret knowledge will get one to higher levels of heaven when they die.[49]

Many cult leaders claim this knowledge and authority and use it to give them control. An example of this is how the Jehovah's Witnesses rehearse questions and answers from their magazines to interpret the Bible in the way their leaders do, not on their own.

Mary Baker Eddy gives the meaning of the first phrase in the Lord's Prayer, "Our Father which art in heaven," as "Our Father-Mother God, all harmonious."[50]

Supplementing Biblical Authority

New revelation from post-biblical prophets either replaces or is added to the Bible as authority.

Example: The Mormons supplement the Bible with the Book of Mormon, the Doctrine & Covenants and the Pearl of Great Price. Christian Science supplements the Bible with Science and Health with Key to the Scriptures.

Rejecting Biblical Authority

Either the Bible as a whole or texts from the Bible are examined and rejected because they do not agree with other authorities, such as reason or revelation.

Example: The Articles of Faith for the LDS church states, "We believe the Bible to be the Word of God as far as it is translated correctly." [51]They will use the Bible and discuss the Bible until they disagree with something a passage says, and then they will say, "That must be one of the passages that weren't translated correctly."

---

[49] New Age Movement: New Age or Old Occult? http://www.rapidnet.com/~jbeard/bdm/Cults/newage.htm

[50] The Lord's Prayer, Christian Science Quarterly Bible Lessons http://biblelesson.christianscience.com/related-information/the-lord-s-prayer

[51] Pearl of Great Price, Articles of Faith 1:8

Worldview Confusion

Using a statement, verse, or passage from the Bible, applying it to another religion or worldview, and giving it an entirely different meaning from its original and intended meaning.

Examples:

This is what Gnosticism did with Christianity, and they made it into something unrecognizable as Christianity. This is also what many of the groups represented in this book do when they redefine terms, bringing the members to only one conclusion of how to interpret any given passage of Scripture.

The Maharishi Mahesh Yogi interprets "Be still, and know that I am God" as meaning each person should meditate and come to the realization he is essentially Godhood itself.[52]

---

[52] Osho meets with followers of Maharishi Mahesh Yogi, Sat Sangha Salon: An Inquiry in Being https://o-meditation.com/osho/osho-meets-with-followers-of-maharishi-mahesh-yogi/

CHAPTER 5

Mormonism and Scripture Twisting

Becoming Gods

I have said, Ye [are] gods; and all of you [are] children of the most High. (Psalm 82:6)

Jesus answered them, Is it not written in your law, I said, Ye are gods? (John 10:34)

The LDS claim is the Hebrews were more technically Henotheists that believe in one God but acknowledge the existence of other gods. When the Jewish reforms came later under Hezekiah and other kings, the Hebrews became monotheist and then edited their Scriptures.

Jesus quotes an Old Testament scripture to the Pharisees, "You are gods," which referred to children of the Most High. This would have included not only Jesus but the Pharisees. Unless the LDS are willing to believe the Pharisees were gods while they were still alive, this can't mean what they want it to mean.

The Hebrew word Elohim is used in several different ways. Most of the time, it is speaking of the one true God. Even in LDS terminology, they teach Elohim is the personal name of Heavenly Father, so there is a contradiction when dealing with Psalm 82 when it refers to other Elohim.

In the Old Testament, Moses in Exodus 7 and a couple of other places, is referred to as an Elohim to Pharaoh. Yet LDS do not teach Moses was a literal member of the Divine Council. Here is an example of a human judge who would die as a human, which is what is said in Psalm 82.

The other problem that exists with interpreting Psalm 82 as referring to other gods is Yahweh declares these other gods would die like humans. Unless one believes the LDS interpretation that God is subject to the priesthood, and can be removed from Godhood, this is a problem.

> **For though there be that are called gods, whether in heaven or in earth, (as there be gods many, and lords many,) (1 Corinthians 8:5)**

Many of these misinterpretations can be resolved by looking at the whole passage of Scripture. The verse before and the verse after clears this particular misinterpretation up by saying while many are called gods, there is only one real God.

Below are some other verses that can be used to challenge the idea there are other gods, or there is a Divine Council, or even the LDS view the Godhead consists of three separate gods.

Isaiah 44:6 speaks of two beings, God and the Lord.

> **Thus saith the LORD the King of Israel, and his redeemer the LORD of hosts; I [am] the first, and I [am] the last; and beside me [there is] no God. (Isaiah 44:6)**

Isaiah 43:10-11 says there are no other gods formed before or after him.

> **Ye [are] my witnesses, saith the LORD, and my servant whom I have chosen: that ye may know and believe me, and understand that I [am] he: before me there was no God formed, neither shall there be after me. I, [even] I, [am] the LORD; and beside me [there is] no saviour. (Isaiah 43:10-11)**

Bible translations do some harm. In a debate between James White and Martin Tanner about the possible existence of other gods, Martin Tanner quoted from the Good News Translation of Psalm 82 which says, "God stands in the Divine

Council."[53] This gives the impression the Israelites were like the Canaanites and other surrounding groups that taught the Most High God presided over a Divine Council of other legitimate gods.[54]

These groups also point to the Dead Sea Scroll translation of Deuteronomy 32 to teach God appointed other gods over the nations after disinheriting them at Babel and Yahweh adopted Israel as his chosen people.[55]

The terminology these groups point to as speaking of the Divine Council can be easily interpreted as references to angels, such as "sons of God" and "heavenly hosts."

Some have called Joseph Smith the master religious synthesizer. He would take passages nobody had a clear interpretation of, and build them into entire belief systems.

Some examples:

Pre-Existence

Hebrews 12:9 - Father of our spirits

> **Furthermore we have had fathers of our flesh which corrected [us], and we gave [them] reverence: shall we not much rather be in subjection unto the Father of spirits, and live? (Hebrews 12:9)**

Acts 17:28 - We are his offspring

> **For in him we live, and move, and have our being; as certain also of your own poets have said, For we are also his offspring. (Acts 17:28)**

Jeremiah 1:5 - Before humans were in their mother's womb, God knew them

> **Before I formed thee in the belly I knew thee; and before thou camest forth out of the womb I sanctified thee, [and] I ordained thee a prophet unto the nations. (Jeremiah 1:5)**

---

[53] Can Men Become Gods? James White vs Martin Tanner https://youtu.be/x-Lg8ncs24
[54] Heiser, Michael, The Divine Council http://www.thedivinecouncil.com/HeiserIVPDC.pdf
[55] Heiser, Michael, Deuteronomy 32:8 and the Sons of God http://www.thedivinecouncil.com/DT32BibSac.pdf

Joseph Smith took those concepts and formed a theology we all existed as literal spirit children of heavenly father before coming to this earth.

As Christians, we can easily show Joseph Smith must be wrong in his interpretation of these verses by citing a few other verses:

> **And he said unto them, Ye are from beneath; I am from above: ye are of this world; I am not of this world. (John 8:23)**

Jesus is expressing the contrast between himself and humanity. I am from above. You are from below. I am not of this world. You are of this world. I am the Son of God. I was sent from heaven. (We did not all descend from heaven).

> **Howbeit that [was] not first which is spiritual, but that which is natural; and afterward that which is spiritual. (1 Corinthians 15:46)**

First, we have our natural bodies, and then we get our spiritual body.

Baptism for the Dead

> **Else what shall they do which are baptized for the dead, if the dead rise not at all? why are they then baptized for the dead? (1 Corinthians 15:29)**

What scholars do know from the context is this is something the Christians weren't practicing. They know this because Paul uses "I, we, you" language all throughout this passage, and all of the sudden Paul uses "they" when he refers to those who were being baptized for the dead.

Paradise and Spirit Prison

For the LDS person, the LDS church teaches people go to the Spirit World, either to Paradise or Spirit Prison. Both of those terms are used in Scripture, and Joseph gave them new definitions and meanings.

By which also he went and preached unto the spirits in prison;
(1 Peter 3:19)

Every single occurrence, except for one, where it is clarified, when the word spirit is used in the plural in the Bible, it is used to speak of evil spirits. The word for preach is the general "proclamation." I believe this links back to Genesis 6 and the evil spirits who were in the days of Noah before the flood.

For for this cause was the gospel preached also to them that are
dead, that they might be judged according to men in the flesh,
but live according to God in the spirit. (1 Peter 4:6)

This passage simply teaches the "dead" people mentioned had the gospel preached to them while they were still physically alive. They since have died, but they were made alive in the Spirit.

And beside all this, between us and you there is a great gulf fixed:
so that they which would pass from hence to you cannot; neither
can they pass to us, that [would come] from thence. (Luke 16:26)

The rich man is calling out to Abraham asking for a drop of water on his tongue. Abraham responds by saying, "There is a great gulf fixed, so that those who would pass from us to you cannot." One cannot pass from one side of the Spirit World to the other. Therefore, no Mormon missionaries are traveling from Paradise to Spirit Prison. And if that is the case, then nobody in Spirit Prison can receive the baptism for the dead done on their behalf in Mormon temples.

Jesus Submitting to the Father

The LDS, and many of the other groups discussed in this book, love to point out verses such as the following to show Jesus was not equal with the Father, and therefore can't be God, and can't be the second person in the Trinity:

Then answered Jesus and said unto them, Verily, verily, I say unto
you, The Son can do nothing of himself, but what he seeth the

> **Father do: for what things soever he doeth, these also doeth the Son likewise. (John 5:19)**

> **I can of mine own self do nothing: as I hear, I judge: and my judgment is just; because I seek not mine own will, but the will of the Father which hath sent me. (John 5:30)**

> **Ye have heard how I said unto you, I go away, and come again unto you. If ye loved me, ye would rejoice, because I said, I go unto the Father: for my Father is greater than I. (John 14:28)**

> **Jesus saith unto her, Touch me not; for I am not yet ascended to my Father: but go to my brethren, and say unto them, I ascend unto my Father, and your Father; and to my God, and your God. (John 20:17)**

All of those things Jesus said because he was in our place. From the LDS mindset, Jesus came to get his body, to finish his assigned task, so that he could progress to Godhood. For Christians, as Philippians 2 says, Jesus emptied himself of his Godhood to become one of us to stand in our place. Scripture says he was tempted in every way like we are, yet without sin.[56] Jesus felt the full weight of temptation because he never gave in. We all as human beings tap out to temptation at some point. Jesus never did. So Jesus can sympathize with us in our weaknesses because he was truly one of us and truly stood in our place. He was able to truly "become sin" so we might become "the righteousness of God."[57]

Jesus took on an additional nature. He took on human flesh. When he did that, he agreed to do it entirely "in the will of God" and "by the power of the Holy Spirit." Jesus indeed modeled the life we can have in him. He lived life the same way we, as his believers, can.

This is Jesus saying, in this flesh, on this earth, I submit myself to the Father, so that I can play this role. This in no way takes away from John, Paul, Peter and the other New Testament writers saying Jesus is God.

---

[56] Hebrews 4:15

[57] 2 Corinthians 5:21

CHAPTER 6

Ancient Heresy, American History and the Cults

Ancient Heresies

Gnosticism + Arianism + Restoration Movement = Mormonism

Gnosticism + Metaphysical Movement = Christian Science

Gnosticism + Psychology = Scientology

Arianism + Adventism = Jehovah's Witness

Restoration Movement + Discipleship Movement = International Church of Christ

Adventism = Seventh Day Adventist

Communal Living = Twelve Tribes

Charismatic Movement + Metaphysical Movement = New Apostolic Reformation

Restoration Movement + Charismatic Movement = United Pentecostal Church International

Discipleship Movement = Great Commission Churches

Let's connect the dots of theology and church history concerning the groups being discussed in this book. In the chart above I list both the ancient heretical factors that influenced the formation of these modern-day groups as well as particular phenomena in American history that also played a part in the creation of these groups. Some of these groups have deep roots in ancient heresies while others are relatively recent phenomena that had a significant influence on their origins and beliefs.

Two ancient heresies play a considerable role in the foundation of these cults, Gnosticism and Arianism.

Gnosticism has two significant components. The first is dualism, which means all matter is evil and everything spiritual is good. The other main characteristic of Gnosticism is secret knowledge. Gnosis is the Greek word for knowledge.[58] That is why this movement has become known as Gnosticism. Gnosticism was around before Christianity, but it did what Hinduism and Islam have subsequently done, as well as other religions, and that is to swallow up Christianity as part of their system and make it part of it.[59]

Christianity doesn't fit Gnosticism at all, but Jesus was thrown in the middle of it, and several secret gospels were written. These secret gospels are being plugged prominently today.[60]

The first group that was influenced by Gnosticism is Mormonism.[61] The whole thrust surrounding obtaining Celestial Glory revolves around the temple ceremony. In the temple ceremony, one learns all the secret handshakes, tokens and covenants of the priesthood necessary for them to get past the guardian sentinels, so to speak, in the afterlife. When they die, one cannot gain entrance to the Celestial Kingdom and progress to become gods without this secret knowledge. That is purely a Gnostic idea.[62]

The other groups profoundly influenced by Gnosticism is Christian Science and Scientology.[63] [64] Christian Science borrows the Gnostic dualistic belief all matter is evil and teaches matter is an illusion.[65] A teaching made famous by the film "The Matrix." Scientology borrows from the secret knowledge component of Gnosticism.

---

[58] The Gnostic World View: A Brief Summary of Gnosticism http://gnosis.org/gnintro.htm

[59] Ninan, M.M., Emergence of Hinduism from Christianity, p. 99

[60] The Nag Hammadi Library http://gnosis.org/naghamm/nhl.html

[61] Owens, Lance, Joseph Smith: America's Hermetic Prophet, Gnosis: A Journal of Western Inner Traditions, Spring 1995

[62] Oakes, Jason, Gnosticism and Mormonism https://drive.google.com/file/d/0ByFtvrDqTG6JS DF0czg0bXh2aWc/view

[63] Christian Science: A non-Christian Religion http://www.letusreason.org/cults18.htm

[64] Scientology and Gnosticism http://www.bible.ca/scientology-gnostic-roots.htm

[65] A Study of Denominations: Christian Science http://www.astudyofdenominations.com/denominations/science/

The other major ancient player was Arius, who represented the other side of the Nicene Council. The Council of Nicaea will be discussed in detail later in this book. Alexander brought the idea of the Trinity and Arius brought the catchphrase "there was when he was not" about Jesus.[66] The followers of Arius taught Jesus was greater than the angels and greater than humans, but there was a time when he was not. That he is, in fact, a created being. The language of the "begotten" Son of God, the "firstborn" of all creation, while biblical, took on a whole new meaning for the followers of Arius.

The Jehovah's Witnesses are, in reference to their belief about the relationship between Jehovah and Jesus, the direct descendants of Arius as they are teaching what Arius taught.[67]

The LDS also teaches Jesus is a literal spirit child of Elohim, as Lucifer was, as all humanity is.[68] They teach he is the one through whom God created the worlds.

These are the ancient connections. What about the connections to phenomena in American history?

American History

When the founders came to America, some specific moments began to take prominence. One of these was the Restoration Movement, started by Thomas and Alexander Campbell, which taught the church needed to be restored. The church had gone apostate or had become so corrupted there was no hope of reform from the inside. They also taught the creeds needed to be abandoned because they were human products of this corrupt church.[69]

---

[66] Arianism http://www.newadvent.org/cathen/01707c.htm

[67] Dorsett, Tommy, Modern Day Arians: Who are They? http://www.watchman.org/articles/other-religious-topics/modern-day-arians-who-are-they/

[68] Porter, Bruce D. and McDermott, Gerald, Is Mormonism Christian?https://www.firstthings.com/article/2008/10/003-is-mormonism-christian

[69] Mallett, Robert, Restoration Movement: "What Do You Mean, Restoration Movement?" http://www.thecra.org/about us/restoration movement

The Restoration Movement was highly influential on the LDS. In fact, one could say the LDS are the direct ancestors of the Restoration Movement.[70] All Joseph Smith added to this way of thinking was a new Scripture to restore what was lost.

This movement also indirectly brought us the International Church of Christ, which broke off the mainline denominational Church of Christ and Christian Church movement.[71] There are instrumental and non-instrumental branches of the denominational Church of Christ. The Restoration Movement also brought us the Disciples of Christ.

Because the American continent was believed to be a new undiscovered world, there was a feeling by some this might be the New Jerusalem.[72] This idea brings with it the idea Jesus was going to come back very, very soon. Once this belief took root, people started calculating when Jesus was going to come back. This brought us William Miller and the Great Disappointment of 1844.

After the Great Disappointment, two groups formed: The Seventh Day Adventists and Jehovah's Witnesses.[73] Both Ellen White and Charles Taze Russell were part of William Miller's Bible Student movement. They both came up with solutions to the theological problem created by the Great Disappointment.

The next American phenomena that influenced the formation of these groups was the Metaphysical Movement. Phineas Quimby was unintentionally influential in turning Christianity into a scientific system. His work planted the seeds for both Mary Baker Eddy of Christian Science and E.W. Kenyon from the Word of Faith movement.[74]

The Charismatic Movement brought a renewal of the Spirit of God, but it also brought with it a dangerous tendency to allow experience to supersede the Bible as the basis for truth. Some branches started questioning significant doctrines such as the Trinity while other branches began re-establishing the offices of apostles and

---

[70] The LDS Restorationist movement, including many Mormon denominations http://www.religioustolerance.org/lds.htm

[71] The Churches of Christ, the Christian Churches, the Disciples of Christ http://www.equip.org/article/the-churches-of-christ-the-christian-churches-the-disciples-of-christ/

[72] Yahweh's Kingdom of America http://kingdomhereamerica.blogspot.com/p/america-new-jerusalem.html

[73] The Great Disappointment https://www.gci.org/history/disappointment

[74] The Word of Faith, Positive Confession... as applied to Prosperity and Healing http://www.inplainsite.org/html/word_of_faith.html

prophets. This brought us groups such as the United Church of Christ International and the New Apostolic Reformation.

The 60's brought the communal living movement with people wanting to live in a community and share their worldly possessions. These groups misinterpreted Acts 2 when many new Christians from surrounding areas were staying in Jerusalem to get grounded in their faith. People started to live in a community and share their worldly possessions to make sure all needs were met. Groups like the Twelve Tribes teach this practice as normative for all Christians.[75]

In response to seeing many fall away from the faith, many churches started focusing on discipleship. Some churches took this too far, giving authority to the one discipling to make major life decisions for the discipler. Some of these churches started teaching that every believer has a covering, and if we fall outside that covering, bad things will begin to happen in our lives. These abuses brought us groups such as the International Churches of Christ, the New Apostolic Reformation and Great Commission Churches.

The last significant movement that gave these groups roots in America was the popularization of psychology. It used to be people would go to the pastor and the church if they needed counseling. Now they go to psychologists. This gave Scientology a foothold, which is glorified psychology, or at least psychological thinking as Scientology is not acknowledged as legitimate science or psychology.[76]

I hope this helps show the way these groups are a reflection of ancient heresies and more recent movements in American history. As Solomon said, there is indeed nothing new under the sun.[77]

---

[75] The Radical Life of Acts 2:44 http://www.twelvetribes.com/pt-br/node/2353

[76] Vox, Ford, Scientology vs. Psychiatry: A Case Study, The Atlantic, July 2, 2012

[77] Ecclesiastes 1:9

CHAPTER 7

Can You Be Saved If …

One of the most important things we can settle in our minds and our hearts is the answer to the question, "What must a person believe, and what practices are required, for a person to be saved?" On the group end of things we would ask, "What must a group believe or practice, to be considered Christian?"

One of the reasons this is important is once we settle the answer to this question, it will set us free from feeling the need to discuss and argue and convince people about almost 99% of the essential points one could discuss with these groups. In fact, about 99% of the topics this book covers. Quite honestly, it's good to be ready with an answer on these topics, but Christianity is about the gospel and how to come into a relationship with Jesus Christ.

I want to share my answers to these questions and how I came to these answers.

As I have been working with LDS people, God has taught me much about his grace, and he's also helped me clarify what are essentials and what are not. There are a couple of key moments that have helped me along the way. I have had conversations with several people, but one conversation in particular stretched me. I got into a dialogue, and still do occasionally, with a New Testament professor at Brigham Young University named Shon Hopkin. My conversations with Shon have forced me to ask the question, "If somebody believed x,y or z, could they be a Christian?" That is why I called this chapter "Can you be saved if …?"

I started to ask questions like, "If somebody believed in the Book of Mormon, could they be saved?" "If they were still part of The Church of Jesus Christ of Latter-day Saints, could they be saved?" "If they hold to continuing revelation or baptism for the dead, could they be saved?" "Could they be saved if they believed in a pre-existence?" All these different types of scenarios started running through my head.

I also started questioning why Christians would exclude the LDS, JW's and fill in the blank group from Christianity and their claim to Christianity when there are mainline Christian groups who share the similar teachings.

The other moment that shaped my answer was hearing the testimony of Jerald and Sandra Tanner.[78] If one is new to researching cults, and particularly the LDS, they need to know about Jerald and Sandra Tanner. Jerald has passed on, but Sandra is continuing their work through Utah Lighthouse Ministry, and they have a bookstore across from the minor league baseball park in Salt Lake City. One can find pretty much any book dealing with these groups through their ministry, and their website, www.utlm.org, is phenomenal when researching LDS.

When Jerald and Sandra were first together as a couple, Jerald was asking some tough questions about Mormonism's history and credibility. Both of them came from pretty prestigious families within the LDS church. Sandra is a direct descendant of Brigham Young. Sandra went on a journey with Jerald to visit all of the splinter groups that had broken off from the LDS church because they were starting to believe the mainline LDS church wasn't all it claimed to be. But they thought one of these splinter groups would be able to help them.

One of these splinter groups still held to the Book of Mormon, but they taught the gospel, and they had no problem with the idea Jesus paid for our sins on the cross. Jerald and Sandra became born again and accepted Jesus as their Savior as a result of attending meetings of this splinter LDS group. For a long time, Jerald and Sandra Tanner were born again Christians, yet still believed the Book of Mormon was true. They still held, to a certain extent, that at least in the beginning, Joseph Smith was a true prophet of God. It was only later, as they started uncovering more and more information and started their ministry they rejected the Book of Mormon as well,

---

[78] Tanner, Jerald & Sandra, Excerpts from The Changing World of Mormonism http://www.utlm. org/testimony/chworldtestimony.htm

and Joseph Smith entirely. But by that time, they had been born again Christians, and believing all the right things for the right reasons, for several years.

So after hearing this, I began asking things like "Can one be saved if they don't believe in the Trinity?" "Can one be saved if they don't believe in the virgin birth?" "Can one be saved if they believe in evolution?" "Can one be saved if they believe Jesus already came back and they're a Preterist?" "Can one be saved if ... fill in the blank?"

Few verses in the Bible explicitly state unless a person believes these doctrines, they cannot call themselves a Christian. Here are the verses:

> **Ye are my witnesses, saith the LORD, and my servant whom I have chosen: that ye may know and believe me, and understand that I am he: before me there was no God formed, neither shall there be after me. (Isaiah 43:10)**

> **I said therefore unto you, that ye shall die in your sins: for if ye believe not that I am he, ye shall die in your sins. (John 8:24)**

> **And if Christ be not raised, your faith is vain; ye are yet in your sins. (1 Corinthians 15:17)**

> **But though we, or an angel from heaven, preach any other gospel unto you than that which we have preached unto you, let him be accursed. (Galatians 1:8-9)**

> **For by grace are ye saved through faith; and that not of yourselves: it is the gift of God: Not of works, lest any man should boast. (Ephesians 2:8-9)**

> **And every spirit that confesseth not Jesus Christ is come in the flesh is not of God: and this is that spirit of antichrist, whereof ye have heard that it should come; and even now already is it in the world. (1 John 4:3)**

The conclusion I have arrived at as I read the gospels and the New Testament, and I continue to have these conversations, is this. The gospel is Jesus died for our sins according to the Scriptures, he was buried, and he rose from the dead according to the Scriptures. This is what the Apostle Paul taught in 1 Corinthians 15:1-4. Paul said this is the gospel he received, and this is the gospel he had passed on to the Corinthians. He then clarified in Galatians if anybody preaches another gospel, let them be accursed.[79]

A person must believe Jesus is both truly God and truly man to be saved. I say that because Jesus said in John 8 unless you believe "I AM," you will die in your sins.[80] One must believe Jesus is God because only God can pay an eternal price for their sins. Their sins can't be forgiven by another guy who happened to be a good guy dying for them. Jesus had to be God, or else he can't die as a payment for sins.

One must also believe Jesus is truly human because if Jesus wasn't a man, he couldn't die as a payment for sins. He had to be a kinsman of Adam. He had to be able to stand in the place of humanity fully.

One must believe Jesus is truly God and truly man, and as a result of that, he lived a sinless life. They must believe Jesus died as a payment for sins. They must believe Jesus rose from the dead, physically and bodily. That is important because it all has to do with the resurrection. Jesus was a model for the resurrection of believers by his physical and bodily resurrection. One must trust in Jesus and Jesus alone for their salvation, meaning they don't add a single solitary thing, In fact, one must believe it is impossible for them to add anything to what Jesus has already done. If one believes those things in their heart, and they confess them with their mouth, they shall be saved.[81] More than that, they are saved. They have eternal life. They have the Father, Son and Holy Spirit dwelling inside of them.

So what that means is one can have issues with the Trinity. They can be a modalist. They can have issues with the Holy Spirit being God. They can confuse the role between the Father and the Son. They can believe Jesus was killed on a stake. They can believe many things. They can believe in many different aspects of the beliefs these different groups hold and have that born again experience. When they are given a new spirit, a new mind and a new heart, and they are given eternal life, it is a guarantee God is going to save them.

Here's the rub of that. If somebody has genuinely given their life over to Jesus Christ, God has come into their heart, and he's going to guide them into all truth.

---

[79] Galatians 1:8-9

[80] John 8:24

[81] Romans 10:9-10

And over time they are going to turn away from certain things they did in the past. They're going to believe differently than they did in the past. They are going to struggle if they're in an unbiblical church and they're teaching false doctrines. They're going to struggle if they're reading other books teaching doctrine contradictory to the Bible. It's going to take time, but they are going to come out of those churches. But the reality is there are saved people within the LDS church, within the JW's, within the Seventh Day Adventist. In fact, within the Seventh Day Adventists, there is probably a large number of people who are saved. Within Scientology, well, I don't know about that one.

What I am saying is this. It's important to know where that individual is coming from. Because they may be a part of an organization that is entirely false, but they do believe those things I said, and there's a vast difference between talking to somebody who is born again and somebody who is not.

Here's the other side. It has been confusing to me as to why we are so insistent as Christians that these groups should not be allowed to call themselves Christian. I'm in complete agreement with that by the way. But I don't understand why mainline denominations of Christianity teaching works-righteousness, even if it's baptism they are trusting to save them, that is works-righteousness are allowed to call themselves Christian when that is one of the distinctive of Christianity of a worldview, setting it apart from all others. Even if they are trusting baptism to save them, that is works-righteousness. If they are trusting in having to speak in tongues to be saved, that is works-righteousness. That is something beyond. If they are teaching people they have to sell everything they have and live in a commune to be saved, that is adding to what Jesus has done. If they're telling people they have to believe in young earth creation and a pre-tribulation rapture to be saved, that is adding to what Jesus has done. There are so many groups and denominations out there teaching things like this. The fundamentalist groups of all the major denominations teach these things. There are some reformed, some Baptist, some from all sorts of different groups. They believe some extreme things. They teach people they have to believe x,y, or z or they have to do or not do x,y, or z to be saved or to maintain their salvation.

We need to start being consistent as Christians. We have to start standing up for Christianity, and the core teachings that make us Christians, and be clear in our message that this is the gospel, and if anyone preaches any other gospel than this, then they are not saved.

CHAPTER 8

You Might Be a Cult If …

After teaching this class for two years at Bethel Seminary, I noticed a pattern of questions from the students in my class related to why certain groups were included in our course material and other groups were not. Some students started suggesting we look at Christianity as a spectrum from Orthodoxy to Cult, and every group falls somewhere along that spectrum. In other words, some groups might be considered a cult while others are deemed false teachers or quirky Christians.

Part of the dilemma for my students was the fact some of them discovered they were a part of one of the groups we were discussing as a class. Some of them realized they were part of a group that matched the description of a cult found in this section of the course material.

The other problem one runs into when asking this question is some of the groups discussed in this book deviate significantly from accepted historic core doctrines of Christianity. Others vary little. Some of these groups practice unhealthy group dynamics such as mind control while others don't. Should all of these groups be lumped under the same category?

While I had no problem with the idea of this spectrum, I asked myself how one would determine which category a group should be considered.

What I have done in this chapter is compile the material from this section - What is a Cult? - of the book and turned it into a questionnaire.

Here's how the questionnaire works. You will notice there is an outer-most group of numbered questions or criteria (1-7). Answer these questions first. If the answer is "yes," mark "yes." If the answer is "no," mark "no." If you do not know enough information to answer yes or no, place a ? next to that question.

If you answered "yes" to all seven main questions, you don't need to go any further. This is definitely a cult.

Answer the sub-questions for any questions or criteria you answer "yes" or placed a? next to. Ignore the sub-questions for those you answered "no." Repeat the process until completed.

When you have completed the questionnaire, tally up the amount of "yes" answers. I would also suggest doing more research on those you have placed a ? next to until you can answer yes or no. All main categories and sub-categories add up to 59 possible points. Ascribe a point for every "yes" answer. From there, one can figure out what percentage away from Orthodoxy the group in question is on the spectrum.

1. Your group practices mind control

    A. B - Behavior Control
        •   Your group has a uniform
        •   Group members or leaders make important decisions for you
        •   Health code
        •   Time regulation
        •   Bizarre rituals and ordinances
        •   Financial obligations or commitments
        •   Regulate relationships and who you spend your time with

    B. I - Information Control
        •   Only allowed to read information produced by the group
        •   Group withholds information, lies, changes history and/or bends the truth
        •   Pyramid style doctrines (milk vs. meat)
        •   Encourage members to spy on one another
        •   New revelations trump old ones
        •   Hide leaders false prophecies and/or immoral behavior

- Always some worldwide conspiracy against the group

C. T - Thought Control
  - You are not allowed to ask questions
  - You are taught thought killing techniques
  - You are taught contention is of the devil
  - There is no legitimate reason for leaving the group
  - Attack the person instead of the information
  - Put doubts on the shelf
  - Dismiss facts because they are scary

D. E - Emotional Control
  - Emotions are the ultimate source of truth
  - Use their family and their peers to manipulate their emotions and to keep them from leaving
  - Social consequences if you leave the group
  - Heavy use of fear and guilt
  - Good feelings are from God and bad feelings are from Satan
  - Irrational fears are implanted subconsciously of ever leaving or questioning the group
  - Unethical use of confession
  - Use of one's past sins to manipulate them
  - Never forgiveness or absolution of sins without complete obedience
  - Double bind

2. Your group has one central leader
   E. Who received their authority from God
   F. Speaks on God's behalf
   G. Is never wrong
   H. Must always be followed
   I. The leader interprets Scripture for you

3. Your group has unique teachings outside core Christian doctrines
   J. One God

K. Deity of Christ

L. Humanity of Christ

M. The Gospel

N. The physical bodily resurrection of Christ

O. Salvation by grace alone through faith alone

4. Your group becomes dependent upon the writings of the founder and/or current leader

P. Living prophet

Q. Continuing revelation

R. Additional Scriptures

5. Your group believes in a complete apostasy

S. The Bible has been corrupted

T. Your group is the one true church

U. Your group is the only one with the authority to act on God's behalf

6. Scripture Twisting

7. Re-defining of Christian and biblical terminology

SECTION 2

OVERVIEW OF THE CULTS

But though we, or an angel from heaven, preach any other gospel unto you than that which we have preached unto you, let him be accursed. (Galatians 1:8)

CHAPTER 9

The Church of Jesus Christ
of Latter-day Saints

(Mormons; LDS)

LDS Plan of Salvation

I'm going to touch on some of the aspects of the LDS plan of salvation. This is their gospel or their plan of happiness. The plan begins with God, but their God has not always been God.[82] Their God was once a man on another planet, like we are. Through obedience to the LDS church and gospel, this same plan of salvation, and submission to another God, he has earned his way up to being God of our planet.

The LDS church teaches all humans pre-existed before our earthly lives as literal spirit children of our Heavenly Father Elohim. In fact, the firstborn spirit child was Jesus. Jesus had another brother named Lucifer. Jesus and Lucifer, before the council of the gods, presented two conflicting plans of salvation, and Jesus' gospel was

---

[82] Becoming Like God https://www.lds.org/topics/becoming-like-god? Lattin, Don "Musings of the Main Mormon," San Francisco Chronicle, Apr. 13, 1997; see also Biema, David Van, "Kingdom Come," Time, Aug. 4, 1997, p. 56

chosen.[83] He was chosen to be the Savior of our world. Because he was chosen, Lucifer got upset and started a war against our heavenly father Elohim. A third of us as spirit children joined on his side, a third sided with Jesus, and a third stayed neutral.[84] The third that sided with Lucifer got cast out of heaven without bodies. This is important because a body, and coming to this earth, is essential to become a God or become exalted. So those third automatically have their exaltation stunted. They will never progress beyond that point. The righteous third were born into good, noble families. The neutral third were born into less fortunate circumstances.

Those of us who stayed in heaven wait our turn to come to this earth, and to be born with a human body. The purpose of life on our earth is a time of testing.[85] It's a time when we are either going to overcome this world, overcome temptation, overcome our sinful bent toward things, or we're going to side again with Lucifer.

After this life on earth, we've either become perfect, or we have not. We've accepted the LDS gospel or did not receive the LDS gospel. When we die we go to the spirit world. Everyone goes to one of two places. We either go to Paradise, or we go to Spirit Prison.[86]

The reason why the LDS church has temples is because they do some important things in them, at least from their point of view. In those temples, they get baptized by proxy on behalf of a dead relative.[87] So they can get baptized in the name of Grandpa Joe, and then Grandpa Joe, in Spirit Prison, has a chance to accept the LDS gospel from missionaries sent from Paradise to Spirit Prison. Grandpa Joe, if he receives the LDS gospel and the baptism done on his behalf by proxy, is now able to enter Paradise,

---

[83] Jesus Christ, Our Chosen Leader and Savior https://www.lds.org/manual/gospel-principles/chapter-3-jesus-christ-our-chosen-leader-and-savior?
Abraham 3:27; Moses 4:1–4

[84] Introduction to the Revelation of St. John the Divine
https://www.lds.org/manual/new-testament-seminary-teacher-manual/introduction-to-the-revelation-of-st-john-the-divine?lang=eng
Moses 4:1-4

[85] The Purpose of Life to be Proved https://www.lds.org/ensign/1971/12/the-purpose-of-life-to-be-proved?
Doctrine & Covenants 130:19-34

[86] The Post-Mortal Spirit World https://www.lds.org/manual/gospel-principles/chapter-41-the-postmortal-spirit-world?

[87] Baptism for the Dead https://history.lds.org/article/doctrine-and-covenants-baptisms-for-the-dead?
Doctrine & Covenants 127

and then start progressing on toward exaltation. Another thing that takes place in their temples is LDS get sealed as families, as husbands and wives, along with their children, for all time and eternity. The Mormon church does not teach marriage is until death, but for all time and eternity.[88]

The LDS church teaches everyone is going to come to a final judgment. The LDS church teaches Jesus died to overcome physical death for all people, but in contrast to orthodox Christian teachings, his death only makes it possible for us to achieve exaltation.[89] So they will say we've all been saved by grace, but exaltation is a different matter. And when they say exaltation, they are talking about their belief in three levels of heaven. The LDS church teaches everyone is going to go to heaven because Jesus died.[90] It's a matter of where they are going to spend eternity.

The LDS teach there are three levels of heaven. The highest level is the Celestial Kingdom. That's for those who have repented of all of their sins, they have performed all of their covenants they have made here on earth in the temple and the LDS church.[91] These are the ones who have progressed to the point where they are ready to become gods themselves. They will then have their spirit wives, and they will give birth to their spirit children, and they will send a Savior to a world, and the whole process will play over again.

Those who didn't quite make it to the highest level go to the Terrestrial Kingdom. This includes not just LDS people, but all faithful people who are good, moral people.[92] They just have not become perfect. They either have not repented of their sins, or they have never been a part of the LDS church.

The third and final level of heaven is the Telestial Kingdom. It is for those who we culturally believe "should" go to hell.[93] These are the "horrible" people of the world, i.e. the people who live without law, the people who were murderers or thieves, spent

---

[88] Marriage https://www.lds.org/topics/marriage? Doctrine & Covenants 131:1-4

[89] What Think ye of Salvation by Grace https://speeches.byu.edu/talks/bruce-r-mcconkie_think-ye-salvation-grace/

[90] Jesus Christ Redeems All Mankind from Temporal Death https://www.lds.org/manual/teachings-joseph-f-smith/chapter-10?

[91] Doctrine & Covenants 76:50-70, 92-96

[92] Doctrine & Covenants 76:71-80, 91, 97

[93] Doctrine & Covenants 76:81-90, 98-106, 109-112

much time in prison, etc… In other words, we determine the level of heaven we will end up in by the law we have been willing or unwilling to keep.

Outer Darkness is a separate category. The people who go to Outer Darkness are those who have received the full knowledge of the truth and then walked away from it. What that translates to is those who were members of the LDS church and left. Sometimes what they mean by this term are those who left and actively fight against the church. Sometimes the term is used to mean people who have gone through the temple and then left the church and fight against the church. Some LDS members want to be more gracious than others. Those who go to Outer Darkness are called apostates, and they have been taught God is through with them.[94]

The Apostasy

The Mormon church teaches Jesus came to this earth and established his church. When he established his church, it was based upon the concept of priesthood, which is the authority to act on God's behalf. The authority of the priesthood is bigger than God from the Mormon viewpoint. God used to be a man and became a God, and we're following the same pattern. God has to follow the laws of the priesthood and other laws set in motion far before his existence.[95]

Jesus established priesthood authority and gave us the Scriptures. He passed this authority on to his apostles, then persecution broke out, the apostles died, and priesthood authority was not transferred to others. The priesthood authority was then taken from the earth, which means the true church was taken from the earth.[96] Along with that, the LDS church teaches plain and precious truths were taken out of the Scripture by malicious scribes who didn't like certain things Jesus taught.[97] So the LDS church teaches a complete apostasy happened on this earth. It happened shortly after the death of the apostles and got progressively worse over time.

---

[94] Doctrine & Covenants 76:30-49

[95] Alma 13:7–8; Doctrine & Covenants 84:17–18

[96] Doctrine & Covenants 124:28

[97] 1 Nephi 13:34-40

Joseph Smith

Apostasy continued to be the state of the church until the early 1800's when a 14-year-old boy named Joseph Smith went out into the woods during a revival meeting happening in his neighborhood. He was praying and asked God which church he should join. His testimony is God the Father and Jesus appeared to him and said, "All of the churches are an abomination. You shouldn't join any of them. I'm going to restore the true church through you. One of the ways I'm going to restore the church is through an angel named Moroni."[98]

The Book of Mormon

As Smith was praying, the angel Moroni appeared and eventually showed Joseph where some golden plates were buried near his home in upstate New York. Joseph uncovered the plates, and he was given the supernatural ability to translate them. These plates were supposed to be the recorded history of the people living in the Americas before all of the history we know about. The LDS church teaches the Native American Indians came from a group of Israelites who left during the captivity, and they came over to the new world and established a whole new empire.

The father of the family that left was named Lehi. His two prominent sons were Nephi and Laman. Laman was not a good son, and Nephi was. Nephi's descendants became known as the Nephites, and they fought for truth. The Lamanites were the bad seed. Eventually, these two tribes, which were vast kingdoms, fought against each other. The Lamanites wiped out the Nephites. The last standing Nephite was a man named Moroni. This is the same Moroni who gave the plates to Joseph Smith.

Joseph Smith told everybody where the Bible had been corrupted, the Book of Mormon restored all which was lost in the apostasy. He said a man would get closer to God through the teachings of the Book of Mormon than any other book. It was the most correct book on the face of the earth.[99]

The LDS article of faith says, "We believe the Bible to be Word of God, as far as it is translated correctly." That is followed up with "and we also believe the Book of

---

[98] First Vision Accounts https://www.lds.org/topics/first-vision-accounts?
Joseph Smith History 1
[99] Book of Mormon Introduction

Mormon to be the Word of God." [100]What that means is the LDS church teaches the Book of Mormon is pure, untainted, and the most accurate book. At the same time, the LDS church teaches the Bible is not to be trusted because it has been corrupted and tainted.

Something I need to note is they don't word this article of faith correctly. The LDS do not teach the Bible has been mistranslated. They teach the Bible hasn't been transmitted correctly. They teach the original words of the Scriptures haven't been preserved for us today.

Joseph Smith claimed to be able to translate, and one of the things he did is retranslate the Bible. The finished product is the Joseph Smith Translation, or the Inspired Version, as Mormons know it. [101] The interesting thing is Mormons still use the LDS published version of the King James Version, which gives reference to the Joseph Smith Translation.

Salvation by Works

Even in pre-existence, our coming to earth, and our position on this earth, the geographical place, the time period we live, is all based on works we did in the pre-existence. We have already earned our place in the here and now. This life is a time of testing. It's a time when people are either going to join the LDS church or reject it. They're either going to be an active Mormon, or they're going to be an inactive Mormon. They're either going to be able to go through the temple and be sealed together with their family for all time and eternity, or they're not going to be able to do that. People are either going to repent of their sins, or they're not. All of those decisions are going to influence where one will spend eternity.

The LDS church teaches Jesus died so everybody could go to a heaven of some kind. That's what they mean by the term "saved by grace." [102] Joseph Smith said even the lowest level of heaven is so great one would kill themselves to go there right now. [103]

[100] Articles of Faith 1:8

[101] Joseph Smith's Inspired Translation of the Bible https://www.lds.org/ensign/1972/12/joseph-smiths-inspired-translation-of-the-bible?

[102] "The Family: A Proclamation to the World," p. 129.2 Nephi 25:23

[103] Journal of Charles W. Walker

In the final judgment, we are going to be judged by which law we have kept, and that will determine which level of heaven where we will spend eternity.

Multiple Gods

The LDS church, even within the Godhead, has multiple gods because the LDS church teaches God the Father has become our God. They have Jesus, who is the Savior of this world, and through his efforts, he has earned his way up to Godhood as well. [104] The Holy Ghost is a strange figure, who doesn't have a body yet, which is against Mormon theology because the LDS church teaches a physical body is essential to become a God and become exalted. The Holy Ghost has never received a body, but he somehow earned his right to become a God. [105]

It doesn't make much sense to Christians because LDS talk about Elohim being the one God we worship, but they also have Jesus and the Holy Ghost whom the LDS church teaches are actual gods. So what they teach is called the Godhead. The LDS church teaches three gods we interact with in our world, one of which we primarily worship because he is our actual father.

But there are infinite numbers of gods in the universe we have no idea how many there are. We have no idea who the first God was. We have no concept of that. And there will be an infinite number of gods after us because we can potentially, if we make it to the Celestial Kingdom, become a God ourselves.

So we are not dealing with a strictly monotheistic religion when we talk about the LDS church. We're talking about a polytheistic scheme of things, and within our world, and what we have been told about through Scripture, there is a Father, Son and Holy Ghost who are three separate gods.

LDS God	**Christian God**
Body of flesh and bones	Spirit
Not eternal	Eternal
Once a man	Uncreated
Not Trinity	Trinity

---

[104] LDS interpretation of Revelation 3:21

[105] The Guide to the Scriptures: Holy Ghost, https://www.lds.org/scriptures/gs/holy-ghost
Doctrine & Covenants 130:22

Godhead is three separate gods	One God, three persons
Worship only Heavenly Father	Worship Father, Son and Holy Spirit
Not omnipresent	Omnipresent
Not omnipotent	Omnipotent
Not omniscient	Omniscient
Multiple gods	One God
Humans can become gods	Shares his glory with no other

I also wanted to highlight something about the LDS view of God, because this makes the LDS church so unique and so far removed from Christianity. The Bible, if one were to sum it up, says God is Spirit,[106] God is eternal,[107] God is Trinity,[108] God is omnipotent,[109] omnipresent and omniscient,[110] and there is one God.[111] Mormonism teaches God has a body of flesh and bones,[112] God is not eternal.[113] He was once a man, like we are. He is not Trinity. The LDS church teaches the Godhead, God the Father, God the Son and God the Holy Ghost are three separate gods, and God the Father is the one we worship because we are his spirit children. Because he has progressed to become a God and is still progressing, the LDS church does not teach God is omnipresent because he has a body of flesh and bones. The LDS church does not teach he is omnipotent because he is subject to priesthood authorities and his Heavenly Father, which is greater than him. He is not omniscient because he is still progressing in his knowledge. The LDS church does not teach there is one God. In fact, they teach there are countless numbers of gods who have gone before the God we worship, as well as the belief we can potentially become gods ourselves, which means there could be countless numbers of gods after us.

---

[106] John 4:24

[107] Psalm 90:2

[108] 1 John 5:7

[109] Ephesians 1:19

[110] Psalm 139

[111] 1 Timothy 2:5

[112] Doctrine & Covenants 130:22

[113] In Eliza R. Snow Smith, Biography and Family Record of Lorenzo Snow, p. 46
"The Grand Destiny of Man," Deseret Evening News, July 20, 1901, p. 22

Key Historical Markers

In 1820, Joseph Smith claimed he had his first vision experience. He was attending the revivals happening during the Second Great Awakening and hearing all of the discussion amongst the sects, and the differences between them, and he went out into the woods and claimed he asked God which church he should join. And then God the Father, and Jesus, both in separate bodies, appeared to Joseph and answered his question by saying, "You should join none of them. All of their creeds are an abomination." [114] And that's where the first inkling Joseph Smith is supposed to be the vehicle to restore the true church of Jesus Christ to the face of the earth appears.

The year 1823 is when he claimed to have been visited by an angel named Moroni. Moroni, as we've discussed, was the last living Nephite, and he's the one who buried the golden plates. He is the last author or editor of the Book of Mormon. Then he became an angel, appeared to Joseph Smith, and told him where the golden plates were buried near his home in upstate New York in one of the Native American burial grounds with which everybody was so fascinated.

It wasn't until 1827 Moroni gave Joseph Smith permission to access the plates, and in 1829, Joseph Smith claimed to have been visited by John the Baptist, restoring unto him the Aaronic Priesthood.[115] Later on that year, he claimed to have been visited by Peter, James and John, who restored unto him the Melchizedek Priesthood.[116]

In 1830, Joseph Smith published the Book of Mormon and started the Church of Christ, which is what the church was called at the beginning. In 1844, Joseph Smith was martyred according to the LDS. He was killed in Carthage Jail.

Brigham Young didn't win control of most of the Mormons until 1845, as there was a power struggle, including William Bickerton, Sydney Rigdon, Granville Hedrick, Joseph Smith III, James Strang and Brigham Young. There were more break-offs from the main group later over the issue of polygamy, which is why there are many different polygamist, or fundamentalist, groups of Latter-day Saints.

---

[114] Joseph Smith - History 1:19

[115] Doctrine & Covenants 13

Joseph Smith—History 1:68–72

[116] Doctrine & Covenants 27:12-13

Also, there is the Reorganized Church of Latter-day Saints, which now has become the Community of Christ. They have become more Christian. They have made many changes in their doctrine, coming much closer to Christianity. This is because they rejected many of Joseph Smith's later visions, and they didn't follow Brigham Young. They still hold on to the Book of Mormon as Scripture. But the Book of Mormon, as we will see later in this book, is much more Christian than Mormon.

There are many more splinter groups out there. This is why one can't necessarily label somebody because they relate to the Book of Mormon or Joseph Smith as a prophet. We need to get to know the individual we are talking to and find out what they believe personally.

Terminology

Something making it difficult to talk with members of cults is they often use the same terminology as Christians, but they mean entirely different things when they say those terms. With Mormons in particular, it is easy to walk away after asking a series of salvation and gospel-related questions believing the LDS person we are talking with is saved. However, if one took the time to ask follow-up questions as to what that person meant by the terms they used, they would find a different God, Jesus, salvation, heaven, etc… being discussed. It would be a different conversation even though the same words were used.

So here is a sample of some keywords to be aware of their LDS meanings:

Adam - The physical father of human beings. Also known as Michael the archangel or the Ancient of Days (Doctrine & Covenants 116).

Atonement - Jesus' death on the cross which allows for all human beings to be resurrected, and makes salvation possible through repentance of sins and keeping covenants made with God.

Aaronic Priesthood - The first level of priesthood in the LDS church held typically by Junior High age boys (Doctrine & Covenants 107:1, 6, 10).

Baptism - The means by which sins are washed away. Must be performed by proper priesthood holder, in the right location and in the proper way in to be effective.

Bible - Viewed as Scripture only as far as it is translated correctly. It is taught in the Book of Mormon plain and precious truths were removed from the Bible. One of four standard works within the LDS church (Bible, Book of Mormon, Doctrine & Covenants, and Pearl of Great Price). The KJV is the official Bible of the LDS church.

Bishop - The LDS version of a Christian pastor over a local ward. They are to be unpaid.

Celestial Kingdom - The highest level of heaven where God and Christ dwell, and where one can be exalted to Godhood. One must repent of their sins and keep all covenants made within the temple in to go to this level of heaven.

Church - The LDS church, which is the only true church due to its priesthood authority and structure.

Damnation - Differs depending on the person. Some would only refer to Outer Darkness as damnation while others would view damnation as anything less than becoming a God.

Elohim - The name of Heavenly Father.

Exaltation (Eternal Life) - Becoming a God.

Fall - A necessary transgression of Adam allowing human beings to procreate and move toward exaltation.

God - A being who has achieved exaltation. The LDS church teaches there have been an infinite amount of gods from eternity past and will continue to be for eternity future. LDS will state Heavenly Father is the only God they have to do with. (Doctrine & Covenants 130:22-23)

Godhead - LDS terminology for the Father, Son and Holy Ghost, which the LDS church teaches are three separate gods, all of which became a God at some point in time.

Gospel - The LDS plan of salvation

Heaven - Everybody except for apostate Mormons goes to a level of heaven. The lowest level is the Telestial Kingdom. The middle level is the Terrestrial Kingdom. The highest level is the Celestial Kingdom.

Hell - Temporary holding place for those who are awaiting entrance into the Telestial Kingdom (Doctrine & Covenants 76: 84-85, 106).

Holy Ghost (Holy Spirit) - Member of the Godhead. Became a God though never receiving a physical body. One receives the Holy Ghost through the laying on of hands by a proper priesthood holder following baptism.

Jehovah - The name of Jesus in the Old Testament.

Jesus - Literal firstborn spirit child of Heavenly Father. Spirit brother to Lucifer and all human beings. Member of the Godhead. Jehovah in the Old Testament. Given the title and role of Savior for this earth.

Kingdom of God - Celestial Kingdom in heaven. The LDS church on earth.

Marriage - A covenant made between a man and a woman, when performed in an LDS temple by a proper priesthood authority, that lasts for all time and eternity. (Doctrine & Covenants 132:15-20)

Melchizedek Priesthood - The higher level of priesthood usually held by males 18 years or older. (Doctrine & Covenants 107)

Pre-Existence - Our existence as spirit children in heaven before coming to this earth.

Salvation - General salvation refers to the resurrection of all human beings. Individual salvation must be attained through repentance of all sins and keeping all covenants made to God.

Satan (Devil) - Spirit child of Heavenly Father who leads a war in heaven after his plan of salvation was rejected. Was cast to earth with his followers without a physical body.

Scripture - Bible, Book of Mormon, Doctrine & Covenants, Pearl of Great Price.

Temple - Physical buildings where endowments, sealings, and baptisms for the dead are performed, allowing LDS members who partake and keep these covenants to progress to the Celestial Kingdom.

Trinity - The LDS church does not teach the Trinity. They view this as teaching three gods. The LDS church teaches the Trinity was created at the Council of Nicaea by the apostate church.

CHAPTER 10

Jehovah's Witnesses

(Watchtower Society; JW's)

General Overview

A lot of things about the Jehovah's Witnesses are common knowledge. They don't celebrate holidays.[117] They don't participate in saluting the flag, voting, politics or war activities. The Watchtower teaches its members not to receive blood transfusions.[118] The Old Testament and the New Testament talk about not consuming blood.[119] Don't eat meat with the blood in it. The Jehovah's Witnesses interpret those passages to mean Christians should not receive blood transfusions. They have backed off this doctrine some in the recent past, but there is much peer pressure amongst the ranks not to take blood.

They discourage going on to higher education. They limit contact with non-Jehovah's Witnesses, friends and family. They keep their members within their little group, and they try to make sure people are not talking with people outside of the

---

[117] Young, Nathan, Should Christians Celebrate Religious Holidays? - Chapter 16 https://youtu.be/T56edT2Nh2I

[118] Young, Nathan, Biblical stance on Blood Transfusions - Chapter 13 https://youtu.be/R7137WXJDvU

[119] Acts 15:29

group and making friends with people outside of the group unless, of course, they're witnessing and trying to bring them into the Jehovah's Witnesses.

They forbid critical thinking and disagreeing with the governing body. The governing body is the group of men who write the doctrines of the Watchtower Society. If one disagrees with the leadership, that doesn't go well for them. They forbid reading literature critical of the group.

They forbid non-Jehovah's Witness religious broadcasting at church attendance, and they have mandatory door-to-door proselytizing. They're pressured into a certain amount of door-to-door witnessing, and they have to write down all of their hours and turn it in. They go to their Kingdom Hall, which is their version of church, almost every single day, and they have Bible studies.

What are their Bible studies like? They pretty much avoid reading the Bible. They have their own version of the Bible. It's called the New World Translation. As one may suspect, they've modified many passages in the Bible. Cutting and snipping and pasting and changing things as they go. It still looks like the Bible. It still feels like the Bible, but important things are missing. But there are still many good Bible passages intact the Jehovah's Witnesses have missed. We'll get into how we can use these verses to help them understand true Christian doctrine later in this book.[120]

They get together and study, for the most part, Watchtower magazines. The same ones they hand us at the door. Where do those come from? In Brooklyn, New York, where their organization is headed up, they have a group of men called the governing body. It's about 10-15 men, and they run this organization. They design all of the doctrines and employ many writers who write these magazines, and they deal out these magazines that answer questions Jehovah's Witnesses want to know and teach them doctrine slowly. Every week they've got they've got a few articles, they've got questions, they've got answers; Covering a wide range of different little subjects. They will read these magazines, and then recite the answers it gives. It's an indoctrination process, through repetition. Repetition is good, but they repeat over and over again these answers in these magazines, and it gets these doctrines stuck in their heads.

They are discouraged from looking into the older Watchtower magazines. Their old magazines are filled with contradictions. Their old doctrines contradict their new doctrines. Their old magazines have all kinds of false prophecies that never came true.

---

[120] Young, Nathan, The BIBLE - A Book from God - Chapter 2 https://youtu.be/SrR83jRv3LQ

The Jehovah's Witnesses have mispredicted various aspects of the end of the world in 1914, 1917, 1918, 1925, 1975.[121]

What do they Believe?

What do Jehovah's Witnesses teach concerning Jesus? The Watchtower teaches Jesus is God's Son, as do we, but inferior to the Father.[122] Also, the Watchtower teaches Christ was the first creation of God.[123] The Watchtower teaches Jesus was created. [124]They teach Christ died on a stake, not on a cross.[125]

The Watchtower teaches Christ's human life was paid as a ransom for obedient humans.[126] When you're talking to them about salvation by grace alone, many times they'll give lip service, and they'll agree, but that is not what they teach.[127] The Watchtower teaches Christ died on a stake, and it was to give all of humanity a chance. This covered up Adam's sin. It gives humanity a chance to win salvation through their works and obedience. It provides us with the opportunity to work our way into salvation.[128]

The Watchtower teaches Jesus was raised from the dead as an immortal spirit person.[129] The Watchtower teaches Jesus is the archangel Michael.[130]The Watchtower teaches the Kingdom under Christ will rule the earth with righteousness and peace.[131]

---

[121] Changed Dates: Failed Predictions, http://www.jwfacts.com/watchtower/1800s.php

[122] The Bible's Viewpoint: Is Jesus God? http://wol.jw.org/en/wol/d/r1/lp-e/102013444

[123] Reasoning: Trinity, http://wol.jw.org/en/wol/d/r1/lp-e/1101989276?q=jesus+first+creation&p=par

[124] Young, Nathan, Who is JESUS CHRIST? - Chapter 4A https://youtu.be/ft5CopzXITk

[125] Insight, Volume 2: Torture Stake, http://wol.jw.org/en/wol/d/r1/lp-e/1200004456

[126] Insight, Volume 2: Ransom, http://wol.jw.org/en/wol/d/r1/lp-e/1200003640

[127] Young, Nathan, The Ransom, God's greatest Gift - Chapter 5 https://youtu.be/3vqCduwwtgk

[128] Bodine, Marian, A Beginner's Guide to Witnessing to the Jehovah's Witnesses http://www.equip.org/article/a-beginners-guide-to-witnessing-to-the-jehovahs-witnesses/

[129] The Watchtower (2014): The Resurrection of Jesus - Its Meaning for Us, http://wol.jw.org/en/wol/d/r1/lp-e/2014842?q=resurrection+of+jesus&p=par

[130] Who is Michael the Archangel? https://www.jw.org/en/publications/books/bible-teach/who-is-michael-the-archangel-jesus/

[131] Listen to God and Live Forever: Part 9 When Will Paradise Come? https://www.jw.org/en/publications/books/listen-and-live/when-will-paradise-come/

The Watchtower teaches the Kingdom brings ideal living conditions to earth.[132] The Watchtower teaches the earth will never be destroyed, or de-populated.[133] The Watchtower teaches God will destroy the present system, the present world, in a great battle called Har-Mageddon.[134]

The Watchtower does not teach hell.[135] They do not teach there is an eternal punishment for those who are non-believers. In fact, the founder of the Jehovah's Witnesses, Charles Taze Russell, stated Christians belief in hell was his main reason for starting this new group. The Watchtower teaches rather than eternal punishment, the wicked will be destroyed or annihilated. Concerning the same lack of hell, those who God approves of, those who have worked out their salvation through many good works and works and works, will receive their eternal life.[136]

Also, concerning the end times, the Jehovah's Witnesses have been teaching since well before 1914 we were at the time of the end.[137] They've been talking about the end of the world for a long time. The Watchtower teaches the death of humans is due to Adam's sin, and we do too, but we also say spiritual death, as well as physical death, is due to Adam's sin.[138]

Another thing the Watchtower teaches is the human soul ceases to exist at death.[139] Their resurrection is a bodily resurrection, which is a contradiction since the Watchtower doesn't teach Jesus rose physically in bodily form.

---

[132] Young, Nathan, What is God's Kingdom? - Chapter 8 https://youtu.be/zyLZoJk7bfo

[133] Awake! December 2014: The Bible's Viewpoint - The Earth, https://www.jw.org/en/publications/magazines/g201412/the-earth/

[134] Young, Nathan, False Predictions by Jehovah Witnesses - Chapter 10 https://youtu.be/cFJSe-TmuwM

[135] What is Hell? Is it a Place of Eternal Torment? https://www.jw.org/en/bible-teachings/questions/what-is-hell/

[136] Witnessing to Jehovah's Witnesses – what is the key? https://www.gotquestions.org/witnessing-Jehovahs-Witnesses.html

[137] What Does the Bible Really Teach? APPENDIX 1914—A Significant Year in Bible prophecy https://www.jw.org/en/publications/books/bible-teach/1914-significant-year-bible-prophecy/

[138] Romans 5:14

[139] Awake! December 2015 The Bible's Viewpoint: The Soul https://www.jw.org/en/publications/magazines/g201512/the-soul/

Concerning hell, the Watchtower teaches the word hell is referring to mankind's grave, the common grave. So when one is dead and buried, that's hell. So everybody gets their grave time, or hell time.[140]

The Watchtower teaches only 144,000 people get to go to heaven and rule with Christ. They call this the John class.[141] The door to heaven for those 144,000 have closed.[142] There is already 144,000 according to the Jehovah's Witnesses who have been sealed to go to heaven, and the rest can only hope to be resurrected and live an eternal life in these bodies on this planet. And God's going to charge them to fix the earth after Har-Mageddon.[143] So they live their whole life in these bodies while getting tired, cutting their fingers while they're doing work, catching a cold, etc.[144]

The Watchtower believes one's prayers must only be directed to Jehovah, through Christ.[145] They also observe the Sabbath on Saturday. They make a big deal about clergy class and titles. For example, calling somebody a deacon, a pastor, a bishop, is not something they would do. They think that's improper.

The Watchtower teaches Christians must give public testimony to scriptural truth. The Watchtower teaches Christ came invisibly in 1914, and that's when his Kingdom was established in heaven. It was predicted, and this is one of the false prophecies, Jesus would return in 1914.[146] Well, it didn't happen, so right after 1914, they were scrambling to discover how they could cover up this blatant false prophecy. People were leaving their church in droves, and the way they found they could cover up this false prophecy was to say Jesus came invisibly and is now setting up his Kingdom. They made a big deal out of it, and had people waiting on their roofs for Jesus to come back, selling their stuff, expecting Har-Mageddon was right around the corner. They led their people to believe that, and then, when it didn't happen, they said, "We never said that. It must have been local leaders of Kingdom Halls that said that. We

---

[140] Tips on Witnessing to Jehovah's Witnesses https://christiananswers.net/evangelism/beliefs/jehovahswitness.html

[141] The Watchtower (Study Edition) January 2016: "We Want to Go With You" https://www.jw.org/en/publications/magazines/watchtower-study-january-2016/we-want-to-go-with-you/

[142] Young, Nathan, Heaven & Hell (Where are the Dead?) - Chapter 6 https://youtu.be/v408-PJgAMI

[143] Young, Nathan, Are we living in "The Last Days?" - Chapter 9 https://youtu.be/Pzj0_DNYFhk

[144] Comfort, Ray, How to Witness to a Jehovah's Witness https://www.crosswalk.com/faith/spiritual-life/how-to-witness-to-a-jehovahs-witness-1408500.html

[145] Does God Have a Name? https://www.jw.org/en/bible-teachings/questions/gods-name/

[146] The Time is At Hand (1911 ed), p. 239 Zion's Watch Tower 1894 Jul 15, p. 226

never said Jesus was going to come back and bring Har-Mageddon. We were only saying Jesus was going to come back invisibly and set up his Kingdom."[147] But the prophecies say otherwise.

Charles Taze Russell

To touch on a few more items from a historical basis. Charles Taze Russell was the founder of the Jehovah's Witnesses. He was a Bible student and was a student of William Miller, and he did go through the Great Disappointment of 1844. It wasn't until 1879 he founded the Watchtower organization and started publishing materials that later would become the Watchtower magazine and the Awake magazine familiar to many people. He died in 1916, and it was then Judge Rutherford took over the organization. It was in 1931 he transitioned the name of this group from Bible students to Jehovah's Witnesses.[148]

I also want to highlight again the teaching of Jesus, which sets Jehovah's Witnesses apart from mainline Christianity by great lengths. They follow the teachings of a man named Arius. At the Council of Nicaea, Arius was the main contender to Alexander. He denied the doctrine of the Trinity, instead claiming Jesus was a created being and inferior to the Father. His main catchphrase was "there was a time when he was not" about Jesus, believing he is not equal with God.[149] They emphasized there was one God and Jesus was a higher creation of God. In fact, he was the first creation of God, and it was through Jesus God created all "other" things besides Jesus. The Watchtower does teach Jesus is Michael the Archangel, and the title Archangel signifies his unique role of being over the angels, and he is separate from the angels. He has a special place, but he is not in fact God.

---

[147] Watchtower 1993 Jan 15, p. 5

Awake! 1973 Jan 22, p. 8

[148] Piper, John, How to Talk to Jehovah's Witnesses About Jesus https://www.desiringgod.org/messages/in-the-beginning-was-the-word/excerpts/how-to-talk-to-jehovah-s-witnesses-about-jesus

[149] Church History, by Socrates of Constantinople, Book I, Ch. 5

Terminology

Armageddon: The total world battle, pronounced as Har-Mageddon, that Jehovah's Witnesses teach will take place soon. Jesus and the Watchtower Society will prevail over all organizations and people not affiliated with them.

Anointed class: The 144,000 that will rule and reign with King Jesus in heaven.

Bethel: This is the designation given to the official headquarters of the Watchtower Bible and Tract Society, located at 25 Columbia Heights, Brooklyn, NY.

Bloodguilt: When guilt is acquired through bloodshed, support of blood-guilty organizations, eating or drinking blood, failing to preach the good news.

Christendom: Protestant and Catholic groups which Jehovah's Witnesses represent false Christianity formed at the Council of Nicaea under Constantine.

Circuit: A group of 20 Jehovah's Witness congregations, with a circuit overseer over them.

Circuit assembly: Individual Jehovah Witness congregations.

Circuit overseer: Official leader of the circuit.

Disfellowship: When a member gets removed, usually for one year, following which is an opportunity for reinstatement.

District overseer: Supervisor of several circuits.

Expelling: Excommunication of unfaithful members. Under some circumstances, the member can be reinstated through repentance.

Faith: "To maintain a firm faith requires putting up a hard fight for it, resisting men who could plunge one into immorality, combating the works of the flesh, avoiding the snare of materialism, shunning faith-destroying philosophies and traditions of men, and above all, looking 'intently at the Chief Agent and Perfecter of our faith, Jesus.'"[150]

---

[150] Aid to Bible Understanding, p. 562

Gentile times: Jehovah's Witnesses teach this is the period (from 607 B.C. to 1914 A.D.) when Jews were in disfavor with Jehovah.

Good will person: This is a person who is interested in Bible study and is a prospective member of Jehovah's Witnesses. Those who are not interested are called goats.

Great crowd or other sheep: People faithful to Jehovah, but not going to heaven because they are not one of the 144,000. They will live in paradise on earth.

Hell: The common grave. There is no eternal punishment, but non-believers are annihilated.

Impalement (of Jesus): Jehovah's Witnesses teach Jesus was impaled on a stake, not crucified on a cross. They teach the idea of a two-piece cross was adopted from the pagans in the third century.[151]

New World Translation of the Holy Scriptures (NWT): The NWT is the official translation of the Old and New Testaments by the Watchtower.

People's Pulpit Association: The first Jehovah's Witness president organized this movement in 1909. The name was changed to the Watchtower Bible and Tract Society in 1939.

Publisher: Jehovah's Witnesses who sell Watchtower literature door-to-door and serve the Watchtower as directed.

Salvation: Attained by dedicating one's life to Jehovah and living the lifestyle prescribed by the Watchtower. Jesus died to make salvation possible by living a life of good works.

Theocracy: Belief Jehovah is running the Watchtower organization through the Governing Body.

---

[151] Aid to Bible Understanding, p. 824-825

Trinity: The Watchtower teaches the Trinity is a false doctrine created at the Council of Nicaea under Constantine. They teach Jesus is a created being lesser than Jehovah and the Holy Spirit is God's active force.[152]

Year: In prophecy, it "is often used in a special sense as the equivalent of 360 days (12 months of 30 days each)." It is also called a time and sometimes a day (see Genesis 7:11, 8:3-5).[153]

---

[152] Young, Nathan, What is the TRUTH about God? - Chapter 1 https://youtu.be/_wYRJ2g9xmY
[153] Aid to Bible Understanding, p. 1677-1678

CHAPTER 11

First Church of Scientology

(Scientology)

The Backstory of Humanity

Once upon a time, 75 million years ago, there was an alien galactic ruler named Xenu. Xenu was in charge of all the planets in this part of the galaxy, including our planet earth, except in those days, it was called Teegeeack. Now Xenu had a problem. All of the 76 planets he controlled were overpopulated. Each planet had an average 178 billion people. He wanted to get rid of all the overpopulation. So he had a plan. Xenu took over complete control with the help of renegades to defeat the good people and the loyal officers. Then, with the help of psychiatrists, he called in billions of people for income tax inspections, where they were instead given injections of alcohol and glycol mixed to paralyze them. Then they were put into space planes that looked exactly like DC-8's, except they had rocket motors instead of propellers. These space planes flew to earth where the paralyzed people were stacked around the bases of volcanoes, in their hundreds of billions. When they finished stacking them, then H-bombs were lowered into the volcanoes. Xenu then detonated all the H-bombs at the same time, and everyone was killed.

The story doesn't end there. Since everyone has a soul, called a Thetan in this story, then they had to trick the souls into not coming back again. While the hundreds of billions of souls were being blown around by the nuclear winds, he had special electronic traps that caught all the souls in the electronic beams. These electronic beams were like sticky fly paper. After he had captured all these souls, he had them packed into boxes and taken to a few huge cinemas. There all the souls had to spend days watching special 3D motion pictures that told them what life should be like, and many confusing things. In this picture, they were shown false pictures and told they were God, the devil and Christ. In this story, this process is called implanting. When the films ended, and the souls left the cinema, these souls started to stick together. Since they had all seen the same film, they thought they were all the same people. They clustered in groups of a few thousand. Now because there were only a few living bodies left, they stayed as clusters and inhabited these bodies. As for Xenu, the loyal officers finally overthrew him, and they locked him away in a mountain on one of the planets. He's kept in by a force field, powered by an eternal battery, and Xenu is still alive today.[154]

Signs of a Cult

Scientology matches signs of a cult. They do have one single human leader who calls the shots, the dogma, the theology, their belief system, their rules. This cult is abusive to its members. There is mind control over its members. If one is merely a surface dabbler, checking it out, they won't be exposed to this material, but if one gets involved heavily with this movement, they will be isolated from the rest of the world, from their friends, from their family. Those ties are severed. If one questions this movement, if they question dogma, the beliefs of Scientology, those questions will be discouraged, suppressed, and they might even be labeled a suppressive person. Some people will be removed from this cult. Those who are removed are demonized, and those who leave the cult are demonized. If one is a member of this cult, and somebody leaves the cult, they are not to associate with this defector, this heretic, this suppressive person.

---

[154] Long Before Xenu: Scientology's Actual Origin Story as Told by a Former Member http://tonyortega. org/2015/07/24/long-before-xenu-scientologys-actual-origin-story-as-told-by-a- former-member/

A Religion for Movie Stars

It is a strange movement. Many know of Scientology because of some of its celebrity members. Scientology is known for roping in celebrities. People like Kirstie Alley, Tom Cruise, John Travolta, and so many more. They are known for attracting celebrities and then using them to bring in other people.

Steamrolling

Scientology is known for its aggressive litigation. If one speaks ill of their movement, if they try to expose them, they've been known to sue people, and they will sue them silly. They will sue them out of house and home. They will do everything and anything to take down their opposition.

Another tactic of Scientology is to go after people's websites. Scientology is the only group that has successfully gone after the IRS and caused the IRS grief. One of their tactics is to steamroll. Scientology will do this against people that oppose them. They will bring all kinds of false accusations against them, and they will steamroll them with so many false accusations, litigation, so much, the person who is opposing Scientology will throw up their hands and give up. They can't handle it all, and they give up. They get tired, and they decide not to attack the group.

South Park is one of the first groups who brought opposition of Scientology, was critical of their claims and their beliefs, and at the end of the show, they said, "Sue me," challenging Scientology. Scientology didn't do anything, and that was when the cork was popped out of the bottle, and articles started coming out right and left critical of Scientology's worldview, and all of the craziness and scandals came out in the open.

L. Ron Hubbard

The movement was started by L. Ron Hubbard, born March 13, 1911, and he was a popular pulp fiction science fiction writer in the 30's and 40's. But things seemed to take a turn during a science fiction convention in New Jersey, somewhere around 1949. L. Ron Hubbard said this, in front of an audience, he announced, "Writing for a penny a word is ridiculous. If a man really wanted to make a million dollars, the best way would be to start his own religion."[155] I should note there are various versions of the story around that quote and Scientology officially denies Hubbard ever said it. One year later, L. Ron Hubbard released Dianetics, which is seen as the Bible for Scientology. It's their book, their Scriptures. Dianetics: a modern science, a modern health. A few years after that, the First Church of Scientology was opened in California. That was February 18, 1954.

L. Ron Hubbard was a pathological liar. So much has been written about this man from people who lived around him, who knew him personally, who walked with him day to day, and have written about him and said, "For a long time I thought this guy was for real. The more time I spent with him, the more I realized, he was perhaps a little bit brilliant, articulate, but mad and a pathological liar."[156] L. Ron Hubbard at times has claimed or called himself, a nuclear physicist. He's not a nuclear physicist. In fact, he failed his only class on molecular and atomic physics. L. Ron Hubbard also, while married to his wife Margaret Grubb Hubbard, pretended to be a bachelor to Sarah Northrup Hollister, and ended up marrying her. She claimed sleep deprivations, beatings, strangulations, kidnapping of her child and fleeing to Cuba, and Ron counseling her to commit suicide.[157]

Many of L. Ron Hubbard's space opera stories were borrowed from his science fiction books, with the names changed, or the scenarios changed. Many things also came from L. Ron Hubbard's own life.

Dianetics

Dianetics was originally intended to be a new psychotherapy, and it was not expected to become the foundation for a new religion. Hubbard defined this Dianetics as a spiritual healing technology, an organized science of thought. He did submit papers outlining these principles in his book Dianetics to the Journal of American Medical Association and the American Journal of Psychiatry in 1949. All of it was rejected. Every time his methods of helping people out have been reviewed by various psychiatry associations, medical communities and the like, they have all been rejected and denounced as anything scientific. When one gets to know the writings of L. Ron

---

[155] Start a Religion http://www.don-lindsay-archive.org/scientology/start.a.religion.html

[156] Gardner, Martin, "Propheteering business," Nature. 331 (6152), p. 125–126.

[157] http://www.spaink.net/cos/LRH-bio/sara.htm

Hubbard and those who knew him, they find most of everything he said of himself is pure fantasy.

What do they Believe?

What does Scientology teach? As far as the mind goes, it is divided into three divisions. According to Scientology, there is the analytical mind. This mind is the part of the mind that works like a perfect computer. It never makes mistakes. It is the "I" of the person. It is the part of the mind where rational decisions are made, the rational mechanism, is responsible for consciousness. It is the good part of the mind. It is the part of the mind that does everything. It's the part of the mind we want to develop.[158]

The second part of the mind is the reactive mind. It works on a stimulus/response basis. Some liken the reactive mind to the subconscious. The reactive mind is thought to absorb all pain and emotional trauma, and then the reactive mind holds these mental pictures, images of this trauma or past experiences. Scientology calls these mental pictures engrams. That is a term that is going to be used several times as we go on. These engrams are the single source of aberrations and psychosomatic ills.

The third part, the somatic mind, is directed by the reactive and analytical minds. The somatic mind controls the body on a physical level. The somatic mind keeps the body regulated and functioning. In other words, it keeps the body ticking.[159]

How does this hold together? Why is this important, or even worth mentioning? This forms the foundation of why Scientology does what it does. There is this battle that seems to take place in the mind. It occurs when the reactive mind interferes with the analytical mind. The analytical mind is desired to be at the wheel. The reactive mind can cause a "moment of unconsciousness." A person can be fully awake during this, but when it does, the mind will take a mental snapshot of everything happening and store it. These are, once again, called engrams. These will cause one to react in certain ways to certain stimuli.

Hubbard said it this way. "Suppose, as an example of an engram, and its effects on the spirit. Mr. A has a tonsillectomy. During the operation, the surgeon, who wears glasses, comments to a nurse, 'You don't know what you're doing.' Mr. A recovers, and

---

[158] The Parts of the Mind, http://www.scientology.org/what-is-dianetics/basic-principles-of-scientology/the-parts-of-the-mind.html

[159] The Somatic Mind, http://www.ronthephilosopher.org/phlspher/page49.htm

a few months later, has an argument with his employer, who also happens to wear glasses, who says, 'You don't know what you're doing.' Mr. A suddenly feels dizzy, stupid, and gets a pain in his throat. There is installed a disk, a conditioned semantic response, which affects the Thetan."[160]

So here we see Hubbard saying we have these traumatic events, the reactive mind takes a snapshot of this event and certain things that happen during this event, and then later on in life, something similar happens, almost like a deja vu moment, but things are a little bit different. The reactive mind takes control or interferes with the analytical mind. What would have been a more calculated, controlled, rational response can be muddied from these engrams, these snapshots, that somehow got stuck inside the hard drive of the brain. It's messing up how one would typically react to certain stimuli.

The solution is to get somehow rid of these engrams, these reactive mind snapshots, of other events influencing analytical thinking, one's ability to make good analytical decisions.

Let's talk about the state of man. Mankind is an immortal being called a Thetan. These Thetans are not originally from earth. Man is trapped by matter, energy, space and time, also referred to by Scientologists as M.E.S.T.[161] Scientology gets much of their theology from Buddhism and Hinduism.[162] Scientology teaches reincarnation. Salvation for Scientologists comes through a process called auditing, where through auditor questions, the auditor will guide them to consciously re-experience painful or traumatic events in their past, to free themselves of these limiting effects of these events. This is how they get cleared of these engrams.[163]

Reincarnation can be involved with these engrams. These engrams don't necessarily have to be from this life.[164] They can be engrams, or memories, from previous lives. The goal is, from these auditing sessions, to clear a person from all of these engrams.

---

[160] Martin, Walter, Kingdom of the Cults, p. 341

[161] What is the Scientology Thetan? https://scientologyanswers.wordpress.com/category/what-is- the-scientology-thetan/

[162] Scientology's Relationship With Eastern Religious Traditions, Journal of Contemporary Religion, Vol. 11, No. 1, 1996, p. 21, http://www.bible.ca/scientology-eastern-religions-Kent.htm

[163] Salvation with Scientology, https://scientologyanswers.wordpress.com/2007/10/16/salvation-with- scientology/

[164] Scientology and Past Lives: Was L. Ron Hubbard Actually Serious? http://tonyortega.org/2012/12/08/scientology-and-past-lives-was-l-ron-hubbard-actually-serious/

Each one of these sessions to go in and speak to an auditor is a fee for service basis. They call it a donation. It's much more than a donation. With each audit, there are higher and higher costs associated. When a person first starts out, it's pretty cheap, but with each successive time they go into get another level of clear, it costs them more and more and more. That is why this faith has become a cash cow. It can costs people hundreds of thousands of dollars to get a state of clear from Scientology. It makes sense now why this is a celebrity religion because one has to have some money to pull this off. Like typical cults, they will talk people into selling their house, giving their inheritance, to reach this state of clear.

If one reaches a state of clear, they will gain superpowers, because they will have escaped matter, energy, space and time (M.E.S.T.). Hubbard claimed they would develop superpowers, X-men powers, over the world around them because they will have escaped it.[165]

The electro-psychometer, E-meter, is used during auditing sessions. In the early days, it resembled a lie detector test. It is a box that measures electrical activity. The prospective member has to hold two little cans. They would have a wire going back, and resistance is measured between the cans. A small current is passed through them and resistance is measured through these cans. The auditor will ask the prospective member questions, and as he's asking questions, he's looking for the needle to move on his E-meter. When this happens, he has touched on an engram. Then he'll start probing and asking questions about this event. It almost has a feeling of a scientific nature to it, like there is something there to it.

At one point the FDA raided some offices and confiscated their e-meters because Scientology was claiming they were medical devices.[166] Now they have to refer to them something along the lines of a religious device. Scientology claims they are purely religious artifacts now.

The auditor will continue to ask questions until there are no more readings on his e-meter, at which point it is assumed the prospective member has been freed of that engram because they are no longer showing any electrical resistance through these tin cans they are holding.

---

[165] These are the superpowers Scientologists are paying big bucks to attain, http://tonyortega. org/2015/02/11/these-are-the-superpowers-scientologists-are-paying-big-bucks-to-attain/
[166] Secrets of Scientology: The E-meter, https://www.cs.cmu.edu/~dst/E-Meter/

They call this process the "bridge to total freedom."[167] It is the quest to becoming clear. Once one becomes clear, all sorts of amazing things happen.

What is a Thetan? As far as Christianity is concerned, the closest thing would be the soul, the true identity of a person. This Thetan is intrinsically good. It's omniscient. Every person has a person has a Thetan that is omniscient inside of them.[168] This Thetan is divine but has forgotten its divinity. These Thetans were the ones who brought the material universe into being, mainly for their pleasure. The universe had no real independent reality. It got its form, its reality, from the Thetans, this collective of Thetans. Almost like in Hinduism, where each person has a spark of the divine in them, and they seek to, through yoga and meditation and mantras, and offering sacrifices to various Hindu gods, and other things, they are trying to get back to that knowledge of divinity.[169] They hold this in common with the New Age.

Hard to imagine. A God somehow forgot it was once a God.

The goal is to become an operating Thetan, at which point one transcends M.E.S.T. and gains special powers when they go clear. Supposedly, many, many, many people have gone clear. The world has not seen anybody come out of Scientology with special X-men powers to transcend M.E.S.T. Of all the people who have spent tens of thousands of dollars, why aren't there more people who are saying they have reached this status and can show us their powers? Such as, "I can levitate. I can move things with my mind. I can travel through space at the speed of light. I can astral travel at will. I can read minds." We should see a little Avengers team coming out of Scientology, but we don't, because it's not real.

These Thetans agreed their creation was good. But, at some point, these Thetans got so into their creation, that somewhere along the line over an extended period, they forgot they were divine and started putting more and more stock in the idea they were a part of this creation. Now Scientology comes along as a Savior to help everybody re-establish the link with their divinity, and become clear, operating Thetans.

What do Scientologists teach about the cross? Scientology has a version of the cross. Imagine a traditional cross, but imagine an x over the point where the vertical

---

[167] What is the Bridge in Scientology? https://www.scientology.org/faq/background-and-basic-principles/what-is-the-bridge-in-scientology.html

[168] The Thetan, http://www.scientology.org/what-is-scientology/basic-principles-of-scientology/the-thetan.html

[169] Ankerberg, John and Weldon, John, Encylopedia of New Age Beliefs, p. 530

and horizontal bars meet. But it's more of a star in the shape of an x. Scientology says the horizontal bar of the cross represents the material universe, and the vertical bar is the spirit. So the spirit is to be seen rising triumphantly, ultimately transcending the turmoil of the physical universe, to achieve salvation.[170]

Scientology also has a logo that might be familiar. It looks science fiction-esque. It is the letter S, along with two triangles which are diagonally leaning to the S. The top triangle is referred to as the KRC triangle. K for knowledge, R for responsibility, C for control. Then there is this lower triangle, called the arc triangle. A for affinity, R for reality and C for communication.[171]

Another thing worth mentioning about Scientology is their abusive tactics. There have been many shows exposing Scientology. Scientology is known for its brainwashing tactics.[172] For example, there have been many examples of people on their Sea Org ships who have been labeled a suppressive person. Or, one does something against the rules of the Sea Org, and they will put them in solitary confinement, starve them, or other strange and abusive tactics.[173]

Scientology denies the existence of hell. They categorically deny the existence of God and the Bible.[174] L. Ron Hubbard was much opposed to Christianity.[175] If anything, he gravitated toward the occult. He was good friends with Jack Parsons.[176] He ended up stealing Jack Parsons' girlfriend. He had some interesting connections with Aleister Crowley as well.[177]

---

[170] What is the Scientology Cross? http://www.scientology.org/faq/background-and-basic-principles/what-is-the-scientology-cross.html

[171] What does the Scientology Symbol, the S and Double Triangle, Represent? http://www.scientology.org/faq/background-and-basic-principles/what-does-the-scientology-symbol-represent.html

[172] Brainwashing and Thought Control in Scientology -- The Road to Rondroid, Understanding Scientology, by Margery Wakefield, chapter 14, https://www.cs.cmu.edu/~dst/Library/Shelf/wakefield/ us-14.html

[173] Sea Org, http://exscientologykids.com/sea-org-2/

[174] What Christians Need to Know about Scientology, https://www.cs.cmu.edu/~dst/Library/Shelf/wakefield/christians.html

[175] L. Ron Hubbard's Thoughts on Christianity, https://youtu.be/sk03n7rMJ1o

[176] The strangely true connection between Scientology, the Jet Propulsion Lab, and Occult Sorcery, http://io9.gizmodo.com/5978746/the-strangely-true-connection-between-scientology-the-jet-propulsion-lab-and-pagan-sorcery

[177] L. Ron Hubbard Speaks about Aleister Crowley, https://youtu.be/h3yfsbi4L70

As far as Jesus goes, he was merely a good teacher. There were elements of implants. When the Thetans were implanted with fake memories, and the concept of Christianity was part of the brainwashing. Jesus is part of a by-product of a brainwashing operation done by Xenu.

Scientology teaches multiple gods, and some gods are over other gods.[178] L. Ron Hubbard mentions in several of this writings there are other gods. But he never gets in-depth on who these gods are. He mentions them in passing. He never spends much time on who's in charge, if anybody. L. Ron Hubbard was polytheistic in his beliefs.

As far as sin goes, Scientology teaches mankind is inherently good. They are born good, and they are pretty much good their whole lives. They make bad decisions from time to time.[179]

L. Ron Hubbard despised Christians and the Scriptures telling him he is a sinner that needs to repent.

Terminology

Auditing – Sessions a member has with an auditor to get rid of engrams.

Blow – Leaving Scientology

Clear – When all engrams have been successfully removed and a member has transcended M.E.S.T. (Matter, Energy, Space, Time)

Dianetics – L. Ron Hubbard's first book describing his spiritual healing technology which became the philosophical and methodological foundation for Scientology when it became a religion.

Disconnection – Severing ties with all friends and family members who are unsupportive of Scientology.

---

[178] Does Scientology have a Concept of God? https://www.scientology.org/faq/scientology-beliefs/what-is-the-concept-of-god-in-scientology.html

[179] Does Scientology Believe Man is Sinful? https://www.scientology.org/faq/scientology-beliefs/does-scientology-believe-man-is-sinful.html

E-meter – Device created in the 1940s by Volney Mathison,[180] an inventor and early collaborator with L. Ron Hubbard. Used during auditing sessions to measure engrams.

Engram – Trauma in the reactive mind causing hindrance to the analytic mind. The purpose of auditing sessions is to remove these engrams.

Fair Game – L. Ron Hubbard's prescribed method of retaliation against those who oppose or speak negatively of Scientology.

Operating Thetan – A Scientologist who has reached the second level in Scientology's version of salvation. There are eight sub levels which gradually reveal the deepest secrets of the church, including the creation story.

Reactive mind – The subconscious half of the human mind containing a person's involuntary impulses. The goal of auditing is to clear the engrams that operate the reactive mind, allowing the analytic mind to function fully.

Suppressive person – Anybody at odds with or actively opposing Scientology.

Thetan - Invisible part of a human being, similar to the soul or spirit in other religions.

Xenu – The dictator of a Galactic Confederacy who brought billions of people to Earth and massacred them with hydrogen bombs 75 trillion years ago. The story of Xenu is revealed in Operating Thetan level three.[181]

---

[180] The True Inventor of the E-Meter, https://www.cs.cmu.edu/~dst/E-Meter/volney.html
[181] OT III Materials, http://exscientologykids.com/ot3/

Chapter 12

First Church of Christ, Scientist

(Christian Science)

What do they Believe?

There is no life, truth, intelligence or substance in matter. All is infinite mind, in its infinite manifestation. For God is all in all. Spirit is mortal truth. Matter is mortal error. Spirit is the real and eternal. Matter is the unreal and temporal. Spirit is God and man is his image and likeness. Therefore man is not material. He is spiritual.[182] Many people confuse Christian Science with Scientology and faith healing. They get confused with New Age practices and also Eastern religions.

They present themselves as a restoration of primitive Christianity as a demonstrable scientific system.[183]

What one finds in Christian Science reading rooms are various publications, the works of Mary Baker Eddy. Her name is the most well known in this movement. She founded Christian Science. One will find various publications on proofs, or testimonies, of people being healed by Christian Science. Another thing to note is they

---

[182] Eddy, Mary Baker, Science and Health, Chapter XVII - Glossary, 591:6
[183] Epps, Henry, The Consummation of the Ages vol III, p. 84

have several major publications published throughout the world, such as the Christian Science Monitor, which is a newspaper. They have the Christian Science Journal and Christian Science Sentinel. They are prolific when it comes to creating content.

Christian Science is neither Christian nor science.

Christian Science does not teach Jesus is God.[184] They don't teach Jesus died on a cross, nor do they teach his blood atones for our sins. They don't teach Jesus rose from the dead bodily.[185] They don't teach salvation as we see it.[186] They have a different view of salvation. They don't teach Jesus' bodily ascension.[187] They don't teach Jesus is going to return someday.[188] They do not teach the Trinity.[189] They don't teach hell or sin. Christian Science teaches sin, evil, the devil, death and disease are illusions.[190] They don't teach suffering is real. They don't teach God created a material universe. They teach this entire universe is an illusion.[191] They don't teach the virgin birth as the Bible sets forth. They do have a virgin birth, but it is so different than what the Bible talks about.[192] They teach Jesus was a fallible man. Demons are bad thoughts.[193] They do not teach the word of God is infallible. So it's not divinely inspired. It's full of corruptions. [194]But they also teach Science and Health with Key to the Scriptures is inspired and without error.[195] This was Mary Baker Eddy's key work. They view Mary Baker Eddy as a prophet, and their Scriptures are now above the Bible.

Christian Science teaches the traditional view of the Trinity is polytheism. They teach creation, all we see, all this matter, is an illusion. God did not create a material

---

[184] Eddy, Mary Baker, Science and Health, Chapter XVII - Glossary, 589:18

[185] Eddy, Mary Baker, Science and HealthChapter II - Atonement and Eucharist

[186] Eddy, Mary Baker, Science and Health, Chapter XVII - Glossary, 593:21

[187] Eddy, Mary Baker, Science and Health, Chapter II - Atonement and Eucharist, 34:27

[188] Eddy, Mary Baker, Science and HealthChapter XVI - The Apocalypse

[189] Beliefs and Teachings, http://www.christianscience.com/what-is-christian-science/beliefs-and- teachings

[190] Eddy, Mary Baker, Science and Health, Chapter XVII - Glossary, 588:1

[191] Eddy, Mary Baker, Science and HealthChapter IX - Creation

[192] Cook, Barbara, Virgin birth: beyond history, a living spiritual idea, The Christian Science Journal, December 1988, Volume 106, Issue 12

[193] Eddy, Mary Baker, Science and Health, Chapter XVII - Glossary, 584:18

[194] Eddy, Mary Baker, Science and Health, Key to the Scriptures

[195] Eddy, Mary Baker, Science and Health, Contents - Preface

universe, but rather the creation is the unfolding of spiritual ideas and their identities in the mind of God. They don't teach Jesus is God.

How do they Worship Together?

Their version of prayer is much different than ours. They aren't asking God for help. Christian Science does not teach prayer is communicating with a personal God.[196] They don't use doctors, at least, not as often as we do. They prefer to use Christians Science practitioners for healing.[197] Going to the doctor is frowned upon. It's not official doctrine to not use doctors or medicines or immunizations. They don't observe any ordinances like the Lord's Supper or baptism.

They use the Bible, but they don't follow the typical customs of Christianity. Their church services are divided. They have a little section of time where they have Bible readings. The Bible readings are not expounded on at all. Then they read excerpts from Mary Baker Eddy's book.

Mary Baker Eddy

Mary Baker Eddy started Christian Science. It was influenced with some major illnesses in her life.[198] She had a spinal weakness, and this caused seizures, and she also had some other health problems as well. These health problems influenced her as time goes on to come up with the doctrine and form the First Church of Christ Scientist.

As an adult, Mary became involved with various forms of the occult, including spiritism. She sometimes fell into a deep trance, where sometimes people would ask her for advice on various matters. She claimed she experienced various encounters during the night, including strange rapping sounds and seeing dead people by her bedside. She sometimes received messages from the dead.[199]

---

[196] Eddy, Mary Baker, Science and Health, Chapter I - Prayer

[197] Eddy, Mary Baker, Science and Health, Chapter VI - Science, Theology, Medicine

[198] What is Christian Science? http://www.christianscience.com/what-is-christian-science

[199] A Course in Miracles: Spirituality or Spiritism? http://www.neirr.org/MIRACLES.htm

Phineas Quimby

Then enters a character named Phineas Quimby. He's like a faith healer. He was a metaphysical healer, and he was known for his particular view of sin, sickness, disease and death existing only in the mind. He taught wrong thinking, or false beliefs caused disease. Mary Baker Eddy went to him to hopefully heal her back. On November 7, 1862, she believed her back had been healed. In 1866, she had a nasty fall on some icy pavement, and she believed she was instantly healed when the healing truth dawned upon her senses.

It is believed by many that Mary Baker Eddy plagiarized many sections of Phineas Quimby's book.[200] Phineas Quimby referred to his system sometimes as Science of the Christ or Science and Health. Mary Baker Eddy wrote her book Science and Health with Key to the Scriptures. She comes to the point where illness, death and disease is in the mind, and positive thinking can cure it.

This probably sounds familiar because it has found its way into the Christian church. There was a book by Rhonda Byrne called Rahasya - The Secret which has become popular because of people like Oprah Winfrey. By thinking positively and tapping into the cosmic energies, one can bring about change in their life.

It's interesting to note several of Phineas Quimby's students went on to found the New Thought Movement, which has now spawned other movements like Religious Science and the Unity Church. These movements are considered precursors of the contemporary New Age Movement.

Other Influences

Mary Baker Eddy despised Calvinism, and she disagreed with the final judgment and also hell, or eternal punishment.[201] Her father was a Calvinistic preacher. Mary and her dad had many disagreements. She argued with her dad often, especially during her teenage years, and this formed her ideas on her faith that was to be birthed in 1866.

Another person who influenced her thoughts concerning this future movement was a woman named Ann Lee. She recognized divinity as both masculine and

---

[200] Phineas Pankhurst Quimby, Father of New Thought http://phineasquimby.wwwhubs.com/

[201] Dunbar, Rosalie E., Calvinism, Christian Science, and God's Elect, The Christian Science Monitor, March 30, 2010

feminine, our Mother/Father God. Christian Scientists often refer to God as Father/Mother.[202]

"Creed" of Christian Science

Mary allowed herself to be represented as the equal and successor to Christ, like a Christian Science version of the Pope.[203] She was okay with this. Her loyal followers revered her. She wanted to be called Mother Eddy. Christian Science is based on a pantheistic worldview. They have a view God is all in all. They have a quotation they often recite. "All is infinite mind in its infinite manifestations for God is all in all."[204]

Their logic goes something like this:

"If God is Spirit, and God is all, then non-Spirit (matter) does not exist."

1) God is all in all.
2) God is good. God is mind.
3) God, Spirit, being all, nothing is matter.
4) Spirit is the real and eternal. Matter is the unreal and temporal.
5) If God is life, and God is all, then non-life (death) does not exist.
6) If it is true man lives, this fact can never change in science to the opposite belief man dies.
7) Life is real, and death is the illusion.
8) If God is healthy, and God is all, then non-healthy (sickness) does not exist.
9) Man is never sick for mind is not sick, and matter cannot be.
10) If God is good, and God is all, then non-good (evil) does not exist.

From these, all the doctrines of Christian Science follow. Judgment and wrath are bad thought processes bring consequences on the people of the world. Evil is not real, and God did not create evil or sin. Sin is a bad thought process.[205]

---

[202] Klein, Janice, Ann Lee and Mary Baker Eddy: The Parenting of New Religions, The Journal of Psychohistory 6.3, Winter 1979, p. 361

[203] Bailey, Joshua, Christian Science and its Revelator, The Christian Science Journal, April 1889, p.1

[204] Eddy, Mary Baker, One Cause and Effect http://www.endtime.org/library/mbe/one cause and effect.html

[205] Eddy, Mary Baker, Science and Health, Chapter XIV - Recapitulation

Terminology[206]

When one reads these terms and their meanings to Christian Science and then applies them to the Bible, the Bible becomes a disaster area as one cannot make heads or tails of anything. Everything is metaphorical. It becomes impossible to read and make any sense out of it.

Angels - God's thoughts passing to man. An inspiration of goodness, purity that counters evil and material reality.

Atonement - At - one - ment, lifting the whole man into Christ consciousness. The biblical account is metaphorical and not real.

Baptism - The ongoing daily purification of thought and deed.

Eucharist - Spiritual communion with God, celebrated with silent prayer and Christian living. It is a submergence in Spirit.

Blasphemy of the Holy Spirit - The belief God created disharmony in the world.

Body - The form of expression of both Spirit and soul. It is the apparent materialization of the limits of soul as influenced by a person's conscious development in Christian Science principles.

Christ - The divine idea man. Jesus was not the Christ, but a perfect representation of the Christ consciousness that is the true and higher self of every person. Christ is the manifestation of everything good and true. The realization of divine principle. A Christian Scientist can say, "I am Christ." Jesus and the Christ are two separate beings. New Agers and other groups have similar concepts. Jesus was a man, and Christ, this divine idea, this mindset, came upon him, and he became Jesus the Christ.

Creation - A product of divine mind. Divine mind is another name for God Christian Scientists use. There is only one reality that emanates and is part of the divine mind. Anything not in harmony with the divine mind is not a reality, but a lack of understanding of the principles of divine mind brought about by people.

---

[206] Boehm, Michael, What is Christian Science? 04, Christian Science Terms and Definitions episode 151, http://www.sermonaudio.com/sermoninfo.asp?SID=73012224033

Devil - Evil, a lie, error. He is an entity, not a person, and has no existence. A belief in sin, sickness and death.

Evil spirits - False beliefs.

Flesh - An error of physical belief. A supposition life, substance and intelligence are in matter. An illusion.

God - Spirit, who is ever-present, all-knowing, all-powerful and good. God is the Father/Mother God. Other names for God are Divine Mind, Soul, Principle, Life, Truth, Love. To the Christian Scientist, God is the governing principle of the universe to which a person must harmonize his belief system.

Gods - Mythology; a belief life, substance, and intelligence are both mental and material; a supposition of sentient physicality; the belief infinite Mind is infinite forms; the various theories that hold mind to be a material sense existing in the brain, nerve, matter; suppositious minds, or souls, going in and out of matter, erring and mortal.

Healing - Accomplished by correct thinking according to Christian Science principles. A change of belief that effects physical symptoms.

Heaven - Not a literal place of eternal bliss, but a harmonious condition of understanding where a person's consciousness is in harmony with Divine Mind. Harmony, the reign of Spirit, government of divine principle.

Hell - Mortal belief; error; lust; remorse; hatred; revenge; sin; sickness; death; suffering and self-destruction; self-imposed agony; effects of sin.

Holy Spirit - The divine science. It's the Spirit of God and is only discernable and knowable through his spiritual awareness. It's an emanation, a presence, a law of God in action. There is a sense where the Holy Spirit is not a being at all, but rather a thought process, a harmonious mindset one achieves.

Jesus' Stripes - The rejection of error. It has nothing to do with the beating Jesus received in the flesh.

Knowledge - The evidence of pain from the five corporeal senses. Mortality, beliefs and opinions. It's the opposite of spiritual truth and understanding. Material reality is non-existent. It's only an interpretation of Divine Mind. Even though a person may feel pain or sickness, it does not exist.

Mortal Mind - Nothing claiming to be something, for mind is immortal. Error creating errors.

Pastor - The combined books of the Bible with Science and Health with Key to the Scriptures.

Personhood - An aspect and reflection of Divine Mind.

Prayer - Contemplation and internalization of divine truths. The taking hold of God's willingness. An affirmation of God's being in relation to man. Prayer from the Christian Science perspective does not ask God to intervene, but rather a process of learning more of God's spiritual reality.

Resurrection - Spiritualization of thought. A new and higher idea of immortality or spiritual existence. Material belief yielding to spiritual understanding.

Salvation - Life, truth and love, understood and demonstrated as supreme over all. Sin, death and sickness are destroyed.

Sickness - False understanding giving the appearance of reality by the unfaithful and ignorant of divine principle and mind.

Sin - Not understanding and behaving according to divine law of God, and the law of our being.

Soul - Man's consciousness; that which he has apprehended or developed out of Spirit; both consciousness and subconsciousness.

Spirit - Another name for God; divine substance, mind, divine principle; everything good; Christ.

Wrath - The working out of the law of God's being upon a person. It is not God's judgment upon a sinner.

CHAPTER 13

International Church of Christ

(ICOC; Boston Church of Christ; Multiplying Movement)

My Personal Experiences with this Group

I've had a couple of run-ins with this group over the years. The first of which was when I was in college at Hope International University. I was with a Bible study that would go out on the campus of Fullerton College witnessing. We would also have prayer meetings and Bible studies. We had a book table that was set up for anybody who was interested in getting information about the group, Christianity and the gospel. One day there was an entire group of people that came over to our table, and they paired up with us, one on one, and started arguing with us. And that group was part of the International Church of Christ group on campus. Some might know this group as the Boston Church of Christ or Los Angeles Church of Christ.

I encountered them in Chicago as well. One time, when living there, my wife and I got invited to church. I found out that it was with the Church of Christ, and I was wondering if it was the good Church of Christ or not so good Church of Christ. When we got to church, the first thing anybody said to us was, "Who invited you?" When we told them, they ushered us down to the front as this individual was performing a special song during the worship service. It was pretty obvious to me from the way they were asking the question and what I saw around me that this was the not so good Church of Christ. But it was good to have that experience of knowing what their worship services were like.

Going back to that first experience at the book table, there was one individual from that group that ended up coming back later by himself and asked if he could talk to one of us. He ended up giving his life over to the biblical Jesus that day, leaving that group and becoming part of our group. We watched as this man got harassed by other members of this group.

I had another interesting encounter with this group. I got to meet one of the key leaders of the group in that area. He had an interesting name. Something like Geo or something like that. I was talking with him for quite a while, and then all of the sudden, two girls seemed to come out of nowhere. They started joining in on the conversation, and it became clear after a while that these two girls were hitting on the people in my group, and I came to find out later that this is a strategy that ICOC doesn't have any problem employing when trying to recruit people. In fact, it's referred to as flirty fishing, made popular in the 1960s and 1970s by the Children of God. They are popular when it comes to the college-age level. They are active on college campuses.

What do they Believe?

They are also known as the Boston Church of Christ, the Crossroads Movement, Multiplying Ministries, the Discipling Movement, the International Church of Christ, the London Church of Christ, the San Diego Church of Christ, etc.

As far as doctrine goes, they teach the Bible as the inerrant, infallible Word of God. They are Trinitarian. They teach the resurrection of Jesus and the sacrificial atonement. The Boston Church of Christ is the only true church. And that is a dangerous teaching. They teach baptismal regeneration, meaning baptism is necessary for salvation, and baptism in their church, with a proper understanding that baptism saves is required for salvation.

They practice heavy discipleship. What I mean by heavy discipleship is that every person in the church is supposed to have somebody discipling them and somebody they are discipling lower than them, or newer to the group than them. Discipleship isn't just teaching the basics, or opening the Bible and studying it together. It's who

I should marry, what job should I have, what should I do with my life, where should I live. All of those types of questions and more would be under the scrutiny of the person who is their discipler, and they would have the authority in their life to tell them the answer to all of those questions.

Unquestioned submission to authority is another trademark of this group.

History

The group's distant origins go back to 1967 in Gainesville, Florida under Charles Lucas. He started a program called the Multiplying Ministries program, which was successful. The movement we're concerned with here started in the Crossroads Church of Christ in Florida in 1985 by Kip McKean, who had been trained in the discipling methodology by Mr. Lucas from Charleston, Illinois early in the movement. Kip later moved to Massachusetts and using the methodology, the church began to grow. In the first year, 103 people were baptized in their church. In the second year, 200 were baptized. Third year, 256. Fourth-year 368. In 1982, the Boston Movement began planning their pillar churches. These are churches in key cities throughout the world. The first two were established in Chicago and London. In 1986, the program called reconstruction was undertaken whereby trained International Church of Christ ministers replaced ministers in established Church of Christ churches. This caused problems among this organization, but it helped to solidify this group.

Structure

Kip McKean is the unquestioned leader, and under Kip are the elders. Under the elders are the evangelists, then zone leaders, then house church leaders, which is obsolete in most congregations, and last, assistant Bible talk leaders. These leaders govern by consensus, but Kip McKean gives them direction.

Regarding authority and submission, elder Al Baird, one of the uppermost leaders in the Church of Christ, wrote a series of articles distributed to the Boston Church of Christ which said, "Let us begin our discussion of submission by talking about what it is not. It is not agreeing. When one agrees with the decision that was made, he does not have to submit to anything. By definition, submission is doing something one has been asked to do that he would not do if he had his own way. Submission is not outward obedience, but It includes a wholehearted giving up one's desires. Submission is not conditional. We submit to authority, not because the one in authority deserves it, but because the authority comes from God, so therefore, in reality, we are submitting to God."[207]

Origins

Church of Christ should sound familiar from the previous chapters covering The Church of Jesus Christ of Latter-day Saints and the movement in the early 1800s in America called the Restoration Movement. It was started by Thomas and Alexander Campbell, along with some contemporaries, and it was the idea that the true church of Jesus Christ needed to be restored to the earth. Then somewhere along the line, and they disagreed on when, the church had gone apostate, and there was a need to return to New Testament Christianity, the early church, and the model that is present within the book of Acts.

Going back to the book of Acts, they started incorporating baptismal regeneration, and this is true of any Christian Church, Church of Christ, Disciples of Christ, and all the other movements that began with the Restoration Movement.

Within the Church of Christ, there is the Instrumental Church of Christ and Non-Instrumental Church of Christ. The International Church of Christ is also non-instrumental. They do not implement any musical instruments in their worship services. Why? Because they say it is not to be found in the New Testament. The idea behind the Restoration Movement was that anything that is not found in the New Testament they would not do and anything that is found in the New Testament, they would do.

And most of these churches, Churches of Christ, will require people to be re-baptized in their church, even if they have been previously baptized, and by baptized, I mean immersed, as a believer, after they have believed.

---

[207] Authority and Submission, parts III, V and VII as quoted in Jones, Jerry, *What Does The Boston Movement Teach?* p. 59-63

Distinctives

1) Heavy discipleship.

2) Distinction between Christian and disciple. They get people in by asking, "Are you a Christian, or are you a disciple?" A disciple is one who would fully submit, they are wholehearted in the church.

3) They are the one true church that can teach the truth, truly disciple, and truly help one come into a relationship with Jesus Christ.

CHAPTER 14

Seventh Day Adventist

(SDA)

Are they a Cult or Not?

Are they a cult, or are they not a cult? The late Dr. Walter Martin, during the beginning of his ministry, claimed they were a cult, but toward the end of his ministry, he started claiming they were not a cult. Rather, they were Christians with some different and aberrant beliefs.

What do they Believe?

Seventh Day Adventists teach one must worship on the Sabbath, Saturday. They teach from sundown on Friday to sundown on Saturday is the Sabbath. They meet on the Sabbath, and they try to follow some of the Old Testament laws concerning the Sabbath.

Seventh Day Adventists teach Jesus is Michael the Archangel., however, not in the same way as Jehovah's Witnesses. They teach Michael was the title of Jesus in the

Old Testament, but Jesus has always been and always will be co-equal and co-eternal with God.[208]

Seventh Day Adventists teach three phases of the atonement. The death on the cross is phase one. In 1844, Jesus entered into a time that is referred to as the Investigative Judgment, which is phase two. The third part of the atonement is the scapegoat, who they refer to as Satan. On the day of judgment, Satan will have all of the believers' sins placed upon him. So Satan plays a part in the atonement.[209] Seventh Day Adventists teach Ellen G. White is a prophet. They try as much as they can to follow the Kosher law.

Origins

Seventh Day Adventism started with William Miller in the 1800s. He started out as a Deist, but he converted to Christianity in 1816, and he became a Baptist. He also became involved in the Second Coming, talking about the end times and when Christ would return. This is important because he came up with a theory about when Christ would return that had a significant impact on Seventh Day Adventist teachings.

William Miller did not start the Seventh Day Adventists. He had some ideas that Ellen G. White picked up and ended up in their theology later on. William Miller, reading Daniel 8:14, came up with a theory Jesus would return somewhere around 1843 to 1844. He came up with it this way.

> **Then I heard one saint speaking, and another saint said unto that certain [saint] which spake, How long [shall be] the vision [concerning] the daily [sacrifice], and the transgression of desolation, to give both the sanctuary and the host to be trodden under foot? And he said unto me, Unto two thousand and three hundred days; then shall the sanctuary be cleansed. (Daniel 8:13-14)**

So William Miller came up with a theory Jesus was going to return in 2,300 years from the rebuilding of the sanctuary. The decree was issued to rebuild Jerusalem in

---

[208] Christ, Michael, and Archangel, Questions on Doctrine, Question 8 http://www.sdanet.org/atissue/books/qod/q08.htm

[209] 28 Fundamental Beliefs, http://szu.adventist.org/wp-content/uploads/2016/04/28 Beliefs.pdf

457 B.C. From there one would count 2,300 years into the future and land somewhere around 1843 to 1844. This lead to the Great Disappointment because everybody was expecting Jesus to return on that day - another failed prophecy about Jesus' coming on a certain day like those made by Harold Camping, the Watchtower and others.

He finally came up with a date and declared that it was going to happen on October 22, 1844. Several people quit their jobs, sold everything, and were standing on the roofs of their houses in all white linen with their arms raised and ready for Christ to show up.

We're not supposed to know the day or hour. Jesus didn't even know. They're all standing on the roof of their houses, and Jesus doesn't come back. That day went down in history as the Great Disappointment.

After this happened, the Millerites, as they were called, broke up. He stopped pushing his prophecies. He realized he had played the role of a false prophet. He threw in the towel and gave up on his ministry. But that didn't stop some of his followers.

History

Now enter in Hiram Edson. On October 22nd, was the Great Disappointment. The morning after, October 23rd of 1844, Hiram Edson was walking through a cornfield, and he was praying and asking God why this happened. And then he claimed he had a vision. He received new light, and in his vision, he was informed Jesus was not to show up in 1844, but rather he moved from one part of heaven to a different part of heaven. He moved into the sanctuary, the Most Holy Place, to cleanse the sanctuary. Jesus moved into this Most Holy Place, and the Investigative Judgment began. In this Investigative Judgment, Jesus is reviewing all of the records of heaven. He's trying to find out who's been naughty and nice. He must review all of them and complete this Investigative Judgment before he can return.

Hiram Edson was one of the founders of the Seventh Day Adventist movement. There were three, maybe four, notable characters in the beginning or foundation of this movement. William Miller came up with the idea Jesus was going to return in 1844, and then he stopped his career as a false prophet. He gave that up, and these other characters stepped in, picked up the ball and ran with it.

Another key person was Joseph Bates. He was a seaman. Joseph Bates also taught the Investigative Judgment. He heard about the Investigative Judgment idea of Hiram

Edson. He was a strong proponent that New Testament believers should be following the Sabbath. So he was the one who brought the Sabbatarian concept to the Seventh Day Adventists.

He was also the man who brought in the health-conscious attitude to the Seventh Day Adventists. Joseph Bates became known as the apostle of the Sabbath.[210]

Ellen G. White

There are many founders of this group. Ellen G. White is the main one, the most notable one. She does claim to be a prophet, and the movement claims that she is a prophet even though she had several false prophecies.

Ellen G. White is by far the most influential character in the Seventh Day Adventist movement. She's the one who got this thing rolling.

Ellen White was born on November 26, 1827, and died on July 16, 1915. When she was young in school, somebody threw a rock at her and hit her in the face. It messed up her nose and put her in a coma for several weeks. The reason I bring this up is that it's quite possible that some or all of her visions had something to do with this. As later physicians note, they diagnosed her with brain injuries later on in life.[211]

Ellen G. White had many different visions. She uttered some prophecies in these visions. These prophecies turned out to be false prophecies. She did not breathe during the entire period of a vision that ranged from 15 minutes to 3 hours. Her pulse beat regularly, and her countenance remained pleasant as in the natural state. She was unconscious of everything transpiring around her and viewed herself as removed from this world and in the presence of heavenly beings. These descriptions were attested to by several different witnesses.[212]

---

[210] Joseph Bates, Adventist Pioneer Library, Volume1, Number 3 http://www.aplib.org/?page id=104

[211] Peterson, Donald I., MD, Visions or Seizures, Was Ellen White the Victim of Epilepsy? http://www.whiteestate.org/issues/visions.html

[212] I Am Quite Certain That She Did Not Breathe http://www.truthorfables.net/visions-no-breath-1.htm

False Prophecies

Ellen G. White has uttered many false prophecies, and that places her in the camp of a false prophet. Ellen White predicted Jesus would return in 1845. This ended up going around in the churches. It was the big buzz. She didn't come up with an exact date, but she said he would return in June of 1845. That came and passed, and Jesus never returned. That was not the only time she predicted his return. She predicted Jesus would come back in 1844, then 1845, then 1849.[213]

Joseph Bates announced that the time of trouble had begun. In 1850, Ellen G. White said the mighty shaking had commenced, referring to the end, the time of tribulation. To round out what she was saying, her husband was also claiming when Jesus said, "Come out her, my people,"[214] referring to Babylon, that this departure was already completed. "Babylon, the nominal church, has fallen. God's people have come out of her. She is now the habitation of devils and the hold of every foul spirit and the cage of every unclean and hateful bird."[215]

Ellen G. White said, "My accompanying angel said, 'Time is almost finished. Get ready, get ready, get ready. Now time is almost finished, and what we have been years learning, they will have to learn in a few months.'"[216]

Ellen G. White said, "I saw that the time for Jesus to be in the Most Holy Place was nearly finished."[217] So the Investigative Judgment was almost finished back in 1850.

Lastly, Ellen G. White predicted the end would be sometime that all those present and alive during 1856 would not all pass away before Christ returned. She said, "I was shown the company present at the conference. Said the angel, 'Some food for worms. Some subjects of the seven last plagues. Some will be alive and remain upon the earth to be translated at the coming of Jesus.'" [218]That was in 1856. That's over 150 years ago.

---

[213] Corner, Dan, Ellen G. White Fact Sheet http://www.evangelicaloutreach.org/white.htm

[214] Revelation 18:4

[215] White, James, Present Truth, 1850

[216] White, Ellen G., Early Writings, p. 64-67

[217] Ellen G. White Writings, To Those who are receiving the seal of the living God, January 31, 1849 http://text.egwwritings.org/publication.php?pubtype=Periodical&bookCode=Broadside2&lang=en&year=1849&month=January&day=31&m=1&paragraphReferences=1

[218] Regarding Some Food for Worms Statement http://ellenwhite.org/content/file/regarding-some- food-worms-statement#document

Soul Sleep

The idea of soul sleep goes back to a Methodist preacher named George Storrs.[219] Around 1837, a Baptist preacher read a tract written by a deacon Henry Gru from Pennsylvania.[220] It was about conditional immortality or soul sleep. The teaching of soul sleep is as follows. No conscious part of a human being survives death. The soul is nothing more than the Greek word for soul, pneuma. They see it as breath. So when one dies, that part of them returns to God is breath. After one dies, that's it. Lights out. Done. Then, when the resurrection happens, these bodies are resurrected. God breathes the breath of life into them and fills this being, the body that looks like that individual's body, with all of the thoughts, memories of the original person that once was. Then comes the judgment, whether for eternal life or annihilation.

Charles Taze Russell of the Jehovah's Witnesses, early on, before he had even started the Watchtower, was a follower of William Miller. He was a Millerite. He also subscribed to the teachings of George Storrs. One could say Charles Taze Russell was loosely affiliated with the Adventists. He was almost one of them for a while. Then, because he had some disagreements with the editor, he left the editorial staff of the Midnight Crying Herald of the Morning and started the Watchtower.

The Clear Word Bible

The Clear World Bible is a paraphrase. It is a commentary on the Word of God. It flows like the Bible, but it's a commentary because the author will insert his/her own beliefs right into the text.[221]

---

[219] Origins of the Doctrine of Soul Sleep and Annihilation in Adventism http://sogentlybroken.blogspot.com/2008/09/adventist-teaching-on-soul-sleep.html

[220] Champions of Conditional Immortality in History http://www.truthaccordingtoscripture.com/documents/death/champions-of-conditional-immortality.php#.WBdKYuErIXo

[221] Slick, Matt, The Clear Word Bible https://carm.org/clear-word-bible

Annihilation

After Jesus comes back, there is a great resurrection, where everybody comes back to life, the good and the bad. The good, those who have followed after Christ, who have trusted in Christ, will move on to everlasting life. Those who have rejected Christ are going to be annihilated. Like the Jehovah's Witnesses, Seventh Day Adventists teach one cataclysmic moment for each person where they are burned up. It might be painful, but it's going to be a fairly quick judgment, and then they are gone. There is no more conscious torment. They are gone gone, never to come back, never to be seen or heard from again, and their judgment is final. It's done, it's over with, and they are simply not conscious enough to worry about it for the rest of eternity.[222]

Shut Door Doctrine

Ellen G. White was also teaching the Shut Door Doctrine. She was teaching that from that moment, October 22, 1844, nobody else could get saved.[223] Jesus is already judging everybody. He's going through the books, and nobody else can be saved. That is not what Seventh Day Adventists teach now. The Shut Door Doctrine is now being reinterpreted and understood to be concerning the sanctuary, and not the fact nobody else can be saved. Ellen G. White said in The Great Controversy, "Attended by heavenly angels, our Great High Priest enters the Holy of Holies, and there appears in the presence of God to engage in the last acts of his ministration on behalf of man. To perform the work of Investigative Judgment, and to make atonement for all who are shown to be entitled to its benefits. In the day of the final atonement and Investigative Judgment, the only cases considered are those of the professed people of God."[224]

Investigative Judgment

One of the things Ellen White said is that Christ is closely reviewing the records in this book, and investigating those who have taken the name of Christ who are entitled

---

[222] Seventh Day Adventists http://www.eaec.org/cults/seventhdayadvent.htm

[223] Olson, Robert W., The "Shut Door" Documents http://www.whiteestate.org/issues/shutdoor.html

[224] White, Ellen G., The Great Controversy, p. 480

to its benefits.[225] That is a troubling statement. In other words, we have to do all these works. One gets the feeling from this Investigative Judgment, and many Seventh Day Adventists feel this way, that it is through their good works that they can be entitled to take the name of Christ. In other words, Adventists are left with this uncertain feeling as to whether or not their sins have truly been forgiven.

Scapegoat

Ellen G. White taught that the scapegoat in the Old Testament on the Day of Atonement was representing Satan. Satan takes part in the Atonement of God's people. Satan becomes the sin-bearer for the Seventh Day Adventists. Here are a few quotes from her. "It was seen also, that while the sin offering pointed to Christ as the sacrifice and the High Priest represented Christ as a mediator, then we have the Scapegoat, which typified Satan, the author of sin, upon whom the sins of the truly penitent will finally be placed, when the High Priest, by virtue of the blood of the sin offering, will remove the sins from the sanctuary, he placed them upon the scapegoat. When Christ, by virtue of his own blood, removes the sins of his people from the heavenly sanctuary at the cross of his ministration, he will place them upon Satan, who, in the execution of the judgment, must bear the final penalty. The Scapegoat was sent into a land not inhabited, never to come again into the congregation of Israel. So will Satan be forever banished from the presence of God and his people and he will be blotted from existence in the final destruction of sin and sinners."[226]

This scapegoat and the final day of atonement is phase three, as Seventh Day Adventists see it.

Mind Control

Below are some statements made regarding mind control practices used within the Seventh Day Adventist church:

"When I was in 5th grade at Fresno Adventist Academy our teacher told our class that SDA's should be identifiable when in public by anyone looking at them. The

---

[225] Take the SDA Truth Challenge https://www.nonsda.org/study4.shtml
[226] White, Ellen G., The Great Controversy, page 422

body needed to be fully covered, and no jewelry or makeup should be worn. She even gave pointers on proper haircuts for the boys and hairdos for the girls. It was way far out... I have a close friend who never even heard of Ellen G. White until after she became SDA. She was told by her SDA "Bible teacher" to make her first time in the Adventist church the Sabbath of her baptism, to not attend the SDA church until then because to do so would only cause her to become confused because the teachings she would hear on Saturdays at the church were way more complicated than what she was learning in her home during the weekly studies. As a result, she had never even heard of Ellen G. White until after signing on the bottom line. Nor had she even been told that as an Adventist she was forbidden to consume beer, her favorite beverage. She read the baptismal vows, and it said something about not using alcohol. She asked the minister about this, and he told her the baptismal vows were suggestions and not rules and she could be an SDA and continue drinking if she wanted. Needless to say, she did not stay SDA long."[227]

"Some of our workers have taken courses in hypnotic mind-control exercises, with the purpose in mind of using them on our people. The stated purposes are to teach pastors and church members new methods of working with people, to bring them back into active church attendance. What is needed is heartfelt revival and reformation in our own lives and churches first. Let us get rid of the worldly entertainment, clothing, diet, and education."[228]

"An advanced instructor-level course In how to teach these mind-changing, hypnotic procedures will be [was] given to our leaders In Takoma Park, Maryland, on May 5-10, 1991. One of the first to speak up was a layman in the Oregon Conference, Terry Ross by name."[229]

"We are told that these skills will include: fogging, negative inquiry, neuro-linguistics, paraphrase, perception check, story polarization listening, interpersonal gap, process to debrief calls, stop action role play, renegotiation, closure play role, return tracks, and religious journey interview."[230]

---

[227] Mind Control Test http://www.formeradventist.com/discus/messages/5371/3856.html?1139517170

[228] Hypnotism Within the Adventist Church http://www.sdadefend.com/Spiritualism-invasion/Hypnotism.htm

[229] Ross, Terry, You Are Growing Sleepy, p.9

[230] Hypnotism Within the Adventist Church http://www.sdadefend.com/Spiritualism-invasion/Hypnotism.htm

[231]"In Lifton's criteria for deciding whether a church is a cult or not, he looks at whether the church has a charismatic leader who controls, interrogates and bullies its members. The Seventh Day Adventist church has no such leader. Instead, it has an interesting phenomenon about it; instead of a leader doing this, the members fulfill this function themselves. If a church member is caught breaking one of the many rules, they face social retribution for their sin. Most conservative Christians look at SDA's and see them as extreme, as while other churches will judge you for much bigger choices, SDA's will judge each other harshly for seemingly small, random and arbitrary 'rules.'"

"Another interesting thing about the church is there is no room to dissent. If you chose to keep all of the Adventist rules except you chose to continue to eat ham, then most conservative SDA's would have to declare you sinful, your actions worldly, and your blatant disregard for God's health laws mean God would not save you, and you would die the eternal death."

"Add to this the fact conservative churches don't leave much room for interpretation of the scriptures; you are rigidly expected to obey all the 28 Fundamentals. Add to this that within the 28 Fundamental beliefs you then have additional sub-rules within those rules that you need to keep. Take rule #20, the Sabbath – general consensus is that wading in water on Sabbath is OK, but swimming is not. These are unlisted rules and are things you need to pick up from experience/reading. This makes it extremely difficult to keep them all, which means many members live in fear of breaking the rules and live in a constant state of guilt."

"Another "cult-like" characteristic that the church exhibits is that it controls the information that its members hear. It manages this by removing the situations where SDA's have to interact with non-SDA's in any meaningful way. Consider the life of a typical Seventh Day Adventist:

They are born in an SDA Church
They attend only SDA schools from pre-school through college
They are then employed in a SDA institution
They will marry an SDA spouse
They then retire in an SDA retirement village."

---

[231] Seventh Day Adventist Cult - Oppressive and Destructive http://leavingsda.com/ seventh- day-adventist-cult/

"Everything that contradicts the SDA church is 'planted' by Satan. If someone came to me and gave me a good explanation about why the SDA churches theological beliefs didn't make sense, I would be told 'be wary of listening to anyone but the church. Satan is deceptive and he can make things seem appealing. It is safest not to go to any other church at all, and to not debate these things.' I would then be barred from going to the other church meeting. This was not just my experience. Other adults outside my family told me this many times, and Adventists who have left will tell you similar stories."

Terminology

Flesh food - meat

Health Message - Diet and lifestyle teachings of Ellen G. White. Referred to as "the right arm of the gospel," and used as a form of proselytizing.

Great Controversy - Jesus is in a cosmic battle with Satan and humans help Jesus win.

Investigative Judgment - Divine judgment of professed Christians has been in progress since 1844.

Pen of Inspiration - The writings of Ellen G. White.

Present Truth - The revelations of Ellen G. White and the teachings of the SDA Church.

The Testimonies - Ellen G. White's writing, but in particular a set of nine books titled, "Testimonies for the Church."

CHAPTER 15

Twelve Tribes

My Experiences with this Group

I encountered this group one year at the Harvest Crusade in Anaheim, California. We had gone with a youth group I was leading at the time. As we were leaving the stadium, there were many different groups waiting out in the parking lot. They were passing out flyers, hoping to catch people in a vulnerable time as they were searching for the truth. Possibly those who had recently accepted Jesus as their Savior who would be open to the suggestion of selling everything they have and moving to a commune that is gathered in several areas around the world. They have locations in Argentina, Australia, Brazil, Canada, Czech Republic, France, Germany, Spain, United Kingdom and the United States. This group identifies themselves as the Twelve Tribes.

It became clear as I was reading the literature that they were calling people to be like Abraham, commanded by God to leave his family and go to the land that he would show him.[232] Like the early church that had all things in common after the Day of Pentecost and thousands were giving their life over to Jesus from all different regions who were now in Jerusalem.[233] Like Jesus said to that rich young ruler, "Sell

---

[232] Genesis 12:1

[233] Acts 2:44; 4:32

all you have, and come follow me. That is the one thing you lack for eternal life."[234] The Twelve Tribes take that command seriously and teach this as required. If one is going to follow Jesus, and if one is going to have salvation, then they are going to sell all of their possessions, and they are going to give them into the common purse of the Twelve Tribes community where God leads them.

What do they Believe?

From their website, here are some of their beliefs.[235] The Twelve Tribes teach fairly orthodox views of God and Jesus. They refer to Jesus as Yeshua. They teach Jesus paid for our sin over the course of three days and three nights as he was suffering in hell, and as he cried out to the Father, the Father granted his request, returning his soul and spirit to his body, and he rose from the dead.

The Twelve Tribes teaches Jesus will return when his people are perfect and become like him. They teach this is done through living life for others in a community of believers. Particularly, their community. Somebody hears the gospel from a worthy member of their community, and then they are given faith, and that faith allows them to obey, and obedience means selling all they have and moving into the community with them. If one does this, then they will become like Jesus. When the whole community, and all the sum of their communities, have become like Jesus, then Jesus will return and set up his Millennial Kingdom.

They share a common life with a common purse.

They call themselves the Twelve Tribes, not because they believe they are literal Israel, but because they teach the body of Christ is organized into twelve distinct regions throughout the world. Each one of those represents a tribe of Israel.

The Twelve Tribes teaches there are three distinct categories of people, and there's going to be three distinct destinations regarding their eternity. There's a group that they refer to as the unjust and filthy, and these have lived their own life even against their conscience. They're bad and know they're bad, and don't care that they're bad, and do what they want. That group is going to go to hell. Those who heard the gospel by a worthy member of their community and rejected it are going to hell as well.

---

[234] Matthew 19:21; Mark 10:21; Luke 18:22

[235] Our Life and Beliefs http://twelvetribes.org/articles/our-life-beliefs

The second group is called the Righteous, composed of people who never had the opportunity to hear the gospel, but they live according to their conscious. These are good people who never had the opportunity to hear the gospel. I guess in a rather small group, one would have to make an exception for those who don't have a chance to hear the gospel. This group is worthy of the second death, but the Twelve Tribes teaches their first death paid for their sins. Now they live under the rulership of the Holy, which is our third category.

The Holy are the ones who heard the gospel and responded to it by selling everything they have and joining in community with them. They were baptized and cried out unto the name of the Lord to save them. They lived for God, not themselves. As a result of all of their faith and obedience, they are going to be part of the Holy. That group of the Holy is made up of those who are going to rule with Jesus Christ in heaven over the Righteous.

There is a pattern with several of these groups of different levels of heaven. I think it is interesting that both with the LDS and the Twelve Tribes if people never hear the gospel in this life, they find themselves in some ways better off in the next life than those who have heard the message and rejected it. With the LDS, that person can accept that message in Spirit Prison and have somebody who is living be baptized on their behalf, allowing them to progress to the higher levels of heaven. Also with the LDS, those who die before the Age of Accountability, which is eight years old, go immediately to the Celestial Kingdom, the highest level of heaven. With the Twelve Tribes, a person who does not hear the message, but is a good person, will go to their middle level of heaven.

Distinctives

Another distinction that I saw was that they hold cafes, stores, bakeries, delis, farms, hotels. They have businesses in the world. It's that they don't want their people living in the world. They want them to make money in the world so that they can bring it back into the community. I don't know if I've been familiar with any of their stores or items, but they are out there.

The other distinction I found on their website is that men wear beards and have their hair back. Women have distinct clothing. They don't participate in electronics. Similar to the Amish or Mennonite communities, or the Hutterites, and those were other movements going on here in America that set them apart as distinct.

CHAPTER 16

New Apostolic Reformation

(NAR)

The New Apostolic Reformation (NAR) is a title originally used by C. Peter Wagner to describe a movement within Pentecostal and charismatic churches.[236] The New Apostolic Reformation is one of the most significant, broadest and most potent movements within Christianity today, but most Christians have probably never heard of it.[237] Even those who attend churches that are a part of this movement have probably never heard the term New Apostolic Reformation before. This is because there is no headquarters, organization or leadership, but instead, this is a movement of like-minded churches who rally together under unofficial, yet key leaders, who identify themselves as modern-day apostles and prophets.[238] The New Apostolic Reformation gains most of its growth by recruiting pastors of independent congregations and nondenominational churches, assimilating members from other

---

[236] New Apostolic Reformation https://en.wikipedia.org/wiki/New_Apostolic_Reformation

[237] Gilley, Gary, The New Apostolic Reformation An Examination of the Five-Fold Ministries Part 1 http://tottministries.org/the-new-apostolic-reformation-an-examination-of-the-five-fold-ministries-part-1/

[238] What is the New Apostolic Reformation? https://www.gotquestions.org/New-Apostolic-Reformation.html

churches through cell group meetings and frequent church planting, including foreign missions around the globe.[239]

Roots

However, this movement did not have its origins with C Peter Wagner's label of New Apostolic Reformation. There are many common teachings and practices from the New Order of the Latter Rain in the late 40's and early 50's. Before that, it made its presence felt in the early days of the century among early Pentecostals.[240] Some have equated NAR with the Third Wave of Pentecostalism which emphasizes power evangelism, healings and spiritual warfare. This movement was led by John Wimber and the Vineyard Movement in the 1980s.[241]

As far as the essentials of the Christian faith, you will not find a lot of deviation within the New Apostolic Reformation. They do believe that Jesus is God, the gospel and salvation by grace through faith. It is not in the core doctrines that they fall into error, but in the peripheral doctrines, and in practice.[242]

Distinctives

According to C Peter Wagner and other NAR leaders, several distinct traits characterize NAR's core teachings and practices, even if leaders or churches deny they have anything to do with the NAR brand. Those are 1) Five-fold ministry 2) Unity 3)

---

[239] New Apostolic Reformation https://en.wikipedia.org/wiki/New_Apostolic_Reformation

[240] G. Raymond Carlson, personal letter to Jewel Van de Mewre http://web.archive.org/web/20130529041702/http://members.ozemail.com.au/~rseaborn/New_Apostolic_Reformation.html

[241] Gilley, Gary, The New Apostolic Reformation An Examination of the Five-Fold Ministries Part 1 http://tottministries.org/the-new-apostolic-reformation-an-examination-of-the-five-fold-ministries-part-1/

[242] Boehm, Michael, New Apostolic Reformation Exposed 01 What Does the NAR Believe Episode 452 https://www.sermonaudio.com/sermoninfo.asp?SID=1119132127181

Extra-biblical revelation[243] 4) Seven Mountain Mandate[244] [245] [246] 5) Supernatural signs and wonders.[247]

Five-Fold Ministry

Pastors and churches within the New Apostolic Reformation teach the five-fold ministry in Ephesians 4:11-13 must be restored for the church to be triumphant in spiritual warfare, bringing unity to the church and establishing the Kingdom of God on earth. They teach and have affirmed modern-day apostles and prophets. These apostles and prophets are equal to the biblical apostles and prophets in role and authority. Since God commissioned these new apostles, their authority may not be questioned.[248]

Many people have not yet heard of the New Apostolic Reformation by that formal name, but when they start hearing the names of organizations and leaders, they will say they have heard of the International House of Prayer in Kansas City,[249] or Bethel Church in Redding, California.[250] Popular teachers associated with the New Apostolic Reformation include C. Peter Wagner, Rick Joyner, Mike Bickle, Lou Engle, Todd Bentley, Bill Johnson, Che Ahn and Kim Clement.[251] [252] [253]

These apostles and prophets are to govern the church and reveal new truths, unleashing God's miraculous power and advancing his kingdom on earth. They

---

[243] The Six Hallmarks of a NAR Church http://www.piratechristian.com/berean-examiner/the-six-hallmarks-of-a-nar-church

[244] Gilley, Gary, The New Apostolic Reformation An Examination of the Five-Fold Ministries Part 1 http://tottministries.org/the-new-apostolic-reformation-an-examination-of-the-five-fold-ministries-part-1/

[245] Wilder, Forrest, "Rick Perry's Army of God," *Texas Observer*, August 2, 2011

[246] New Apostolic Reformation https://www.gotquestions.org/New-Apostolic-Reformation.html

[247] Wilder, Forrest (12 August 2011). "As Texas Gov. Rick Perry Enters GOP Race, New Exposé Reveals His Close Ties to Radical Evangelicals," *Democracy Now*. Retrieved 14 October 2013.

[248] The Six Hallmarks of a NAR Church http://www.piratechristian.com/berean-examiner/the-six-hallmarks-of-a-nar-church

[249] http://www.ihopkc.org/

[250] http://bethelredding.com/

[251] New Apostolic Reformation https://www.gotquestions.org/New-Apostolic-Reformation.html

[252] Oakes, Jason, People of the Free Gift, Bill Johnson: Cult Leader, False Teacher or Christian? https://youtu.be/DS1BRM0x0WE

[253] http://harvestim.org/

believe that we as Christians are mandated to practically and supernaturally take dominion over every aspect of our lives, from education and government to the demonic.[254]

According to the International Coalition of Apostolic Leaders (ICA) website,[255] the aspiring apostle must be nominated by two existing apostles who can show that he meets the ICA's criteria. There are some fees to pay as well.[256]

Here are some other passages that are often cited:

> And he gave some, apostles; and some, prophets; and some, evangelists; and some, pastors and teachers; For the perfecting of the saints, for the work of the ministry, for the edifying of the body of Christ: Till we all come in the unity of the faith, and of the knowledge of the Son of God, unto a perfect man, unto the measure of the stature of the fulness of Christ: (Ephesians 4:11-13)

> And are built upon the foundation of the apostles and prophets, Jesus Christ himself being the chief corner [stone]; (Ephesians 2:20)

> And God hath set some in the church, first apostles, secondarily prophets, thirdly teachers, after that miracles, then gifts of healings, helps, governments, diversities of tongues. (1 Corinthians 12:28)

Unity

According to C. Peter Wagner, God's people can only ever return to pure Christianity as seen in the early church if they "recognize, accept, receive and minister in all the spiritual gifts, including the gift of apostle."[257]

---

[254] Purdom, Georgia, NAR: The Fastest-Growing Counter-Christian Movement Most Haven't Heard Of https://answersingenesis.org/blogs/georgia-purdom/2017/01/25/na-fastest-growing-counter-christian-movement/

[255] https://www.icaleaders.com/

[256] Buettel, Cameron & Johnson, Jeremiah, The Apostles Who Don't Do Anything: The New Apostolic Reformation https://www.gty.org/library/blog/B131118

[257] Cannistraci, David, Apostles and the Emerging Apostolic Movement, p. 12

The NAR teaches that only when every Christian and church has submitted to NAR leadership will true unity be achieved, the church will take its rightful place of authority over the "mountains" of dominion and Jesus will return.

As the church unifies behind the apostles, the NAR teaches these leaders will develop greater and greater supernatural powers. Eventually, this will include the ability to perform mass healings and suspend the laws of physics. These signs are meant to encourage a massive wave of converts to Christianity. These apostles are also destined to be recipients of a great wealth transfer in the end times, which will enable the church to establish God's kingdom on earth.[258]

Extra-Biblical Revelation

NAR apostles and prophets are believed to receive messages from God and speak for God in the same sense as the biblical apostles and prophets, putting their words on the same level of importance, if not greater due to being more current and relevant, as the biblical text. This naturally causes, as we described in section #1 - What is a cult?, greater authority of the leadership, a lower view of the Bible and a dependence upon the leadership among the members.

Rick Joyner says this about those who are concerned about theology and what the Bible says, testing the spirits, "Some pastors and leaders who continue to resist this tide of unity will be removed from their place. They will become so hardened that they will become opposers and resist God to the end. Some that were used greatly of God in the past have become too rigid in doctrinal emphasis."[259]

Bill Johnson has said, "While doctrine is vitally important it is not a strong enough foundation to bear the weight of His glory that is about to be revealed through true unity."[260] When NAR leaders teach the church must achieve unity, they are referring to Apostolic Unity, which they believe is referring to Christians submitting to NAR apostles. When all the Christians in a particular city recognize and submit to the authority of the local apostles, then unity has been achieved in that city.

---

[258] New Apostolic Reformation https://www.gotquestions.org/New-Apostolic-Reformation.html

[259] Boehm, Michael, New Apostolic Reformation Exposed 01 What Does the NAR Believe Episode 452 https://www.sermonaudio.com/sermoninfo.asp?SID=1119132127181

[260] Johnson, Bill, Bill Johnson: "Apostolic Teams: a Group of People Who Carry the Family Mission" http://www.elijahlist.com/words/display word/7083

One leader within this group, Brian Simmons, believed that he was called by God to create another translation of the Bible, known as the Passion Translation. Here's what Brian says about this translation on the official website:

The Passion Translation is a new, heart-level translation that expresses God's fiery heart of love to this generation using Hebrew, Greek, and Aramaic manuscripts, merging the emotion and life-changing truth of God's Word.

"So why another translation? The reason is simple: God longs to have his Word expressed in every language in a way that unlocks the passion of his heart. The goal of this work is to trigger inside every reader an overwhelming response to the truth of the Bible, revealing the deep mysteries of the Scriptures in the love language of God, the language of the heart."[261]

Brian also says this on the Bible Gateway website about the Passion Translation. "The message of God's story is timeless; the Word of God doesn't change. But the methods by which that story is communicated should be timely; the vessels that steward God's Word can and should change. One of those timely methods is Bible translation. Bible translations are both a gift and a problem. They give us the words God spoke through his servants, but words can be poor containers for revelation because they leak! The meanings of words change from one generation to the next. Meaning is influenced by culture, background, and many other details. Imagine how differently the Hebrew authors of the Old Testament saw the world three thousand years ago from the way we see it today!

You will notice at times TPT italicizes certain words or phrases. These highlighted portions are not in the original Hebrew, Greek, or Aramaic manuscripts but are implied from the context. We've made these implications explicit for the sake of narrative clarity and to better convey the meaning of God's Word."[262]

As I pointed out in section #1 - what is a cult?, it is only a matter of time before a group that believes in continuing revelation, modern-day apostles and prophets and the need for something to be "restored" to Christianity, will create a translation of the Bible, using their terminology or creating new scripture from their modern-day revelations. This is precisely what Brian Simmons and the NAR have done.

---

[261] Simmons, Brian, The Passion Translation https://www.thepassiontranslation.com/
[262] Simmons, Brian, Version Information
https://www.biblegateway.com/versions/The-Passion-Translation-TPT-Bible/

Beyond that, I want to point out the danger of one man creating a translation of the Bible, especially when their goal is not to render a word-for-word translation, but a thought-for-thought translation, adding words where necessary and having an express agenda going into the translation process.

Seven Mountain Mandate

Apostolic leaders are working to bring the Gospel of the Kingdom of Heaven to Earth. They do this through a revelation known as the Seven Mountain Mandate. They believe it is the mission of the church, and their right as apostles and prophets, to take dominion of earthly kingdoms or "mountains." These "mountains" have been identified as government, media, entertainment, education, business, family, and religion. Leaders often talk of city building and organize prayer walks to pray against demonic strongholds.[263]

Supernatural Signs and Wonders

The Apostles and Prophets within the New Apostolic Reformation place a greater emphasis on dreams, visions and extra-biblical revelation than they do on the Bible, claiming that their revealed teachings and reported experiences, including trips to heaven, face-to-face conversations with Jesus and visits by angels, cannot be proven by the 'old' Scripture.[264]

The NAR teaches that the body of Christ coming to spiritual maturity will be able to defeat death itself. This teaching became known as the "Manifest Sons of God." The NAR teaches that a company of overcoming believers known as "the sons of God" will be manifested upon the earth with never dying spiritual bodies before the return of Christ.[265]

---

[263] New Apostolic Reformation (NAR) https://bereanresearch.org/dominionism-nar/

[264] New Apostolic Reformation (NAR) https://bereanresearch.org/dominionism-nar/

[265] Steinkamp, Orrel, The New Apostolic Reformation http://web.archive.org/web/20130529041702/ http://members.ozemail.com.au/~rseaborn/New_Apostolic_Reformation.html

Spiritual Abuse

While they are not the only ones, NAR apostles, prophets and pastors teach what is known as covering theology. This is the belief that every believer has a "covering," or another Christian they are called to submit to. The way this plays out is believers within a church are required to submit to the Pastor of that church and that Pastor is called to submit to the leadership of a NAR apostle in their area. Those NAR apostles are called to submit to an apostle with more authority. Without a named central leader, one wonders where this chain ends.

While God does call us to submit to the authority that he has placed over us, where this gets dangerous is the belief and teaching that if one steps outside their "covering," they are of the devil and bad things will begin to happen in their life, perhaps even risking their salvation.[266]

Many have come out of this movement who have described characteristics of a cult, particularly mind control and abuses of authority detailed in Section #1 - What is a Cult?[267]

Scripture Twisting

How are they twisting and misinterpreting these passages? All three passages say nothing about governing offices. In the case of Ephesians 4:11-13, it's merely listing various types of leaders God has given to build up the church. It doesn't state that they must hold governing offices. In fact, it doesn't even list all the leaders that God has given to the church. For instance, it says nothing about deacons though they are discussed in other passages in the Bible.[268] So it would be an incorrect interpretation of this passage to teach the church must have five ongoing governing offices including apostles and prophets.

Again in Ephesians 2:20, nothing about governing offices. One does not build a foundation more than once. In 1 Corinthians 12:28, it simply lists different persons

---

[266] Boehm, Michael, New Apostolic Reformation Exposed 01 What Does the NAR Believe Episode 452 https://www.sermonaudio.com/sermoninfo.asp?SID=1119132127181

[267] Boehm, Michael, The Largest Christian Cult You've Never Heard Of with M Barbara Hansell https://www.sermonaudio.com/sermoninfo.asp?SID=103162143161

[268] 1 Timothy 3:8

that God has given the church, which includes not only apostles and prophets but also lists speaking in tongues or helps. Not even NAR leaders would say there should be a formal office of speaking in tongues, so they can't use this verse to argue for the office of apostle or prophet.

Test of an Apostle

How can we know whether the NAR apostles are legitimate? The Bible lists specific requirements for apostleship. The word apostle in Greek means one who is sent. Many are sent by churches even today, but the twelve apostles of Jesus were sent and given their authority directly by him.[269] This was also true of the Apostle Paul. That is why it was required that apostles be a physical eyewitness of the resurrected Christ.[270] They must be able to authenticate their apostleship with miraculous signs.[271] They must be able to support in Scripture any new teachings and practices they bring.[272] They must have an exemplary personal character and quality of ministry.[273]

Conversely, Paul tells us in 2 Corinthians that false apostles are characterized by greed, arrogance, self-promotion, superficiality, outward appearance, speaking skills, twisting the scripture, preaching a different Jesus and a different gospel.[274]

Test of a Prophet

Scripture also gives clear criteria as to whether one who claims to be a prophet is from God or not. If they make a prediction, it must come to pass as predicted.[275] The prophet's words must line up with revelation already given by God.[276] Their life must not be characterized by greed, drunkenness, idolatry or sexual immorality.[277]

---

[269] Mark 3:14; Luke 6:13; Acts 1:2; 10:41; Galatians 1:1

[270] Acts 1:22; 1 Corinthians 9:1; 15:7-8

[271] Matthew 10:1; Acts 2:43; 5:12; 2 Corinthians 12:12; Hebrews 2:3-4

[272] Acts 17:11

[273] 1 Timothy 3

[274] 2 Corinthians 11-12

[275] Deuteronomy 18:21-22

[276] Deuteronomy 13:1-4

[277] 1 Timothy 3

Terminology

Apostles - Modern-day apostles with the same authority as biblical apostles.

Dominionism/ Kingdom Now - NAR apostles and prophets teach it is the task of the church — under the leadership of apostles and prophets — to take dominion of the earth.[278]

Five-Fold Ministry — Apostles, prophets, evangelists, pastors and teachers based on Ephesians 4:11-13.

Identificational Repentance - A term coined by John Dawson in Healing America's Wounds[279] to describe a prayer which identifies with and confesses before God the sins of one's nation, city, people group, church or family.[280]

Manifest Sons of God - One of most radical teachings in the NAR movement is known as the "Manifest Sons of God." According to this teaching, the people who continue to receive the new revelation given by NAR apostles and prophets will gain more and more supernatural powers until they eventually become "manifest" or unveiled as "sons of God." These manifested sons of God will overcome sickness and death and execute God's judgments on earth.[281]

Prophets - Modern-day prophets with the same authority as biblical prophets.

Seven Mountain Mandate - government, media, family, business/finance, education, church/religion, and arts/entertainment.

Supernatural Powers - NAR leaders teach they and their followers will develop vast supernatural powers and will perform miracles that will surpass those performed by

---

[278] Wagner, C. Peter, Dominion; Bill Hamon, Prophetic Scriptures Yet to Be Fulfilled

[279] Dawson, John, Healing America's Wounds

[280] 'Identificational Repentance' - Repenting for the Sins of Our Ancestors http://www.jmm.org.au/articles/11659.htm

[281] Hamon, Bill, Apostles, Prophets and the Coming Moves of God, p. 265-266

the biblical apostles and prophets[282] and even those performed by Jesus during his earthly ministry.[283] These miracles will include amazing feats such as healing every single person inside hospitals and mental institutions simply by laying their hands on the buildings and having command of the laws of nature, including gravity.[284]

---

[282] Joyner, Rick, The Final Quest, p. 137, 145

[283] Wagner, C. Peter, Dominion!, p. 107

[284] Joyner, Rick, The Apostolic Ministry, p. 41

CHAPTER 17

United Pentecostal Church International

(UPCI; Oneness Pentecostals)

History

There[285] are around five million Oneness Pentecostal type churches. The largest of them is the United Pentecostal Church International, with somewhere around 28,000 churches worldwide.

United Pentecostal Church International, comes from the Assembly of God movement. Sometime around the early 1900s, several of the Assembly of God pastors started holding to a belief that the Father, Son and Holy Spirit were all the same person or being and that God manifests himself in three different modes, but as the same person. This is a belief called Modalism, teaching in the Old Testament, God manifested himself as the Father, and in New Testament times, God manifested himself as the Son. God came down to earth in the form of a human. Jesus had a human nature and also a God nature. Then after the resurrection, God now exists as the Holy Spirit.

---

[285] Boehm, Michael, Youth Apologetics Training, Unbiblical Doctrines of Oneness Pentecostals http://www.sermonaudio.com/sermoninfo.asp?SID=66132312245

In the 1900s, many of the Assembly of God pastors started subscribing to this belief. Around 1916, a meeting was pulled together to debate this issue. Many of the Assembly of God pastors stood firm in the doctrine of the Trinity as the Bible teaches it, but about 156 of the 585 pastors broke off the Assembly of God movement because of this sharp disagreement.

Baptism in the Name of Jesus Only

A doctrine the United Pentecostal Church International teaches is one must not be baptized in the name of the Father, Son and Holy Spirit as Matthew 28:19 teaches, but rather in Jesus' name alone. They teach the doctrine of the Trinity is a pagan doctrine. They also believe right now Jesus is no longer in his human body. God is right now manifesting himself as the Holy Spirit. Jesus is not standing at the right hand of the Father in heaven.[286] They believe Jesus is God the Father and the Holy Spirit. They believe Jesus is the name of God. They also believe Jesus did not pre-exist as the Word.

Many Oneness Pentecostals have a mistaken view of what Trinitarians believe. They believe we have a polytheistic view of God, believing in three different gods.

Baptism and Tongues Necessary for Salvation

The United Pentecostal Church International denies justification by faith alone. They teach to be saved, one must be baptized. They believe if one doesn't manifest with the gift of tongues, they are not saved. In other words, if one doesn't speak in tongues, the Holy Spirit didn't come upon them, and if the Holy Spirit didn't come upon somebody, they could not be saved. They also believe if Oneness Pentecostal ministers have not baptized a person, their baptism is not valid. Some of them believe if one is not a Oneness Pentecostal, they are not saved. Many of these beliefs were not taught by anybody within Christian history before this movement in the early 1900s.

---

[286] Matthew 22:44

Bible Passages Commonly Used

Below are some of the verses the United Pentecostal Church International commonly uses to teach the doctrine of being baptized in the name of Jesus only:

Then Peter said unto them, Repent, and be baptized every one of you in the name of Jesus Christ for the remission of sins, and ye shall receive the gift of the Holy Ghost. (Acts 2:38)

(For as yet he was fallen upon none of them: only they were baptized in the name of the Lord Jesus.) (Acts 8:16)

And he commanded them to be baptized in the name of the Lord. Then prayed they him to tarry certain days. (Acts 10:48)

When they heard this, they were baptized in the name of the Lord Jesus. (Acts 19:5)

And now why tarriest thou? arise, and be baptized, and wash away thy sins, calling on the name of the Lord. (Acts 22:16)

Matthew 28:19 Not in the Original Text

The following verse, used by Trinitarians as evidence of one God (singular name) who exists in three co-equal, co-eternal persons (Father, Son and Holy Spirit), the United Pentecostal Church International believes was added much later and was not in the original text of Matthew:

Go ye therefore, and teach all nations, baptizing them in the name of the Father, and of the Son, and of the Holy Ghost: (Matthew 28:19)

"In the Name Of"

When one looks at the phrase "in the name of" or "in someone's name" in the Bible, it carries more of a meaning of "in the authority of." Like when someone says, "Stop in the name of the law." Here are some examples:

And when they had set them in the midst, they asked, By what power, or by what name, have ye done this? Then Peter, filled with the Holy Ghost, said unto them, Ye rulers of the people, and elders of Israel, If we this day be examined of the good deed done to the impotent man, by what means he is made whole; Be it known unto you all, and to all the people of Israel, that by the name of Jesus Christ of Nazareth, whom ye crucified, whom God raised from the dead, [even] by him doth this man stand here before you whole. (Acts 4:7-10)

But that it spread no further among the people, let us straitly threaten them, that they speak henceforth to no man in this name. And they called them, and commanded them not to speak at all nor teach in the name of Jesus. (Acts 4:17-18)

Saying, Did not we straitly command you that ye should not teach in this name? and, behold, ye have filled Jerusalem with your doctrine, and intend to bring this man's blood upon us. ... And to him they agreed: and when they had called the apostles, and beaten [them], they commanded that they should not speak in the name of Jesus, and let them go. (Acts 5:28, 40)

But Barnabas took him, and brought [him] to the apostles, and declared unto them how he had seen the Lord in the way, and that he had spoken to him, and how he had preached boldly at Damascus in the name of Jesus. And he was with them coming in and going out at Jerusalem. (Acts 9:27-28)

But when they believed Philip preaching the things concerning the kingdom of God, and the name of Jesus Christ, they were baptized, both men and women. (Acts 8:12)

And this did she many days. But Paul, being grieved, turned and said to the spirit, I command thee in the name of Jesus Christ to come out of her. And he came out the same hour. (Acts 16:18)

Claimed Spiritual Abuse

Many individuals have come out of the United Pentecostal Church International who have shared their testimonies of various types of abuse they experienced. Here are some of the things they experienced and shared:[287]

Controlling

"Within the United Pentecostal Church International, there is a grocery list of what they can and can not do."

Here are some examples:

1. Don't cut your hair
2. No makeup
3. No jewelry
4. No nail polish
5. No dancing
6. No pants
7. No shorts

"The pastor there always cut people down and was very mean."

"Year by year things changed as far as it being a sin or not."

"Holiness often means the way people dress."

---

[287] United Pentecostal Church International Visitor Comments http://cultbustersgalactica.yuku.com/topic/100/United-Pentecostal-Church-International-CULT#.WPmQXlMrlXp

"I experienced that same control once, over every part of my life."

"I was always told what I could/could not do, who I could/could not date/marry, wear/not wear, and who I would honor/not honor."

"I do believe in Jesus [despite] the oppressive torment I endured. I know those years I was a zombie at the UPC I had no joy 95% of the time--just horrible condemnation."

"We later left because we were not allowed to make our own decisions. They didn't want my son to play any sports, no swimming--the last straw came when they were upset over us putting our daughter in a Christian school (she was in public school) because we didn't consult the pastor first."

Indoctrination

"I was amazed at how indoctrinated I became in such a short time."

Punishment for leaving the group

"The condemnation, shunning, the unspoken message that Satan has deceived a person for leaving. To 'backslide' is to choose to stop living for God."

"After I left and went to an Assemblies of God church some of the UPCI members said we couldn't be friends."

"We have gone through hell emotionally and socially after leaving."

"I can relate to everything said about this religion, mind control, emotional abuse, threats and the ostracizing of people that leave."

The One True Church

"The UPCI teaches only they have the 'truth,' and every other denomination is not saved."

"My church felt that it was so ultra-holy that it would not even fellowship with other churches of the same denomination."

"I don't believe that all of the UPCI churches or pastors would go to such extremes, but they all claim that only Oneness believers will enter heaven."

Freethought discouraged

"These men often put down women, sabotage freethought, are unable to defend 'Holiness Standards' either biblically or historically."

"Our former pastor has to be one of the most extreme. He was controlling, manipulative, demanding and isolated us through constant intimidation and fear."

CHAPTER 18

Great Commission Churches

(GCAC; GCI; GCM; GCC; GCLA; GCE)

I had never heard of Great Commission Churches until a student of mine called my attention to her previous experience in this group as part of her assignments for the Understanding the Cults class I was teaching for Bethel Seminary San Diego.

Practice, Not Doctrine

I want to make something clear as I begin this chapter. I do not categorize GCC as a cult based on doctrine. To my knowledge, they teach as an organization, as well as individual churches, the core doctrines of Christianity as discussed in Section 1 - What is a Cult?, of this book. It is their practices, which match many of the things described in that same section, that cause me to come to the conclusion this group is a cult.

Origins

[288] [289]The Great Commission Association of Churches (GCAC), formerly Great Commission International (GCI), is an association of Christian churches in the United States, Canada, Latin America, and Asia. Most of these churches are less than twenty years old and originated with a group of Christians at Southern Colorado University who set out to preach the Gospel and so fulfill the Great Commission. [290]GCI, GCM, and GCAC are used interchangeably to describe the same organization. From Colorado, they reached out to other campuses across the country. The goal of those few men, and of the men and women who eventually chose to labor with them, was to "reach the world" with the Gospel of Jesus Christ in their generation and in doing so, glorify him. To reach that goal, they modeled their churches as nearly as possible after the New Testament church, and took the Lord's command literally to "Go."

During the 1970s and 1980s, some secular newspapers wrote articles accusing churches in the movement of being a cult. As a result of an article in a college newspaper, author William Watson included Great Commission in a book he wrote on cults.[291] Watson has since written a retraction letter that can be found on the Great Commission Churches website.[292]

[293]The largest of these organizations today is Great Commission Churches (GCC). Other associated organizations include Great Commission Ministries (GCM), Great Commission Latin America (GCLA), and Great Commission Europe (GCE).

---

[288] Hopler, John, An Example of How False Information Can Spread http://gccweb.org/about/how-false-information-can-spread/

[289] A Statement Recognizing Early Errors and Weaknesses in the Development of the Great Commission Association of Churches http://ae32b6f7a6ad6f5ae1f0-a966d7fcbad4fbcd7d1dccf3fb abbb92.r98.cf2.rackcdn.com/uploaded/e/0e4539571 1442587016 errors-weakness-final.pdf

[290] GCM Warning: An Evaluation of Great Commission Ministries http://gcmwarning.com/History.aspx

[291] Watson, William, A Concise Dictionary of Cults and Religions

[292] Watson, William http://gccweb.org/abou t/how- false-information-can-spread/

[293] Great Commission Churches http://www.worldlibrary.org/articles/great commission churches #cite note-Orthopraxy-86

Roots

[294]In 1965, 20-year-old Jim McCotter (James Douglas McCotter) left his home in Colorado Springs, Colorado and moved to Greeley, Colorado in an attempt to recreate the New Testament Church, a church model he believed no existing Christian denomination was emulating fully.

McCotter, whose family's religious background was with the Plymouth Brethren, has stated that his desire to form the movement stemmed from his belief that God had shown him in the Bible's Book of Acts a strategy instructing Christians on how God wanted to use church planting to "reach the world for Christ" within one generation. This strategy came to be known as the "Heavenly Vision,"[295] and was a cornerstone belief of the early movement. McCotter also believed that the Bible was instructing every Christian to emulate the actions of the Apostle Paul's life as he imitated Christ and that this was the model life for all Christians to imitate based upon Paul's exhortation in 1 Corinthians 11:1.

Early members believed they were returning to the lost lifestyle of the first century Christians. This lifestyle included a devotion to discipleship which has been criticized and compared to the "Shepherding Movement."[296]

After arriving in Greeley, McCotter attended and began sharing his faith at the University of Northern Colorado campus. The movement eventually spread to other cities in Colorado, as well as Las Cruces, New Mexico, in the form of missions or "works."

During basic training at Fort Polk, Louisiana, McCotter met Dennis Clark, and on McCotter's return from Vietnam in 1970 he met Herschel Martindale. Clark and Martindale would become two of the founders of the movement in the summer of 1970.

---

[294] Great Commission Churches http://www.worldlibrary.org/articles/great commission churches #cite note-Orthopraxy-86

[295] Resources on the Great Commission Church Movement http://gcxweb.org/Misc/MikeRoyal- 06-28-1985.aspx

[296] The Shepherding Movement http://abusivechurch.org/the-shepherding-movement-2/

"Blitz Movement" Begins

[297]In 1970, under the leadership of Jim McCotter, Dennis Clark, Herschel Martindale, and others, approximately 30 college-age Christians embarked on a summer-long evangelical outreach known as "The Blitz" to several university campuses in the Southwestern United States. These two or three-day events used singing, tract distribution, and sidewalk canvassing to draw crowds and spread the word. As the movement expanded, additional mission outreaches and training conferences took place. In the late 1970s, selected newspapers, former members, and select watchdog groups began to criticize the movement's practices publicly. This continued into the 1980s and early 1990s.

Great Commission International

[298]In 1983, Great Commission International (GCI) was formed. Led by Jim McCotter and Dennis Clark, it was created to provide services such as publishing and fundraising for the developing association. That summer, GCI launched the first summer Leadership Training conference which attracted college students for a summer of intensive training in evangelism and discipleship. The LT program continues today under the leadership of Great Commission Ministries.

In the mid 80's, several ex-leaders staged a conference "to help other ex-members to recover from the emotional and psychological damage they'd experienced" in Great Commission churches.[299] Some of these former leaders went on to form the world's first and only accredited cult recovery center, Wellspring Retreat.[300]

In late 1986, founder Jim McCotter announced his resignation from GCI, stating a desire to utilize his entrepreneurial abilities in an attempt to influence secular media for Christ. Two years later, McCotter moved to Florida and has not since attended a church affiliated with the movement.

---

[297] Great Commission Churches http://www.worldlibrary.org/articles/great commission churches #cite note-Orthopraxy-86

[298] Great Commission Churches http://www.worldlibrary.org/articles/great commission churches #cite note-Orthopraxy-86

[299] Ross, Rick. "Just Who Is Jim McCotter?" North & South Apr. 2002.

[300] www.wellspringretreat.org

GCAC and GCM Formed

[301] In 1989, Great Commission International changed its name to the Great Commission Association of Churches (GCAC) and is known today as Great Commission Churches (GCC). Also in 1989, Great Commission Ministries (GCM), under the initial leadership of Dave Bovenmyer, was formed. It aimed to "mobilize people into campus ministry by training them to raise financial support and by equipping them for campus ministry."

Attempted Correction

[302] Since the 1980s, God has led pastors in Great Commission Churches to make significant changes. In 1991, they conducted Project Care, a movement-wide effort to reconcile with any who had a grievance. This included the writing of the 1991 Errors and Weaknesses Paper where GCC pastors acknowledged errors and imbalances from the past. Since then, they claim to have set a higher standard in servant leadership, personal and organizational accountability, responding to criticisms with humility and empathy, and unity with the body of Christ. GCC became a member of the National Association of Evangelicals and the Evangelical Council for Financial Accountability.[303]

Self-Admitted Abuses

GCC has admitted to several different forms of abuse, including a prideful attitude, improper response to criticism, an elitist attitude, misapplication or misinterpretation of Scripture, failing to distinguish between a command, principle or preference, authoritarian or insensitive leadership, lack of emphasis on formal education, a belief that every man should become an elder, etc...

---

[301] Great Commission Churches http://www.worldlibrary.org/articles/great commission churches #cite note-Orthopraxy-86

[302] Hopler, John, Responding to Criticisms http://gccweb.org/about/responding-to-criticisms/

[303] Callahan, Frank, Great Commission Church Withdraws from NAE https://www.culteducation.com/group/1046-great-commission-international/13279-great-commission-church-withdraws-from-nae.html

Criticisms and Abuses

Several research organizations, including the American Family Association and the Council on Mind Abuse, classified the movement as a "cult" during this period.[304] In 1992, Group Publishing's Group Magazine published an article titled "How to Spot an Abusive Church"[305] where Great Commission was mentioned as the first example. Larry Pile has since written a retraction letter that can be found on the Great Commission website.[306]

In the 90's, around the time the church error statement was made, the organization began to appear in numerous books on abusive churches, including Cult-Proofing Your Kids, Recovery From Cults: Help for Victims of Psychological and Spiritual Abuse,[307] and Churches that Abuse.[308] The movement's practices have also been discussed in research papers, including a University of Virginia Master's Thesis whose research included interviews with 274 ex-members, and a Trinity Evangelical Divinity School Master's Thesis on aberrant Christian churches.[309] Ronald Enroth has since written a retraction statement that can be found on the Great Commission website.[310]

In 1989, officials of the University of Guelph banned the movement from campus following a three-month investigation of the group's activities.[311] This was the first organization banned from that campus in its 25-year history.[312]

---

[304] Pile, Larry. "The Making of a Cult Counselor." Wellspring Journal Vol. 9 Issue 2 (Summer 2000).

[305] Enroth, Ronald. "How to Spot an Abusive Church." Group Magazine Mar. 1992.

[306] Pile, Larry http://gccweb.org/ about/ history/reconciliations/

[307] Langone, Michael D., Recovery from Cults: Help for Victims of Psychological and Spiritual Abuse

[308] Enroth, Ronald, Churches That Abuse

[309] Butz, Martin, "An inquiry into the paradox of aberrant Christian churches: orthodoxy without orthopraxy," Trinity Evangelical Divinity School, 1991

[310] Enroth, Ronald http://gccweb.org/d r-enroth- and-gcc/

[311] "Bible club evicted from U of Guelph campus: Group accused of authoritarianism, cult-like control over members," Toronto Globe and Mail, 27 Sep. 1989.

[312] Zilliox, Jr., Larry, and Larry Kahaner. Factual Analysis of the Operations and Activities of Great Commission Inc. and James Douglas McCotter. KANE Associates International, Inc., 1990.

Behavior Control

"People have tailored their lives around this church. They have chosen careers that would allow them to move with the church. They refuse to move to a town that doesn't have a GCM church. They choose a wife or husband based on that individual's commitment to GCM. We were told at our fall retreat that 'If you are not totally committed to your local church, you lack courage.' And that 'every time you change church families, you are damaging a part of your soul forever.' . . . The difference between GCM and 'the Church' referred to in the New Testament has become blurred in many areas. Great Commission Ministries is only a small piece of 'the Church'. . . But the mindset seems to be that GCM is the way. It is the church. GCM has the answers, has the best way to do things, and other churches are seen as sub-par. Other churches will not get you as close to God as a GCM church will. Whenever such attitudes cropped up the first thing I felt was fear. Should I feel this, too? Should I not? Proverbs 3:34 scared me a lot. 'God opposes the proud but gives grace to the humble.' I used to struggle a lot with this in my conversations with God. Was this real pride I was encountering? If so, what was I supposed to do? Was this really an army I could fight in, or would even want to fight in?"

"Because [Jenny] chose to leave the church for a few months on a travel job, she was expected by leaders to fail in her Christian walk. The assumption was that she would be unable to find a GCM church where she was going, thus she would lose her faith. Similar expectations were verbalized about three of my other friends. There is no trust in other churches at all."

"It was at this time, that I reflected on all of my other concerns with this church: The monopolization of time – many retreats, conferences, meetings, accountability groups. The marginalization of women – there are few places for women to serve other than in the kitchen, the nursery, and with other women. The pressure to grow the numbers, and the de-emphasis of making lifelong friends. People become tools and projects. Many, many sermons on submission, unity, obedience – messages that suit an unhealthy church's purpose well! The pressure to spank and only spank your children. The silent conformity to homeschooling, women at home, courtship, and even vocabularies – Core members are very much alike, in my opinion."[313]

---

[313] Pile, Larry, Statement about Great Commission Association of Churches/Great Commission Ministries http://gcxweb.org/Misc/LarryPile-03-11-2006.aspx

Information Control

[314]"A version of George Orwell's double-think is applied to everything. Any reading material critical of GCI was satanic; anyone who criticized the Elders was manipulated by the devil. We were instructed to go about 'capturing' naughty thoughts by consigning all critical ideas to the demonic. I found myself in constant war with myself. The Satan I jumped at--tried to jump over--was my own shadow. Any search for counsel would bring bibliolatry into play. Whenever anything challenged the GCI worldview, we were taught to answer with scripture--in our heads or, better, aloud."

"No legitimate group needs to lie or mislead you about what they practice or believe. Any group which says you must belong to their organization to be saved is almost certainly a cult. Be very suspicious of any group claiming to be better than all the others. A religious group may say other groups following the same religion are OK, but they are the ones who have a better grasp of the truth and they are superior to the rest. This is often a subtle version of exclusivism. Character Assassination is a sure sign of a cult. Cult members are usually very fearful of disobeying or disagreeing in any way with their leadership. Healthy organizations, however, are not threatened by openly debating issues. Beware of 'instant friends,' remember true friendships develop over time. Beware of a group that tells you who you can and cannot see. If you are instructed by a group not to read information critical of the group, then that is a sign of a cult. Legitimate groups have nothing to fear from their members reading critical information about them. Is information you expected to be kept confidential reported to leadership? If so, then it's a cult. Never-ending compulsory meetings and tasks is a sign of a cult. Beware of any group where there appears to be a spy network. Be very cautious even if, or especially if, they are spying on you for your own good."

"We were told that all we needed was the Bible (but our interpretation better match up with approved doctrine)!"[315]

---

[314] Dickerson, Matthew, The Culture of Control: Inside Great Commission (Part 2) http://gcxweb.org/Articles/Touchstone-05-1992-b.aspx

[315] Pile, Larry, Statement about Great Commission Association of Churches/Great Commission Ministries http://gcxweb.org/Misc/LarryPile-03-11-2006.aspx

Thought Control

"A common theme in interviews we conduct is that GCM strongly discourages any outside Christian counseling, even on issues it has nobody trained to handle. Quite often what happens when someone finally does get outside counseling, the counsellor recommends they find another church. This may explain their reluctance."

"We were overwhelmed with our two special needs children. We tried to talk to certain people, and their response was, 'You know what your problem is? You need to serve more. You are focusing too much on yourself. You are not Christ-like, because when Christ found out his cousin John had been beheaded - he then fed the 5000!' That compounded the problem and we sought a biblically based counselor, and when it came up ... I was specifically reprimanded for getting counsel outside of the church. Our small group leader was excessively offended to the point of confronting us and saying, 'You should not have gone outside of our church!'"

Emotional Control

"If you asked counsel you were expected to follow it, or else you were considered disobedient to God. If someone higher up counseled you to do something, they were your 'spiritual authority' and thus God in his sovereignty had placed them above you, and so you were thought to be disobeying God if you disobeyed them. The verse used quite often to back this theology up was: Obey your leaders and submit to them, for they watch on behalf of your souls.[316] Nobody was trusted to be able to hear from God on their own, and thus people's lives were lived in submission to what their spiritual leader decided was best for them. Wasn't always a bad thing as some people needed guidance, however it pretty much discouraged you from developing any functional relationship with God, and was very legalistic and controlling due to the way it was presented as God's will and not a pastor's advice."

---

[316] Hebrews 13:17

SECTION 3

TACTICS

And Paul, as his manner was, went in unto them, and three sabbath days reasoned with them out of the scriptures, Opening and alleging, that Christ must needs have suffered, and risen again from the dead; and that this Jesus, whom I preach unto you, is Christ. (Acts 17:2-3)

TACTIC #1

Using Jesus as our "Common Ground"

CHAPTER 19

"I'm a Christian Too"

I want to paint a scenario. It's one most Christians have probably experienced, or at least it will sound familiar. A knock comes on the door. Two young men who are dressed in white shirt, nice tie, a nameplate saying Elder _____. Maybe it's a family or a couple of ladies that come to the door. No particular uniform. But they say they are a representative of The Church of Jesus Christ of Latter-day Saints, or perhaps the Jehovah's Witnesses, Kingdom Hall, or Watchtower Society. They invite the person who answers the door to have a discussion about Jesus with them, and in the midst of getting to know them, what comes out is they're a Christian, and from the lips of the person at the door comes, "I'm a Christian too!" It doesn't have to be a missionary but could be a friend or a conversation at the park.

Sometimes this exchange can take an adversarial tone, where they say, "You don't think I'm a Christian, do you?"

What does one do at that moment that won't put up a barrier, won't put up a wall, but tells them the truth, tells them how one feels?

I find many times this situation comes up and the cult member is trying to make you feel uncomfortable as a Christian. The Christian is claiming the cult member falls outside the boundaries of Orthodox Christian doctrine. So sometimes Christians pull back when this happens because they don't want things to become confrontational.

What does one do at this moment?

One of the most significant tactics I have found with these groups is to leverage this moment to invite them into a conversation about Jesus. What he did and said as recorded in the four gospels contained in the Bible. The reason is that all of these groups want to claim Jesus, or claim Christianity, but many of them don't know what Jesus taught, or what the Bible teaches. I want to focus on the gospels mainly because they are all about the life, ministry and teaching of Jesus. The gospels are where we learn about the death and resurrection of Jesus, which is the gospel. They are the foundational documents, the manifesto, for Christianity. Especially when one reads those red letters.

I prefer to use the King James Version. Why? Because this is the Bible, if the particular group you are talking to uses a Bible, that they will use. They might only use their own group's translation, which are all train wrecks. Being a good missionary means making Jesus the stumbling block and removing all others. I'm not going to cover everything. There is a great series called Reasoning from the Scriptures by Ron Rhodes using this very tactic more systematically through the entire Bible with most of the groups described in this book.[317] There are other books written by former members of these groups that do the same exact thing that I'm doing. The Scripture is loaded with answers for these various groups. It's my conviction that the Holy Spirit anticipated every single heresy when he gave us the Bible. Even if the particular false teaching was not something being taught in Bible times, the Holy Spirit finds a way to word things so it answers every single one of the modern-day heresies and objections.

---

[317] Reasoning from the Scriptures Ministries http://www.ronrhodes.addr.com/

CHAPTER 20

Passages in the Gospels Related to Authority

The Apostasy

Most of the groups categorized as a cult teach there was an apostasy of the church at some point and the true church needed to be restored to the earth. They claim that the true church had disappeared from the face of the earth, the Bible had been tainted, the authority of the early church disappeared and needed to be restored. So what does Jesus say about that?

> **And I say also unto thee, That thou art Peter, and upon this rock I will build my church; and the gates of hell shall not prevail against it. (Matthew 16:18)**

Jesus is teaching that Hell, or Hades, cannot stand before the onslaught of the church. And that is what the claim of the apostasy is making. These false groups may say Jesus was saying the church ultimately won't be overcome by Hades. But Jesus is speaking in offensive terminology, not defensive. The gates of a city were what an army would storm when they were attacking the city. Jesus was saying the gates of hell will not be able to withstand the attack of the church. This doesn't mean the church is going to bring in the Kingdom of God, or that things are going to become better and better. The Scripture does say things would become worse and worse, and there would be an apostasy. But Jesus would never allow for the church as a whole, that he is building, to be overcome by Satan. And it's not up to us. It's not that we failed because we were in charge. Jesus is in charge, and Jesus is fully capable of preserving his church.

> **Heaven and earth shall pass away, but my words shall not pass away. (Matthew 24:35)**

This is one of a plethora of Scriptures from Genesis to Revelation that says God's word will not fail. It is perfect. He will preserve it. God's word will never pass away. There will never be a point in time where the gospel is not available to men. There was never a time where the entire church vanished off the face of the earth. There is never a time where the Scripture was tainted to the point where the original is not discernable and "plain and precious truths" were removed from the Scriptures. And if this did happen, then Jesus is a false prophet. And if Jesus was a false prophet, not only is their group in trouble but ours as well.

> **Forasmuch as many have taken in hand to set forth in order a declaration of those things which are most surely believed among us, Even as they delivered them unto us, which from the beginning were eyewitnesses, and ministers of the word; It seemed good to me also, having had perfect understanding of all things from the very first, to write unto thee in order, most excellent Theophilus, (Luke 1:1-3)**

Luke is declaring the painstaking labor he went through to bring his gospel to us. He interviewed every source he could find to make sure he had done all the research needed. He then made his best effort to present the events in chronological order. Luke is the only gospel that attempts to do this, which will come up when we talk about "contradictions" in the Tactic #4: Why Should We Trust the Bible? tactic discussed in this book.

Luke is a historical document using more medical terminology than Hippocrates, the father of modern medicine.[318] This shouldn't surprise us because Luke is a

---

[318] Hobart, William Kirk, The Medical Language of St. Luke, p. 52-53

physician. In fact, he might have been Paul's personal physician assigned to him as a prisoner on his way to Rome to testify to Caesar.[319]

Luke was acknowledged by Sir William Ramsay, who set out to discredit the Bible using Luke and Acts as his sole travel guide and ended up converting to Christianity. He concluded Luke was a "historian of the first rank."[320] Luke has more specific mentions of locations, rulers, customs, details, etc. than any of the other gospels, which helps us to date the events as well as locate the places mentioned. A forger simply wouldn't take the time, or have the desire, to mention all of these details. These false groups want us to believe God brought us his word, established his church, etc. and then allowed it to fall into complete apostasy for hundreds or thousands of years.

> **The law and the prophets [were] until John: since that time the kingdom of God is preached, and every man presseth into it. And it is easier for heaven and earth to pass, than one tittle of the law to fail. (Luke 16:16-17)**

This is a repeat of what Jesus had already said. "Think not that I came to destroy the law, but fulfill it, for I tell you not one jot or tittle will pass from the law until all is fulfilled."[321] Jesus is repeating what the Bible teaches repeatedly. God's Word cannot fail. Psalm 138:2 says, "I have reverenced my word, even above my name." God would not have allowed the Word of God to vanish from the face of the earth for 1500 years until a fourteen-year-old came on the scene who could restore it back to the earth, and do it, no less, through another scripture.

Authority

A question that was asked of Jesus is often the same question that is asked of me by members of these different groups.

---

[319] Franz, Gordon, Luke The Physician: with "Medicine for the Souls" http://www.biblearchaeology.org/post/2014/01/23/Luke-The-Physician-with-Medicine-for-the-Souls.aspx#Article

[320] Ramsay, Sir William, St. Paul the Traveller and the Roman Citizen, p. 4

[321] Matthew 5:17

And when he was come into the temple, the chief priests and the elders of the people came unto him as he was teaching, and said, By what authority doest thou these things? and who gave thee this authority? (Matthew 21:23)

The authority to do what we do. To teach, preach, and baptize, comes through Jesus Christ, who is God, who said, "All authority in heaven and earth has been given unto me, and I commission you to make disciples of all nations and baptize them in the name of the Father, Son and Holy Spirit, and teach them to obey everything I have commanded you. And I will be with you even unto the end of the age."[322]

This is the same God who brought us into existence. It's the same God who breathes life into us. It's the same God by way of him speaking, who calmed the waves and the sea. Who spoke, and different individuals were healed. Who spoke, and demons were cast out of people. It's the same Jesus who spoke and gave us his authority. We don't need to hold a priesthood. We don't need to have hands laid on us. We don't need to be baptized in the name of Jesus only. We don't need to be a part of any particular church said to be the one true church. None of those things is where we get our authority. Our authority comes straight from the lips of Jesus to us. And that's why we can do what we do.

Hear another parable: There was a certain householder, which planted a vineyard, and hedged it round about, and digged a winepress in it, and built a tower, and let it out to husbandmen, and went into a far country: And when the time of the fruit drew near, he sent his servants to the husbandmen, that they might receive the fruits of it. And the husbandmen took his servants, and beat one, and killed another, and stoned another. Again, he sent other servants more than the first: and they did unto them likewise. But last of all he sent unto them his son, saying, They will reverence my son. But when the husbandmen saw the son, they said among themselves, This is the heir; come, let us kill him, and let us seize on his inheritance. And they caught him, and cast [him] out of the vineyard, and slew [him]. When

---

[322] Matthew 28:18-20

the lord therefore of the vineyard cometh, what will he do unto those husbandmen? They say unto him, He will miserably destroy those wicked men, and will let out [his] vineyard unto other husbandmen, which shall render him the fruits in their seasons. (Matthew 21:33-41)

This parable was spoken directly to the Pharisees. And Jesus was describing them, as the religious leaders, for having slain all of the prophets that God had sent into his vineyard. The vineyard is Israel. Isaiah 5, as well as other passages, establishes this truth. He said, "Last of all, he sent unto them his Son, saying, 'They will receive my Son.'" Jesus was calling them on the fact they were going to reject and kill him too. And the vineyard was going to be taken from them and given to those who will be good stewards. Of John the Baptist, Jesus said the law and prophets prophesied until John. Hebrews 1:1 says in times past God spoke through the prophets, but in these last days he has spoken by his Son. There are no more prophets. There is no more need for official apostles or prophets or any of that stuff. God has spoken to us through his Son. Jesus is our High Priest.[323] He is our Apostle. He is our Prophet. He is our King.[324] He is everything. There is no need for another. There is only one mediator between God and man, and that is the man Christ Jesus.[325]

Beware the Counterfeits

For many shall come in my name, saying, I am Christ; and shall deceive many. ... And many false prophets shall rise, and shall deceive many. ... Then if any man shall say unto you, Lo, here [is] Christ, or there; believe [it] not. For there shall arise false Christs, and false prophets, and shall shew great signs and wonders; insomuch that, if [it were] possible, they shall deceive the very elect. (Matthew 24:5, 11, 23-24)

---

[323] Hebrews 3:1

[324] Acts 17:7

[325] 1 Timothy 2:5

What are the criteria for a false prophet? Deuteronomy 13 and 18 tells us. If they lead people to follow other gods, or if something they say is going to happen doesn't happen, they are a false prophet. Don't listen to them. Put them to death. A tactic some use is to go through the false prophecies of these various groups and leaders to show they are false prophets or false groups. We are taking another tactic in this book, focusing on whether what their leaders and Scriptures are teaching are matching up with what God has previously revealed, particularly the words of Jesus. Do the words of Joseph Smith, Charles Taze Russell, Ellen G. White, L. Ron Hubbard, Mary Baker Eddy, etc. match with the words of Jesus?

Jesus is our Prophet

This is for all groups claiming specific authority roles within the church, whether they be apostle, prophet, high priest, elders, brethren, etc...

For all the prophets and the law prophesied until John. (Matthew 11:13)

Hear another parable: There was a certain householder, which planted a vineyard, and hedged it round about, and digged a winepress in it, and built a tower, and let it out to husbandmen, and went into a far country: And when the time of the fruit drew near, he sent his servants to the husbandmen, that they might receive the fruits of it. And the husbandmen took his servants, and beat one, and killed another, and stoned another. Again, he sent other servants more than the first: and they did unto them likewise. But last of all he sent unto them his son, saying, They will reverence my son. But when the husbandmen saw the son, they said among themselves, This is the heir; come, let us kill him, and let us seize on his inheritance. And they caught him, and cast [him] out of the vineyard, and slew [him]. When the lord therefore of the vineyard cometh, what will he do unto those husbandmen? They say unto him, He will miserably destroy those wicked men, and will let out [his] vineyard unto other

husbandmen, which shall render him the fruits in their seasons.
(Matthew 21:33-41)

The Old Testament prophet was how the whole dynamic worked until John the Baptist. Then Jesus became the one through whom God spoke. Jesus is the ultimate revelation of God.[326] Are there prophets in the New Testament? Some people are referred to as prophets or even people who have the gift of prophecy or have a manifestation of prophesying, but they are not a prophet in the Old Testament sense.[327] That ended with John the Baptist, and Jesus makes that clear. Hebrews 1:1 makes it even more apparent.

Modern-Day Apostles

And Jesus said unto them, Verily I say unto you, That ye which have followed me, in the regeneration when the Son of man shall sit in the throne of his glory, ye also shall sit upon twelve thrones, judging the twelve tribes of Israel. (Matthew 19:28)

Question. If there were at the same time twelve apostles in Israel, and then Jesus came over to the American continent, and he chose twelve more apostles, and each of them was supposed to pass on that office after they died, and on top of that, there are modern-day apostles, why are there only twelve thrones judging the twelve tribes of Israel? And if only the twelve apostles are going to judge Israel, then who are these modern-day apostles going to judge over? What is their reward? Even in the heavenly city in Revelation 21-22, only the names of the twelve apostles are written on the city gates.

The Bible vs. Tradition

All of these groups seem to have other writings or leaders who have writings or Scriptures or translations of Scriptures that they put on par with the Bible. And Jesus said that is not a good thing. This is what happened in his day, with tradition poured

---

[326] Hebrews 1:1-2
[327] Acts 21:10

upon tradition and commentary upon commentary of God's word. So the person who was trying to discern God's word had a hard time doing so.

And that is what goes on in most of these groups. They keep changing the rules and the doctrine, to the point where it becomes hard trying to maintain a conversation about some of these things. That is why I don't discuss official doctrine. I want to key into that individual and go with what they are saying. Now, I might bring up what their church teaches from time to time to see how that individual reacts, but that isn't my focus.

> **Howbeit in vain do they worship me, teaching [for] doctrines the commandments of men. For laying aside the commandment of God, ye hold the tradition of men, [as] the washing of pots and cups: and many other such like things ye do. And he said unto them, Full well ye reject the commandment of God, that ye may keep your own tradition. For Moses said, Honour thy father and thy mother; and, Whoso curseth father or mother, let him die the death: But ye say, If a man shall say to his father or mother, [It is] Corban, that is to say, a gift, by whatsoever thou mightest be profited by me; [he shall be free]. And ye suffer him no more to do ought for his father or his mother; Making the word of God of none effect through your tradition, which ye have delivered: and many such like things do ye. (Mark 7:7-13)**

It's interesting to me that with most of these groups who fall heavy into legalism, what I find when I read the gospels is if you insert, for example, an LDS person, in the place of the Pharisees, it fits most often like a glove. And this is what the issue is. Like I've said before. It's not that they claim to have additional or modern-day revelation. It's when that revelation is contradicting what God has previously and revealed through his word creating a problem. And when that happens, these groups will take the new over the old, and they are taught that is the way God operates. If one is going to reach members of these groups, they have to be able to break through that mindset.

> **In the mean time, when there were gathered together an innumerable multitude of people, insomuch that they trode one**

upon another, he began to say unto his disciples first of all, Beware ye of the leaven of the Pharisees, which is hypocrisy. (Luke 12:1)

This is a message for all people. We shouldn't pretend to be someone we aren't. One's identity doesn't rest in how good a person they are, the role they play in church, how people see them, what they expect of them, or any of that. Don't give into any of that. The Pharisees pretended to be righteous. They pretended to be all together. They acted like they were doing everything God asked them to do. And they weren't. And they knew that they weren't. But they put on a mask, and as long as the outward presence was clean, they were okay with that, and they let people believe that. The Pharisees even allowed people to believe they were better people.

CHAPTER 21

Passages in the Gospels Related to Salvation by Grace Alone through Faith Alone

Every single one of the groups discussed in this book is different from Christianity in that they teach individuals have to do something to earn their salvation. They have to work alongside Jesus as if he is co-Savior. Below are several passages in the gospels that teach salvation is by grace alone, through faith alone, and not by works.

Author and Finisher

But he that shall endure unto the end, the same shall be saved. (Matthew 24:13)

How does this fit in with this idea of faith alone, Jesus being the one who saves us, and not our efforts? Is this verse teaching that we have to keep ourselves saved and in good standing with God, or else one can lose their salvation. I don't think so.

Jesus is saying one can tell the true believers from the false believers because false believers fall away. They weren't trusting in the right things to save them or weren't believing for the right reasons. When hard times come, some fall away. When false teachers come, some fall away. When different things in life come, or the cares of the world come, some fall away. John, in his epistle, said if some went out from us to show they were never really of us.[328] And he was talking about the false teachers. That is what Jesus is getting at in this passage. In the midst of persecution, the one who endures to the end will be saved. Another way of looking at this is to hear him say, "If I have a hold of you, you will endure to the end. I have you in the palm of my hand," as he said in John 10.

Boast in Jesus

Notwithstanding in this rejoice not, that the spirits are subject unto you; but rather rejoice, because your names are written in heaven. (Luke 10:20)

The names of the apostles, and by extension, anybody who believes, are already written in heaven. We have eternal life.

Faith Alone

He that believeth and is baptized shall be saved; but he that believeth not shall be damned. (Mark 16:16)

Is Jesus telling us in this verse we have to be baptized in water to be saved? I don't think it is. There are some who would debate whether or not this was in the original manuscripts of Mark. I personally believe it was. I think there are reasons to believe it was. I don't want to get into that here. But this verse does not seal any case you have to be baptized to be saved. On the positive end, Jesus said, "he who believes and is baptized shall be saved," but on the negative side he said, "he who does not believe will be condemned." So belief is the thing that is emphasized, and baptism is the thing one does out of the answer of a good conscience as Peter said.[329] It doesn't save you. It doesn't forgive sins.

---

[328] 1 John 2:19
[329] 1 Peter 3:21

> **And these signs shall follow them that believe; In my name shall they cast out devils; they shall speak with new tongues; (Mark 16:17)**

Is Jesus saying we need to speak in tongues to be saved? No. Jesus is referring to something that will be happening with believers, but Paul's writings tell us through rhetorical questions that not all believers have the same gifts or speak in tongues.[330] Each is given gifts according to where God placed you in the body.[331] Not all need to speak in tongues to fulfill the opportunities that God gives them. Others do need to speak in tongues to take advantage of opportunities that God gives them to preach the gospel.

> **And he said to the woman, Thy faith hath saved thee; go in peace. (Luke 7:50)**

I have to confess that when I was going through the gospels, this was a gem that I had yet to discover. This is Jesus proclaiming to this woman that her faith, and faith alone, has saved her. That is awesome!

> **And I say unto you, Ask, and it shall be given you; seek, and ye shall find; knock, and it shall be opened unto you. For every one that asketh receiveth; and he that seeketh findeth; and to him that knocketh it shall be opened. If a son shall ask bread of any of you that is a father, will he give him a stone? or if [he ask] a fish, will he for a fish give him a serpent? Or if he shall ask an egg, will he offer him a scorpion? If ye then, being evil, know how to give good gifts unto your children: how much more shall [your] heavenly Father give the Holy Spirit to them that ask him? (Luke 11:9-13)**

Matthew's gospel talks about how we know how to give good gifts as humans. We know a gift is not earned but rather is given because we love that person and simply want them to have what we are giving them. For them to make it theirs, they simply

---

[330] 1 Corinthians 12:30

[331] Romans 12:4-8

have to receive the gift we are offering them. They aren't trying to figure out what they did to earn the gift, or figure out how to pay us back.

Luke tied this idea into the giving of the Holy Spirit and said that it is available for the asking. The Holy Spirit is given the moment one believes. It's the empowering force by which everything in the Christian life happens. The Holy Spirit is available for the asking.

> **Two men went up into the temple to pray; the one a Pharisee, and the other a publican. The Pharisee stood and prayed thus with himself, God, I thank thee, that I am not as other men [are], extortioners, unjust, adulterers, or even as this publican. I fast twice in the week, I give tithes of all that I possess. And the publican, standing afar off, would not lift up so much as [his] eyes unto heaven, but smote upon his breast, saying, God be merciful to me a sinner. I tell you, this man went down to his house justified [rather] than the other: for every one that exalteth himself shall be abased; and he that humbleth himself shall be exalted. (Luke 18:10-14)**

I can't think of something Jesus could have taught that would have been more to the point when it comes to the LDS. If one substitutes an LDS person here in the place of the Pharisee, it fits like a glove. They fast at least once a month. They give tithes of all they possess. And they are looking, even to their fellow LDS people, and saying, "God, thank you I'm not committing the same sins as the man standing over there." And they look on everybody else with an attitude of superiority because they are a part of the one true church. I like how it says, "He prayed with himself."

Then there is the tax collector, despised by society, who is simply asking, "God, be merciful to me, a sinner." And he went away justified, meaning as if he had never done the crime. He is now right with God.

> **And Jesus said unto him, Receive thy sight: thy faith hath saved thee. (Luke 18:42)**

Jesus said, present tense, "Thy faith has saved you." At that moment, Blind Bartimaeus was saved. And that wasn't even what he was asking for.

> **And one of the malefactors which were hanged railed on him, saying, If thou be Christ, save thyself and us. But the other answering rebuked him, saying, Dost not thou fear God, seeing thou art in the same condemnation? And we indeed justly; for we receive the due reward of our deeds: but this man hath done nothing amiss. And he said unto Jesus, Lord, remember me when thou comest into thy kingdom. And Jesus said unto him, Verily I say unto thee, To day shalt thou be with me in paradise. (Luke 23:39-43)**

The thief on the cross had no opportunity to speak in tongues or be baptized, yet Jesus said he was saved. Jesus said, "You will be with me in Paradise."

The LDS teach Paradise is where the righteous go after this life, and they go there and wait until the final resurrection of the dead when they are assigned to one of the three levels of glory. From that perspective, they would say Jesus went to Paradise that day, and the thief on the cross went with him to that place, and this passage doesn't necessarily say he was guaranteed a place in heaven. I don't think a case can be made for that. If one examines all of the places where Paradise is spoken of in the Bible, it is equated with the presence of God. Paradise is implied in the Garden of Eden narrative.[332] Paradise is mentioned in the new Eden in Revelation.[333] Paul was caught up to Paradise in 2 Corinthians 12 and equates that with the third heaven.[334]

This is also a great way to get the LDS to see this because, in the LDS mind, the Third Heaven is the Celestial Kingdom. Going back to this verse, to be consistent, they would have to believe Jesus said to this thief that he was going to the Celestial Kingdom. There is no way to reconcile that with Mormon theology. He wasn't baptized, didn't receive the laying on of hands, didn't receive the Holy Ghost, didn't receive any callings, didn't go through the temple, wasn't sealed as a family unit, or anything meriting the Celestial Kingdom from a Mormon perspective.

Where did Jesus go when he died? This is another interesting question, and one I'm going to have some fun with here.

---

[332] Genesis 2-3

[333] Revelation 2:7

[334] 2 Corinthians 12:2, 4

People debate about this, even within Christianity. Where did Jesus go? Some scriptures insinuate he went into the heart of the earth.[335] There are Scriptures like this that insinuate Jesus went back to his Father. He went to heaven. Some passages talk about him releasing righteous believers from the Old Testament through his righteous death.[336] Some verses insinuate Jesus was proclaiming his victory to evil spirits.[337] My point is this. Something has gone untouched by anything that I've seen. Jesus' spirit was set free from his body while he was in the grave for three days. His Spirit, being God, is omnipresent.[338] So Jesus could have been in all of those places doing all of those things at the same time.

> **That whosoever believeth in him should not perish, but have eternal life. For God so loved the world, that he gave his only begotten Son, that whosoever believeth in him should not perish, but have everlasting life. For God sent not his Son into the world to condemn the world; but that the world through him might be saved. (John 3:15-17)**

What does one have to do to get eternal life? They have to believe. Jesus doesn't list anything else. On the other side, if they don't believe, they don't have eternal life.

> **Jesus answered and said unto her, If thou knewest the gift of God, and who it is that saith to thee, Give me to drink; thou wouldest have asked of him, and he would have given thee living water. (John 4:10)**

The gift of God is Jesus. Sometimes we get confused and think that the gift of God is eternal life. We receive Jesus, and everything God has to give he gives with Jesus. If one receives Jesus, they have received everything God has to give. There is nothing left to earn.

---

[335] Psalm 16:10; Acts 2:27

[336] Psalm 68:18; Ephesians 4:8

[337] 1 Peter 3:18-20

[338] Psalm 139:7

> **He that believeth on the Son hath everlasting life: and he that believeth not the Son shall not see life; but the wrath of God abideth on him. (John 3:36)**

If one doesn't have Jesus, they are condemned already. The wrath of God abides on them. God doesn't look at progress. He asks if we have his Son or not. He who believes on the Son "has," present tense, eternal life. Once a person has Jesus, there is no giving away or taking away of eternal life.

> **Verily, verily, I say unto you, He that heareth my word, and believeth on him that sent me, hath everlasting life, and shall not come into condemnation; but is passed from death unto life. (John 5:24)**

If a person believes in Jesus Christ, they have everlasting life, and they shall not come into condemnation. This is present tense, not some future thing that we can look forward to only if we have done enough to have been counted worthy.

> **Then said they unto him, What shall we do, that we might work the works of God? Jesus answered and said unto them, This is the work of God, that ye believe on him whom he hath sent. (John 6:28-29)**

For those who want to emphasize works, Jesus tells us what the work is, and it's belief in him. However, when one emphasizes the words on the front end of this passage, they will find Jesus is even taking this a step further and saying it's God's work that we believe. We are told elsewhere by Paul that faith is a gift of God. When we exercise faith, it is God's work, not ours. Who's faith is it? It's the faith of Jesus given to us so that we might come into a relationship with God.[339]

> **And many other signs truly did Jesus in the presence of his disciples, which are not written in this book: But these are written, that ye might believe Jesus is the Christ, the Son of God; and that believing ye might have life through his name. (John 20:30-31)**

---

[339] Galatians 2:16

John tells us he wrote his gospel for the express purpose that we would believe Jesus is the Son of God. And through that belief, we might have life through his name. Again, that's present tense life. Eternal life. Through our belief in Jesus Christ.

Forgiven More, Love More

> There was a certain creditor which had two debtors: the one owed five hundred pence, and the other fifty. And when they had nothing to pay, he frankly forgave them both. Tell me therefore, which of them will love him most? Simon answered and said, I suppose that [he], to whom he forgave most. And he said unto him, Thou hast rightly judged. ... Wherefore I say unto thee, Her sins, which are many, are forgiven; for she loved much: but to whom little is forgiven, [the same] loveth little. (Luke 7:41-43, 47)

Religion teaches the more one does for God, and the less they sin, the better standing they are going to have with God. Jesus flips this around in this scenario. He said the one who has more sin forgiven will love him more. Those who think they are already okay could care less about Jesus.

Grace as a Model for Life

> And forgive us our debts, as we forgive our debtors. (Matthew 6:12)

Jesus is saying the way God forgives us is the same way we are supposed to forgive others.

Imagine one has a friend that has offended them, and that friend apologizes. Imagine if one approached this situation the way the LDS and other groups teach we obtain forgiveness from God. They would have to tell that friend when they apologize, "The only way I would know you are truly sorry is if you never do that again, and I will only know that when you die. Before you die, you still can do it again. After you die, then I will be able to forgive you." Even under these circumstances, you would never know whether they repeated the act. They might have done it, but decided to find another friend because they didn't find forgiveness.

If ye then, being evil, know how to give good gifts unto your children, how much more shall your Father which is in heaven give good things to them that ask him? (Matthew 7:11)

God is the model gift giver. Christmas is a great time to emphasize this idea of gifts. Think about a father who pays good money that he has earned for gifts for his children. He puts them under the tree. The kids are all excited. On the gift is a note saying, "As soon as you mow the lawn, you can have this gift," or "As soon as you do the dishes, you can have this gift." That's not a gift anymore, is it?

We know what a gift is. We know how to give good gifts. Jesus said that if we know how to give good gifts, how much more does the Father know how to give good gifts to us. That gift is his son.

Heal the sick, cleanse the lepers, raise the dead, cast out devils: freely ye have received, freely give. (Matthew 10:8)

This verse is the basis for my ministry, People of the Free Gift. "Freely you have received. Freely give." Again we see God modeling salvation and forgiveness for us. We are supposed to be like him, give like him. The way we do that is by giving freely, which is only possible if we have received freely.

Therefore is the kingdom of heaven likened unto a certain king, which would take account of his servants. And when he had begun to reckon, one was brought unto him, which owed him ten thousand talents. But forasmuch as he had not to pay, his lord commanded him to be sold, and his wife, and children, and all that he had, and payment to be made. The servant therefore fell down, and worshipped him, saying, Lord, have patience with me, and I will pay thee all. Then the lord of that servant was moved with compassion, and loosed him, and forgave him the debt. But the same servant went out, and found one of his fellowservants, which owed him an hundred pence: and he laid hands on him, and took [him] by the throat, saying, Pay me that thou owest. And his fellowservant fell down at his feet, and besought him, saying, Have patience with me, and I will pay thee all. And he

would not: but went and cast him into prison, till he should pay the debt. So when his fellowservants saw what was done, they were very sorry, and came and told unto their lord all that was done. Then his lord, after that he had called him, said unto him, O thou wicked servant, I forgave thee all that debt, because thou desiredst me: Shouldest not thou also have had compassion on thy fellowservant, even as I had pity on thee? And his lord was wroth, and delivered him to the tormentors, till he should pay all that was due unto him. So likewise shall my heavenly Father do also unto you, if ye from your hearts forgive not every one his brother their trespasses. (Matthew 18:23-35)

There are a couple of things to point out in this powerful parable. First, the slave owed a far, far greater debt. An insurmountable amount of money. And he was forgiven. And notice it was after he made the offer, "Please don't throw me into prison. I promise I'll pay you back." But he was forgiven the debt. God does not accept offers of repayment. He only forgives the debt we owe before him. You can't do it by trying to earn it. He only gives it as a gift.

Second, the first debtor found the man who owed him a small debt, and exacted it of him. And when the second debtor offered to pay back a far more modest amount, he denied him and threw him into prison.

Then the man who was owed the original debt came back and said, "Really?" This shows where his heart was. To not forgive the debt others owe to us is showing we don't understand the debt God forgave us. We don't need to make too much out of the condition of forgiveness because it shows a heart of humility and a knowledge of who we are before God. To truly repent of our sins and be forgiven by God, and then to turn around and not forgive the offense others have done to us, shows that we don't understand the grace that was shown to us.

God's forgiveness is the model. Implementing a works-righteousness mentality in our interpersonal relationships would be ridiculous. If God didn't forgive us until the final judgment day, and do so upon conditions of repentance, then Jesus would be telling us to not forgive anybody because one never know until the end whether others have repented.

> **Then said he also to him that bade him, When thou makest a dinner or a supper, call not thy friends, nor thy brethren, neither thy kinsmen, nor [thy] rich neighbours; lest they also bid thee again, and a recompence be made thee. But when thou makest a feast, call the poor, the maimed, the lame, the blind: And thou shalt be blessed; for they cannot recompense thee: for thou shalt be recompensed at the resurrection of the just. (Luke 14:12-14)**

Jesus is saying, "Here's what I want you to do. I want you to not do things for people who can do them back for you. I want you to do things for people who can't do them back for you. I want you to forgive people who don't deserve forgiveness. I want you to love people who don't deserve love. I want you to give to people who can't give back. I want you to include people who can't repay you." That is the model Jesus gave us. That's because it is what we has done for us. What gets us rewards in heaven is when we allow the Spirit of God to live his life out through us. When we do, what we do will be in his will, his timing, his strength, done in his motives, his desires. That's what gets us rewards. Ultimately, when we stand before God and get rewarded in heaven, it is because Christ is the one who is getting rewarded. It's all about him. There's nothing about what is going to get rewarded that is ours or we can lay claim to. Nothing.

Lost and Found

> **And he said, A certain man had two sons: And the younger of them said to [his] father, Father, give me the portion of goods that falleth [to me]. And he divided unto them [his] living. And not many days after the younger son gathered all together, and took his journey into a far country, and there wasted his substance with riotous living. And when he had spent all, there arose a mighty famine in that land; and he began to be in want. And he went and joined himself to a citizen of that country; and he sent him into his fields to feed swine. And he would fain have filled his belly with the husks that the swine did eat: and no man gave unto him. And when he came to himself, he said, How many**

hired servants of my father's have bread enough and to spare, and I perish with hunger! I will arise and go to my father, and will say unto him, Father, I have sinned against heaven, and before thee, And am no more worthy to be called thy son: make me as one of thy hired servants. And he arose, and came to his father. But when he was yet a great way off, his father saw him, and had compassion, and ran, and fell on his neck, and kissed him. And the son said unto him, Father, I have sinned against heaven, and in thy sight, and am no more worthy to be called thy son. But the father said to his servants, Bring forth the best robe, and put [it] on him; and put a ring on his hand, and shoes on [his] feet: And bring hither the fatted calf, and kill [it]; and let us eat, and be merry: For this my son was dead, and is alive again; he was lost, and is found. And they began to be merry. Now his elder son was in the field: and as he came and drew nigh to the house, he heard musick and dancing. And he called one of the servants, and asked what these things meant. And he said unto him, Thy brother is come; and thy father hath killed the fatted calf, because he hath received him safe and sound. And he was angry, and would not go in: therefore came his father out, and intreated him. And he answering said to [his] father, Lo, these many years do I serve thee, neither transgressed I at any time thy commandment: and yet thou never gavest me a kid, that I might make merry with my friends: But as soon as this thy son was come, which hath devoured thy living with harlots, thou hast killed for him the fatted calf. And he said unto him, Son, thou art ever with me, and all that I have is thine. It was meet that we should make merry, and be glad: for this thy brother was dead, and is alive again; and was lost, and is found. (Luke 15:11-32)

So many things are going on in this passage, but I want to point out a couple of things. The son asks for his inheritance, and he wasted it. This whole scenario would have been repugnant in Jewish society because he utterly disgraced the father. The son comes to an end of himself, and said, "Even the servants in my father's house are doing better than this." He prepares a speech which revolves around him not being worthy to be called his father's son but begging him to make him a servant. He goes home. His father sees him and runs to him. Fathers didn't run in that day. It was a sign of disgrace and disrespect. The father runs to him and embraces him. The son started into the speech he had prepared, and the father didn't even listen to his speech or respond to it. He said he wants the best party thrown for his kid. He was lost, but now he's found. The father didn't know whether he was dead or alive.

Then there is the older son, who had not left, who didn't waste his inheritance, who was there the whole time and was doing what the father said. Notice the son said, "I haven't broken any commandments that you've given me." That's probably not true. But that aside, the father said, "Rejoice with me. Come into the party." The son refused to come into the party. He won't come into the party, showing he is not willing to follow this command, which contradicts the claim he has made.

What the father said is, "All I have is yours." What we see in this older son is a model of Christians, who are saved, but they don't take advantage of the gifts that God has given them. They don't care about the things of God. This is a sad case because this was an obedient son. One who was doing what he was supposed to do. But he wasn't enjoying any of it. He wasn't taking advantage of anything that was available to him. And he wouldn't join in the party to celebrate what his father was doing. This is such a sad state, and one legalism ultimately breeds. Contempt for those who aren't good enough. Legalism causes one to fall into either pride or despair.

Not as the World Gives

Peace I leave with you, my peace I give unto you: not as the world giveth, give I unto you. Let not your heart be troubled, neither let it be afraid. (John 14:27)

One of the things that helped me understand grace was to contrast the way the world gives from the way God gives. Jesus said, "I don't give the way the world gives." The world gives, but they're not really giving. They expect repayment. They say it's going to be free, and it's not really free. There are always strings attached. There's always a commitment that's down the road. There's always an exchange of goods. Jesus doesn't give the way the world gives. He gives without thought of repayment. In fact, if one tries to earn what God desires to give, or pay for it, they can't receive what he wants to give.[340] He gives exclusively as a gift, and he gives to people who cannot repay him.[341]

Our Inability to Do Good

Even so every good tree bringeth forth good fruit; but a corrupt tree bringeth forth evil fruit. A good tree cannot bring forth evil fruit, neither [can] a corrupt tree bring forth good fruit. (Matthew 7:17-18)

A good man out of the good treasure of his heart bringeth forth that which is good; and an evil man out of the evil treasure of his heart bringeth forth that which is evil: for of the abundance of the heart his mouth speaketh. (Luke 6:45)

What Jesus is saying is there are good trees and bad trees, and good fruit can't be obtained out of a bad tree, nor can bad fruit be obtained out of a good tree. Before we accept Jesus and the gift that he gives us, we are bad trees. We cannot bring forth good fruit. We cannot say we are good people. That is not true. Sinful desires, sinful motives taint everything we do. He makes us and calls us good, and then we bring forth good fruit.

And Jesus said unto him, Why callest thou me good? none [is] good, save one, [that is], God. (Luke 18:19)

In reference to whether it is possible for humans to save themselves, or play a part in their salvation, Jesus answers, "There is only one who is good, and that's God."

John answered and said, A man can receive nothing, except it be given him from heaven. (John 3:27)

---

[340] Romans 11:6

[341] Luke 14:12

A gift cannot be received unless it is given. Salvation, Jesus, eternal life, repentance, faith. All of these things are described as a gift. In other places, God said that if one tries to earn a gift, they can't receive it because it's only given as a gift.[342]

> **Jesus answered them, Verily, verily, I say unto you, Whosoever committeth sin is the servant of sin. (John 8:34)**

Anyone who desires to earn salvation and get in by their absence of sin or their abundance of good works? Jesus said that if we sin, we are a servant of sin. That's our identity. That's our status. That's our eventual destiny. Where do servants of sin go when they die? They get judged and go to hell.

> **And Jesus said, For judgment I am come into this world, that they which see not might see; and that they which see might be made blind. And [some] of the Pharisees which were with him heard these words, and said unto him, Are we blind also? Jesus said unto them, If ye were blind, ye should have no sin: but now ye say, We see; therefore your sin remaineth. (John 9:39-41)**

There is a contrast given in this passage. Jesus came to save sinners. A considerable requirement is that one has to know they are sick. They have to know they are not well for a doctor to treat them. So Jesus told the Pharisees that if they were able to acknowledge they were sinners and they were blind, he would be able to cure them and save them. But because they insisted on saying they see, their sin remained.

> **I am the vine, ye [are] the branches: He that abideth in me, and I in him, the same bringeth forth much fruit: for without me ye can do nothing. (John 15:5)**

The question is, "Do we believe this?" When it comes to our status before we come to Christ, we believe it, but I don't know if we believe it as Christians after we accept Jesus. Jesus said apart from him, we can do nothing. There is no good work we can claim. Nothing. From start to finish, all of the resources involved. All of the situational happenstances involved. Everything, from start to finish, was him and only him.

---

[342] Romans 11:6

**If ye keep my commandments, ye shall abide in my love; even as
I have kept my Father's commandments, and abide in his love.
(John 15:10)**

An excellent question one can ask members of the groups discussed in this book is, "Can you keep his commandments? Really?" If one depends on themselves and their efforts as a means of getting them to heaven, I have bad news for them. Nobody can. As good as a person tries to be, as many self-help things as they do, as much behavior modification, as much accountability as they have, they cannot, and will not, fully keep his commandments. And even if they manage to, what are they going to do about all of the commandments that they broke before they reached that point? Honestly, are they going to trust in themselves, or are they going to trust Jesus?

Pictures of Salvation

**But when he saw the wind boisterous, he was afraid; and beginning
to sink, he cried, saying, Lord, save me. (Matthew 14:30)**

This verse describes Peter's statement after he saw Jesus walking on water. He said he wanted to walk on water too. Jesus told him to step out of the boat. And at first, Peter was walking on water. But then he looked at the waves and the storm, and he started to sink. And he cried out one thing. "Jesus, save me!" He didn't say, "Jesus, teach me how to save myself," "Jesus, help me save myself." He said, "Jesus, save me." Sometimes, when we talk about salvation, we forget that the verb form of that word is save. Somebody only cries out, "Save me" when they can't save themselves. That is the job of the Savior. Not to help save, but to save.

The Call to Rest

**Come unto me, all [ye] that labour and are heavy laden, and I will
give you rest. (Matthew 11:28)**

When I dug into the Greek on this one, I found something fascinating. When you look at those words "for I will give you rest" in Greek, the fuller translation would look something like this: "Come unto me, all ye who labor and are heavy laden, and I

163

will cause you to cease from any movement or labor for you to collect your strength."
And I would encourage you to compare what I said with Hebrews 4:10, where it talks
about Jesus being our rest and entering into his rest.

The Least is the Greatest

**At the same time came the disciples unto Jesus, saying, Who is
the greatest in the kingdom of heaven? And Jesus called a little
child unto him, and set him in the midst of them, And said,
Verily I say unto you, Except ye be converted, and become as
little children, ye shall not enter into the kingdom of heaven.
Whosoever therefore shall humble himself as this little child,
the same is greatest in the kingdom of heaven. (Matthew 18:1-4)**

This is the opposite of what these groups teach. These groups teach one has to advance
to a certain level of spiritual maturity, or even perfection before they can become
worthy or have counted themselves as having repented. Jesus is saying to all of the
adults in the room who were caretakers and trusted by God with taking care of these
little children to humble themselves. And when they humble themselves, then they
can go to heaven.

**When thou art bidden of any [man] to a wedding, sit not down
in the highest room; lest a more honourable man than thou be
bidden of him; And he that bade thee and him come and say to
thee, Give this man place; and thou begin with shame to take
the lowest room. But when thou art bidden, go and sit down in
the lowest room; that when he that bade thee cometh, he may say
unto thee, Friend, go up higher: then shalt thou have worship in
the presence of them that sit at meat with thee. For whosoever
exalteth himself shall be abased; and he that humbleth himself
shall be exalted. (Luke 14:8-11)**

All of the works-righteousness groups discussed in this book base this teaching on
becoming more worthy, becoming more able to be exalted. All of them sit in the
higher seats and presume to hold authority and priesthoods and roles and offices and

functions within their churches. Or they participate in certain rituals that others aren't able to participate in, such as secret knowledge, handshakes and tokens. They commit oaths and covenants before God they are trusting in to get them to that higher seat. Jesus said, "Sit in the lowest seat." Realize who you are. All of our works are as filthy rags.[343] Become poor in spirit.[344] Then comes exaltation to the higher position.

The Mission of Jesus

And she shall bring forth a son, and thou shalt call his name JESUS: for he shall save his people from their sins. (Matthew 1:21)

One can read this as almost a prophetic word. Jesus is going to save his people from their sins. The job of Jesus is to save people from their sins. There is no need to save people who can save themselves, or better their situation. People who need saving and know they need saving are those who are saved.

And when the Pharisees saw [it], they said unto his disciples, Why eateth your Master with publicans and sinners? But when Jesus heard [that], he said unto them, They that be whole need not a physician, but they that are sick. But go ye and learn what [that] meaneth, I will have mercy, and not sacrifice: for I am not come to call the righteous, but sinners to repentance. (Matthew 9:11-13)

Here again, Jesus clarified and said that it is not those who think they are doing okay, who believe they are good people, that he came for. He came for those who realize they have a need, who know they are sinners, who have a need for a Savior.

For the Son of man is come to save that which was lost. (Matthew 18:11)

Did Jesus accomplish his mission, or did he not? Is Jesus the one who saves, or is it us, or some mixture or combination? Jesus came to save that which was lost. That was his mission.

---

[343] Isaiah 64:6

[344] Matthew 5:3

Even as the Son of man came not to be ministered unto, but to minister, and to give his life a ransom for many. (Matthew 20:28)

Jesus' life is the ransom, not our life, not our works, not our effort. We aren't even playing a part in the ransom. The picture of a ransom is that one has been held captive and there is a price that is hanging over their heads. God is the one who pays that price. Not us. He sets the captive free. We didn't free ourselves. The picture is clear.

For this is my blood of the new testament, which is shed for many for the remission of sins. (Matthew 26:28)

Jesus' blood is the New Covenant and is for the remission of sins. That is the basis of the New Covenant. It's never an agreement, like many of the other covenants in the ancient world, where there would be two parties and both parties would have to make promises and have to keep those promises. Our part in the New Covenant is receiving the gift. In fact, it is emphatically stated that receiving a gift is the only way you will ever receive anything from God. (Romans 4:4-5; 11:6) Some of the groups discussed in this book de-emphasize the cross. The LDS teach Jesus atoned for our sins in the Garden of Gethsemane when he shed his blood. And that's not at all what the New Testament says. It never points to the Garden. It always points to the cross.

The Jehovah's Witnesses change the cross into a stake. It sounds minor, but they are diminishing the cross. By doing so, they can start de-emphasizing what Jesus did on the cross, and his ability to pay for all of our sins. And from that point, it makes sense they would teach a Jesus who is not able to save them from all their sins.

For the Son of man is not come to destroy men's lives, but to save [them]. And they went to another village. (Luke 9:56)

Legalism, trying to live by the law, trying to have enough good works, ends up destroying lives. Because nobody ever knows when they have done enough or they are good enough for God to save them. We're all held in suspense until judgment day. And when you look at the standards, nobody is going to make it. The law brings death, but Jesus came to give life and to save us.[345]

---

[345] Oakes, Jason, "I'm a Christian Too!" part 1 https://youtu.be/DuHQ19PmsrM

And Jesus said unto him, This day is salvation come to this house, forsomuch as he also is a son of Abraham. For the Son of man is come to seek and to save that which was lost. (Luke 19:9-10)

This is Zaccheus, the tax collector. Once again we have the tax collectors as the heroes. This day salvation has come to this household. Zaccheus was seeking Jesus. Furthermore, Jesus said he's going to be at work within Zaccheus' household for salvation.

Jesus also repeats that he came to seek and to save that which was lost. Are we going to allow him to save, or keep trying to save ourselves?

The Necessity of Relationship

Not every one that saith unto me, Lord, Lord, shall enter into the kingdom of heaven; but he that doeth the will of my Father which is in heaven. Many will say to me in that day, Lord, Lord, have we not prophesied in thy name? and in thy name have cast out devils? and in thy name done many wonderful works? And then will I profess unto them, I never knew you: depart from me, ye that work iniquity. (Matthew 7:21-23)

This has been a troubling passage to many, and the LDS love this verse because they think that it's saying one has to do, do, do to get into heaven. That's not what this passage is saying. It's not emphasizing the do. It's emphasizing the know. Do you have a relationship with Jesus? There is a verse that clarified what Jesus meant. The Apostle Paul said in 1 Corinthians 8:3 "But if any man love God, the same is known of him." So what Jesus was saying is, "You never loved me."[346]

Then shall the kingdom of heaven be likened unto ten virgins, which took their lamps, and went forth to meet the bridegroom. And five of them were wise, and five [were] foolish. They that [were] foolish took their lamps, and took no oil with them: But the wise

---

[346] Oakes, Jason, Jason Oakes - Sharing Jesus with the Cults - Communicating Grace to the Religious Mind https://youtu.be/vRkosO1Iob8

167

took oil in their vessels with their lamps. While the bridegroom tarried, they all slumbered and slept. And at midnight there was a cry made, Behold, the bridegroom cometh; go ye out to meet him. Then all those virgins arose, and trimmed their lamps. And the foolish said unto the wise, Give us of your oil; for our lamps are gone out. But the wise answered, saying, [Not so]; lest there be not enough for us and you: but go ye rather to them that sell, and buy for yourselves. And while they went to buy, the bridegroom came; and they that were ready went in with him to the marriage: and the door was shut. Afterward came also the other virgins, saying, Lord, Lord, open to us. But he answered and said, Verily I say unto you, I know you not. Watch therefore, for ye know neither the day nor the hour wherein the Son of man cometh. (Matthew 25:1-13)

This is another passage where the key phrase is "I know you not." The key is a relationship, not what they did or didn't do. Again, we have to go to Paul's statement in the middle of his letter to the Corinthians, where he said:

But if any man love God, the same is known of him. (1 Corinthians 8:3)

If we love God, then we are known by him.

The Prayer of Jesus

Then said Jesus, Father, forgive them; for they know not what they do. And they parted his raiment, and cast lots. (Luke 23:34)

Was the prayer of Jesus answered? When Jesus said, "Father, forgive them," he's praying to the Father sincerely that those who crucified him would be forgiven. We have to ask the question as to whether the prayer of Jesus was answered in the affirmative or not for those who were willing to receive God's forgiveness?[347]

---

[347] Oakes, Jason, The Gospels: Salvation by Grace Alone Through Faith Alone https://youtu.be/xKswJ2y1FbY

The Priority of Heaven

I say unto you, that likewise joy shall be in heaven over one sinner that repenteth, more than over ninety and nine just persons, which need no repentance. (Luke 15:7)

This is a priority statement. Jesus is saying he will go after the one instead of the ninety-nine. Granted, the ninety-nine who don't need to repent probably refers to the Pharisees, who were saying they were fine and didn't have need of Jesus. But it's still a priority statement. Jesus said there is more rejoicing in heaven over the one who repents than the ninety-nine who are already there.[348]

The Requirement of Moral Perfection

But I say unto you, That whosoever is angry with his brother without a cause shall be in danger of the judgment: and whosoever shall say to his brother, Raca, shall be in danger of the council: but whosoever shall say, Thou fool, shall be in danger of hell fire. ... But I say unto you, That whosoever looketh on a woman to lust after her hath committed adultery with her already in his heart. ... Be ye therefore perfect, even as your Father which is in heaven is perfect. (Matthew 5:22, 28, 48)

I want to emphasize the standard Jesus was laying out to escape judgment. In other words, Jesus would take two different routes in his teaching. The first was to lay out the full standards of the law and bring people to an awareness of their sin, their inability to save themselves and their need for a Savior. Then he would point to himself as the source of salvation and rest through faith in the work he came to accomplish, and that was his death and resurrection as a payment for our sins. For believers, who have been filled with the Holy Spirit, we look back to the teachings of Jesus as a basis for how we are to live because we love Jesus, not to earn salvation.

---

[348] Is salvation by grace through faith alone? https://www.neverthirsty.org/bible-qa/qa-archives/question/is-salvation-by-grace-through-faith-alone/

The Book of Mormon includes the Sermon on the Mount almost verbatim.[349] The only difference is Jesus was supposed to have been preaching this sermon to the inhabitants of the American continent. The Sermon on the Mount with the absence of Jesus' other teachings would lead one to believe their only hope was sinless perfection, and this is what the LDS church teaches as the only means of obtaining celestial glory and dwelling again with Heavenly Father.[350]

Let's take a few verses and lay out what the standard is if one is trying to obtain salvation by the keeping of the law or sinless perfection. Have you ever called somebody a fool? Have you ever lusted after somebody who was not your spouse? Jesus said that if we have, we are in danger of judgment and hell fire. Then Jesus said that one needs to be perfect as their father in heaven is perfect.

The LDS love verse 48 and teach one has to reach sinless perfection. But most LDS individuals water this verse down to mean "if you try to be perfect," or the Book of Mormon version which says, "we are saved by grace after all we can do."[351] This view sees Jesus as extending his grace to fill the gap between our best effort and sinless perfection. But that isn't what Matthew 5:48, or several other LDS scriptures teach. You can't have it both ways. One either tries to obtain salvation through sinless perfection, or they accept Jesus' payment for their sins as a free gift.

While LDS want to believe one needs to obtain sinless perfection, none of them believe they have done this, or know anybody who has, or even heard of anybody who has. That is why some have called this the "impossible gospel."[352] We can use this as a springboard to assure LDS that they can "know" that they've been forgiven and have eternal life.[353]

> **And thou shalt love the Lord thy God with all thy heart, and with all thy soul, and with all thy mind, and with all thy strength: this [is] the first commandment. (Mark 12:30)**

---

[349] 3 Nephi 12-14

[350] Asher, Jeff, Salvation By Grace Through Faith http://www.padfield.com/2000/faith.html

[351] 2 Nephi 25:23

[352] Questions for the LDS on the Impossible Gospel of Mormonism http://www.4mormon.org/questions-for-lds-on-the-impossible-gospel-of-mormonism/

[353] 1 John 5:13

This is the first commandment. To love the Lord thy God with all your heart, soul, mind and strength. If one was asked if they could do this, or if they are doing this if they say yes, there is a problem with pride.[354]

The Wages of Sin is Death

There were present at that season some that told him of the Galilaeans, whose blood Pilate had mingled with their sacrifices. And Jesus answering said unto them, Suppose ye that these Galilaeans were sinners above all the Galilaeans, because they suffered such things? I tell you, Nay: but, except ye repent, ye shall all likewise perish. Or those eighteen, upon whom the tower in Siloam fell, and slew them, think ye that they were sinners above all men that dwelt in Jerusalem? I tell you, Nay: but, except ye repent, ye shall all likewise perish. (Luke 13:1-5)

Jesus is saying the whole idea of categorizing sins as greater than other sins is not right. We are all sinners who deserve to die and suffer the wrath of God. Jesus is saying we all need to repent and come to him so he can forgive us of our sins, no matter what they are.[355]

We are All the Same Before God

For the kingdom of heaven is like unto a man [that is] an householder, which went out early in the morning to hire labourers into his vineyard. And when he had agreed with the labourers for a penny a day, he sent them into his vineyard. And he went out about the third hour, and saw others standing idle in the marketplace, And said unto them; Go ye also into the vineyard, and whatsoever is right I will give you. And they went their way. Again he went out about the sixth and ninth hour, and

---

[354] By Grace Alone Through Faith Alone https://www.ligonier.org/learn/devotionals/grace-alone-through-faith-alone/

[355] What does it mean that salvation is by grace through faith? https://www.gotquestions.org/by-grace-through-faith.html

did likewise. And about the eleventh hour he went out, and found others standing idle, and saith unto them, Why stand ye here all the day idle? They say unto him, Because no man hath hired us. He saith unto them, Go ye also into the vineyard; and whatsoever is right, [that] shall ye receive. So when even was come, the lord of the vineyard saith unto his steward, Call the labourers, and give them [their] hire, beginning from the last unto the first. And when they came that [were hired] about the eleventh hour, they received every man a penny. But when the first came, they supposed that they should have received more; and they likewise received every man a penny. And when they had received [it], they murmured against the goodman of the house, Saying, These last have wrought [but] one hour, and thou hast made them equal unto us, which have borne the burden and heat of the day. But he answered one of them, and said, Friend, I do thee no wrong: didst not thou agree with me for a penny? Take [that] thine [is], and go thy way: I will give unto this last, even as unto thee. Is it not lawful for me to do what I will with mine own? Is thine eye evil, because I am good? So the last shall be first, and the first last: for many be called, but few chosen. (Matthew 20:1-16)

This parable deals with a couple of different issues. One of them is harsh feelings those who are in religion, or legalism, or works based righteousness systems, feel about so-called deathbed conversions, like the thief on the cross. That scenario isn't one these groups believe in, much less embrace, as do biblical Christians. Some of these people who the master hired at the end of the day got paid the same amount as those who had been working all day.

This parable also teaches it's not about when one gets saved, how much work they've put in, how much they've done plays into the ultimate prize or plan, which is salvation. It has to do with the vineyard owner being intrinsically good, and him calling us to work in his vineyard. God is the owner of the vineyard. Jesus is the Son of the landowner. That interpretation would fit the other parables as well.[356]

---

[356] Lesson 14: Salvation by Grace through Faith Alone (Ephesians 2:8-9) https://bible.org/seriespage/lesson-14-salvation-grace-through-faith-alone-ephesians-28-9

Chapter 22

Passages from the Gospels Related to the Afterlife

Hell

And fear not them which kill the body, but are not able to kill the soul: but rather fear him which is able to destroy both soul and body in hell. (Matthew 10:28)

And if thy hand offend thee, cut it off: it is better for thee to enter into life maimed, than having two hands to go into hell, into the fire that never shall be quenched: Where their worm dieth not, and the fire is not quenched. And if thy foot offend thee, cut it off: it is better for thee to enter halt into life, than having two feet to be cast into hell, into the fire that never shall be quenched: Where their worm dieth not, and the fire is not quenched. And if thine eye offend thee, pluck it out: it is better for thee to enter into the kingdom of God with one eye, than having two eyes to be cast into hell fire: Where their worm dieth not, and the fire is not quenched. (Mark 9:43-48)

Jesus is quoting from a reference in Isaiah, and what he said was, "Where their worm dieth not, and their fire is not quenched."[357] This passage is referring to the individual who is cast into hell, and yes, the punishment is eternal, but also, that individual, who is punished, is eternal. There is no annihilation. Hell is eternal. Their punishment is eternal.

Multiple Destinations for the Righteous?

The Jehovah's Witnesses teach 144,000 are going to go to heaven, and the rest of the Jehovah's Witnesses are going to a restored earth. The Twelve Tribes teach a similar thing in their theology where those who "really" believed what Jesus wanted them to do will go to a higher level of glory, whereas those who are well-meaning, good intentioned moral people are going to go to their "Terrestrial Kingdom," because it's still heaven, but they are going to serve the Twelve Tribes people. The LDS also have three levels of heaven, two of which are reserved for those who would be considered religious, moral, law-abiding people.

> **But I say unto you, I will not drink henceforth of this fruit of the vine, until that day when I drink it new with you in my Father's kingdom. (Matthew 26:29)**

Jesus said he is going to drink wine with his followers in his Father's kingdom. I guess one could say he was talking to his disciples and that he was talking to them exclusively. Technically I think he's talking to all believers. He said he was going to come back so believers could be where he was.[358] To go into his Kingdom is to go where Jesus is. The same thing as "today you'll be with me in Paradise."[359] To be in heaven to a Christian means to be where Jesus is. The Jehovah's Witnesses, if they teach Jesus is going to dwell in heaven, then those who are on the earth won't be with Jesus. The LDS, if they teach Jesus is going to dwell in the Celestial Kingdom, then those who aren't there won't be with Jesus.

---

[357] Isaiah 66:24
[358] John 14:1-3
[359] Luke 23:43

One can call it a degree of heaven, a reward, or inheritance, or whatever they want to. But it's not heaven if it's not with Jesus.

Rewards and Inheritance

Discussing future rewards and inheritance trips up many Christians because they don't know how to articulate a difference between their beliefs and an LDS person who teaches three levels of heaven, and having to do certain things to enter into the celestial kingdom and enter into glory. Or the Jehovah's Witnesses who teach only 144,000 will go to heaven while the rest of believers will inherit the earth. Believers get tripped up when it comes to this idea of rewards and inheritance. The Bible discusses this concept several times. And sometimes we start saying things like, "Well, salvation is free, but we do earn rewards by our performance." That doesn't sound much different than what these groups are saying. This topic will be discussed further in the Tactic #3: Communicating Grace to the Religious Mind section of this book.

> **Fear not, little flock; for it is your Father's good pleasure to give you the kingdom. (Luke 12:32)**

The thing that most people miss when we talk about inheritance, rewards, crowns, ruling and reigning with Christ, is that it is not earned. They are all gifts. They are spoken of in the language of gifts. The kingdom is said to be something God gives, and something we receive.[360] In the same way, a person can accept or reject salvation, a Christian, a believer, can accept or reject, many different good gifts that God wants to give us, and already has offered to us. We need to receive them simply.

On a day to day level, give us this day our daily bread.[361] The opportunity to open God's word and hear from him. The opportunity to utilize the gifts, the talents and abilities that he's given us as believers. The opportunity to open our mouth when he provides us with an opportunity to preach the gospel. All of those are gifts that he wants to give us. He even said that we have not because we ask not.[362] There are things we simply say no, and we do it for all sorts of different reasons. We say no,

---

[360] Luke 12:32; Mark 10:15

[361] Matthew 6:11

[362] James 4:2

or later, or make up excuses, or pretend we don't hear him. Ultimately, all of those things cumulatively add up to opportunities that God is giving us to become more like him. And as we become more like him, he then, in the Kingdom, gives us an opportunity to have an inheritance, to rule and reign with him.[363] Several of Jesus' parables talk about this.

When we stand before the Judgment Seat of Christ, Paul said there are some that will suffer loss.[364] The church in Philadelphia is advised by Jesus not to let anyone "take" their crown.[365] Paul said that he has a crown that is laid up for him.[366] He said he runs the race so he won't be disqualified.[367] All of these terms are the language of gift even though it uses the language of rewards. Every good thing that we do comes from the desire to do good which God places within us. It comes from the motive of love that Paul said compels us.[368] Believers possess the power: the source of power, the ability to control and choose the right thing to do, as well as the physical strength to carry out that power.[369] All of those are gifts given to us by God, without whom, we wouldn't be able to do anything.[370] So to say we earned, or we can lay claim, to any good gift, including ruling and reigning with Christ, is utter nonsense.

Second Chance after Death

This is a topic that not only groups who are considered false by Christians teach, but many mainstream, and otherwise orthodox Christians teach. I have to admit that I've never understood the logic behind this teaching. I couldn't imagine anybody, after they die, going to an afterlife, or standing before the throne of God, or going to a place of torment, and not realizing that they were wrong, not changing their mind and repenting, and saying, "Please, I'll do anything. Get me out of here." But the way those who hold to this teaching articulate this idea, they believe people are

---

[363] Matthew 25:21

[364] 1 Corinthians 3:15

[365] Revelation 3:11

[366] 2 Timothy 4:8

[367] Galatians 2:2; Philippians 2:16

[368] 2 Corinthians 5:14

[369] Ephesians 6:10

[370] John 15:5

so stubborn that people can suffer in hell for years and years, even a thousand years, and then come to a place where they finally realize and admit that they were wrong. Then God is going to let them into heaven after suffering so long in hell.

Jesus shut the door on this whole issue.

> **There was a certain rich man, which was clothed in purple and fine linen, and fared sumptuously every day: And there was a certain beggar named Lazarus, which was laid at his gate, full of sores, And desiring to be fed with the crumbs which fell from the rich man's table: moreover the dogs came and licked his sores. And it came to pass, that the beggar died, and was carried by the angels into Abraham's bosom: the rich man also died, and was buried; And in hell he lift up his eyes, being in torments, and seeth Abraham afar off, and Lazarus in his bosom. And he cried and said, Father Abraham, have mercy on me, and send Lazarus, that he may dip the tip of his finger in water, and cool my tongue; for I am tormented in this flame. But Abraham said, Son, remember that thou in thy lifetime receivedst thy good things, and likewise Lazarus evil things: but now he is comforted, and thou art tormented. And beside all this, between us and you there is a great gulf fixed: so that they which would pass from hence to you cannot; neither can they pass to us, that [would come] from thence. Then he said, I pray thee therefore, father, that thou wouldest send him to my father's house: For I have five brethren; that he may testify unto them, lest they also come into this place of torment. Abraham saith unto him, They have Moses and the prophets; let them hear them. And he said, Nay, father Abraham: but if one went unto them from the dead, they will repent. And he said unto him, If they hear not Moses and the prophets, neither will they be persuaded, though one rose from the dead. (Luke 16:19-31)**

This is not a parable. People are not named in parables. Jesus was talking about something real.

There were two compartments to Hades before Jesus came and died for our sins. There was Abraham's Bosom. It was a place of comfort. Those who were waiting faithfully for the Messiah to forgive them of their sins, and died in faith, went to Abraham's Bosom. Those who rejected Yahweh were in a place of torment. That place of torment is still the place where people go who reject Jesus, while they are waiting for their formal sentencing, at which time they will be cast into the Lake of Fire, which Jesus referred to as Gehenna.

There are two sides, and there is an interchange between the Rich Man and Abraham, which first of all tells me that we don't go into soul sleep after we die. These are conscious individuals. They can feel things. They can communicate. They can see the other side. They could see the reality of both choices.

The rich man called out to Abraham and said, "Would you be able to send Lazarus with one drop of water to give me a moment of relief from my torment?" Abraham said to him, "Sorry, he can't." First of all, you made your choices in your life. Lazarus made his choices. Now you're bearing the fruit of those choices. What you sowed you will reap. Second, he said there is a great gulf fixed. They could see between the two sides and interchange between the two sides, but nobody is going from one side to the other. It's not going to happen.

To clarify, no missionaries are going down from Paradise into Spirit Prison, preaching the gospel, and offering people the chance to have people offer baptism for the dead or family sealings to get them into the Celestial Kingdom. I want to make that clear.

But, then Abraham said, "Because of that great gulf, those who would pass from here to you cannot. Neither can they pass to us who would come from your side." So he makes it clear because of this great gulf, even if there were people who wanted to go to the other side to help or to save themselves, they cannot.

Then the Rich Man, after he realizes his fate is sealed, said, "Well, can you help me with my brothers? Can you send somebody up there to the earth and help them to understand?" Abraham said, "They have the law and the prophets, and the law and the prophets are sufficient to condemn individuals if they won't listen. Even if somebody rose from the dead, they wouldn't listen to them either." Ironic since Jesus rose a man named Lazarus from the dead, and all the Pharisees could think about was how bad that was for PR, and decided to kill him again. When Jesus rose from the dead, they didn't say, "Oh wow, he was right." They said, "Let's say the apostles stole the body." There is no second chance after death. Abraham makes it even more apparent by saying this life is the chance and we have everything we need to believe. God's given us every chance to believe, and if one dies in unbelief, there is no second chance after death.

Second Coming

The Second Coming is a big, big deal with some of these groups, especially those coming from the Adventist movement. Many of their leaders such as William Miller, Charles Taze Russell, Judge Rutherford, Ellen G. White all predicted, falsely I might add when Jesus was going to come back.

> **But of that day and [that] hour knoweth no man, no, not the angels which are in heaven, neither the Son, but the Father. (Mark 13:32)**

> **Watch therefore: for ye know not what hour your Lord doth come. (Matthew 24:42)**

Charles Taze Russell, the founder of the Jehovah's Witnesses, was over-fascinated with the Great Pyramid at Giza and taught that Melchizedek built it, and taught that the tunnels and passageways were able to predict when Jesus was going to come back. I wonder why he was wrong. Jesus said, in his humanity, that even he didn't know the timing. It is in the book of Revelation when Jesus tells us God did reveal to him what was going to happen before he is coming.

Soul Sleep

Seventh Day Adventists and Jehovah Witnesses teach the concept known as Soul Sleep.

> **Marvel not at this: for the hour is coming, in the which all that are in the graves shall hear his voice, And shall come forth; they that have done good, unto the resurrection of life; and they that have done evil, unto the resurrection of damnation. (John 5:28-29)**

This is a passage that the Adventist groups use to show when we die, we go in the ground, we stay in the grave until the resurrection happens. Then, when the resurrection happens, we come out of the grave and go to the judgment seat and find out whether we're going to go to heaven or hell. This is an excellent example of taking one verse and making too much out of it. Because many other verses talk about Paul's struggle of being torn between dying and being with Christ and living and continuing his ministry here on earth, and not being able to decide which is better.[371] You can't reconcile that with soul sleep. It is not better to go into the grave in a state of unconsciousness if one can continue living and go further in their ministry. That doesn't make sense.

We need to understand time to be the physical property that it is, where past, present and future are all happening at the same time. We also need to acknowledge heaven is where God dwells in eternity. If we can agree on these two concepts, then it's possible that the person who passed away two-thousand years ago, the person who passed away last week, the person who dies right now and the person who is raptured five years from now, all arrive at the throne of God at the same moment. I know that's a mind-blower, but it's a possibility that I throw out there from the vantage point of physics, and has to do with this whole issue of soul sleep.

Do we fall into a state of unconsciousness when we die, or do we go immediately to a destination?

> **And whosoever liveth and believeth in me shall never die. Believest thou this? (John 11:26)**

This verse has to do with both Soul Sleep and with the faith vs. works conversation. If we believe in him, we're never going to die. These groups might argue that this verse doesn't address soul sleep, but dying. Dying, they would say, is ceasing to exist or something of that nature.

---

[371] Philippians 1:21-24

CHAPTER 23

Passages in the Gospels Related to General Miscellaneous Issues

Repentance

Take heed to yourselves: If thy brother trespass against thee, rebuke him; and if he repent, forgive him. And if he trespass against thee seven times in a day, and seven times in a day turn again to thee, saying, I repent; thou shalt forgive him. (Luke 17:3-4)

What is repentance? Some of these groups, such as LDS, define repentance as forsaking all of your sins. What they mean by forsaking our sins is that one can't repent of one sin, but they must repent of all sins to repent. Spencer Kimball, one of the former prophets of the LDS church, wrote in Miracle of Forgiveness that if one has to repent or confess sins, then they haven't repented. It's not until one reaches a point where they don't ever do any of those things, or think about doing those things, that they have repented.[372] [373]

---

[372] Kimball, Spencer W., Chapter 4: The Miracle of Forgiveness Teachings of Presidents of the Church: Spencer W. Kimball, p. 34–45

[373] Doctrine & Covenants 58:43

What does Jesus say? He said it's possible that a person would have to repent seven times in a day for the same thing. That means they did it, they repented, they did it again, they repented again, etc. So all repentance means is a change of mind, change of direction, where we turn from our sins and turn toward Christ. It doesn't mean one physically doesn't do all those things. Now, is that what the intention is? Is that where a person's heart should be? Yes. I don't want to do this again. Everybody would question whether the person Jesus is hypothetically referring to was repenting or not, but Jesus said that he repented. He expressed sorrow for what he did. And why does he do it again? Because we are fallen human beings. We can only change from the power of sin by the power of Jesus inside of us, not by ourselves.

Sabbath

The Sabbath is an important issue to the Seventh Day Adventists, LDS, and Jehovah's Witnesses, all of which teach believers should be keeping the Sabbath. Some within the Seventh Day Adventists teach worshipping on any other day than Saturday is taking the mark of the beast.

> **At that time Jesus went on the sabbath day through the corn; and his disciples were an hungred, and began to pluck the ears of corn, and to eat. But when the Pharisees saw [it], they said unto him, Behold, thy disciples do that which is not lawful to do upon the sabbath day. But he said unto them, Have ye not read what David did, when he was an hungred, and they that were with him; How he entered into the house of God, and did eat the shewbread, which was not lawful for him to eat, neither for them which were with him, but only for the priests? Or have ye not read in the law, how that on the sabbath days the priests in the temple profane the sabbath, and are blameless? But I say unto you, That in this place is [one] greater than the temple. But if ye had known what [this] meaneth, I will have mercy, and not sacrifice, ye would not have condemned the guiltless. For the Son of man is Lord even of the sabbath day. And when he was departed thence, he went into their synagogue: And, behold, there was a man which had [his]**

hand withered. And they asked him, saying, Is it lawful to heal on the sabbath days? that they might accuse him. And he said unto them, What man shall there be among you, that shall have one sheep, and if it fall into a pit on the sabbath day, will he not lay hold on it, and lift [it] out? How much then is a man better than a sheep? Wherefore it is lawful to do well on the sabbath days. Then saith he to the man, Stretch forth thine hand. And he stretched [it] forth; and it was restored whole, like as the other. (Matthew 12:1-13)

Jesus points to the fact all of these people who say one shouldn't work on the Sabbath, if they are facing the loss of one of their animals, they will violate the Sabbath to save that animal. And Jesus points out that these extra additions to the Sabbath are not God's standards, but man's standards have been added to what God established concerning the Sabbath. Once again he points out their hypocrisy by saying, "If you can do this, I can do this."

And it came to pass, that he went through the corn fields on the sabbath day; and his disciples began, as they went, to pluck the ears of corn. And the Pharisees said unto him, Behold, why do they on the sabbath day that which is not lawful? And he said unto them, Have ye never read what David did, when he had need, and was an hungred, he, and they that were with him? How he went into the house of God in the days of Abiathar the high priest, and did eat the shewbread, which is not lawful to eat but for the priests, and gave also to them which were with him? (Mark 2:23-26)

And he entered again into the synagogue; and there was a man there which had a withered hand. And they watched him, whether he would heal him on the sabbath day; that they might accuse him. And he saith unto the man which had the withered hand, Stand forth. And he saith unto them, Is it lawful to do good on the sabbath days, or to do evil? to save life, or to kill? But they held their peace. And when he had looked round about on them

> **with anger, being grieved for the hardness of their hearts, he saith unto the man, Stretch forth thine hand. And he stretched [it] out: and his hand was restored whole as the other. And the Pharisees went forth, and straightway took counsel with the Herodians against him, how they might destroy him. (Mark 3:1-6)**

Jesus is the Lord of the Sabbath. The Sabbath was a sign and seal of the covenant that God made with Israel. The whole point of the Sabbath was to point forward to Jesus, our Messiah, who is our rest. The book of Hebrews goes into great detail about this subject. In fact, Tactic #6 discussed later in this book is based on the book of Hebrews.

He who entered God's rest has ceased from his labors.[374] Jesus would say later, "Come unto me, all you who labor and are heavy laden, and I will give you rest."[375] Jesus is our rest. He is our Sabbath. The Sabbath was made for man, not man for the Sabbath.[376] Paul would say, "Let one man consider one day holy. Let another consider every day alike. Let each be fully convinced in his own mind."[377] In this way, keeping the Sabbath becomes an issue of conscience where each believer is to follow the leading of the Holy Spirit in their life, come to their own convictions, but not convince others that they are wrong in their personal convictions on this issue.

> **And immediately the man was made whole, and took up his bed, and walked: and on the same day was the sabbath. The Jews therefore said unto him that was cured, It is the sabbath day: it is not lawful for thee to carry [thy] bed. He answered them, He that made me whole, the same said unto me, Take up thy bed, and walk. (John 5:9-11)**

> **Moses therefore gave unto you circumcision; (not because it is of Moses, but of the fathers;) and ye on the sabbath day circumcise a man. If a man on the sabbath day receive circumcision, that the law of Moses should not be broken; are ye angry at me, because**

---

[374] Hebrews 4:10

[375] Matthew 11:28

[376] Mark 2:27

[377] Romans 14:5

I have made a man every whit whole on the sabbath day? Judge not according to the appearance, but judge righteous judgment. (John 7:22-24)

Circumcision was performed on the Sabbath. Jesus was after the heart of the Sabbath, which was a picture fulfilled in him, and the rest we can have in him. It isn't about a specific day or taking the mark of the beast, or anything like that.

Sin

The concept of sin needs to be emphasized and explained to those groups that mix some form of pseudo-science with some false form of Christianity. Specifically, Christian Science, teaching sin is simply bad thoughts representing the illusion of physical reality. Also Scientology, which calls sin "engrams," and these are simply traumatic experiences that trigger reactive responses that hold us back from realizing the inner Thetan, or divine being, we are.

It's harder to speak to these types of groups from the Bible because they don't respect it the way the other groups do. If they do look at the Bible, they have redefined all of the terms that it's hard to have an intelligent conversation about the Bible with them. Remember to keep having them define their terms and asking them follow-up questions to get them to think for themselves and see the contradictions and logical fallacies for themselves.

From that time Jesus began to preach, and to say, Repent: for the kingdom of heaven is at hand. (Matthew 4:17)

The purpose of sharing these verses is to start a discussion, but also to allow the Bible to speak for itself. The Bible is filled with references to itself having power in and of itself because it is the Word of God. We need to unleash its power, even if we are dealing with individuals that don't respect it or trust it the way we do as Christians. We will deal more with the trustworthiness of the Bible in Tactic #4 - Why Should We Trust the Bible.

CHAPTER 24

Passages in the Gospels Related to Miscellaneous Christian Science Issues

And when he had fasted forty days and forty nights, he was afterward an hungred. (Matthew 4:2)

Christian Science teaches Jesus was the model person. But here, he was hungry. It was not an illusion.

And Jesus went about all Galilee, teaching in their synagogues, and preaching the gospel of the kingdom, and healing all manner of sickness and all manner of disease among the people. And his fame went throughout all Syria: and they brought unto him all sick people that were taken with divers diseases and torments, and those which were possessed with devils, and those which were lunatick, and those that had the palsy; and he healed them. (Matthew 4:23-24)

Jesus didn't say to them, "This is all an illusion. It's a trick. You're all part of the matrix. You need to say, 'There is no spoon.'" Instead, he healed real diseases and cast out real demons.

A small sample of medical conditions listed in the Gospels:

1. Vexed with a demon (Matthew 15:22)
2. Lame, blind, dumb, maimed (Matthew 15:30)
3. Lunatick (Matthew 17:15)
4. Dropsy (Luke 14:2)

There are many other specific illnesses Jesus healed in the gospels. Sometimes the person manifested physical symptoms, and sometimes it was a spiritual reality, and Jesus cast out demons. These were real people suffering from real illnesses and real demons.

> **And he asked him, What [is] thy name? And he answered, saying, My name [is] Legion: for we are many. ... And forthwith Jesus gave them leave. And the unclean spirits went out, and entered into the swine: and the herd ran violently down a steep place into the sea, (they were about two thousand;) and were choked in the sea. ... And they come to Jesus, and see him that was possessed with the devil, and had the legion, sitting, and clothed, and in his right mind: and they were afraid. (Mark 5:9, 13, 15)**

Christian Science teaches demons are bad thoughts, but this passage doesn't make any sense at all if that is the case. Jesus was casting out bad thoughts and putting the bad thoughts into the swine. The swine then ran off the cliff and died. The bad thoughts are talking back to Jesus. They are begging him and bargaining with him. That speaks of personhood. That speaks of identity. It doesn't speak of a thought. A thought can't do those things. This passage would make no sense if that were the case.

> **And as [Jesus] passed by, he saw a man which was blind from [his] birth. And his disciples asked him, saying, Master, who did sin, this man, or his parents, that he was born blind? Jesus answered, Neither hath this man sinned, nor his parents: but that the works of God should be made manifest in him. (John 9:1-3)**

Jesus shows that a disease can be for the glory of God. It's not always something one has created in their mind and has to overcome.

CHAPTER 25

Passages in the Gospels Related to Miscellaneous Jehovah's Witness Issues

The Wise and Discreet Slave

And the Lord said, Who then is that faithful and wise steward, whom [his] lord shall make ruler over his household, to give [them their] portion of meat in due season? Blessed [is] that servant, whom his lord when he cometh shall find so doing. Of a truth I say unto you, that he will make him ruler over all that he hath. (Luke 12:42-44)

This passage is not talking about the Watchtower. It wasn't talking about Charles Taze Russell in the beginning, and it's not talking about the Watchtower now. Jesus was giving a generic parable, and he was talking about servants. The passage goes on to say there was potential for this servant not to be doing what they were supposed to and even to be beaten with few or many stripes. This is talking about servants of the Most High God, and whether we are doing what we are supposed to be doing. What are we supposed to be doing? Not works. We're supposed to be allowing him to live out his life through us. We're supposed to become less so he can become greater.[378] Like Paul said, "It is no longer I who live, but Christ who lives in me."[379]

Was the Resurrection of Jesus Physical or Spiritual?

But after I am risen again, I will go before you into Galilee. (Matthew 26:32)

And go quickly, and tell his disciples that he is risen from the dead; and, behold, he goeth before you into Galilee; there shall ye see him: lo, I have told you. (Matthew 28:7)

Jesus physically died, he physically rose, and physically met with the disciples in Galilee.

And came out of the graves after his resurrection, and went into the holy city, and appeared unto many. (Matthew 27:53)

This passage is talking about how many of the Old Testament saints' bodies rose from the graves, and they started walking through the streets of Jerusalem. Now if that doesn't get your attention, I don't know what will. This might be a good verse to use when reaching out to those who like vampire and zombie movies, those in witchcraft or the occult. If one explains to followers of these particular movements that zombies started walking through the streets when Jesus died on the cross, they might get their attention.

If Old Testament saints physically walked through the streets of Jerusalem, then why would there be only a spiritual resurrection of Jesus?

Saying, Sir, we remember that that deceiver said, while he was yet alive, After three days I will rise again. Command therefore that the sepulchre be made sure until the third day, lest his disciples come by night, and steal him away, and say unto the people, He

---

[378] John 3:30
[379] Galatians 2:20

> **is risen from the dead: so the last error shall be worse than the first. (Matthew 27:63-64)**

The enemies of Jesus, the religious leaders, approached Pilate and asked for extra guards at the tomb because Jesus claimed he would rise from the dead.[380] Pilate said, I think with a smile on his face, "Make it as sure as you can." The Pharisees were priming the pump for the lie they would tell later about the disciples stealing the body.[381] Pilate told them to make the tomb as sure as they can. He gave them a full guard. He put a Roman seal on the tomb. It would take multiple men to roll away the stone in front of the tomb. Jesus was embalmed at this point. There is no way to simply explain all this by saying the disciples came and stole his body.

If Jesus spiritually rose from the dead, none of the resurrection accounts make any sense. It's all physically based. It's all geared toward keeping a physical body from being stolen.

> **And, behold, there was a great earthquake: for the angel of the Lord descended from heaven, and came and rolled back the stone from the door, and sat upon it. (Matthew 28:2)**

Why did the angel move the stone if it was a spiritual resurrection? The angel could have explained Jesus' body vanished and he went back to the Father.

> **But they were terrified and affrighted, and supposed that they had seen a spirit. And he said unto them, Why are ye troubled? and why do thoughts arise in your hearts? Behold my hands and my feet, that it is I myself: handle me, and see; for a spirit hath not flesh and bones, as ye see me have. And when he had thus spoken, he shewed them [his] hands and [his] feet. (Luke 24:37-40)**

If Jesus was an apparition, and he was appearing to them in visions, he wouldn't have scars all over him, and he wouldn't be telling people to reach out and touch him. A spirit has not flesh and bones. Jesus, in his resurrection body, had flesh and bones. He had scars. In fact, when he talks to Thomas, he said, "Touch the wounds on my hands

---

[380] Matthew 12:40-41
[381] Matthew 28:13

and my feet and thrust your hand into my side." I don't think we have a grasp of what Jesus' body looked like after the crucifixion, or even in his resurrected body. There is one place in the resurrection accounts where it says Jesus intentionally appeared in different forms.[382] This may answer some questions as to why some didn't recognize Jesus immediately when he appeared to them. Mary thought he was the gardener. Even when he appeared to the disciples when they were fishing on the shore, it says "none dared ask him who he was because they all knew it was the Lord."[383] There are many reasons why they might not have recognized them, at least at first. Did Jesus always have a huge gash in his side as he appeared to Thomas, or did he appear to Thomas intentionally this way?

If the disciples were making up the account of the resurrection, they would not have included embarrassing details about women being the first witnesses of the empty tomb or they not recognizing who Jesus was, or experiencing doubt and fear when Jesus appeared to them. These are all signs of honesty that one wouldn't make up if they wanted others to believe their story.

This raises another question. Does God have a body of flesh and bones as Doctrine & Covenants, the LDS Scripture teaches?[384] Absolutely not. How do we know that?

A = God

B = Spirit

C = flesh and bones

So ...

A = B (God is spirit)[385]

B does not = C (A spirit has not flesh and bones)

---

[382] Mark 16:12

[383] John 21:12

[384] Doctrine & Covenants 130:22

[385] John 4:24

So ...

A does not = C (God does not have flesh and bones)

Now, if the cult member is thinking when you walk them through this, they might come up with their own equation.

D = Jesus

C = D (Jesus had flesh and bones)

So ...

A does not = D (Jesus cannot be God)

But, as we have discussed several times earlier in this book, Jesus said this as a resurrected human. So Jesus at this moment is not God. He is also human. Nowhere after he is ascended do we find him appearing in a physical resurrected body of flesh and bones with scars. Some metaphors imply Jesus might still have his scars, but we are also to Jesus was restored to the glory he had with the Father before the world began.

So Jesus having flesh and bones, and saying spirit has not flesh and bones, and saying God is spirit does not mean you can turn that around and say Jesus can't be God because he had flesh and bones. The Bible is clear Jesus took on human flesh and the image of man to become one of us, stand in our place and die for our sins.

> **I am the door: by me if any man enter in, he shall be saved, and**
> **shall go in and out, and find pasture. (John 10:9)**

It's interesting Jesus was continually referring to the fact he was going to die and rise from the dead after three days. And the disciples were clueless regarding this. Why? I guess it's because the Holy Spirit guides us into all truth and they didn't have the Holy Spirit yet. If Jesus didn't physically rise from the dead, how did they see him? How would they have even known it ever happened?

> **But Thomas, one of the twelve, called Didymus, was not with**
> **them when Jesus came. The other disciples therefore said unto**

him, We have seen the Lord. But he said unto them, Except I shall see in his hands the print of the nails, and put my finger into the print of the nails, and thrust my hand into his side, I will not believe. And after eight days again his disciples were within, and Thomas with them: [then] came Jesus, the doors being shut, and stood in the midst, and said, Peace [be] unto you. Then saith he to Thomas, Reach hither thy finger, and behold my hands; and reach hither thy hand, and thrust [it] into my side: and be not faithless, but believing. (John 20:24-27)

Jesus appeared to Thomas in a physical body. There's no way of getting around this from this passage. Jesus would later say a spirit has not flesh and bones. The whole idea of a spiritual resurrection is purely a Gnostic influence that says material is evil, so Jesus couldn't have resurrected in a physical body. It's not looking at what Jesus said, but making things up according to what you want to believe or what you think makes sense. It is an absolute refusal to admit that you are wrong.

The Jehovah's Witnesses teach Jesus physically resurrected from the dead. They teach his body vanished and he spiritually went to be with the Father again.

CHAPTER 26

Passages in the Gospels Related to Miscellaneous LDS Issues

Burning of the Bosom

Burning of the Bosom refers to the moment when one prays and asks if the Book of Mormon is true or if the LDS church is the true church and God supposedly manifests himself by passing through them, and when he does, they are supposed to feel a burning in their bosom. This concept is also discussed in the Tactic #2 - Have you Prayed about the Book of Mormon section of this book.

> **And they said one to another, Did not our heart burn within us, while he talked with us by the way, and while he opened to us the scriptures? (Luke 24:32)**

Is this a case of that burning of the bosom? I don't think it is. Why? Because these guys already believed in Jesus. They were heartbroken because they didn't understand the fullness of what Jesus came to do. They were still stuck in that they needed to believe in his resurrection. The Scripture goes on to say the Bereans were more noble because they received the word with all readiness of mind, but they searched the Scriptures daily to prove whether these things be so.[386] The Bible calls us to test the

---

[386] Acts 17:11

spirits to see if they come from God.[387] It gives certain criteria, such as if people don't believe certain things about Jesus, then they are not genuine believers. This criterion was discussed in the "Can You Be Saved If ..." section of this book. If something contradicts previous Scripture, it doesn't matter how much our hearts burn within us. [388]Yes, in this case, their hearts burned within them. What was that like? We don't know. But this wasn't a normative or prescriptive passage explaining what happens to all believers. It happened to these two individuals. And this wasn't even the moment when they realized who Jesus was. That came later when Jesus broke the bread.[389]

Exaltation

Jesus answered them, Is it not written in your law, I said, Ye are gods? If he called them gods, unto whom the word of God came, and the scripture cannot be broken; Say ye of him, whom the Father hath sanctified, and sent into the world, Thou blasphemest; because I said, I am the Son of God? (John 10:34-36)

This is a massive can of worms, and I'm not going to unpack this here fully. If you want more information on this topic, or want more information on how one can respond to this, I have an in-depth article on this topic.[390] I was also interviewed about this topic on the Youth Apologetics Training podcast.[391] I also discuss this passage in other sections of this book. The article, by the way, came as a result of a conversation I had with an LDS apologist that wrote an article on this verse on the FairMormon. org website.

I'm going to give you a shortcut to this one. Who was Jesus speaking to in this passage? The Pharisees. So, if you take what Jesus is saying literally, you would have to conclude that the Pharisees were, at the time Jesus was speaking to them, present

---

[387] 1 John 4:1

[388] Deuteronomy 13:1-3

[389] Luke 24:30-31

[390] Oakes, Jason, Why I Don't Believe Psalm 82:6 And John 10:34 Teach The LDS View Of Exaltation https://drive.google.com/file/d/0ByFtvrDqTG6JUTE4QWdXU0NXMEk/view?usp=sharing

[391] Are Christians Becoming More LDS (Mormon)? / Michael Heiser and Ancient Near Eastern Texts https://youtu.be/ewoDnYtYdVM

tense gods. If you can't say that, then you can't make a case about humans becoming gods from this verse.

Families are Forever

This is a considerable catchphrase for the LDS church. You see it in the temple visitor centers. They teach marriage, and family units, are not just for this life, but exist and have a purpose for all time and eternity.

> **For there are some eunuchs, which were so born from [their] mother's womb: and there are some eunuchs, which were made eunuchs of men: and there be eunuchs, which have made themselves eunuchs for the kingdom of heaven's sake. He that is able to receive [it], let him receive [it]. (Matthew 19:12)**

This is a foreign concept to an LDS person. If you are on this topic, this is a great Scripture to take them to, and ask them, "How would that look in your church? How would somebody make themselves a eunuch for the Kingdom of Heaven's sake?" In other words, they are doing a good thing by not marrying and not procreating. They are advancing the Kingdom of God by not marrying and not having kids. How does that work?

> **Then come unto him the Sadducees, which say there is no resurrection; and they asked him, saying, Master, Moses wrote unto us, If a man's brother die, and leave [his] wife [behind him], and leave no children, that his brother should take his wife, and raise up seed unto his brother. Now there were seven brethren: and the first took a wife, and dying left no seed. And the second took her, and died, neither left he any seed: and the third likewise. And the seven had her, and left no seed: last of all the woman died also. In the resurrection therefore, when they shall rise, whose wife shall she be of them? for the seven had her to wife. And Jesus answering said unto them, Do ye not therefore err, because ye know not the scriptures, neither the power of God? For when they shall rise from the dead, they neither marry, nor are given**

in marriage; but are as the angels which are in heaven. (Mark 12:18-25; Luke 20:27-36)

LDS would teach Jesus was simply saying marriages are not going to be performed in heaven, but he would honor those already done here on earth. So those who were sealed in the temple here on earth, he would honor. A key question Jesus could have asked is, "Were any of them married in the temple?" Because the first man that she had married in the temple would be the one whose wife she would be according to the LDS. If the proposed situation was reversed, and it was a man who had seven wives, then all of them could have been married and sealed in the temple for all time and eternity according to the LDS. Several of the current LDS apostles and prophets have done that. They've been sealed to multiple women in the temple after the subsequent one died. That's the way they would look at it, and they would say they are going to practice polygamy in eternity. So this would have been a non-sensical question. If any of them were married in the temple, that's the one she would have been married to.

Jesus never answered their question. He just said, "There is no marriage in heaven. Your question is a fallacy in and of itself. Families are not forever."

Suppose ye that I am come to give peace on earth? I tell you, Nay; but rather division: For from henceforth there shall be five in one house divided, three against two, and two against three. The father shall be divided against the son, and the son against the father; the mother against the daughter, and the daughter against the mother; the mother in law against her daughter in law, and the daughter in law against her mother in law. (Luke 12:51-53)

I don't see any Scripture where Jesus said the opposite of this, where he said he came to unite families and show them how they can live together forever in eternity, or the need for them to be sealed as family units within the temple. None of that happened. On the opposing side, there are several Scriptures where Jesus is turning away his own family when they come to correct him when they think he went too far or maybe wanted him to spend more time with them. Jesus clarified his mission, and he emphasized time and time again that family is not biological, but spiritual. To be the family of God means one accepts him, and that person is adopted into his family.

> **Whosoever putteth away his wife, and marrieth another, committeth adultery: and whosoever marrieth her that is put away from [her] husband committeth adultery. (Luke 16:18)**

This passage speaks against a practice of the LDS church. If the husband or wife finds themselves married to somebody who falls out of worthiness, specifically if one spouse joins the LDS church, or one spouse leaves the LDS church, the church will let some time pass, put on the full court press trying to get the other spouse in the church or back in the church. But if they are unsuccessful, they will counsel, and I can testify to this from several people who have shared their story with me, the faithful partner to divorce their spouse and remarry somebody who is worthy and can be sealed to them in the temple. That way a woman can be called forth on the day of resurrection by her husband or the man can find a woman worthy of being one of their Goddess wives. So the LDS church encourages people to commit adultery according to Jesus.

> **And as it was in the days of Noe, so shall it be also in the days of the Son of man. They did eat, they drank, they married wives, they were given in marriage, until the day that Noe entered into the ark, and the flood came, and destroyed them all. (Luke 17:26-27)**

As it was in the days of Noah, so shall it be at the coming of the Son of Man. When Jesus comes, that's the day compared to the day Noah got in the ark, when marriages stopped.

God Has a Body of Flesh and Bones

> **And Jesus answered and said unto him, Blessed art thou, Simon Barjona: for flesh and blood hath not revealed [it] unto thee, but my Father which is in heaven. (Matthew 16:17)**

If you use simple logic:

A = Flesh and blood

B = revelation

C = Father in heaven

So in this case:

A does not = B (flesh and blood did not reveal)

B = C (Father in heaven did reveal)

So:

A does not = C (Father in heaven is not flesh and blood)

> **God [is] a Spirit: and they that worship him must worship [him] in spirit and in truth. (John 4:24)**

When Jesus was speaking with the woman at the well, he said, "God is a spirit," which means part of his essential nature. LDS would say this verse does say "God is only a spirit" because their Scripture teaches, that God has a body of flesh and bones as tangible as man's. (Doctrine & Covenants 130:22) Jesus would later clarify that a spirit has not flesh and bones, further emphasizing that God is distinctly different from us in nature.

Jesus Born in Jerusalem?

> **Now when Jesus was born in Bethlehem of Judaea in the days of Herod the king, behold, there came wise men from the east to Jerusalem, ... And they said unto him, In Bethlehem of Judaea: for thus it is written by the prophet, And thou Bethlehem, [in] the land of Juda, art not the least among the princes of Juda: for out of thee shall come a Governor, that shall rule my people Israel. (Matthew 2:1, 5-6)**

In the Book of Mormon, supposedly in a prophetic utterance, the Messiah is said to be born in Jerusalem.[392] LDS scholars and apologists are trying to make a case it says

---

[392] Alma 7:10

the "county" of Jerusalem, but the words "region," "county," etc. are not used in that passage. Furthermore, ancient documents don't use that terminology the way we do in English today. I believe this was simply an error, a slip-up, on Joseph Smith's part, when he was compiling the Book of Mormon. To be honest, I don't think Christians would make too much of a big deal about this if LDS scholars would simply admit that. But they don't, because ultimately they know this puts a black dot, amongst many other black dots, on the credibility of the Book of Mormon.

Jesus Conceived by Heavenly Father

Now the birth of Jesus Christ was on this wise: When as his mother Mary was espoused to Joseph, before they came together, she was found with child of the Holy Ghost. ... But while he thought on these things, behold, the angel of the Lord appeared unto him in a dream, saying, Joseph, thou son of David, fear not to take unto thee Mary thy wife: for that which is conceived in her is of the Holy Ghost. (Matthew 1:18, 20)

This is an idea that was taught by several LDS leaders of the past and is still taught in several LDS manuals used in their Sunday worship services. They teach the Holy Ghost did not conceive Jesus, but rather Heavenly Father and Mary conceived Jesus like every other human is conceived by their father and mother.

This passage teaches the Holy Ghost is the Father, so to speak, of Jesus. As we stated earlier, this is another example of the names, titles, attributes and works of God being ascribed to each member of the Trinity as if they lay exclusive claim to them.

No Paid Clergy

Nor scrip for [your] journey, neither two coats, neither shoes, nor yet staves: for the workman is worthy of his meat. (Matthew 10:10)

Jesus sent out the twelve on missions in groups of two, and he tells them he will take care of them by saying, "A worker is worthy of his wages." The LDS teach if you are being paid for your work for God, then you are working for Satan.[393] This is hypocritical because the LDS pay several different roles within their church, but they structure them as reimbursements.[394] Some of these add up to quite a bit of money. By the way, some of the early revelations that Joseph Smith had regarding this contradict this idea. Joseph received revelation that some roles should be paid for their duties.[395]

Outer Darkness

LDS teach Outer Darkness is reserved exclusively for those who have been fully enlightened, meaning those who were part of the LDS church and left the church. Sometimes what they mean by that are those who left and actively fight against the church. Sometimes it means only people who have gone through the temple and done certain other things and then left the church and fought against the church. Some want to be more gracious than others.

> **For [the kingdom of heaven is] as a man travelling into a far country, [who] called his own servants, and delivered unto them his goods. And unto one he gave five talents, to another two, and to another one; to every man according to his several ability; and straightway took his journey. Then he that had received the five talents went and traded with the same, and made [them] other five talents. And likewise he that [had received] two, he also gained other two. But he that had received one went and digged in the earth, and hid his lord's money. After a long time the lord of those servants cometh, and reckoneth with them. And so he that had received five talents came and brought other five talents, saying, Lord, thou deliveredst unto me five talents: behold, I have gained beside them five talents more. His lord**

[393] The Dangers of Priestcraft, Teaching Seminary Preservice Readings Religion 370, 471, and 475, p. 106-111 https://www.lds.org/manual/teaching-seminary-preservice-readings-religion-370- 471-and-475/the-dangers-of-priestcraft?lang=eng

[394] Lindbloom, Sharon, Mormon Business: Paying the Church's Unpaid Clergy, January 18, 2017 http://www.mrm.org/mormon-business-paying-its-unpaid-clergy

[395] Doctrine & Covenants 42:71-73; 75

said unto him, Well done, [thou] good and faithful servant: thou hast been faithful over a few things, I will make thee ruler over many things: enter thou into the joy of thy lord. He also that had received two talents came and said, Lord, thou deliveredst unto me two talents: behold, I have gained two other talents beside them. His lord said unto him, Well done, good and faithful servant; thou hast been faithful over a few things, I will make thee ruler over many things: enter thou into the joy of thy lord. Then he which had received the one talent came and said, Lord, I knew thee that thou art an hard man, reaping where thou hast not sown, and gathering where thou hast not strawed: And I was afraid, and went and hid thy talent in the earth: lo, [there] thou hast [that is] thine. His lord answered and said unto him, [Thou] wicked and slothful servant, thou knewest that I reap where I sowed not, and gather where I have not strawed: Thou oughtest therefore to have put my money to the exchangers, and [then] at my coming I should have received mine own with usury. Take therefore the talent from him, and give [it] unto him which hath ten talents. For unto every one that hath shall be given, and he shall have abundance: but from him that hath not shall be taken away even that which he hath. And cast ye the unprofitable servant into outer darkness: there shall be weeping and gnashing of teeth. (Matthew 25:14-30)

Jesus mentions outer darkness a few times, and these references only appear in Matthew's gospel.[396] No doubt this is a debatable topic. Most people equate Outer Darkness with hell. The phrase in Greek means the "darkness outside." If you look at the parables, you have servants, friends, and other analogies which used to describe believers. Most of these passages describe somebody inside a physical location and then being asked to leave or being cast outside. Outer Darkness sounds much different than "the darkness outside." It's the difference between a person missing out on something or burning in everlasting flames.

---

[396] Matthew 8:12; 22:13; 25:30

The Outer Darkness is not something reserved for apostates. In this case, the servant was simply scared. To me, it's the equivalent of somebody who is a believer but doesn't do anything with their faith. They don't take advantage of the gifts that God has given us, and it goes to the idea of Stunted Grace that will be discussed in the Tactic #3 - Communicating Grace to the Religious Mind - section of this book. Stunted Grace refers to those things God intends to give us, the gifts that he wants to bestow on us, and we pass up for a number of reasons. This guy had the gift but didn't use it, because he was afraid. We don't know if he was honest about his motive. But he's cast into Outer Darkness. The others are welcomed into the joy of the Lord.

I do believe there are things in heaven that we're going to miss out on if we haven't been receptive to what God wants to do in our lives. And there will be those who rule and reign with Christ in his Millennial Kingdom, and some who don't. Sometimes we think of salvation as eternal life, and it's so much more than that. What God wants to do through us, and in us, is far more than giving us a spot in heaven and reserving that for us. He wants to gain talents through us. He wants to use us to bring him glory. He wants to involve us in what he's doing, as a good Father would.

The idea that the LDS have of Outer Darkness is unscriptural.

Pearl of Great Price

Again, the kingdom of heaven is like unto a merchant man, seeking goodly pearls: Who, when he had found one pearl of great price, went and sold all that he had, and bought it. (Matthew 13:45-46)

Like the Book of Mormon, and like the Doctrine & Covenants, Joseph Smith taught that the Pearl of Great Price. This is the story behind the books of Abraham and Moses, contained within the book the LDS believe is Scripture called the Pearl of Great Price. There was a salesman of artifacts who was coming to town at a time when some people in the church were starting to question Joseph as a prophet, seer and revelator.[397] A man came to town with some Egyptian artifacts along with some mummies. With the mummies were some manuscripts, and when Joseph Smith

---

[397] Larson, Charles M., By His Own Hand Upon Papyrus: A New Look at the Joseph Smith Papyri

looked at them, he said they were the writings of Abraham and Moses. The LDS purchased them for him. Joseph translated them, and they became the Book of Abraham and the Book of Moses. We thought these manuscripts had been burned in the Great Chicago Fire, but the manuscript Joseph used to translate the Book of Abraham later turned up. This was supposed to be a huge validation for the church, but instead, it turned out to be another embarrassment. Now we understand how to translate Egyptian, scholars were able to verify the document, and it was stated that not one word was accurately translated.

So, was Jesus prophesying about the Pearl of Great Price, a book that was not what it claimed to be? Probably not.

Pre-Existence

Joseph Smith borrowed from Greek philosophy for this belief. The LDS church teaches all people have existed eternally as intelligences, and that matter is eternal.[398] Priesthood authority is eternal.[399] The being we call God can only be said to be eternal in this sense. He was once a man as we are, on another planet, under another God, and he became a God, at which point he birthed every human who has ever lived, and we became his spirit children. It was then vital to our progression we take on the physical bodies we now have and come to this earth so that we can prove ourselves worthy to return to the presence of our Heavenly Father and progress to become gods ourselves.

The other thing you need to understand about the LDS belief in the pre-existence is there were two plans of salvation presented. One was Jesus', the firstborn spirit child of Elohim, our Heavenly Father. He proposed to come as a Savior. Lucifer also presented a plan where individuals would be forced to progress and not have free agency. Jesus' plan was chosen, and Lucifer led a rebellion in heaven against Elohim. One-third of the spirit children sided with Lucifer and were cast down to earth without bodies, forever stunting their progression. These are what we know as demons or evil spirits. One-third of the spirit children fought valiantly and would be born into families where they would learn the truth and be a part of the LDS church, and have an advantage in their progression. One-third were neutral and would be

---

[398] Doctrine & Covenants 131:7-8

[399] Alma 13:7–8; Doctrine & Covenants 84:17–18

born with disadvantages, either because of race, geographic location, or the time when they would be born. They could still find the truth and progress, but they would do so at a disadvantage.[400]

When we came to this earth, we passed through the veil, our memories of the pre-existence were taken away, so this reality needs to be re-taught to us by the LDS church.

> **And he answered them, saying, Who is my mother, or my brethren? And he looked round about on them which sat about him, and said, Behold my mother and my brethren! For whosoever shall do the will of God, the same is my brother, and my sister, and mother. (Mark 3:33-35)**

How does one become a brother or sister to Jesus? Is it through the pre-existence? No, we become family to Jesus through doing the will of the Father.

> **But as many as received him, to them gave he power to become the sons of God, [even] to them that believe on his name: (John 1:12)**

You have to believe in Jesus, which means you receive Jesus. Receive is the language of gift.

> **And no man hath ascended up to heaven, but he that came down from heaven, [even] the Son of man which is in heaven. (John 3:13)**

The language Jesus used all throughout the gospel of John shows that he is unique in his identity and how he came to this earth. Jesus refers to himself as being "sent" from the Father, coming from "above," not of this world, descended from heaven, etc.

> **He that cometh from above is above all: he that is of the earth is earthly, and speaketh of the earth: he that cometh from heaven is above all. (John 3:31)**

---

[400] Lee, Harold B., *Decisions for Successful Living*, p.164-165 http://www.mrm.org/was-ban-a-theory

This statement would be blasphemous if it were not true. Jesus did not say, "I am above all, except for God." He said he was above all.

> **Not that any man hath seen the Father, save he which is of God, he hath seen the Father. (John 6:46)**

If the pre-existence is true, then we've all seen the Father.

> **And he said unto them, Ye are from beneath; I am from above: ye are of this world; I am not of this world. (John 8:23)**

The LDS teach Jesus was talking about their spiritual state. But this would be reading meaning into the text instead of drawing meaning out of the text. He was talking about where he came from vs. where they came from.

> **Ye are of [your] father the devil, and the lusts of your father ye will do. He was a murderer from the beginning, and abode not in the truth, because there is no truth in him. When he speaketh a lie, he speaketh of his own: for he is a liar, and the father of it. (John 8:44)**

Again, the LDS teach Jesus wasn't talking about the actual parents or origins of the Pharisees. However, If the pre-existence were true, Jesus wouldn't say Lucifer was their father because Elohim would still be their Father even if they are rejecting him.

Prophecies of the Book of Mormon

> **And other sheep I have, which are not of this fold: them also I must bring, and they shall hear my voice; and there shall be one fold, [and] one shepherd. (John 10:16)**

This verse is quoted within the Book of Mormon, and it is supposed to be Jesus prophesying of the sheep that he had in the Americas, namely the Nephites and the Lamanites, and that he was going to go after his ministry there to the Americas to preach this same message to them. They believe this to be the source of the Book of Mormon. That is not what Jesus was talking about. He was talking about the

Gentiles. One evidence is the sheep, even over in the Americas, are supposed to still be Israelites that came over in earlier periods. So they would be of the same fold. They would be Israelites. Gentiles are by definition not Israelites.

Seventies

After these things the Lord appointed other seventy also, and sent them two and two before his face into every city and place, whither he himself would come. (Luke 10:1)

The LDS claim Jesus sending out the seventies was a model of church government that he intended to be in his one true church. One would never come to this conclusion unless they believed modern LDS revelation and read it back into this Scripture.

Temples

Again, ye have heard that it hath been said by them of old time, Thou shalt not forswear thyself, but shalt perform unto the Lord thine oaths: But I say unto you, Swear not at all; neither by heaven; for it is God's throne: Nor by the earth; for it is his footstool: neither by Jerusalem; for it is the city of the great King. Neither shalt thou swear by thy head, because thou canst not make one hair white or black. But let your communication be, Yea, yea; Nay, nay: for whatsoever is more than these cometh of evil. (Matthew 5:33-37)

In the temple, the LDS make certain covenants with God. They make covenants that they will pledge all they are, all they have, to Jesus and building up his kingdom. They also receive the power of the priesthood to be upon them and their posterity, which is a scary thing, in context, when one asks whose priesthood they are calling upon themselves.

I should state that it is not wise to discuss the temple ceremony with LDS as they believe everything to be associated with the temple to be sacred and they have made solemn oaths not to discuss anything related to the temple with outsiders.

> **The centurion answered and said, Lord, I am not worthy that thou shouldest come under my roof: but speak the word only, and my servant shall be healed. (Matthew 8:8)**

> **And preached, saying, There cometh one mightier than I after me, the latchet of whose shoes I am not worthy to stoop down and unloose. (Mark 1:7)**

> **John answered, saying unto [them] all, I indeed baptize you with water; but one mightier than I cometh, the latchet of whose shoes I am not worthy to unloose: he shall baptize you with the Holy Ghost and with fire: (Luke 3:16)**

Over and over again in the gospels, we see people declaring that they are not worthy, which is the posture Jesus wants us to take toward him. The LDS do the opposite when they have their temple interview, declaring themselves to be worthy to go through the temple and receive the endowments, make the covenants and receive the priesthood.

In Revelation 5, Jesus is proclaimed to be the only worthy one in heaven or on earth. Our worthiness is tied to Jesus' death and resurrection. Even as a believer, we are not worthy in and of ourselves.

The idea of worthiness related to the temple also creates a contradiction of sorts since LDS are never given assurance of their standing before God. One would think that if they are worthy to enter God's presence in the temple, then they would consider themselves worthy to enter into God's presence in heaven. But this is not the case.

> **And said, This [fellow] said, I am able to destroy the temple of God, and to build it in three days. (Matthew 26:61)**

Jesus prophesied the physical destruction of the temple and spiritual rebuilding of it. If the temple were vitally important to the spiritual well being of his children, God would not have wanted the temple to go away. And he would have had it rebuilt it at some point. I know the LDS think they are rebuilding temples that function the same way as Solomon's temple, but nothing going on in LDS temples is the same as what went on in the original temple in Jerusalem.

And, behold, the veil of the temple was rent in twain from the top to the bottom; and the earth did quake, and the rocks rent; (Matthew 27:51; Mark 15:38)

Some have said it this way. Jesus tore down the veil in the temple, and Joseph Smith put it back up. In LDS temples, before you get into the Celestial Room, there is a separation veil. That's the veil where the hands come out, and LDS learn the tokens, covenants and handshakes of the Melchizedek Priesthood that will get them past the "sentinels" in the afterlife and get them into the Celestial Kingdom. Jesus tore down the separation between the main Sanctuary and the Holy of Holies. Hebrews tells us we can come boldly before the throne of grace to help us in our time of need.[401] But Joseph Smith claimed a separation between God and man still exists by using a temple veil.

We heard him say, I will destroy this temple that is made with hands, and within three days I will build another made without hands. (Mark 14:58)

If God's intention was for the geography to be littered with temples as was the vision of Brigham Young and started by Joseph Smith, then I have a question as to why Jesus, with the temple in Jerusalem, would say, "Physically, this building will be destroyed, and spiritually, it will be risen again." Jesus didn't ever say, and never pointed to a time, when a physical temple needed to be rebuilt and used by the church.

Jesus saith unto her, Woman, believe me, the hour cometh, when ye shall neither in this mountain, nor yet at Jerusalem, worship the Father. (John 4:21)

There was a controversy between the Samaritans and the Jews as to which temple was the right one. Jesus clarified that a time was soon coming when a temple would not be necessary. One of the tell-tale signs that the Book of Mormon is not biblical is that several temples were built, allegedly, in the Americas. If one reads the Old Testament, every attempt to set up another place of worship besides Jerusalem was met with

---

[401] Hebrews 4:16

condemnation by God. All throughout the New Testament, the emphasis is made that Christians, both individually and corporately, are the temple of God.[402] We are the place where Christ dwells, not a physical building made of stone by human hands.

Three Levels of Heaven

The LDS teaches there are the Celestial, Terrestrial and Telestial Kingdoms of heaven. What did Jesus say concerning this?

> **In my Father's house are many mansions: if [it were] not [so], I would have told you. I go to prepare a place for you. (John 14:2)**

The LDS church teaches this verse is talking about different places in heaven. Jesus didn't say that. The word translated "place" means rooms in Greek. There are lots of different rooms, and he has a place for us. That was the emphasis. Not there are different levels of heaven.

> **And if I go and prepare a place for you, I will come again, and receive you unto myself; that where I am, [there] ye may be also. (John 14:3)**

What this means, and what the Bible is unanimous about, is heaven is not about the grand features that are going to be there. It's not about becoming a god yourself. It's about dwelling where Jesus is, where the Father is. It's about being with God, worshipping God, serving God, for all of eternity. That's what heaven is all about. The question is, for those who say they are going to some other level of heaven, or for the Jehovah's Witnesses, those who aren't going to go to heaven, but they are going to be on a glorified resurrected earth, how is that heaven? From a scriptural point of view, if they're not where the Father is, or not where Jesus is, how is that heaven?

---

[402] 1 Corinthians 3:16; 6:19

Tithing

And he looked up, and saw the rich men casting their gifts into the treasury. And he saw also a certain poor widow casting in thither two mites. And he said, Of a truth I say unto you, that this poor widow hath cast in more than they all: For all these have of their abundance cast in unto the offerings of God: but she of her penury hath cast in all the living that she had. (Luke 21:1-4)

Jesus didn't teach tithing. This might be my personal opinion. The New Testament says we should give graciously, hilariously, cheerfully, freely, and not out of compulsion. We should give what God has placed on our hearts. This widow gave of everything she had, and she would have been looked on as a second class citizen in many of these churches or the LDS church. Even in many Christian churches, this would be the case. In contrast, several people were giving much more than this widow. They might even be tithing. But it's not affecting them personally at all. They give without a second thought. We give preferential treatment to individuals who are giving large quantities of money even though it might be 5% of their actual income. But individuals who give hardly any money might be giving 20%, but we tend to treat those individuals different.

Word of Wisdom

And when the scribes and Pharisees saw him eat with publicans and sinners, they said unto his disciples, How is it that he eateth and drinketh with publicans and sinners? (Mark 2:16)

This passage is relevant to discussing the Word of Wisdom for the LDS, or the health codes of the Seventh Day Adventists. Jesus was accused of being a glutton and a winebibber. Was he? No. But he was hanging around these people, and he did partake of these things. A theology that teaches Jesus never drank a glass of wine doesn't mesh well with the gospels.

There is nothing from without a man, that entering into him can defile him: but the things which come out of him, those are they

> that defile the man. If any man have ears to hear, let him hear.
> And when he was entered into the house from the people, his
> disciples asked him concerning the parable. And he saith unto
> them, Are ye so without understanding also? Do ye not perceive,
> that whatsoever thing from without entereth into the man, [it]
> cannot defile him; Because it entereth not into his heart, but
> into the belly, and goeth out into the draught, purging all meats?
> And he said, That which cometh out of the man, that defileth
> the man. For from within, out of the heart of men, proceed evil
> thoughts, adulteries, fornications, murders, Thefts, covetousness,
> wickedness, deceit, lasciviousness, an evil eye, blasphemy, pride,
> foolishness: All these evil things come from within, and defile
> the man. (Mark 7:15-23)

This passage is speaking directly to the Word of Wisdom because they were trying to accuse Jesus of being unclean because of the things he was eating, or because of the fact he washed or didn't wash. He would say they should wash the inside of the cup, and then the outside would be clean also. The Word of Wisdom, as a requirement to go into a temple where secret ceremonies to get you into heaven are taught, does not make one more righteous because they don't drink hot or cold drinks, or meat during certain times, or holding to a health code.

The latter part of what Jesus is talking about is a great passage to take LDS to when they ask you to pray about whether the Book of Mormon is true. The reason why Christians are hesitant to pray about whether the Book of Mormon is true is because they don't put their trust in emotions.

The difference between how LDS and Christians see emotions can be contrasted by picturing a train with three cars. The LDS train has emotions out in front. They put their faith, the second car, in those emotions. Facts are pulling the caboose. The Christian train puts facts first. We place our faith in God based on those facts. Emotions may or may not follow that faith.

There is also an interesting event in LDS history called the Canadian Copyright Episode that can help illustrate this difference. Joseph Smith was trying to find a source for more income, so he sent some of the brethren up to Canada to sell the copyright to the Book of Mormon. He told them he received a revelation that the mission would be successful. They went and failed. They came back and asked, "What happened?" Joseph Smith said, "Some revelations are of God, some are of myself, and some are of the devil."[403] Joseph Smith didn't even know if he could trust what he thought were revelations.

---

[403] Whitmer, David, An Address to All Believers in Christ, p. 31

CHAPTER 27

Passages in the Gospels Related to Miscellaneous Twelve Tribes Issues

Jesus said unto him, If thou wilt be perfect, go [and] sell that thou hast, and give to the poor, and thou shalt have treasure in heaven: and come [and] follow me. (Matthew 19:21)

The rich young ruler came and asked what good thing he had to do to gain eternal life. Jesus tossed out some of the commandments and the man was in denial and claimed he kept all of those since he was young. Jesus points something out to him, the idol of his possessions, and said if he was ready to give that up and follow him, then he could have eternal life. And the man went away sad because he had many possessions and he didn't want to get rid of them.

The Twelve Tribes uses this and teaches as Abraham left and gave up everything and as Jesus asked this man to give up everything, is what we are supposed to do. Is that what Jesus meant?

This was an interpersonal conversation Jesus was having with an individual. We need to be careful in our Bible study that we're not placing individual conversations on a level as if Jesus is speaking to us personally. We have to see from the context what the principles are in relation to the passage, ask whether it's a particular thing that was said to a specific person or group of people, or ask whether God is speaking to us directly. Jesus had a personal conversation with Judas where he told him to do what he had in his heart, which was to betray him for money to the authorities.[404] Are we all supposed to see that as normative and betray Jesus for money, or is there something more to Bible study than that? Are all the promises in the Bible concerning eternal life null and void because of one thing Jesus said to this particular man? Or was he dealing with him on a personal level the way he does with all people? I would say it's the latter.

---

[404] John 13:27

CHAPTER 28

Passages in the Gospels Related to the Trinity

The subject of the Trinity is going to come up when talking with most of the groups discussed in this book. We need to be able to articulate, from the Bible, why we believe in the Trinity. We will discuss this topic more in-depth in Tactic #5 - Explaining the Trinity

Fact #1 - One God

And this is life eternal, that they might know thee the only true God, and Jesus Christ, whom thou hast sent. (John 17:3)

We need to clarify Jesus taught there is one true God. Some of the cults will use this verse to show Jesus taught he is not God, and there is only one true God in heaven. That is not what Jesus was saying. He was affirming there is one true God, but he equates that we need to know the one true God "and" Jesus Christ. So he is still equating himself with this one true God, which would be blasphemy in and of itself if it were not true.

Fact #2 - One God (with multiplicity)

God is Judge

> **For many bare false witness against him, but their witness agreed not together. (Mark 14:56)**

They were looking for witnesses. Could they have one witness? No. Why? Because God established in the law that two or three witnesses shall establish a fact.[405] So multiple witnesses that corroborate each other can stand up in a court of law. God goes even further to say in the Ten Commandments, "You shall not bear false witness."[406] I think if God went out of his way to establish this as a law, then he is holding himself to that standard. If God is then our judge, then he must be more than one witness. So we see Jesus saying, "All judgment has been given to me," but he also talks about God and the Holy Spirit being judge.[407] So what we have here is a case if God is judge, and there have to be two or three witnesses to judge justly, God must be two or three. That sounds similar to the Trinity.

That They Might Be One

> **That they all may be one; as thou, Father, [art] in me, and I in thee, that they also may be one in us: that the world may believe that thou hast sent me. And the glory which thou gavest me I have given them; that they may be one, even as we are one: (John 17:21-22)**

This is another verse some of the groups discussed in this book will point to about the Trinity to dissuade you of that belief. What they would teach is the way Jesus prayed we should be one as the body of Christ is the way he and the Father are one. Not in essence, but in purpose. Not in co-equality, like the Trinity belief would hold to.

---

[405] Deuteronomy 17:6

[406] Exodus 20:16

[407] John 5:22

We think in terms of, we, as separate individual persons, are one in Christ. We are one in the same way Jesus and the Father are one because they are separate persons part of one God. We are separate persons part of one body of Christ. That in Christ, we are interconnected in such a way we are part of the collective body of Christ. That we are intricately connected spiritually to each other the same way we are connected to him, because he is in us, and we are his body. It's complicated, but this is convicting because what it shows us is there should be two visible models of the Trinity here on earth. One is marriage, where the two become one flesh.[408] The other is the body of Christ, where believers are called to be one, even as he is one, and even as we are one with him. This is convicting and sad to realize, that yes, we are one in unity over certain concepts and the things we've been talking about in this book. It is important we unite over those core beliefs, but there is so much division and animosity in the body of Christ. And that is one of the things cults use. Because they have this idea they are the one true church, and there can only be one true church. This is true even within Catholicism, teaching they are the one true church Jesus established. The church is not a brick and mortar building or organization. It is a body of believers and is invisible in reference to those who are true believers. Jesus spoke of this in the parable of the wheat and tares when he said we shouldn't figure out who the real believers are, but rather allow him to sort that out in the end.

What we are doing in this book is identifying the core central doctrines of Christianity, and help save or protect our flock we've been entrusted with, from those who are coming and dressed in sheep's clothing, but are ravenous wolves, like the enemy, who prowls around like a roaring lion seeking whom he may devour.[409] We're trying to prevent believers from being taken with every wind of doctrine.[410]

So, yes, we need to be one, but we also need to protect from the outside influences that might cause believers to stumble.

---

[408] Ephesians 5:31

[409] 1 Peter 5:8

[410] Ephesians 4:14

The Baptism Formula

> Go ye therefore, and teach all nations, baptizing them in the name
> of the Father, and of the Son, and of the Holy Ghost: (Matthew
> 28:19)

Baptize in the name (singular) of the Father, Son and Holy Spirit. They all three share one name. That is talking about three persons in one God.

Fact #3 - Jesus is God

God With Us

> Behold, a virgin shall be with child, and shall bring forth a son,
> and they shall call his name Emmanuel, which being interpreted
> is, God with us. (Matthew 1:23)

Jesus was to be called Emmanuel, meaning "God with us."[411]

Jesus Answers Prayer

> And whatsoever ye shall ask in my name, that will I do, that the
> Father may be glorified in the Son. If ye shall ask any thing in my
> name, I will do [it]. (John 14:13-14)

> And in that day ye shall ask me nothing. Verily, verily, I say unto
> you, Whatsoever ye shall ask the Father in my name, he will give
> [it] you. (John 16:23)

Jesus, on the one hand, said, "Ask in my name, and I will do it," speaking of prayer. Then, later on, in the same discourse with his disciples, he said, "The Father will give it to you. The Father will answer your prayers." Jesus claimed to answer prayers. That's enough of a claim to deity. But then, he claimed the Father answers prayers. Jesus is claiming equality with God.

---

[411] Isaiah 7:14

Jesus Can Forgive Sins

> When Jesus saw their faith, he said unto the sick of the palsy, Son, thy sins be forgiven thee. ... Why doth this [man] thus speak blasphemies? who can forgive sins but God only? ... Whether is it easier to say to the sick of the palsy, [Thy] sins be forgiven thee; or to say, Arise, and take up thy bed, and walk? But that ye may know that the Son of man hath power on earth to forgive sins, (he saith to the sick of the palsy,) (Mark 2:5, 7, 9-10)

> And he said unto her, Thy sins are forgiven. And they that sat at meat with him began to say within themselves, Who is this that forgiveth sins also? (Luke 7:48-49)

Jesus claimed authority to forgive sins. Only one can forgive sins, God.

Jesus Claimed to be the "I AM"

> But straightway Jesus spake unto them, saying, Be of good cheer; it is I; be not afraid. (Matthew 14:27)

> For they all saw him, and were troubled. And immediately he talked with them, and saith unto them, Be of good cheer: it is I; be not afraid. (Mark 6:50)

> Then said Jesus unto them again, Verily, verily, I say unto you, I am the door of the sheep. ... I am the good shepherd: the good shepherd giveth his life for the sheep. (John 10:7, 11)

> Jesus said unto her, I am the resurrection, and the life: he that believeth in me, though he were dead, yet shall he live: (John 11:25)

> They answered him, Jesus of Nazareth. Jesus saith unto them, I am [he]. And Judas also, which betrayed him, stood with them.

> **As soon then as he had said unto them, I am [he], they went backward, and fell to the ground. (John 18:5-6)**

Jesus referred to Himself as "I AM." Those words under "It is I" are ἐγὼ εἰμί in Greek, which means "I AM." Jesus is declaring himself to be the voice of the burning bush that introduced himself to Moses back in Exodus 3, which became the basis for God's unpronounceable name YHWH, or Yahweh.[412]

What I found interesting is there are places where the "ego eimi" is said by others, but there is always another word, such as ὅτι Ἐγώ εἰμι in Greek, which means they were not declaring an identity statement saying "I AM," declaring themselves equal with Yahweh.[413] Jesus was.

> **And Pilate wrote a title, and put [it] on the cross. And the writing was, JESUS OF NAZARETH THE KING OF THE JEWS. This title then read many of the Jews: for the place where Jesus was crucified was nigh to the city: and it was written in Hebrew, [and] Greek, [and] Latin. Then said the chief priests of the Jews to Pilate, Write not, The King of the Jews; but that he said, I am King of the Jews. Pilate answered, What I have written I have written. (John 19:19-22)**

This is not clear from the text, but let me share a conjecture. What I think was going on was Pilate, by the end of the conversation, started realizing who he was dealing with, or at least he might potentially be dealing with whom he thinks he's dealing.[414] So, in spite of the fact he ordered Jesus to be crucified, Pilate wrote this inscription and had it above Jesus' head. He wrote in Hebrew, Greek and Latin, and I'm going to focus on Hebrew. When translated into Hebrew, it could have formed an acrostic. An example of an acrostic is preaching on Faith, and the letter F standing for something, the letter A standing for something, etc. That seems to be what Pilate did. When translated into Hebrew, and written in an acrostic, the first letter would have been Y, or the equivalent in Hebrew of Y. Then you would have H - W - H, spelling out

---

[412] Exodus 3:14

[413] John 9:9

[414] Mark 15:15

YHWH, or Yahweh. The Jewish leaders protested, "Can you please add something to this like he said 'I'm King of the Jews?'" Pilate said I think with a smirk on his face, "What I have written, I have written." I think what it said on the cross in Hebrew in acrostic form, was יְהוָה.

I wouldn't necessarily go here in a conversation, but I wanted to include this for fun.

Jesus Commanded us to Believe in Him

> **Jesus cried and said, He that believeth on me, believeth not on me, but on him that sent me. And he that seeth me seeth him that sent me. (John 12:44-45)**

A person who sees Jesus sees the Father. And again Jesus is not saying, "I am the Father," but said if a person has seen him, they have seen the Father because they are the same.

> **Let not your heart be troubled: ye believe in God, believe also in me. (John 14:1)**

We miss the significance of this passage as Christians to a monotheistic Jewish culture. Jesus said they need to believe in him the same way they believe in Yahweh.

Jesus Commands

> **Teaching them to observe all things whatsoever I have commanded you: and, lo, I am with you alway, [even] unto the end of the world. Amen. (Matthew 28:20)**

Believers are commanded to obey all things Jesus commanded us. Not all things the Father has commanded us. The Ten Commandments were written on stone tablets by God himself.[415] Jesus said his commandments trump God's commandments. Believers are told to listen to what Jesus tells them to do and tell others to do the

---

[415] Exodus 24:12

same. He did not tell us to forget what God had said, but Christianity is based on following Jesus' teachings.

Jesus also said he would be with each believer always. This passage goes on to talk about the Father, Son and Holy Spirit, an example of the Trinity. If Jesus can be with each believer always, he is claiming omnipresence, which is only an attribute of God.

Jesus Did the Work of God

> **But Jesus answered them, My Father worketh hitherto, and I work. Therefore the Jews sought the more to kill him, because he not only had broken the sabbath, but said also that God was his Father, making himself equal with God. (John 5:17-18)**

Ever wonder whether Jesus ever said he was God? Here is an example where the Pharisees said they interpreted what Jesus was saying this way, and Jesus didn't deny it. If Jesus wasn't God, the Pharisees had a right reaction in trying to kill him. But they were wrong. He was God. Here's what Jesus said. "The Father works, and I work."

Jesus Equated Himself with the Father

> **I and [my] Father are one. (John 10:30)**

> **The Jews answered him, saying, For a good work we stone thee not; but for blasphemy; and because that thou, being a man, makest thyself God. (John 10:33)**

Notice he doesn't say "one in purpose." He said "one." I also want to point out the Hebrew word "one" referenced to there being "one God" in the Old Testament is not a static one, meaning one and only one. It's a one with complexity to it. It allows for multiplicity to be within that oneness. Back in Genesis 1, it says, "Let us create man in our image." Even the word Elohim is a plural word. The "im" ending in Hebrew is plural. It is a plural noun always used with a singular verb when it is referring to God.

The Pharisees understood Jesus to be claiming to be equal with God.

Jesus Has All Authority

**And Jesus came and spake unto them, saying, All power is given
unto me in heaven and in earth. (Matthew 28:18)**

I was recently challenged on this verse by an LDS person who was trying to make his
case why Jesus wasn't God. He was saying Jesus said all authority was given to him,
meaning he couldn't be God. He was trying to make it sound like Jesus didn't have
authority before this. So I asked a couple of simple questions:

"Are you prepared to say before this, Jesus had no authority?"

"Are you prepared to say after this moment the Father had no authority?"

Neither of these propositions makes any sense. The truth of the matter is this
verse is proclaiming Jesus' deity when he said he had all authority in heaven and on
earth. If he is not God, there is no way to explain why Jesus has all authority on
heaven and on earth.

Jesus has the Power to Raise the Dead

**For as the Father raiseth up the dead, and quickeneth [them];
even so the Son quickeneth whom he will. (John 5:21)**

Quickeneth is King James for made alive, rejuvenate. So Jesus said the Father gives
life, and Jesus gives life.

Jesus is Called God

**And Thomas answered and said unto him, My Lord and my God.
(John 20:28)**

Jesus is called God. Jesus didn't rebuke Thomas. He didn't tell him, "Hey Thomas,
you're taking this too far. I'm not God. I am the Christ. I am lesser than God." He
accepted the worship and praise and glory Thomas was giving to him at that moment.
If Jesus were not God, this would have been blasphemy and idolatry. And if he's not
God, God should have done something about Jesus receiving worship from Thomas.

Jesus is Eternal

> **And they said unto him, In Bethlehem of Judaea: for thus it is written by the prophet, And thou Bethlehem, [in] the land of Juda, art not the least among the princes of Juda: for out of thee shall come a Governor, that shall rule my people Israel. (Matthew 2:5-6)**

In the prophecy of Micah 5:2, which is what is quoted here, it said the Messiah's origins are "from old, from everlasting." In Hebrew, it means the "vanishing point."[416] This would be another way of expressing the Messiah would be eternal and self-existent.

Jesus is Holy

> **Saying, Let [us] alone; what have we to do with thee, thou Jesus of Nazareth? art thou come to destroy us? I know thee who thou art, the Holy One of God. (Mark 1:24)**

God alone is Holy, so Jesus being referred to as Holy means he is being equated with God.

Jesus is Lord

> **Then saith Jesus unto him, Get thee hence, Satan: for it is written, Thou shalt worship the Lord thy God, and him only shalt thou serve. (Matthew 4:10)**

The Hebrew word here is Yahweh once again, but this verse also said one shall only worship Yahweh. Jesus receives worship on a repeated basis, and he is referred to as Lord or Yahweh. Again, each member of the Trinity receives worship as if they lay exclusive claim to it.

> **The voice of one crying in the wilderness, Prepare ye the way of the Lord, make his paths straight. (Mark 1:3; Luke 3:4; Isaiah 40:3; John 1:23)**

---

[416] Micah 5:2 http://biblehub.com/lexicon/micah/5-2.htm

If there is any question what the word Lord means, all one has to do is look for a New Testament verse including Lord quoting an Old Testament verse. When they look up that Old Testament verse, they will find the Hebrew word YHWH is used, which is the unpronounceable name of God. And it is being ascribed to Jesus in name, title and meaning.

The one John the Baptist was preparing the way for was Yahweh, who came in the form of Jesus.

> **And Jesus answered and said, while he taught in the temple, How say the scribes that Christ is the Son of David? For David himself said by the Holy Ghost, The LORD said to my Lord, Sit thou on my right hand, till I make thine enemies thy footstool. David therefore himself calleth him Lord; and whence is he [then] his son? And the common people heard him gladly. (Mark 12:35-37)**

> **The LORD said unto my Lord, Sit thou at my right hand, until I make thine enemies thy footstool. (Psalm 110:1)**

Jesus was both David's son and his Lord. The Pharisees and Sadducees had asked Jesus a series of questions trying to trick him, and every time they did, Jesus would find a way to dodge the trap and throw the question back on them. After a few of these, Jesus asked his own question. Jesus was pointing to the dual nature of the Messiah, as foretold in the Old Testament. That the Messiah would be God in the flesh, was who Jesus was claiming to be. Jesus quotes from Psalm 110:1, which says, "Yahweh said to my Adonai." There are two different words for Lord in Hebrew. This verse uses both. Yahweh always referred to God. Adonai sometimes referred to God and sometimes not. But this verse refers to two individuals, and Jesus points out, and this stumps the Pharisees.

> **For unto you is born this day in the city of David a Saviour, which is Christ the Lord. ... And it was revealed unto him by the Holy Ghost, that he should not see death, before he had seen the Lord's Christ. (Luke 2:11, 26)**

Jesus is called Lord. Then later Jesus is referred to as the Lord's Christ, meaning there is another Lord, which is the Father. This is a great example of the names, titles, attributes, actions, etc. of God being ascribed to each member of the Trinity separately as if they lay exclusive claim to that particular title, attribute, etc.

Jesus is Omnipresent

> **For where two or three are gathered together in my name, there am I in the midst of them. (Matthew 18:20)**

Jesus claimed to be able to be in multiple locations at once. I'm hesitant to say omnipresent because Jesus doesn't necessarily claim that, but it's easy to extrapolate this passage to mean that. How is this possible unless Jesus was in fact, God? Jesus, while physically on earth, claimed to be able to be in multiple places at once.

Jesus is Savior

> **And my spirit hath rejoiced in God my Saviour. (Luke 1:47)**

> **For unto you is born this day in the city of David a Saviour, which is Christ the Lord. (Luke 2:11)**

> **And said unto the woman, Now we believe, not because of thy saying: for we have heard [him] ourselves, and know that this is indeed the Christ, the Saviour of the world. (John 4:42)**

God is called the Savior.[417] Christ is referred to as the Savior. In Isaiah, God declares, "I alone am your Savior." So there is an equating between Jesus and the Father in the title of Savior.

Jesus is Self-Existing

> **For as the Father hath life in himself; so hath he given to the Son to have life in himself; (John 5:26)**

---

[417] Isaiah 45:21

Jesus is claiming his source of life is not from the Father. It's not from God. Jesus is claiming he has life in himself. The same way the Father has life in himself. Apart from the Trinity, one would be left with two separate gods who lay exclusive claim to the same attributes, titles and things they have done. It doesn't work. The reason why we believe in a Trinity as Christians is because the Bible is clear there is only one God, but it is equally clear the Father, Son and Holy Spirit share the titles, attributes and actions as if they each had done them exclusively.

Jesus is Sinless

He that speaketh of himself seeketh his own glory: but he that seeketh his glory that sent him, the same is true, and no unrighteousness is in him. (John 7:18)

Jesus claimed to have no unrighteousness in him. That's quite a claim. Like C.S. Lewis said, "You have to make a decision. Jesus didn't give you an option. He was either a liar, meaning he knew he wasn't God, but he said he was. Or he was a lunatic who thought he was God, but wasn't. Or he was very God of very God, who he said he was."[418]

Jesus is Worshipped

Saying, Where is he that is born King of the Jews? for we have seen his star in the east, and are come to worship him. ... And when they were come into the house, they saw the young child with Mary his mother, and fell down, and worshipped him: and when they had opened their treasures, they presented unto him gifts; gold, and frankincense, and myrrh. (Matthew 2:2,11)

And, behold, there came a leper and worshipped him, saying, Lord, if thou wilt, thou canst make me clean. (Matthew 8:2)

---

[418] Claims: What did Jesus Christ have to say about himself? http://www.whoisjesus-really.com/english/claims.htm

While he spake these things unto them, behold, there came a certain ruler, and worshipped him, saying, My daughter is even now dead: but come and lay thy hand upon her, and she shall live. (Matthew 9:18)

Then they that were in the ship came and worshipped him, saying, Of a truth thou art the Son of God. (Matthew 14:33)

Then came she and worshipped him, saying, Lord, help me. (Matthew 15:25)

Then came to him the mother of Zebedee's children with her sons, worshipping [him], and desiring a certain thing of him. (Matthew 20:20)

And as they went to tell his disciples, behold, Jesus met them, saying, All hail. And they came and held him by the feet, and worshipped him. ... And when they saw him, they worshipped him: but some doubted. (Matthew 28:9, 17)

But when he saw Jesus afar off, he ran and worshipped him, (Mark 5:6)

And they worshipped him, and returned to Jerusalem with great joy:; (Luke 24:52)

And he said, Lord, I believe. And he worshipped him. (John 9:38)

The Greek word here is προσκυνέω, which means worship.[419] It doesn't mean honor or respect. It means worship.

---

[419] προσκυνέω, Strong's Greek Lexicon www.blueletterbible.org//lang/lexicon/lexicon. cfm?Strongs= G4352&t=KJV

Jesus Shared Glory with the Father

> **And now, O Father, glorify thou me with thine own self with the glory which I had with thee before the world was. (John 17:5)**

Before creation, Jesus shared glory with God. And this is the same God who through Isaiah and other prophets said he would not share his glory with any other.[420] If Jesus was not God, then what he said was either not true, or he is God, part of the one God, Father, Son, and Holy Spirit.

Jesus was Able to Raise Himself from the Dead

> **Jesus answered and said unto them, Destroy this temple, and in three days I will raise it up. (John 2:19)**

The resurrection of Jesus is attributed in various places to the Father, Son, and Holy Spirit as if each of them exclusively lay claim to it. We see the same thing when it comes to the crucifixion of Jesus, the indwelling of the believer, etc.

> **Therefore doth my Father love me, because I lay down my life, that I might take it again. No man taketh it from me, but I lay it down of myself. I have power to lay it down, and I have power to take it again. This commandment have I received of my Father. (John 10:17-18)**

Jesus said, "I have the ability to lay my life down. I have the ability to take it back up again." He is laying claim to his resurrection. Something laid claim and given credit to the Father and the Holy Spirit elsewhere in Scripture. Father, Son, and Holy Spirit, all lay claim exclusively to the resurrection of Jesus.

---

[420] Isaiah 42:8

The Holy Spirit Testifies of Jesus

> **But when the Comforter is come, whom I will send unto you from the Father, [even] the Spirit of truth, which proceedeth from the Father, he shall testify of me: (John 15:26)**

If the Holy Spirit were both subservient to the Father, and the goal was to get people to believe in the Father, the Holy Spirit would not be testifying of Jesus. The Holy Spirit would be testifying of the Father. The fact the Holy Spirit testifies of Jesus points to his divinity.

Things Jesus Claimed Were His

When I examined the Upper Room Discourse, I noticed a pattern. These are the things Jesus claimed were his:

1. My peace (John 14:27)
2. My words (John 14:23; 15:7)
3. My disciples (John 15:8)
4. My love (John 15:9)
5. My commandments (John 15:10)
6. My joy (John 15:11)
7. My friends (John 15:14)
8. My name (John 15:16)

Jesus claimed all these things are his. So, if the Father is greater than him, and this means he is lesser than God, and he was simply playing a role in the plan of salvation, he would have attributed all of these things to the Father. The name of God was held in such high reverence by Jewish culture. They wouldn't even say the name of God and put the vowel markings of Adonai on the word Yahweh in the Old Testament in Hebrew so they wouldn't say Yahweh. Jesus claimed to have equality with the name of God.

You Can't Have the Father Without the Son

He that receiveth you receiveth me, and he that receiveth me receiveth him that sent me. (Matthew 10:40)

All things are delivered unto me of my Father: and no man knoweth the Son, but the Father; neither knoweth any man the Father, save the Son, and [he] to whomsoever the Son will reveal [him]. (Matthew 11:27)

That all [men] should honour the Son, even as they honour the Father. He that honoureth not the Son honoureth not the Father which hath sent him. (John 5:23)

I said therefore unto you, that ye shall die in your sins: for if ye believe not that I am [he], ye shall die in your sins. ... Then said Jesus unto them, When ye have lifted up the Son of man, then shall ye know that I am [he], and [that] I do nothing of myself; but as my Father hath taught me, I speak these things. ... Jesus said unto them, Verily, verily, I say unto you, Before Abraham was, I am. (John 8:24, 28, 58)

He that hateth me hateth my Father also. (John 15:23)

This is a big deal for Jehovah's Witnesses and LDS. Jehovah's Witnesses are big on saying Jehovah God is the only God. They don't worship Jesus, they don't honor Jesus. Jesus said if one doesn't honor the Son, they can't honor the Father. The LDS church teaches Jesus is a God, but Heavenly Father is the only one to whom we direct our worship. Furthermore, Jesus said if one doesn't believe he is the "I AM," meaning he is equal with God, they will die in their sins. The only way to know the Father is if Jesus wants to reveal him, and does reveal him.

Fact #4 - The Holy Spirit is God

The Holy Spirit is referred to as the Spirit of the Father, the Spirit of God, the Spirit of Christ, all throughout the Scriptures. That makes him equal with the Father, with Jesus, with God.

Another "of the same" Comforter

> **And I will pray the Father, and he shall give you another Comforter, that he may abide with you for ever; [Even] the Spirit of truth; whom the world cannot receive, because it seeth him not, neither knoweth him: but ye know him; for he dwelleth with you, and shall be in you. I will not leave you comfortless: I will come to you. ... Jesus answered and said unto him, If a man love me, he will keep my words: and my Father will love him, and we will come unto him, and make our abode with him. (John 14:16-18, 23)**

There are a couple of things brought out by this passage. Jesus, when he's referring to the Holy Spirit, calls him a comforter, and he said, "The Father will send another comforter to you." A question came up at the Council of Nicaea, over the letter i, or iota in Greek, believe it or not. The debate was over whether Jesus was the same substance as the Father or a similar substance of the Father. And the difference between those two words was the letter iota. Now, the cults are always claiming the Council of Nicaea was where the church went wrong and Arius was right.

I find this passage interesting in light of this because in Greek there are two different words translated into English as another. The difference between these words is between saying, "Can you get me a pencil?" and "Can you get me another writing device?" One is asking for the same thing as they have. That is the difference between those two words. Allos in Greek means the same kind. Heteros means a different kind. They are both "another," but one is another of the same kind, and the other is the another of a different kind. When Jesus refers to the Spirit, Jesus said the Father would send another comforter of the same kind. Jesus is answering the question at the Council of Nicaea. The Father, Son and Holy Spirit are all of the same substance.

Homo-ousious is the word describing this in reference to the language of the Council of Nicaea, as opposed to homoi-ousious or hetero-ousious.

The other thing brought out by this passage is in reference to the indwelling of the believer. Who is it that indwells us? Throughout this discourse and even the verses we are covering in this passage, we see Jesus said the Spirit will come in you. This is what we classically think of as the indwelling of the Spirit. But that's not where it stops. Jesus said he would make his home in us, and then he said the Father will come and make his abode in us. The Father, Son and Holy Spirit all indwell the believer. The entire Trinity, the Godhead, dwells in us. That is an amazing reality, which also shows the omnipresence of God. God can simultaneously be in heaven, indwelling every believer on the face of the earth, indwelling the praises of his people, and manifesting himself in various miraculous forms all over the earth, at the same time.

Blasphemy of the Holy Spirit will not be Forgiven

> **Wherefore I say unto you, All manner of sin and blasphemy shall be forgiven unto men: but the blasphemy [against] the [Holy] Ghost shall not be forgiven unto men. And whosoever speaketh a word against the Son of man, it shall be forgiven him: but whosoever speaketh against the Holy Ghost, it shall not be forgiven him, neither in this world, neither in the [world] to come. (Matthew 12:31-32)**

People blaspheme against God, people blaspheme against the Son, and Jesus said they could be forgiven for that. But blasphemy against the Holy Ghost cannot be forgiven. That tells me the Holy Ghost is equal with God.

The Holy Spirit is a Person

As I was going through the Upper Room Discourse, another thing I wanted to point out is the Holy Spirit is a person. As Jesus was talking about the Holy Spirit, and this is probably the most concrete teaching we have on the Holy Spirit from the mouth of Jesus, here's what we find:

1. "He," not "it" language is used (John 14:16)
2. Comforts (John 14:16)

3. Dwells in believers (John 14:16)
4. Teaches (John 14:26)
5. Brings things to remembrance (John 14:26)
6. Testifies of Jesus (John 15:26)
7. Guides you into all truth (John 16:13)
8. Glorifies Jesus (John 16:14)

Greek has not only masculine and feminine but also neuter. So if the Holy Spirit were truly a non-personable force, then Jesus would have spoken of the Holy Spirit in the neuter, not in the masculine.

The Virgin Birth

He shall be great, and shall be called the Son of the Highest: and the Lord God shall give unto him the throne of his father David: ... And the angel answered and said unto her, The Holy Ghost shall come upon thee, and the power of the Highest shall overshadow thee: therefore also that holy thing which shall be born of thee shall be called the Son of God. (Luke 1:32, 35)

Jesus is conceived of the Holy Ghost, but he is called the Son of God, the Son of the Highest. You have an equating of God with the Holy Ghost. The title Son of God also has the connotation of being equated with God, which we will see in other places in the gospels.

Fact #5 - The Father is not the Son; The Son is not the Holy Spirit; The Holy Spirit is not the Father

Jesus is God and was with God

In the beginning was the Word, and the Word was with God, and the Word was God. (John 1:1)

The New World Translation says Jesus was "a God," but this violates the rules of Greek Grammar. The rule here is referred to as Granville Sharp's Rule.[421] The Greek is worded "and God was the Word." There is no getting around this. John is going out of his way to teach us Jesus is God, yet also "with" God at the same time. There is only one way to reconcile this, the Trinity. The Jehovah's Witnesses and the LDS end up with polytheism in their interpretation of these verses.

William Lane Craig also points out New Testament writers were trying hard not to say Jesus was theos in Greek because they didn't want to confuse people into thinking they were saying Jesus is the Father.[422] John 1:1 and a few other verses are the exceptions. Usually, they referred to Jesus as kurios in Greek, which still pointed to YHWH. By doing this, they were stating Jesus is equal with YHWH, yet he is distinct from YHWH. They also do this by equating Jesus with creation, redemption, and other attributes, names, titles, and actions ascribed solely to God in the Old Testament.

Jesus Breathed the Holy Spirit

And when he had said this, he breathed on [them], and saith unto them, Receive ye the Holy Ghost: (John 20:22)

This is regarding modalism. If Jesus is the Father, who is the Holy Spirit, and they change modes, then how, while Jesus was still present, could he breathe on the apostles and have them receive the Holy Spirit?

The Baptism of Jesus

And Jesus, when he was baptized, went up straightway out of the water: and, lo, the heavens were opened unto him, and he saw the Spirit of God descending like a dove, and lighting upon him: And lo a voice from heaven, saying, This is my beloved Son, in whom I am well pleased. (Mathew 3:16-17)

---

[421] Granville Sharp's Rule http://www.theopedia.com/granville-sharps-rule

[422] Craig, William Lane, Doctrine of God: Trinity (Part 3) http://www.reasonablefaith.org/defenders-3-podcast/transcript/doctrine-of-god-trinity-part-3

> **Now when all the people were baptized, it came to pass, Jesus also being baptized, and praying, the heaven was opened, And the Holy Ghost descended in a bodily shape like a dove upon him, and a voice came from heaven, which said, Thou art my beloved Son; in thee I am well pleased. (Luke 3:21-22)**

The Trinity was present at the baptism of Jesus. The Son is physically present, being baptized. The Holy Spirit is coming down in the form of a dove. The voice of the Father comes from heaven saying, "This is my beloved Son. In him, I am well pleased."

This verse shatters modalism, teaching the Father became the Son, who became the Holy Spirit. Each member is present here simultaneously and is represented as unique in their person yet all one as God and equal as God.

The Father is in Jesus, and Jesus is in the Father

> **If I do not the works of my Father, believe me not. But if I do, though ye believe not me, believe the works: that ye may know, and believe, that the Father [is] in me, and I in him. (John 10:37-38)**

> **If ye had known me, ye should have known my Father also: and from henceforth ye know him, and have seen him. Philip saith unto him, Lord, shew us the Father, and it sufficeth us. Jesus saith unto him, Have I been so long time with you, and yet hast thou not known me, Philip? he that hath seen me hath seen the Father; and how sayest thou [then], Shew us the Father? Believest thou not that I am in the Father, and the Father in me? the words that I speak unto you I speak not of myself: but the Father that dwelleth in me, he doeth the works. Believe me that I [am] in the Father, and the Father in me: or else believe me for the very works' sake. (John 14:7-11)**

I want to clarify these passages are not teaching modalism. This is not teaching the Son is the Father, or the Father is the Son. This passage goes on to show the Father is distinct from Jesus, but inseparable. Jesus could say on the one hand if they have seen him, they have seen the Father. If they have seen his works, they have seen the Father's works. But then he turns around and says the Father dwells in him and he dwells in the Father. There are two distinct personages inseparable in their substance, in their co-eternality, in their attributes, and everything about them. Jesus was claiming absolute equality with the Father.

The Spirit Couldn't Come Until Jesus Left

> **Nevertheless I tell you the truth; It is expedient for you that I go away: for if I go not away, the Comforter will not come unto you; but if I depart, I will send him unto you. (John 16:7)**

First of all, who sent the Holy Spirit, the Father or the Son? In other places, Jesus said the Holy Spirit is with you, and he will be in you.[423] What Jesus is talking about when he talks about sending the comforter is the fact the dynamic of New Testament believers is different than Old Testament believers when it comes to the Holy Spirit. In the Old Testament, the Holy Spirit would come upon a person for a particular moment, task, or role. Then, when that particular moment, task or role was done, the Holy Spirit would be removed from that person. In the New Testament, the Holy Spirit, in fact, the entire Trinity, indwells believers, and so, when Jesus is referring to the Comforter coming, he said he couldn't come until he departs. Why? Because the New Testament covenant was based on the shedding of the blood of Jesus for our sins, and that had not happened yet. So Jesus was saying, in sequence, he needed to be arrested, beaten, stand trial, die for our sins, rise again from the dead, and then ascend to his Father. So, after he had ascended to his Father is when he said, "Wait in Jerusalem until the Holy Spirit comes, and he will indwell you," the New Testament concept of the church.[424] So that is what Jesus was saying. He wasn't saying when he goes away he could then manifest himself as the Holy Spirit.

---

[423] John 14:17
[424] Acts 1:4

Fact #6 - Jesus Became Fully Human

Is Jesus an Angel?

A couple of the groups discussed in this book teach Jesus is Michael the Archangel. Seventh Day Adventists still teach the Trinity, and Jesus is eternal, but Michael was a title given to Jesus in the Old Testament. Jehovah's Witnesses teach Jesus was Michael the archangel, became Jesus during his life on this earth, and went back to being Michael the Archangel afterward.

> **When the Son of man shall come in his glory, and all the holy angels with him, then shall he sit upon the throne of his glory: (Matthew 25:31)**

> **Thinkest thou that I cannot now pray to my Father, and he shall presently give me more than twelve legions of angels?; (Matthew 26:53)**

Jesus separated himself from angels. He didn't say he would come as an angel and the angels are also going to come as angels. He didn't equate himself with angels. He equated himself with God, and he would come with angels. And the Father could send angels to his rescue.

Is Jesus Inferior to the Father?

Many of the groups discussed in this book have claimed, if they teach the Trinity, there is a hierarchy within the Trinity, or they teach Jesus was a created being. He was greater than the angels, greater than the humans, but less than the Father, and the Holy Spirit is also less than the Father.

Many of these groups emphasize Jesus is inferior to God, being not of the same substance as God. God created him. He's not equal with God. That he's a spirit child of God, etc… One of the ways they want to prove this is by pointing to verses where Jesus said he is inferior to God. Here's how one can discuss those verses.

> **I can of mine own self do nothing: as I hear, I judge: and my judgment is just; because I seek not mine own will, but the will of the Father which hath sent me. (John 5:30)**

> **Ye have heard how I said unto you, I go away, and come [again]**
> **unto you. If ye loved me, ye would rejoice, because I said, I go**
> **unto the Father: for my Father is greater than I. (John 14:28)**

Was Jesus saying he was not able to do anything? Here's the deal. Jesus is God, but he was also a man. When he came in the flesh, he had to stand fully in our shoes. He had to be fully one of us. He had to be our Kinsman-Redeemer who could truly take our place on that cross and pay for our sins. So, in the flesh, as a human, as he said of us, and our reality, he said, "Of myself, I can do nothing." So Jesus was identifying with us in his humanity. Everything he did he did by the will of God through the power of the Holy Spirit, the same exact way Christians can live by the indwelling of the Holy Spirit. And he did it perfectly, meaning he was sinless. This fact, in and of itself, proves he is God.[425]

When Jesus said statements like these, we are encountering the dual nature of Jesus. He was truly God, but he was also truly man. We need to realize Jesus said these statements when he was here on this earth in our place as one of us. He never said a statement like this in his pre-existent state, or after he had gone back to be with the Father and ascended to glory again. He said in his humanity the Father is greater than he was.

Let's address this idea of a hierarchy within the Trinity. There does seem to be different roles the Father, Son and Holy Spirit play in the plan of salvation, and the way it works out. The Holy Spirit always testifies of Jesus,[426] and Jesus is always pointing to the Father. They always have a co-supportive dynamic. Paul would say in 1 Corinthians 11 the husband is the head of the wife, and Christ is the head of the husband, and God is the head of Christ.[427] But, at the same time, that does not mean they are not equal. We have confused in our culture to be equals, or peers, of the same level and importance, that no system of order or hierarchy can exist. We can see by looking at the world at family structures and organizational structures that are not possible. There has to be order. Paul said in 1 Corinthians 14 God is not a God

---

[425] 1 John 1:5

[426] John 15:26

[427] 1 Corinthians 11:3

of disorder, but of order.[428] God has an order of things, and the fact Christ played a role submitting himself to the Father does not mean he is not God.[429]

> **And about the ninth hour Jesus cried with a loud voice, saying, Eli, Eli, lama sabachthani? that is to say, My God, my God, why hast thou forsaken me? (Matthew 27:46; Mark 15:34)**

> **Jesus saith unto her, Touch me not; for I am not yet ascended to my Father: but go to my brethren, and say unto them, I ascend unto my Father, and your Father; and [to] my God, and your God. (John 20:17)**

Jesus referred to God as "my God." What is going on here? Why is Jesus not referring to God as his father, but also his God? Notice Jesus never refers to God as God until he's on the cross, and when he cries out "My God, my God, why hast thou forsaken me?" [430]What is going on is Jesus, for the first time in all of eternity, has been separated from his father. Why? Paul said he who knew no sin became sin so we might become the righteousness of God. [431]When Jesus died on the cross, he became every sin one can imagine. Every sin that would be committed that is to be committed. Jesus became that sin. The wrath of God was poured out on Jesus for our sin. And that is called a propitiation, a sacrifice that appeases the wrath of a God.[432] And that's what was going on in the passages we are discussing. Sin was judged and punished by God the Father on Jesus on that cross. And because Jesus was sinless himself, he canceled out the punishment because death could not hold him,[433] but he bore the punishment for our sins. But at that moment, the New Testament makes it clear, and even LDS Scriptures make this clear, God cannot look on sin in the least degree of allowance. [434]When Jesus became sin, God had to turn his back on his Son. It was the first moment in all of eternity when the Trinity was separated, at least in a sense.

---

[428] 1 Corinthians 14:33

[429] Philippians 2:5-7

[430] Psalm 22:1

[431] 2 Corinthians 5:21

[432] Romans 3:25

[433] Psalm 16:10

[434] Doctrine & Covenants 1:31

Jesus didn't cease to be God. The Father didn't cease to be God. The Trinity didn't cease to exist. But there was a separation at that moment that forever changed the relationship between the Father and Jesus.

It's interesting to note from the time of the cross forward, Jesus referred to God as his father sometimes, but he also said, "my God."[435] Even in the book of Revelation when he's writing the letters to the seven churches, he uses that terminology again. Something changed in the relationship between Jesus and God at the cross, and it was a price Jesus chose to bear on our behalf. It almost brings me to tears to realize how much it cost him to bear the weight of our sins and to pay the price for our sins. To say his blood, his sacrifice, was not sufficient is complete and utter blasphemy.

Was There a Time When He Was Not?

This is a question from a catchphrase of the past. At the Council of Nicaea, the followers of Arius used the catchphrase, speaking of Jesus, "there was a time when he was not," meaning they taught Jesus was the first creation of God through whom God created everything else, but Jesus is not equal with God.[436]

The same was in the beginning with God. (John 1:2)

Jesus was there in the beginning, like in the Micah reference quoted in Matthew's gospel.[437]

All things were made by him; and without him was not any thing made that was made. (John 1:3)

The Jehovah's Witnesses teach Jesus was the first creation of God. So do the LDS. Christian Science teaches the material world is an illusion not created by God, but by an intermediary. Reminiscent of Gnosticism that taught the physical world is evil and only spirit is good as we discussed in the Ancient Heresy, American Church History and the Cults section of this book. John clarified Jesus made all things. Paul clarified Jesus created all spiritual things and physical things.

---

[435] Revelation 3:12

[436] Arius https://en.wikiquote.org/wiki/Arius

[437] Micah 5:2

No man hath seen God at any time; the only begotten Son, which is in the bosom of the Father, he hath declared [him]. (John 1:18)

Joseph Smith claimed he saw God. He saw both the Father and Jesus Christ. There is no sign in that First Vision account said anything about him feeling sorrow or overwhelmed over his sin in the presence of God, which is what Isaiah, Ezekiel, Paul, John and others felt in every account we find in the Bible when they had a vision of God or were caught up into his presence before the throne of God. They say, "I am a dead man. I am a man of unclean lips.[438] I am not worthy." Also, in the Old Testament, when there were visions of God in the Old Testament, it is called a theophany, and it's clear they see Jesus because God the Father is always referred to as spirit, invisible, unseen, etc.[439]

Let's switch gears a moment on this verse. The Jehovah's Witnesses pick up on this word begotten in reference to Jesus to prove he is a created being and not equal with the Father. The Greek word is μονογενής,[440] and it means the unique, or one and only.[441] It doesn't have to mean begotten as in birthed.

---

[438] Isaiah 6:5

[439] Colossians 1:15; 1 Timothy 1:17

[440] μονογενής Strong's Greek Lexicon www.blueletterbible.org//lang/lexicon/lexicon.cfm?Strongs=G3439&t=KJV

[441] Jesus as Monogenes http://thetrinitydoctrine.com/articles/jesus-as-monogenes/

TACTIC #2

Using the Groups Own Scriptures and Writings to Teach Christian Doctrine

CHAPTER 29

"Have You Prayed About the Book of Mormon?"

What do you say when you're LDS friend challenges you and says, "Have you ever read and prayed about whether or not the Book of Mormon is true?"

This is what is commonly known as the "Moroni Challenge" in the Book of Mormon:

> Behold, I would exhort you that when ye shall read these things, if it be wisdom in God that ye should read them, that ye would remember how merciful the Lord hath been unto the children of men, from the creation of Adam even down until the time that ye shall receive these things, and ponder it in your hearts. And when ye shall receive these things, I would exhort you that ye would ask God, the Eternal Father, in the name of Christ, if these things are not true; and if ye shall ask with a sincere heart, with real intent, having faith in Christ, he will manifest the truth of it unto you, by the power of the Holy Ghost. And by the power of the Holy Ghost ye may know the truth of all things. (Moroni 10:3-5)

The Mormon missionary will challenge you to read the Book of Mormon and pray about it. If it's true, they promise God will manifest truth by passing through you.

You will feel a burning in your bosom, and that will tell you the church is true and you should join it.

As a Christian, we want to have the missionaries come to our door, and we want to build a relationship with our LDS friend, but when it comes down to it, we don't want to take this test. And it's not necessarily because we know the Book of Mormon is true. It's because we know it is not. We know nothing is going to happen, and if it does, we know it is not from a godly source if the Book of Mormon contradicts what God has already revealed in the Bible. And we know this because God does not use feelings to testify to truth.

Feelings in Scripture are often spoken of as contrary to truth.[442] Feelings and emotions are signals to tell us whether something is right or wrong, but more in a safety sense, and to let us know something is wrong. When one feels fear or anger, it's a symptom something is not right. Feelings are good things because they are warning signs we need to deal with inappropriate ways. But we are always told to bring our emotions into captivity to God's thoughts and God's Word.[443]

When I was in high school, when I was friends with Steve, mentioned in the introduction, I had another friend named Kelli. She gave me a Book of Mormon with a nice note to me about how I must have been a valiant spirit in the pre-existence because she saw all these great things in me.

I took the Book of Mormon home, and I started reading it. I read the Introduction and 1 Nephi. I read the Moroni challenge. I read some of the parts she had highlighted for me. I wanted to know if it was true. I remember putting the book down, praying, and asking God, "If this is true, would you please show me."

What happened was a miracle, and I'm not promising this will happen to everyone, but what God said to me was, "What are you doing with this book? You haven't read the Bible yet." It was at that moment I put the Book of Mormon down, picked up the Bible, and started devouring it. And I started seeing God's word change my life, and testify to its truthfulness in ways incomprehensible to me. I know beyond the shadow of a doubt the Bible is the Word of God, and it's not because of anything I've ever felt. And I know the Book of Mormon is not the Word of God, and it's not because of anything I've felt or not felt. It's because of what is true and what is not true.

---

[442] Proverbs 28:26

[443] Ephesians 4:26

Here's the thing most Christians don't realize about the Book of Mormon. The Book of Mormon is more Christian than it is Mormon. What I mean is the Book of Mormon more reflects 19th century American Christianity than it does current LDS doctrine and teaching. Mark Twain[444] and Alexander Campbell[445] and other contemporaries of Joseph Smith commented on the Book of Mormon when it first came out. By the way, the original 1830 Book of Mormon said, "Author and Proprietor Joseph Smith."[446] He owned the copyright, and he intended to make money from that.

The contemporaries said Joseph Smith decided to answer all of the controversies of the 19th century in the Book of Mormon. They said he knew his world well, but it was too bad he doesn't know anything about the ancient American world or ancient Jewish culture. They said this because he makes some horrible errors and oversights in the Book of Mormon.

We will not discuss the following topics. However, I have given sources for further study in the footnotes.

1. The complete lack of archaeological support for the Book of Mormon[447]
2. The historical anachronisms in the Book of Mormon[448]
3. Racism in the Book of Mormon[449]
4. The translation process of the Book of Mormon[450]
5. Stolen passages from the King James Version and other sources contemporary to Joseph Smith[451]

---

[444] Twain, Mark, Mark Twain on the Book of Mormon - 1861 http://www.truthandgrace.com/twainbom.htm

[445] Campbell, Alexander, An analysis of the book of Mormon with an examination of its internal and external evidences, and a refutation of its pretenses to divine authority, Millennial Harbinger February 7th, 1831

[446] Joseph Smith, Junior – Author & Proprietor, The Wayne Sentinel – June 26, 1829

[447] Statement Regarding the Book of Mormon http://www.utlm.org/onlineresources/smithsonianletter2.htm

[448] Lindbloom, Sharon, The Indefensible Book of Mormon http://blog.mrm.org/2015/08/the-indefensible-book-of-mormon/

[449] Curse of Cain? Racism in the Mormon Church Part One http://www.utlm.org/onlinebooks/curseofcain part1.htm

[450] Johnson, Eric, Book of Mormon Translation http://www.mrm.org/book-of-mormon-translation- essay

[451] Baker, Lee, The Proof of Plagiarism in the Book of Mormon http://leebaker.4mormon.org/the-proof-of-plagiarism-in-the-book-of-mormon/

6. What the Bible teaches about trusting the heart[452]

What we are going to discuss is what you should do when your Mormon friend asks you to read and pray about the Book of Mormon.

I have no problems with Christians reading the Book of Mormon. I do have a problem with them praying about it. It's not because God is going to testify to its truthfulness. Anytime one is dealing with anything having its origins in the occult, it's dangerous to open doors. And praying and asking God about something he has told us not to have anything to do with, or one can show otherwise is not from him, is not a good idea. It's opening doors that need to stay shut.

I propose an alternative way of dealing with this otherwise awkward scenario. First of all, turn the tables on the LDS person, and ask them if they have a testimony of the Book of Mormon. They will probably say yes, at which point we can ask them to share it with us. Usually, a testimony of the Book of Mormon is something like: "I know the Book of Mormon is true. I know Joseph Smith is a true prophet. I know Thomas Monson is the current living prophet. I know the church is true. I know God restored his church through Joseph Smith."

Ask them to follow-up and share the story behind that testimony. Ask them questions like how old they were and how they gained that testimony. They are going to love sharing their story. They might get emotional when they share their story. But let them get as emotional as they want because the whole thing is going to play into your favor in the end.

Then, ask them to clarify they believe the Book of Mormon came from God. They will probably say yes. Further clarifying questions that can be asked are:

1. Do they believe the Book of Mormon is true?
2. Do they believe everything the Book of Mormon teaches?
3. Is there anything in the Book of Mormon they don't believe?

They will probably say no, but make sure. They might get frustrated because of the seeming repetition of the questions, but these questions are creating a foundation to build from.

Now what we are going to do is take them to passages in the Book of Mormon that teach orthodox Christian doctrine. These will all be doctrines the LDS church

---

[452] Jeremiah 17:9

currently does not teach, and in some cases, would label as false doctrine. In doing so, we are going to put our LDS friend in a mental conflict between their belief the church is true and their belief the Book of Mormon is true, forcing them to see the contradictions between what the two sources teach, and forcing them to choose. But they will know they can't choose one without losing the other. This conflict within them, otherwise known as cognitive dissonance, is what we want to create. Questions for which they have no answer. A desire to search for the answers to those questions. A heart hungry for the truth.

I want to clarify when I say the Book of Mormon is more like 19th century Christianity than current LDS doctrine. I am not saying the Book of Mormon is Scripture, that it came from God or anything like that. I am simply saying we can use it to help them to come to the biblical truth about God, salvation, Jesus, and other core doctrines related to the gospel.

We need to be prepared to be frustrated any time we have a discussion about the Scriptures with an LDS person. They will always find a way to explain the text that avoids the natural, common sense way of interpreting the text, and either agrees with official LDS interpretation of that verse or find a way for the text not to say what it plainly says.

In light of this, my advice is to ask questions, listen, ask clarifying questions, but don't press too hard. Rather than the different way of interpreting the text coming from you, there are many times when the verse can be typed into www.lds.org and a quote from an apostle or prophet or LDS commentary that agrees with the point needing to be made. In the past, I have found it helpful to ask the same question to other LDS mutual friends. This is a way of asking clarifying questions. But don't press too hard or become confrontational because they will immediately go into a thought killing technique and believe there is a "contentious spirit," which their Scriptures teach is of the devil.[453] If this happens, the LDS person will not be as willing to continue the conversation.

Our goal is to be with them in dialogue for the long haul. We may not win the battle, but Lord willing, we want to win the war. So be patient, kind, considerate and move on to the next topic when needed. If there are enough inconsistencies they have to find a way to explain away, eventually, the shelf will pile up and fall down.

---

[453] 3 Nephi 11:29-30

CHAPTER 30

Passages Related to the Nature of God

Eternality

The LDS church teaches God has not always been God. God was in fact once a man like we are on another planet, and he had a heavenly Father he submitted to. God established a church and sent a Savior. And he obeyed Mormon doctrine, kept his covenants, repented of all his sins and was able to become a God over this world.

So God hasn't always been God. The Mormon God also has a body of flesh and bones. He is not the only God who has ever been. So what does the Book of Mormon teach about God? I should say the Book of Mormon does not teach an accurate view of God. At times it teaches modalism, and at other times it teaches Trinitarianism. But it does not teach God has a body of flesh and bones.

> **For I know that God is not a partial God, neither a changeable being; but he is unchangeable from all eternity to all eternity. (Moroni 8:18)**

If you are an LDS, Moroni is the man. He is the last Nephite standing. He buried the golden plates. He showed up and told Joseph Smith where the golden plates were buried. Moroni is the golden angel with a trumpet on top of most LDS temples. Should Mormons listen to Moroni? Absolutely!

The Mormons have a different concept of eternity. They teach God is eternal in that he will never cease to be God moving forward. They also teach all people are eternal because we existed as intelligences who became spirit children, received our bodies and can go on to exaltation. This is their concept of eternal.

This passage has so many truths. God is not partial. He is not changeable. He has existed from all eternity to all eternity. From a Christian perspective, as far back as one can go, and as forward as one can go, God would always have existed and has always been God. This verse is a huge theological nightmare for the LDS person because they do not teach this. They teach God was once a man, and in fact, Joseph Smith invented that notion in 1844 with something called the King Follet Discourse.[454] It was one of his last sermons before he died. And in that sermon, he said, and with attention to the words in Moroni 8:18. Joseph Smith said, "We have imagined and supposed that God was God from all eternity. I will refute that idea, and take away the veil, so that you may see…"

Think about that Joseph. Where did you imagine and suppose we imagined and supposed this? It's from the Book of Mormon. The same one you dug out of the ground, given by an angel named Moroni. The same Moroni who wrote God is unchangeable from all eternity to all eternity.

> **For behold, God knowing all things, being from everlasting to everlasting… (Moroni 7:22)**
>
> **For behold, the time cometh, and is not far distant, that with power, the Lord omnipotent who reigneth, who was, and is from all eternity to all eternity… (Mosiah 3:5)**
>
> **And he shall be called Jesus Christ, the Son of God, the Father of heaven and earth, the creator of all things from the beginning; and his mother shall be called Mary. (Mosiah 3:8)**

---

[454] Becoming Like God https://www.lds.org/topics/becoming-like-god?lang=eng&old=true

Immutability

God does not change in His being or promises. He is pure actuality with no potentiality. He is perfect and consistent. God is all He is and does not change.

> **By these things we know that there is a God in heaven who is infinite and eternal, from everlasting to everlasting the same unchangeable God, the framer of heaven and earth, and all things which are in them. (Doctrine & Covenants 20:17)**

> **For I know that God is not a partial God, neither a changeable being; but He is unchangeable from all eternity to all eternity. (Moroni 8:18)**

> **For do we not read that God is the same yesterday, today and forever, and in him there is no variableness neither shadow of changing? And now if ye have imagined up unto yourselves a god who doth vary, and in whom there is shadow of changing, then have ye imagined up unto yourselves a god who in not a God of miracles. (Mormon 9:9-10)**

Not A Man

> **And because he said unto them that Christ was the God, the Father of all things, and said that he should take upon him the image of man, and it should be the image after which man was created in the beginning; or in other words, he said that man was created after the image of God, and that God should come down among the children of men, and take upon him flesh and blood, and go forth upon the face of the earth. (Mosiah 7:27)**

Joseph Smith taught in Doctrine & Covenants God has a body of flesh and bones as tangible as man's body.[455] This doctrine was placed into his story of the First Vision

---

[455] Doctrine & Covenants 130:22

with God and Jesus both appearing to him in bodies of flesh and bones.[456] That became the doctrine of God, which is essential, because now if we're going to become like God, we come to this earth, to get bodies, so we can become exalted gods who have physical bodies.

First of all, this is close. This is not quite as modalistic as the other verses. What it is saying is God himself is going to come down to this earth and become a man. Now who is it that did this? Jesus. And it says Christ is God. He is the father of all things. "He shall be called Everlasting Father."[457] God has to take on the image of man. The image we were created with in the beginning when God said, "Let us create man in our image and our likeness."[458] Your LDS friend has been taught the image was physical, our body of flesh and bones with blood is the image of God.[459] We're different than the animals than the plants, and all other things because we have the image of God and those things don't.

If one reads that theology into this passage, they have a huge problem because this passage says God had to take on a physical body. If God already had a physical body, how can he take on a physical body? And if the image of God was physical, then God becoming human and taking on the image of God means God doesn't have something intrinsic within LDS thinking as part of the image of God.

Omnipresence

God transcends space and has no spectral limitations. He is capable of being present with his whole being at every point.

> **By these things we know that there is a God in heaven who is infinite and eternal, from everlasting to everlasting the same unchangeable God, the framer of heaven and earth, and all things which are in them. (Doctrine & Covenants 20:17)**

---

[456] Groat, Joel B., Joseph Smith's Changing First Vision Accounts http://mit.irr.org/joseph- smiths-changing-first-vision-accounts

[457] Isaiah 9:6

[458] Genesis 1:26-27

[459] All Human Beings Are Created in the Image of God https://www.lds.org/ensign/2008/07/all-human-beings-are-created-in-the-image-of-god?lang=eng

Because God is omnipresent within and without His creation, He can present Himself in multiple places at the same time.

God is one essence, He is spirit. He presents Himself to us as three persons, Father, Son and Holy Spirit, That is His way of communicating with us. He is one 'what' (spirit, essence) and three persons(who's).

> **Which Father, Son, and Holy Ghost are one God, infinite and eternal, without end. Amen. (Doctrine & Covenants 20:28)**

Self-Existence

God is a necessary being. He has the ground of His existence within himself. He is uncaused. An uncreated Creator is a mystery, but not an absurd notion.

> **Believest thou that this Great Spirit, who is God, created all things which are in heaven and in the earth? And he said: Yea, I believe that he created all things… (Alma 18:28-29)**

Tri-Unity

What the LDS church teaches is there are three gods we have to do with.[460] There is God the Father, or Elohim. His firstborn spirit child, who is Jesus, or in the Old Testament known as Yahweh. Third is the Holy Ghost, who is an enigma because he still doesn't have a body, and yet he somehow became a God. Three gods, but the LDS are only supposed to direct their worship toward Heavenly Father as our one God.

> **And now, behold, my beloved brethren, this is the way; and there is none other way nor name given under heaven whereby man can be saved in the kingdom of God. And now, behold, this is the doctrine of Christ, and the only and true doctrine of the Father, and of the Son, and of the Holy Ghost, which is one God, without end. Amen. (2 Nephi 31:21)**

---

[460] Godhead https://www.lds.org/topics/godhead?lang=eng&old=true

This verse is a problem for the LDS person. It's a problem simply because other verses talk about God becoming the Son, who becomes the Holy Ghost and are modalistic.[461] But this, and other verses are Trinitarian. And what the LDS person will say is, "One God in purpose," but it doesn't say one in purpose. It says, "Which is one God." One cannot read it as one in purpose. And it says, "This is the doctrine of Christ, the only true doctrine of the Father, Son and Holy Ghost."

> **Which Father, Son, and Holy Ghost are one God, infinite and eternal, without end. Amen. (Doctrine & Covenants 20:28)**

> **And Zeezrom said unto him: Thou sayest there is a true and living God? And Amulek said Yea, there is a true and living God. Now Zeezrom said: Is there more than one God? And he answered No. (Alma 11:26-29)**

> **Now Zeezrom saith again unto him: Is the Son of God the very Eternal Father? And Amulek said unto him: Yea, he is the very Eternal Father of heaven and earth, and all things which in them are; he is the beginning and the end, the first and the last. (Alma 11:38-39)**

> **But every thing shall be restored to its perfect frame, as it is now, or in the body, and shall be brought and arraigned before the bar of Christ the Son, and God the Father, and the Holy Spirit, which is one Eternal God, to be judged... (Alma 11:44)**

> **And thus will the Father bear record of me, and the Holy Ghost will bear record unto him of the Father and me; for the Father and I and the Holy Ghost are one. (3 Nephi 11:36)**

> **Thus saith the Lord; for I am God, and have sent mine Only Begotten Son into the world, and have decreed that he that receiveth him shall be saved, and he that receiveth him not shall**

---

[461] Mosiah 15:2-4

be damned ... Behold, I am Jesus Christ, and I come quickly. Even so, Amen. (Doctrine & Covenants 49:5,28)

And now Abinadi said unto them: I would that ye should understand that God himself shall come down among the children of men, and shall redeem his people. And because he dwelleth in flesh he shall be called the Son of God, and having subjected the flesh to the will of the Father, being the Father and the Son. The Father, because he was conceived by the power of God; and the Son, because of the flesh; thus becoming the Father and Son. And they are one God, yea the very Eternal Father of heaven and earth. And thus the flesh becoming subject to the Spirit, or the Son to the Father, being one God, suffereth temptation, and yieldeth not to the temptation, but suffereth himself to be mocked and scourged, and cast out, and disowned by his people. (Mosiah 15:1-5)

And as I spake concerning the convincing of the Jews, Jesus is the very Christ, it must needs be that the Gentiles be convinced also Jesus is the Christ, the Eternal God. (3 Nephi 26:12)

Arise and come forth unto me, that ye may thrust your hands into my side, and also that ye may feel the prints of the nails in my hands and in my feet, that ye may know that I am the God of Israel, and the God of the whole earth, and have been slain for the sins of the world ... Hosanna! Blessed be the name of the Most High God! And they did fall down at the feet of Jesus and did worship him ... Having authority given to me of Jesus Christ, I baptize you in the name of the Father, and of the Son, and of the Holy Spirit, Amen ···· and after this manner shall ye baptize in my name; for behold verily I say unto you that the Father, and the Son, and the Holy Spirit are one; and I am in the Father, and the Father in me, and the Father and I are one. (3 Nephi 11:14,17,25,27)

And also that ye might know of the coming of Jesus Christ, the Son of God, the Father of heaven and earth, the Creator of all things from the beginning ; and that ye might know of the signs of his coming, to the intent that you might believe on his name. (Helaman 14:12)

And he hath brought to pass the redemption of the world. Whereby he that is found guiltless before him at the judgment day hath it given unto him to dwell in the presence of God in his kingdom, to sing ceaseless praises with the choirs above, unto the Father, and unto the Son, and unto the Holy Ghost, which are one God, in the state of happiness which hath no end. (Mormon 7:7)

CHAPTER 31

Passages Related to Salvation

No Repentance After Death

This truth is taught by the Book of Mormon. It's taught in the Bible. For those LDS that believe they are becoming better, working their way toward repentance and exaltation, not much is going to convince them. It's not our job to convince them. An argument is not going to convince them it's false because that is something they want. In many cases there are family members they have been sealed to, have passed away, and they are looking forward to meeting again. If they are wrong, then those family members were wrong, and they are going to hell. Many things are going through their minds.

But the LDS church does teach the Spirit World we go to after we die is split up between Paradise and Spirit Prison, and some missionaries go from Paradise to Spirit Prison and preach the gospel. On this earth, in LDS temples, LDS people are being baptized on behalf of dead relatives so they can have a chance to receive the gospel, move up into Paradise, and start their process of exaltation.

Here is the problem with that. The Book of Mormon doesn't teach it.

And now, as I said unto you before, as ye have had so many witnesses, therefore, I beseech of you that ye do not procrastinate the day of your repentance until the end; for after this day of life, which is given us to prepare for eternity, behold, if we do

not improve our time while in this life, then cometh the night of darkness wherein there can be no labor performed. Ye cannot say, when ye are brought to that awful crisis, that I will repent, that I will return to my God. Nay, ye cannot say this; for that same spirit which doth possess your bodies at the time that ye go out of this life, that same spirit will have power to possess your body in that eternal world. For behold, if ye have procrastinated the day of your repentance even until death, behold, ye have become subjected to the spirit of the devil, and he doth seal you his; therefore, the Spirit of the Lord hath withdrawn from you, and hath no place in you, and the devil hath all power over you; and this is the final state of the wicked. (Alma 34:33-35)

There's so much in this passage. It is such a powerful passage on so many different levels, but we mainly need to get them to see this passage teaches they only have this life to repent of and forsake their sins if they are hoping to reach the Celestial Kingdom and become a God. Tomorrow is not promised to any of us. They could die right now. Death is not something even remotely in our control. It's in God's control. And this passage says once this life is finished, the opportunity to progress and repent is over. They need to understand if there is a standard they need to get to, they need to get to it now.

They need to see the Book of Mormon doesn't teach what the LDS teaches. Ask them what it means the devil seals one his. If there is any group of people who talk about sealing, it's the LDS church. Ask them what that means. "You've been sealed to your family. What does it mean the devil seals somebody his? What do you have to do to according to this passage to avoid this?"

What Must I Do to Be Saved?

This is a core issue. This is a foundational issue. We're either saved by grace, or we're saved by works. Which one is it? What does the Book of Mormon teach?

Well, the Book of Mormon teaches both. In fact, it's such extremes that this is a great place to challenge them on. I do have friends and people in different ministries that focus specifically on this topic, and they call it the "Impossible Gospel."[462] They will take verses from the Book of Mormon and Mormon Scriptures to challenge people to see their sinfulness using the law to bring them to Christ. Once they realize their need for a Savior, and it's impossible to keep the law, then teach them the good news. And there is nothing wrong with that approach, but sometimes I have found when using this method it is tempting to try too hard to convince people they should believe the Mormon Scriptures teach something different than they currently interpret it to say. I say this because most Mormons I talk to don't fully believe what the passages below seem to teach.

Option A - Repent and forsake all of your sins

> **Yea, come unto Christ, and be perfected in him, and deny yourselves of all ungodliness; and if ye shall deny yourselves of all ungodliness, and love God with all your might, mind and strength, then is his grace sufficient for you, that by his grace ye may be perfect in Christ; and if by the grace of God ye are perfect in Christ, ye can in nowise deny the power of God. (Moroni 10:32)**

This verse uses confusing language, especially for Christians. We hear grace, and we understand grace to be an unmerited, undeserved, favor of God. It's a gift, a free gift. Grace cannot be earned, by definition.[463] But the word grace appears in this passage many times, yet there are conditions upon receiving grace.

> **And now, verily I say unto you, I, the Lord, will not lay any sin to your charge; go your ways and sin no more; but unto that soul who sinneth shall the former sins return, saith the Lord your God. (Doctrine & Covenants 82:7)**

There's a colleague of mine who used to work at Concerned Christians in Mesa, Arizona and was former LDS. He strove for this goal. Each time he took communion

---

[462] Shafovaloff, Aaron, The "Impossible Gospel" Presentation and Its Continued Relevance for Modern Mormonism http://www.mrm.org/impossible-gospel
[463] Romans 11:6

as an LDS, he felt cleansed by the blood of Christ and tried to see how long he could go, and he said sometimes he could go through the rest of the service without sinning again. But every time he sinned, he imagined this sack of sins God was delivering on his doorstep because of this verse. And he would have to start all over again.

Here are some other verses within Mormon Scriptures that teach the "Impossible Gospel:"

> **And the brother of Jared repented of the evil which he had done, and did call upon the name of the Lord for his brethren who were with him. And the Lord said unto him: I will forgive thee and thy brethren of their sins; but thou shalt not sin any more, for ye shall remember that my Spirit will not always strive with man; wherefore, if ye will sin until ye are fully ripe ye shall be cut off from the presence of the Lord. And these are my thoughts upon the land which I shall give you for your inheritance; for it shall be a land choice above all other lands. (Ether 2:15)**

> **"For we labor diligently to write, to persuade our children, and also our brethren, to believe in Christ, and to be reconciled to God; for we know that it is by grace that we are saved, after all we can do." (2 Nephi 25:23)**

> **"Have ye walked, keeping yourselves blameless before God? Could ye say, if ye were called to die at this time, within yourselves, that ye have been sufficiently humble? That your garments have been cleansed and made white through the blood of Christ, who will come to redeem his people from their sins? Behold, are ye stripped of pride? I say unto you, if ye are not ye are not prepared to meet God. Behold ye must prepare quickly; for the kingdom of heaven is soon at hand, and such an one hath not eternal life. Behold, I say, is there one among you who is not stripped of envy? I say unto you that such an one is not prepared; and I would that he should prepare quickly, for the hour is close at hand, and he knoweth not when the time shall come; for such an one is not found guiltless. And again I say unto you, is there one among you that doth make**

a mock of his brother, or that heapeth upon him persecutions? Wo unto such an one, for he is not prepared, and the time is at hand that he must repent or he cannot be saved!" (Alma 5:27-31)

"...for I know that the Lord giveth no commandments unto the children of men, save he shall prepare a way for them that they may accomplish the thing which he commandeth them." (1 Nephi 3:7)

"Keep my commandments continually, and a crown of righteousness thou shalt receive. And except thou do this, where I am you cannot come." (Doctrine & Covenants 25:15)

"...for the Lord cannot look upon sin with the least degree of allowance." (Alma 45:16)

"For I the Lord cannot look upon sin with the least degree of allowance; Nevertheless, he that repents and does the commandments of the Lord shall be forgiven." (Doctrine & Covenants 1:31-32)

"By this ye may know if a man repenteth of his sins—behold, he will confess them and forsake them." (Doctrine & Covenants 58:43)

"And I say unto you again that he cannot save them in their sins; for I cannot deny his word, and he hath said that no unclean thing can inherit the kingdom of heaven; therefore, how can ye be saved, except ye inherit the kingdom of heaven? Therefore, ye cannot be saved in your sins." (Alma 11:37)

So option A is repent and forsake all your sins. Here are the requirements for exaltation.[464] This comes from Gospel Principles, an LDS church manual used in their wards, modern-day, current, to teach LDS the principles of the gospel. The section

---

[464] Gospel Principles, Chapter 47: Exaltation, p. 275-280

heading this is under is "Requirements for Exaltation," with this list. I put this here because it is a helpful visual when challenging an LDS person with these Scriptures because they are going to use grace language over and over again to convince the Christian they believe what Christians believe. But they do not. With this list, ask the following questions:

1. "Do you believe you have to be baptized to be saved? For exaltation?"
2. "Do you have to be a member of the LDS church to be exalted?" They might tell you this is not required, but that's not what their church teaches.
3. "Do you believe you have to go through the temple to be exalted?"
4. "Do you believe you have to be sealed as a family unit in the temple to be exalted?"
5. "Do you believe we have to repent of our sins and forsake all ungodliness to be exalted?"

That question usually prompts a wide variety of answers. Some people realize that's impossible and others are caught in pride, and they will insist this is a requirement.

Equivalent questions can be asked for this entire list:

1. Be baptized
2. Become a member
3. Receive the Holy Ghost
4. Temple endowment
5. Temple marriage
6. Love and worship God
7. Love our neighbor
8. Complete repentance
9. Complete honesty
10. Word of wisdom
11. Baptize the dead
12. Keep the Sabbath
13. Sacrament meetings
14. Love family
15. Family and individual prayer
16. Honor parents
17. Evangelize
18. Study the scriptures

After completing the questions based on the list, ask the LDS person, "How is that by grace? How is that not of works? How is that a gift of God given to me, and not something I have to earn?"

Get them to think about that and challenge them.

Option B - Trust in Christ

And after they had been received unto baptism, and were wrought upon and cleansed by the power of the Holy Ghost, they were numbered among the people of the church of Christ; and their names were taken, that they might be remembered and nourished by the good word of God, to keep them in the right way, to keep them continually watchful unto prayer, relying alone upon the merits of Christ, who was the author and the finisher of their faith. (Moroni 6:4)

The language this verse uses is biblical, "relying upon the merits of Christ alone." "He is the author and finisher of your faith." Here is the thing. If one finds a Mormon who believes that, then they can praise God for that. That is an amazing thing, and what we may have met is somebody who is a born-again Mormon. And if that is the case, what we don't need to do is tell them they need to leave the church immediately. They say it takes an average of about five years from start to finish of the process from the initial seed of doubt to leave the Mormon church. The reason is there are real, substantial consequences for them doing so. There is a series of different things they have to get over. They are risking social things, family things, financial things possibly, standing in the community, friendships. They are also risking Outer Darkness because the Mormon church teaches them as they leave the church they are apostate, and they are going to outer darkness, and those are horrifying things to hold over somebody's head. But that is what the Mormon church does. It holds those things over people's heads. And there are many different factors, and the best thing we can do is to be there for that Mormon person and walk them through. If they're going to be forsaken by people who don't feel the same way as they do, then Christians need to be there for them and help them find another support system. If they are going to lose their family, they need family. If they're going to lose their friends, they need friends. If they're going to lose their job, Christians need to try their best to help them with that. There are real ramifications. That's another reason I say they might as well live in Afghanistan or Tibet because the culture in Utah is so steeped and concentrated in Mormonism, and the consequences are so real for them they might have a hard time leaving the church even after they have embraced Christ. But sooner or later, they need to trust God, like we trusted God in talking with them, that he will continue to work in them. One needs not fear they are going to be pulled back into the church and the doctrine. Once their eyes have been opened, they have been opened. Once their hearts have been changed, they've been changed. Once they are a new creation, they are a new creation. Christians need to trust God. He is sovereign and in control.

Christians need to be there for them and need to disciple them. Start getting into the word with them. Chances are, there are still many beliefs and ways of looking at the world that are still LDS in their mind. We need to walk through that with them. And eventually, a time is going to come when they realize they can't fulfill their callings, they can't share their testimony, they don't relate to other LDS people, and they will want to be around other people who are like them. And they will leave the church. But give it time. Don't pressure them.

CHAPTER 32

Passages Related to Origins of the Church of Jesus Christ of Latter-day Saints

Did the Church Need to be Restored?

J oseph Smith claimed all the churches were an abomination. That God the Father told him so. And that's why the church needed to be restored. We're not talking about reformed as in what Martin Luther and the others did when the church was going a little wacky in some of the things it was teaching. By all means, it was heresy, but the true church remained. There were true believers on the earth. God's true word remained on the earth, and it did not need to be restored. It simply needed to be reformed on the inside, on the institutional level.

So, if the church did not need to be restored, then Joseph Smith was wrong, and there is no reason why we have any need for The Church of Jesus Christ of Latter-day Saints to exist.

> **And assuredly, as the Lord liveth, for the Lord God hath spoken it, and it is his eternal word, which cannot pass away, that they who are righteous shall be righteous still, and they who are filthy shall be filthy still; wherefore, they who are filthy are the devil and his angels; and they shall go away into everlasting fire, prepared for them; and their torment is as a lake of fire and**

> **brimstone, whose flame ascendeth up forever and ever and has
> no end. (2 Nephi 9:16)**

This verse says God's word cannot pass away. The Book of Mormon teaches on the one hand plain and precious truths were taken away,[465] but in other places, it says God's word did not pass away. In fact, both teachings are found in the books of Nephi.

Guess what? The Mormons don't teach hell either, but the Book of Mormon is filled with language about hell. They teach Outer Darkness, but they don't teach hell. So this passage is a problem on a number of levels for them, but ultimately you want to challenge them on this idea that the Book of Mormon says God's word cannot pass away. It is his eternal word. Ask them, "What does that mean to you? And how does that play out with the idea Nephi proposed earlier that the church did pass away, that plain and precious truths were taken from it?" Challenge them on this idea. Which one do they believe? They cannot believe both, but both are found in the Book of Mormon.

Where Did the Book of Mormon Come From?

I stumbled upon this when I was meeting with some LDS missionaries as a teenager. They showed me a prophecy from the book of Isaiah quoted in the Book of Mormon. They claim, and the Book of Mormon claims is a prophecy about the Book of Mormon. There are a couple of Bible passages they claim are prophecies of the Book of Mormon,[466] but this is my favorite, and I love it when they turn here.

This gets into the question "Where did the Book of Mormon come from?" This is a fundamental thing. This is a direct quote from Isaiah 29:4, and it's explained in the Book of Mormon as a prophecy of the Book of Mormon.

> **For those who shall be destroyed shall speak unto them out of the
> ground, and their speech shall be low out of the dust, and their
> voice shall be as one that hath a familiar spirit; for the Lord God
> will give unto him power, that he may whisper concerning them,**

---

[465] 1 Nephi 13:38-40
[466] Ezekiel 37:15-20

> **even as it were out of the ground; and their speech shall whisper out of the dust. (2 Nephi 26:16)**

This verse has a fatal phrase found within it: "Familiar Spirit." This passage also uses the language of peep, mutter, whisper. This is all language of the occult, witchcraft, sorcery.

You need to clarify some things:

1. Do you believe this is talking about the Book of Mormon?
2. Do you believe this is a fulfilled prophecy?
3. What significance does this have for you?
4. Does this verse say the Book of Mormon has a familiar spirit?
5. What do you think that means?

What the LDS person is likely to say is the Book of Mormon has a familiar spirit, meaning it sounds familiar, as in it sounds like the Bible. And that's the way it's supposed to be. The Bible is God's Word in the East, and the Book of Mormon is God's Word in the West. Together, they are two witnesses of Jesus.

There are lots of verses in the Bible that say these same things, but it's better if you show them these things from the Book of Mormon.

> **And when they shall say unto you: Seek unto them that have familiar spirits, and unto wizards that peep and mutter—should not a people seek unto their God for the living to hear from the dead? To the law and to the testimony; and if they speak not according to this word, it is because there is no light in them. (2 Nephi 18:19-20)**

Consider this. That is what the Mormon missionaries are asking people to do. They are encouraging them to read the Book of Mormon and pray about it. But they are also acknowledging the Book of Mormon has a familiar spirit. This passage also equates familiar spirits with wizards, peeping and muttering, seeking the dead, those who have no light in them. So the missionaries are functioning as a wizard in encouraging people to seek the dead.

The LDS person is likely going to say these passages are talking about two different things. Familiar spirit doesn't always mean that.

If they say this, show them these definitions of Familiar Spirit:

Dictionary.com has the following entry - Also called familiar spirit. Witchcraft and Demonology. a supernatural spirit or demon, often in the form of an animal, supposed to serve and aid a witch or other individual.[467]

"The word familiar is from the Latin familiaris, meaning a "household servant," and intended to express the idea sorcerers had spirits as their servants ready to obey their command. Those attempting to contact the dead, even to this day, usually have some spirit guide who communicates with them. These are familiar spirits."[468]

This is why I advised it best not to pray about the Book of Mormon. Don't do it. Don't fall into that trap. It is opening up a door equated in the Book of Mormon itself with wizardry, witchcraft, the occult, demons, and everything contrary to God. It is an abomination. Do not do it. That is why this verse is so precious. The LDS church teaches this is a prophecy of the Book of Mormon. The Book of Mormon says it has a familiar spirit. We've now taken a look at what the Book of Mormon, quoting the Bible, says a Familiar Spirit is.

So ask them:

1. Do familiar spirits sound like a good thing?
2. Do you still think the Book of Mormon has a familiar spirit?
3. What does the Book of Mormon say about somebody who consults familiar spirits?
4. If the Book of Mormon does have a familiar spirit, what should you do?

The natural conclusion they will need to come to is they need to put the Book of Mormon to death. What that means is they no longer listen to it, read it, see it as an authority in their life. They need to walk away from it, and any of the sources that contributed to it, meaning they will need to walk away from Joseph Smith, and The Church of Jesus Christ of Latter-day Saints as well.

---

[467] Familiar Spirit http://www.dictionary.com/browse/familiar--spirit?s=t

[468] What are Familiar Spirits? http://www.gotquestions.org/familiar-spirits.html

Again, don't push any of these things. Let them come to these conclusions themselves, and let the Holy Spirit do the work.

I wish I had video footage of the look on the Mormon missionaries' faces the first time I presented this to them. They went pale like life left them. It shook them to the core. One of them shared their testimony with me. The next week, when they came back, one of them was transferred to another location.

They can't wriggle out of this. They have to admit the Book of Mormon has a familiar spirit because it says it does in connection with a claim the Book of Mormon fulfills biblical prophecy.

I have many friends in Utah, and the town we lived in, Manti, has a temple within it, and many friends have told us it's not uncommon for Mormons, when they are being baptized in Grandpa Fred's name in the temple, Grandpa Fred shows up in the temple. There are stories of little kids who will come in from playing in the backyard and talk about how they were talking to Great Grandma Stephanie. And they don't see anything weird or wrong with that. This indeed is a big problem within the Mormon church, and I can tell you why. It is the doctrine of demons. The idea one can become like God, where did it come from? There are only two places it's mentioned in the Bible, and both of them are attributed to Lucifer, both when he fell[469] and when he encouraged Adam and Eve to fall.[470]

The Apostle Paul tells us even if an angel comes from heaven and preaches another gospel, we shouldn't listen to him.[471] We should consider him accursed.

---

[469] Isaiah 14:14

[470] Genesis 3:5

[471] Galatians 1:8

CHAPTER 33

Using the New World Translation to Teach Christian Doctrine

Now[472] that we spent a good deal of time showing how one can use the book of Mormon to help people in the LDS church come to a belief in true Christian doctrine, we will do the same for the Jehovah's Witnesses using the New World Translation, which is the Jehovah Witness created and approved translation of the Bible.

In this section, we're going to help them understand the Trinity by contrasting the New World Translation and the King James Version. We're going to show them God is more than one person. That God is Father, Son and Holy Spirit.

Jesus is the Alpha and Omega (The First and the Last)

Christ is the God of the Old Testament. He is not the Father, but he is God.

> **Thus saith the LORD the King of Israel, and his redeemer the LORD of hosts; I [am] the first, and I [am] the last; and beside me [there is] no God. (Isaiah 44:6 KJV)**

---

[472] Young, Nathan, Trinity Proven from the NWT https://youtu.be/4OLD1GPbUR0

> **This is what Jehovah says, The King of Israel and his Repurchaser, Jehovah of armies: 'I am the first and I am the last. There is no God but me. (Isaiah 44:6 NWT)**

Here you can see two people are speaking in this verse. Thus says the Lord, the King of Israel, and his Redeemer, the Lord of hosts. I am the first. I am the last. And beside me, there is no God. God is speaking collectively.

> **In the beginning was the Word, and the Word was with God, and the Word was God. (John 1:1 KJV)**

> **In the beginning was the Word, and the Word was with God, and the Word was a God. (John 1:1 NWT)**

The way the New World Translation translates this verse cannot be the case because that would conflict with what God said in Isaiah 44:6 by saying there is no God beside him. The King James translation ties in with verses like "make man in our image, and our likeness."[473] The King James Version says nobody has seen God at any time.[474]

Who is the First and the Last?

> **I am Alpha and Omega, the beginning and the end, the first and the last. Blessed [are] they that do his commandments, that they may have right to the tree of life, and may enter in through the gates into the city. For without [are] dogs, and sorcerers, and whoremongers, and murderers, and idolaters, and whosoever loveth and maketh a lie. I Jesus have sent mine angel to testify unto you these things in the churches. I am the root and the offspring of David, [and] the bright and morning star. (Revelation 22:13-16 KJV)**

---

[473] Genesis 1:26-27

[474] John 1:18; 1 John 4:12

> I am the Al'pha and the O·me'ga, the first and the last, the
> beginning and the end. Happy are those who wash their robes,
> so that they may have authority to go to the trees of life and that
> they may gain entrance into the city through its gates. Outside
> are the dogs and those who practice spiritism and those who
> are sexually immoral* and the murderers and the idolaters and
> everyone who loves and practices lying.' "'I, Jesus, sent my angel
> to bear witness to you about these things for the congregations.
> I am the root and the offspring of David and the bright morning
> star.'" (Revelation 22:13-16 NWT)

The Lord Jesus is speaking in this section. The New World Translation says the same thing, "I, Jesus." Verse 13 says, "I am Alpha and Omega. The first and the last." There can only be one first and last. There cannot be two firsts and lasts. Think of an Olympic race. There might be a photo finish, but there can only be one winner. Jehovah is the first and Jehovah is the last. Jehovah is the Alpha and Jehovah is the Omega. Jesus said he is the Alpha and Omega, the First and the Last. Why? Because Jesus is Jehovah. Jesus is not the Father. Jehovah is three persons. Just as 1 John testifies there are three that bear record in heaven, the Father, Son and Holy Spirit.[475]

> And without controversy great is the mystery of Godliness: God
> was manifest in the flesh, justified in the Spirit, seen of angels,
> preached unto the Gentiles, believed on in the world, received up
> into glory. (1 Timothy 3:16 KJV)

> Indeed, the sacred secret of this godly devotion is admittedly
> great: 'He was made manifest in flesh, was declared righteous in
> spirit, appeared to angels, was preached about among nations,
> was believed upon in the world, was received up in glory.' (1
> Timothy 3:16 NWT)

This verse says God was manifest in the flesh. The Lord Jesus Christ, he paid the price for our sins. It wasn't a man. It wasn't an angel. It was God in the form of his

---

[475] 1 John 5:7

273

Son. God the Son. He came down and died on the cross for our sins. He rose from the dead on the third day. The Lord Jesus died for our sins on the cross of Calvary. The Watchtower has a different Jesus. Paul warns there would be those with a different Jesus and a different gospel.[476] The Watchtower Jesus was an angel who was created, who then became a man, and then again was a spirit creature.

The Lord Jesus, when he rose, said to the apostles, "Touch me and see. A spirit has not flesh and bones as you see I have."[477] What the Watchtower is teaching does not coincide with what the Bible teaches. Jesus Christ is Lord.[478]

The Watchtower are called Jehovah's Witnesses, but they don't understand who Jehovah is.

The Holy Spirit is a Person

[479]Here are a few quotes regarding what the Watchtower has said regarding the Holy Spirit.

"The Holy Spirit is the active force of the living God, which he sends out through his Son, Christ Jesus, and which operates toward Jehovah's people, enlightening and directing his theocratic organization on the earth today as it did in the days of the apostles."[480]

We can see the Watchtower does not teach the Holy Ghost is a person.

"The Holy Spirit is God's power in action, his active force. God sends out his spirit by projecting his energy to any place to accomplish his will."[481]

"The Holy Spirit is used similarly by referring to God's spirit as his "hands," "fingers," or "breath." The Bible shows the Holy Spirit is not a person."[482]

The Watchtower organization cannot be farther from the truth with regard to those quotes. They said the Holy Spirit is not a person. We're going to see what the

---

[476] 2 Corinthians 11:4

[477] Luke 24:39

[478] Philippians 2:11; compare with Isaiah 45:23

[479] Young, Nathan, The Holy Spirit Proven as a Person from the NWT https://youtu.be/ ncDL REHtcGQ

[480] Watchtower 1959, April 1 p. 219

[481] What is the Holy Spirit? https://www.jw.org/en/bible-teachings/questions/what-is-the-holy-spirit/

[482] What is the Holy Spirit? https://www.jw.org/en/bible-teachings/questions/what-is-the-holy-spirit/

Bible says regarding the Holy Ghost. Again we're going to contrast the King James Version with the New World Translation.

Jesus is talking to his disciples about another person who is going to come and do the comforting because the Lord Jesus Christ is going to die on the cross soon. The apostles are a little weary because of what Jesus is saying, and he is trying to comfort them.

> **Howbeit when he, the Spirit of truth, is come, he will guide you into all truth: for he shall not speak of himself; but whatsoever he shall hear, [that] shall he speak: and he will shew you things to come. (John 16:13 KJV)**

> **However, when that one comes, the spirit of the truth, he will guide you into all the truth, for he will not speak of his own initiative, but what he hears he will speak, and he will declare to you the things to come. (John 16:13 NWT)**

The Lord Jesus Christ is introducing the disciples to the person who is coming. The Lord Jesus refers to the Holy Spirit as a "he." If the Lord Jesus were describing an active force, he would use the word "it." He introduced the Holy Spirit as a person. He was explaining who the Holy Spirit is, and he introduced him as a person. He said "he" will guide you into all truth. The Watchtower teaches their organization is spirit-filled, and God is guiding their organization. But Jesus taught the Holy Spirit will guide individuals into all truth. The Watchtower has not spoken the truth in the past. There are over 100 failed prophecies. The book of Deuteronomy tells us if a prophet prophecies something and it doesn't come to pass, that prophet is not of the Lord.[483] The Watchtower is notorious for failed prophecies, yet they still say they are spirit-filled. Jesus said "he" will guide us into all truth. The Bible explains and teaches the Holy Ghost is a person.

> **And I will pray the Father, and he shall give you another Comforter, that he may abide with you for ever; (John 14:16 KJV)**

---

[483] Deuteronomy 18:22

> **And I will ask the Father and he will give you another helper to be with you forever, (John 14:16 NWT)**

Notice the word "another." He said he will give us another comforter. Here we see the Lord Jesus Christ is explaining to the disciples another person is coming. There are three persons mentioned in this verse alone. "I, the Lord Jesus, will pray to the Father, and he will give you another Comforter, that he may abide with you forever." The Lord Jesus Christ is mentioning three persons in that verse alone. Himself, the Father, and the Holy Ghost. He is saying another person will come. The New World Translation explains this as well that another person is coming, and that is the Holy Ghost. The Lord Jesus always referred to the Holy Ghost as a person, and not an "it."

> **For there are three that bear record in heaven, the Father, the Word, and the Holy Ghost: and these three are one. (1 John 5:7 KJV)**

I've introduced the Holy Spirit from Scripture, but now let's look at the attributes of the Holy Spirit.

The Attributes of the Holy Spirit

> **But the Comforter, [which is] the Holy Ghost, whom the Father will send in my name, he shall teach you all things, and bring all things to your remembrance, whatsoever I have said unto you. (John 14:26 KJV)**

> **But the helper, the holy spirit, which the Father will send in my name, that one will teach you all things and bring back to your minds all the things I told you. (John 14:26 NWT)**

So here we see the Lord Jesus Christ is again referring to the Holy Spirit as a person. Not a force. Not God's active force, but a person. The Lord Jesus Christ said the Holy Ghost will teach us all things. So one of the personalities or traits the Holy Ghost has is teaching. A wind, or a force, cannot teach anyone. If a person were waiting in a class for somebody to come in and teach them, they would be waiting for a person.

Jesus is telling us a person is going to come and he will teach. The Bible tells us God cannot lie, [484]and the Holy Ghost will teach believers all things, so the Holy Spirit will guide believers into all truth. Not some truth. All truth.

> **Then the Spirit said unto Philip, Go near, and join thyself to this chariot. (Acts 8:29 KJV)**

> **So the spirit said to Philip: "Go over and approach this chariot." (Acts 8:29 NWT)**

Here we see the Ethiopian Eunuch was reading Isaiah, and as he was reading, he had some questions about the Lord Jesus. So the Holy Spirit guided Phillip and told him to go near to this chariot. A wind, or active force, cannot speak. Only a person can speak. The Spirit said, "Go near and join yourself to this chariot." The Holy Spirit gave instructions, guidance and spoke to Phillip.

> **While Peter thought on the vision, the Spirit said unto him, Behold, three men seek thee. (Acts 10:19 KJV)**

> **As Peter was still pondering over the vision, the spirit said: "Look! Three men are asking for you. (Acts 10:19 NWT)**

As Peter was still pondering and wondering about the vision he had, the Holy Spirit had to alert him and make him aware three people were seeking after him. The Holy Spirit spoke to Peter and said, "Behold, three men seek thee." Only a person can speak to you. In Acts 21, we also read the prophet Agabus came, and the Holy Spirit spoke to Paul through the prophet Agabus to not go back to Jerusalem. This shows not only can the Holy Spirit teach, but the Holy Spirit speaks. The Holy Spirit gives instruction, and the Holy Spirit guides. That can only be a person.

> **But Peter said, Ananias, why hath Satan filled thine heart to lie to the Holy Ghost, and to keep back [part] of the price of the land? (Acts 5:3 KJV)**

---

[484] Titus 1:2

> **But Peter said: "An·a·ni'as, why has Satan emboldened you to lie to the holy spirit and secretly hold back some of the price of the field? (Acts 5:3 NWT)**

Peter, speaking to Ananias, said Ananias had lied to the Holy Spirit. One cannot lie to wind or an active force. Later Peter emphasizes who he lied to by saying, "You have not lied to men, but to God." The Holy Spirit is God. He is not the Father, not the Son, but he is part of the Godhead. God is three persons, but one God.

> **And grieve not the holy Spirit of God, whereby ye are sealed unto the day of redemption. (Ephesians 4:30 KJV)**

> **Also, do not be grieving God's holy spirit, with which you have been sealed for a day of releasing by ransom. (Ephesians 4:30 NWT)**

The Bible tells us we can grieve the Holy Spirit. Christians today have believed in the finished work of the cross at Calvary and realize it was blood poured out for us bringing us remission of sins. Once one has trusted in Christ for their salvation, they are indwelt with the Holy Spirit. But Christians can wander off, and go into a lifestyle that doesn't please the Lord. They don't lose their salvation because they can't lose the Holy Spirit. But they can grieve the Holy Spirit. It is impossible to grieve somebody who doesn't love you. So the Holy Spirit can love and can be grieved. Paul also tells us we can quench the Holy Spirit.

> **Go ye therefore, and teach all nations, baptizing them in the name of the Father, and of the Son, and of the Holy Ghost: (Matthew 28:19 KJV)**

> **Go, therefore, and make disciples of people of all the nations, baptizing them in the name of the Father and of the Son and of the holy spirit, (Matthew 28:19 NWT)**

The Holy Spirit is a person who has a name, and we are to baptize in that name. There are three persons mentioned in this passage, the Father, Son and Holy Spirit. If the Holy Spirit was God's active force, then why would we baptize people in the name of an active force? In fact, if you follow the interpretation of Jehovah's Witnesses, Matthew 28:19 would read "baptize them in the name of Jehovah God, Michael the Archangel and God's active force." It would make more sense if we baptized them in the name of Jehovah God.

The Jehovah's Witnesses teach in regard to this verse: "This verse means a baptism candidate recognizes the authority of Jehovah God and of Jesus Christ, and God's active force."[485]

The Bible doesn't say anything about God's active force. It's talking about the Holy Spirit as a unique person. The Bible teaches and indicates the Holy Spirit is a person and not a force. The Jehovah Witnesses say God is not a person. The Bible says he is.

---

[485] What Does the Bible Really Teach? Chapter Eighteen: Baptism and Your Relationship With God

TACTIC #3

Communicating Grace to the Religious Mind

CHAPTER 34

Communicating Grace to the Religious Mind

This chapter is about grace, and how to communicate grace to a religious person. This topic is one of my favorites to talk about, and my ministry, People of the Free Gift, is all about the free gift of God's grace. It's a ministry, from the beginning, intentionally committed to teaching and preaching the gospel of grace.

Before we get started, there is something I love to do, and it's a telling test regarding where we are when it comes to grace. I want you to put these four terms in order based on when they happen in relation to each other in reference to a person who is seeking Christ.

Forgiveness
Obedience
Faith
Grace

The answer will be at the end of this chapter.

The Way the World Gives

First of all, we're going to talk about the way the world gives. This is based off what Jesus said shortly before he was crucified. He was talking about the comforter who was going to come, and he said:

> **Peace I leave with you, my peace I give unto you: not as the world giveth, give I unto you. Let not your heart be troubled, neither let it be afraid. (John 14:27)**

Jesus said something crucial. He said, "I don't give the way the world gives." That's going to frame our entire conversation because we're going to look at the way the world gives. Then we're going to look at the way God gives.

The best way to look at grace is to look at the word free. We love the word free. There's a love and hate relationship with the word free. I found this out when I first had this concept of People of the Free Gift. I was a pastor in California, and we would have evangelistic events where we gave away free things at public events with an invite to our church. So we would give away free ice cream cones, or otter pops, or bottles of water. It was amazing to see the skepticism on people's faces and how unwilling they were to believe something was free. We wanted to give them something and invite them to church. But, as I started thinking about this, I started taking pictures of every time I saw the word free. Then I started thinking about the message behind what was communicated. What is the theology behind when the world says the word "free."

Free ... service ... if you already have purchased the necessary tools

Example: Free Wifi

Free wifi says it all. All you need is a smartphone or iPad or laptop or some other device that can use wifi. All of these devices cost a lot of money.

So, what if God gave this way? One would have to purchase salvation, and then they would be able to utilize all of the benefits of it.

There is a story in the book of Acts that illustrates this contrast. The apostles were doing many mighty acts, and they came upon a sorcerer named Simon. When Simon saw the mighty works the apostles were doing through the Holy Spirit, he offered to buy that power from them.

> **But Peter said unto him, Thy money perish with thee, because thou hast thought that the gift of God may be purchased with money. (Acts 8:20)**

Peter said, "Your money perish with you because you thought the "gift" of God may be purchased with money." We'll come back to that concept as we go further.

Free ... if you do enough on your end

Example: Free shipping on orders of $100 or more.

We'll give you something free if you do enough on your end. I want you to think about how that would work in a religious setting. We don't have to think hard about this as the Book of Mormon, at least at times, teaches this theology.

> **For we labor diligently to write, to persuade our children, and also our brethren, to believe in Christ, and to be reconciled to God; for we know that it is by grace that we are saved, after all we can do. (2 Nephi 25:23)**

I want you to think about that phrase. There's a pretty famous speech given at BYU by Brad Wilcox.[486] He talked about this girl at BYU who was troubled by the gap between what she could do and what she was doing. He confused her because he was trying to tell her she didn't have to do anything, but then pointed her to Scriptures that told her all the requirements of the LDS gospel. She walked out more confused, in my opinion than when she went in.

What if we went to the beach, and we saw a lifeguard applying the same theology the LDS church teaches, or some people in the world believe. I'll save that person who is drowning if they do enough on their end. The lifeguard wouldn't be able to do much. He's not that powerful to save. He's not like Jesus, who the author of Hebrews said he can save to the uttermost. [487]He's not that good, so he can't come out to the drowning person. But if they get back to him, halfway, then he can get them back to shore safely. Do we want that lifeguard? No! That lifeguard would be fired immediately. Neither is the idea we get free stuff once we've done enough on our end the way God gives. But it's the way the world gives.

---

[486] Wilcox, Brad, His Grace is Sufficient https://youtu.be/yLXr9it pbY

[487] Hebrews 7:25

Free ... but everything afterward costs something

Example: Free engine light check.

I don't think there is anybody that sees this and thinks, "Wow, I get to have that checked out for FREE." No, we're thinking, "I wonder how much this is going to cost me."

Granted, we appreciate the diagnostic is free, but we know whatever they find and need to fix is going to cost us. In fact, in the graphic above, they tell you as much.

This is why the letter of Galatians was written. Many Christians think Galatians is about salvation by grace, but not quite. In Galatia, many had accepted the gospel, but after Paul left, Judaizers came into town and started telling these new believers they can't be saved unless they are circumcised and keep the law of Moses. Paul is writing them to challenge the idea they have to do things to maintain the salvation they received for free.

> **This only would I learn of you, Received ye the Spirit by the works of the law, or by the hearing of faith? Are ye so foolish? having begun in the Spirit, are ye now made perfect by the flesh? (Galatians 3:2-3)**

Having begun with a free gift, now you think you have to buy your way into God's blessings and God's favor. He only works through certain people, and they have to earn it. That's not the way God gives, but it's the way the world gives.

Free ... if you earn it.

Example: Free tokens for grades.

That's not free. That's earning it. And we understand, but they throw the term "free" with it to draw us in. Here are two passages every Christian and religious person needs to understand.

> **And if by grace, then [is it] no more of works: otherwise grace is no more grace. But if [it be] of works, then is it no more grace: otherwise work is no more work. (Romans 11:6)**

**Now to him that worketh is the reward not reckoned of grace,
but of debt. But to him that worketh not, but believeth on him
that justifieth the ungodly, his faith is counted for righteousness.
(Romans 4:4-5)**

If a person went to work and they were handed a paycheck, and their boss said, "Enjoy the gift," they would say something like, "I worked 40 hours for this money. Could I have done nothing and still received this?" They would be offended.

Likewise, if a kid opened up his Christmas gifts only to find a note on them saying, "Once you mow the lawn, you can have your gift," they would be confused.

We understand implied in the word gift is the idea it is free. We did not earn it. Likewise, we understand the concept of earning, and to call it a gift would be confusing and offensive.

Likewise, Paul said if we attempt to earn righteousness, then we can't get it because God only gives righteousness as a gift. We have to receive righteousness, and we do so through the finished work of Jesus on the cross in paying for our sins.

So that's the way the world gives. But Jesus said, "Don't worry. I don't give the way the world gives." Praise God for that. Grace means grace. It means free gift. In fact, Jesus further explained how he does give.

**Heal the sick, cleanse the lepers, raise the dead, cast out devils:
freely ye have received, freely give. (Matthew 10:8)**

Jesus advises his apostles to give the same way they received. FREE.

Why Grace?

Once I began having clarity as to what grace means and how God gives differently than the world gives, I started asking "Why grace?" I know that's a silly question, and God doesn't have to give me an answer, but I feel like he did.

God was giving us a model that will affect every area of our lives.

God desires a relationship with us

Ever had a friend who became the boss? As George said on Seinfeld, "Worlds are colliding. George is getting upset." Both relationships are different and can easily cause a conflict between the two parties. One can't stand in judgment over somebody and still have a close intimate relationship with them. It doesn't work that way.

Here's an example. What does one do when they see a police car behind them? Most people do the same thing. It doesn't matter if they're breaking the law or not. It doesn't matter if they are speeding or not. They tap on the breaks, check their mirrors, and drive the way they did when they were taking the test at the DMV.

I recently had a change of mind about this. I used to be a California driver who sees the speed limit as a suggestion, and it's all about the flow of traffic. Then I moved to Utah where they take this stuff seriously. After getting a few tickets, I started using cruise control. Now I don't get tickets. But, when I saw a police car behind me, I caught myself still slowing down. I knew I wasn't doing anything wrong. I knew I could contest it if he gave me a ticket. But I was still slowing down. I had to train myself to start living by grace. If one knows they're not doing anything wrong, then they don't have to slow down. They don't have to be afraid of getting a ticket.

> **There is no fear in love; but perfect love casteth out fear: because fear hath torment. He that feareth is not made perfect in love. (1 John 4:18)**

GRACE	RELIGION
Know you have eternal life	Don't know you have eternal life
Don't fear God's judgment	Fear God's judgment
Love God	Can't love God
Keep his commandments	Can't keep his commandments
Back to the top	Back to the top

This is an amazing verse for helping religious people understand grace. They are in the mindset they have to obey God's commands to be saved. The greatest commandment is to love God.[488] John tells us in this verse there is no fear in love because the fear he is talking about has to do with torment (In contrast to fearing God in the sense of reverence). That word torment in Greek is also used in Matthew 25:46 and translated eternal punishment. That means if one fears God's judgment, or put another way if they don't know whether God will judge them or not, or how that judgment will turn out, they don't know they are forgiven, then there still is an element of fear attached to that. To the extent one fears God's judgment, to that extent they can't love God. If they can't love God, then they can't keep the first commandment, and according to works theology, if they can't keep the commandments, they can't be forgiven, which John said was the only way to eliminate the fear of judgment which allows one to love God.

You can continue going around the circle with religious people until they realize there's no way out of the circle unless they tap out, realize their need for a Savior, and trust in the finished work of Christ and Christ alone for their salvation.

This principle is also why parents can't be their kids' best friend. They have to be a parent or be a friend. They can be close to them, but not their friend.

In order to be honest, we need to know we are forgiven

What I find amazing about the story of the prodigal son is when he gets home, his father runs to him.[489] Something men didn't do in those days. He embraces his son. He even makes his other brother jealous. He doesn't want to come into the party.[490] The prodigal son never lost his sonship. No matter what he did, the father welcomed him back into the family, embraced him, and accepted him for who he was.

If one wants complete transparency in their relationships, they need to ask themselves if they are standing in judgment over that other person. If they come back and make things right, am I going to embrace them? Do they know that about us? Are we known as that person? If not, chances are, that person is not going to make things right. They'll make things right between them and God, but not with us.

---

[488] Matthew 22:37

[489] Luke 15:20

[490] Luke 15:28

> **Or despisest thou the riches of his goodness and forbearance and longsuffering; not knowing that the goodness of God leadeth thee to repentance? (Romans 2:4)**

It's not the fact God can punish us. It's not the fact we're accountable to him, that he's sovereign, or the fact he is going to judge us that leads us to repentance. It's his kindness, his mercy and grace. It's because we know there is forgiveness in the arms of a loving God. That's what is so wrong with a religious model that says one has to repent and forsake their sins before they are forgiven. One is forgiven, and then they repent. It changes one's behavior because it's God living on the inside of them changing their behavior and making them more like Jesus.

God is our Model

> **Forbearing one another, and forgiving one another, if any man have a quarrel against any: even as Christ forgave you, so also [do] ye. (Colossians 3:13)**

"As Christ forgave you." Here's a logical question. Consider this as it plays out in our human relationships. What if Christ worked under the model legalists preach, that we're only forgiven after we have repented of all of our sins? If we operated under that model in our relationships, it wouldn't work. For one, the person would never come to us if they knew they weren't forgiven. Second, we wouldn't be able to forgive them until after they died and we had full knowledge they never repeated that action that offended us originally. This model simply can't work in our human relationships. This is the model legalists suggest God operates under.

This same principle applies to other areas of our lives:

1. Love as God loved you
2. Serve as Christ served you
3. Forgive as you have been forgiven
4. Husbands, love your wives as Christ loved the church and gave himself up for her

How many marriages would still be in existence if what that meant was we're only to forgive and love our spouses if they have been obedient to us?

God gets the glory, not us

**For by grace are ye saved through faith; and that not of yourselves:
[it is] the gift of God: Not of works, lest any man should boast.
(Ephesians 2:8-9)**

It's not that we were saved by grace, through faith, and faith itself is a gift of God. Faith itself is essentially grace. And it's not of works, lest any man should boast. Something inevitable if we're saved by a standard of works, or production, or sin or lack of sin, then we're going to constantly be looking around comparing ourselves to everyone else around us.

Many times when you talk to an LDS person, they speak of this concept of Godhood as if we hop on an elevator, and we're behind the God ahead of us. So we'll always worship God when we're a God. They must not have read much Greek mythology, because, in those works, the gods are warring against each other and competing for the attention and obedience of the humans, getting everybody to appease them, have them wrestling with fate and other contradictory issues. What I have in my mind is there is a God ahead of us, so we take out that God. It's human nature, and if humans are becoming gods, that is likely to happen.

What Paul is saying, if one carries these principles out to its logical conclusion, if salvation is based on us doing more than somebody else, we can't help but compare with other people and feel pride in our accomplishments. One would feel like they're in heaven because of what they did, not because of God's grace or because of Jesus' sacrifice. And they would know you're in a better place, better role, because of their works, which were more or better compared to others. And if we feel like we're on pace to take that higher role than others, we can't help but feel like we are better than them.

**Not by works of righteousness which we have done, but according
to his mercy he saved us, by the washing of regeneration, and
renewing of the Holy Ghost; (Titus 3:5)**

It's according to his mercy. It was never meant to be about us, but about him. It's not about our exaltation. It's about his. He always has been, always will be, God.

> **I do not frustrate the grace of God: for if righteousness [come] by the law, then Christ is dead in vain. (Galatians 2:21)**

Paul goes so far as to say if one is trying to get salvation by works of the law or by obedience, then they are frustrating his grace. They are keeping yourself from being able to grab a hold and obtain his grace, his righteousness. Also, if they are doing that, then they are telling Jesus he didn't have to die for them. "It's okay Jesus. I can take the ball and run with it." And he is saying, "No you can't!"

Grace sends us back to save others

The last reason I believe God operates by grace is it sends us back to save others. I love this about grace. Grace sends us back to save others because we realize it was by grace we are saved, so therefore, there before the grace of God go I. The great salvation by grace passage in Ephesians 2 starts like this:

> **And you [hath he quickened], who were dead in trespasses and sins; Wherein in time past ye walked according to the course of this world, according to the prince of the power of the air, the spirit that now worketh in the children of disobedience: (Ephesians 2:1-2)**

Our spirit was dead in transgressions and sins. This was the former identity of every Christian. That person walking down the street doing that horrible thing. That was the Christian, or could have been, had it not been for God's grace. This truth causes us to always fall in love afresh and anew with grace. Because we understand it wasn't about us or something we did. It was all about God and what he did for us. God wants to do that same thing in the life of every individual. Here's the amazing thing. God wants to use us. He's programmed it into his plan of salvation to use us. He didn't have to. He could come over the loudspeakers and say, "This is how you get saved." He could send angels flying overhead in a heavenly broadcast. In fact, he will do that during the events of Revelation.[491] But as the norm, God uses us, fallen,

---

[491] Revelation 14:6

broken vessels to communicate his message. So it always points us back and sends us out to other people so we can save them.

We have been talking about grace. The average religious person, who is carrying a lot of heavy baggage around with them. They are not resting in God's sufficiency. They have not been saved to the uttermost. They have no knowledge they have even been forgiven of their sins.

So let's go back to that grace test we started with, and let's see how we did.

Put these following items in the order they occur in the life of a believer:

Grace

Faith

Forgiveness

Obedience

First of all, it has to start with grace. If we believe the process starts with anything else, we missed it. And I pray by the time we got through looking at all of these truths about grace it would be obvious God always starts with grace. It's extended to all. God's desire and his will is for everyone to come to the knowledge of the truth,[492] for everyone to come to repentance.[493] God extends his grace to all.

Second comes faith. Faith itself is a gift of God,[494] and that's why grace comes first, then faith. It's not about us. It's about him. He gives us the gift of faith, and we either receive it, or we don't. When we put our faith in Jesus, we are forgiven of our sins, all of them, immediately, and everything going to come after. We are forgiven of our sins, not because of anything we have done, but everything to do with what he's done and who he is.

After that, and only after all those things, can you obey God. [495]Because the greatest command is to love the Lord your God with all your heart, soul, mind and strength.[496] One cannot love the one they fear. We fear the one who may be able to punish us. If one has not been forgiven of their sins, they cannot obey.

---

[492] 1 Timothy 2:4

[493] 2 Peter 3:9

[494] Ephesians 2:8

[495] 1 John 4:18

[496] Matthew 22:37

CHAPTER 35

Stunted Grace

In this chapter we're going to talk about stunted grace. And by stunted grace, I'm referring to grace not fully realized in the life of the believer. The thing about stunted grace is all people, to one extent or another, have grace stunted in our life. God has given everything he has to give to us already.[497] It's already out there. It's already offered. It's there for the taking and receiving. But all people, to one extent or another, fall short of receiving that full gift, that full grace God wants to give us in our lives.

A question was posed to me several years ago by my wife. As I was studying grace more in-depth, and as God was revealing his grace more in-depth to me, she asked me, "What about the verses in the New Testament, and in the Old Testament, that seem to talk about rewards for being good or punishment for doing certain things?" Here's an example of what she was talking about:

> **Know ye not that the unrighteous shall not inherit the kingdom of God? Be not deceived: neither fornicators, nor idolaters, nor adulterers, nor effeminate, nor abusers of themselves with mankind, Nor thieves, nor covetous, nor drunkards, nor revilers, nor extortioners, shall inherit the kingdom of God. (1 Corinthians 6:9-10)**

---

[497] Ephesians 1:3

Christians tend to put some sins into categories as worse than others because of passages like this. I have heard many podcasts and sermons, even from pastors and Christians I greatly respect, using this passage to teach if one practices certain sins, they can't go to heaven. That isn't what Paul was saying. The word heaven isn't even in this verse. It talks about the kingdom of God. And even within that, there is a difference between entering the kingdom of God and inheriting the kingdom of God. This talks about inheriting the kingdom of God or not.[498]

He goes even further in the next verse by saying, "Such were some of you."[499] What Paul is addressing is an identity issue. What is your identity? Is it in Christ, or is it in these things? I'm not saying all believers will inherit the Kingdom of God because Paul is saying they won't.

Let's go to the flip side of this. What about verses that talk about rewards, inheritance, crowns, ruling and reigning with Christ?

> **And he that overcometh, and keepeth my works unto the end, to him will I give power over the nations: And he shall rule them with a rod of iron; as the vessels of a potter shall they be broken to shivers: even as I received of my Father. (Revelation 2:26-27)**

One of the problems I have in talking with members of other groups, is they read these types of passages, and then talk about levels of heaven, degrees of glory, even becoming gods one day. Then they will teach one is going to make it or not at the judgment seat. Some would even say there are sins believers have to be purged of after this life before they can get into heaven and inherit the Kingdom of God.

So, what is going on in these verses, and when I talk about stunted grace, what do I mean?

Here's an example from everyday life. Elijah is my middle son. When he turned eight years old, we wanted to celebrate his birthday, we had gifts for him, and we had things we were trying to do. Many stores and restaurants will offer free stuff or discounts on the customer's birthday. One of my favorites is Red Robin. If one is signed up for the Red Royalty, they will receive a free burger on their birthday. Red Robin burgers come with bottomless fries. Depending on the location, kids receive a

---

[498] Purgatory http://www.newadvent.org/cathen/12575a.htm
[499] 1 Corinthians 6:11

free kids meal with a free ice cream sundae. So we wanted to take Elijah to Red Robin and get his free kids meal, and we were able to do that.

But we also knew Denny's gives a free Grand Slam on the customer's birthday, but unfortunately, we were in Idaho at the time when he hit his actual birthday, and there weren't any Denny's locations on our route until we reached Billings, Montana. So we weren't able to avail ourselves of the offer Denny's made to my son on his birthday.

The other thing Elijah received was a gift certificate for $3 from Toys R Us to use on his birthday. He could receive $3 off anything $3 or more. We took him to a Toys R Us we found along the way. There was a particular toy he liked he was looking for. However, Toys R Us didn't have the toy he was looking for. So we weren't able to use the offer in the way Elijah would have liked.

I'm sure there are many other offers out there we didn't know about. So, of all the available offers for FREE things on Elijah's birthday, we were able to use only a fraction of them.

I submit the Christian life is in many ways the same as those offers I mentioned. There are some things God has given us, are available to us, and we don't take advantage of. Sometimes it's because we don't know they are available to us. Sometimes it's because we refuse to take advantage of them.

That is what I call stunted grace. There is stunted grace in this life, and that results, in many ways, in stunted grace in reference to the Kingdom, and in eternity.

There are many Christians who think of the gift of God as being salvation. The gift of God is not salvation. It's not eternal life. It's not forgiveness. The gift of God is Jesus.[500] In fact, one could say the gift of God, what God wants to give us, is everything of him for everything in us. The disconnect is we think of salvation as happening to us somewhere in the past instead of something happening in us and to us.

Blessed [be] the God and Father of our Lord Jesus Christ, who hath blessed us with all spiritual blessings in heavenly [places] in Christ: (Ephesians 1:3)

---

[500] John 3:16

So many times when we are praying as Christians, we pray God would bless us. Or we pray for specific blessings. And we speak in Christian lingo and ask for travel mercies or blessing on our food. There's no blessing God can give us he hasn't already given? The question isn't whether God has given us the blessing as much as whether we have received the blessing. Or perhaps we've rejected the blessing.

> **All scripture [is] given by inspiration of God, and [is] profitable for doctrine, for reproof, for correction, for instruction in righteousness: That the man of God may be perfect, throughly furnished unto all good works. (2 Timothy 3:16-17)**

God's given us in his word everything we need to do everything he has called us to do.

> **For God so loved the world, that he gave his only begotten Son, that whosoever believeth in him should not perish, but have everlasting life. (John 3:16)**

Jesus tells us he's the gift. He's the gift God gave. God has given all of himself for everything we need. And blessed us with every spiritual blessing in Christ.

Let's talk about some examples of stunted grace we see in the Scripture. The first one I see is when James said in his epistle, "You have not because you ask not."[501] In the next verse, James goes on to say sometimes we ask, but ask with selfish motives or false intentions.[502] There are some items God desires to give us, but the reasons we haven't received them is because we haven't asked for them.

James isn't telling believers they received a blank check from God. He qualifies this teaching by reminding us this isn't a game of selfishness. It's about him. We have been brought along on his mission, and he is working through us to conform us into the image of Christ and accomplish his mission in the world. But still, the reality is there are things we don't have because we simply haven't asked for them.

> **Behold, I come quickly: hold that fast which thou hast, that no man take thy crown. (Revelation 3:11)**

---

[501] James 4:3

[502] James 4:4

Crowns, according to this verse, are something "laid up" in heaven. They are laid up in heaven where moth and rust do not corrupt and thieves do not break in and steal. We can let others take our crown. We can forfeit what was already laid up for us and is available to us. A gift that is either going to be received or refused.

> **Therefore when thou doest [thine] alms, do not sound a trumpet before thee, as the hypocrites do in the synagogues and in the streets, that they may have glory of men. Verily I say unto you, They have their reward. (Matthew 6:2)**

Abstained from their reward is a more literal translation of the Greek.[503] Most translations say, "they have received their reward." The word, ἀπέχω in Greek, means to abstain or hold back, from something. It was a choice made by the Pharisees to reject Jesus, and in doing so, would automatically disqualify them from reward. Furthermore, the reason why the Pharisees do all of the things they do is because they want glory from people, and because they want glory from people, they have said, "No thank you," to the glory God wants to give them and bestow upon them.

> **If any man's work shall be burned, he shall suffer loss: but he himself shall be saved; yet so as by fire. (1 Corinthians 3:15)**

This verse is referring to the judgment seat of Christ where believers are going to be judged in reference to rewards. When we stand before Christ, it's not a matter of earning rewards, it's a matter of finding out what rewards we have received, that we are going to inherit. And, a reward, as we said earlier with the crowns, is something one can receive, refuse, have taken from them or lose.

> **There hath no temptation taken you but such as is common to man: but God [is] faithful, who will not suffer you to be tempted above that ye are able; but will with the temptation also make a way to escape, that ye may be able to bear [it]. (1 Corinthians 10:13)**

---

[503] ἀπέχω - Strong's Greek Lexicon Blue Letter Bible www.blueletterbible.org//lang/lexicon/lexicon. cfm?Strongs=G568&t=KJV

Christians sometimes have a self-destructive pattern when they get together, though we all have a common bond of being saved by grace through faith. When we look at Scripture, we find passages addressing our sins, some more serious than others. Or at least we look at them that way. There are some sins most don't struggle with, and we all talk about how bad those sins are, but there are sins most Christians struggle with, and I hear Christians write these sins off as though there is nothing they can do to rid themselves of these sins in their life. It's part of their personality. It's the way they were raised. They brush off what God wants them to do, invited them into, and instead say, "I can't," and in the process, they reject the gift God wants to give them in conforming them into his image.

God has already provided a way out in his providence. That circumstance, temptation or trial the Christian faces has not taken God off guard. He knew it was going to happen. He allowed it to come into our lives. And he's provided a way for us to overcome it. We overcome sin by fully submitting ourselves to him.[504] By fully receiving the gift he wants to give us. And remember, the gift is him. All of him for everything God has called us to do.

Desire

What do we want to do? Ever notice change doesn't occur in one's life because somebody nags at them or wants that change for them? It doesn't happen when they kind of sort of want to get out of trouble or stay out of trouble? Ever realize consequences don't necessarily form character? And the reason is this. We don't change unless we want to. And the only reason we ever want to is because God, in his Holy Spirit, has given us the desire to want to. We see this reality lived out in what the Apostle Paul said in Romans 7.

> **For that which I do I allow not: for what I would, that do I not; but what I hate, that do I. (Romans 7:15)**

Paul goes on to say, "What's wrong with me? Who will save me from this wretched body of evil?"[505] But then he goes on to say, "I thank God, through Christ Jesus our

---

[504] 1 John 5:4-5

[505] Romans 7:24

Lord. So then with the mind I serve the law of God, but with the flesh, the law of sin."[506] It is possible for one to have conflicting desires. There are the desires of the flesh. In terms of emotions, we might even feel these more. Every believer lives with a conflict between their fleshly desires, those immediate cravings, those immediate urges that come upon us, and those temptations are so convincing we think we can take the shortcut and still get the best God wants to give us. But the truth of the matter is those things are always selling us short. It's always Satan bringing up a desire that's within us and putting it in the form of a temptation, and then causing us to give into what he wants us to do, but not what God wants to give us.

Notice something. When Jesus was in the Garden of Gethsemane, he faced one of these moments. What did he pray? Father, if there is any other way, let's take it.[507] He was looking at his circumstances. He knew the physical, emotional and spiritual suffering he would face on the cross, and he sweat, as it were, drops of blood.[508] But in the same prayer, he confessed he was feeling these things and struggling with it and didn't want to do it. But he said, "Nevertheless, not my will, but thine be done." That is the model he gives to us.

Notice Jesus didn't try harder to have different emotions. He didn't try to ignore his emotions. He prayed and asked God to work out the conflict in his emotions. Sometimes we have to do war on our knees, and humbling ourselves and being honest before God. And like Jesus, there is nothing sinful about this. There is nothing wrong with this. In fact, Paul said, "In my weakness, he is strong."[509] Coming before God and fighting the battle on our knees and saying, "God, I'm going to be honest with you. I know your word calls me to do this thing. But I can say in all honesty, I enjoy this other thing. That thing helps me to cope with life's struggles. It helps me to cope with hard days. It helps me to feel good for a while. It helps me to feel better about myself. But that's not what your word says I'm supposed to be doing. So Holy Spirit, would you work within me and conform me into the image of your Son.[510] Please give me the desire to change this? Because Father, I don't like what this sin is doing.

---

[506] Romans 7:25

[507] Matthew 26:39

[508] Luke 22:44

[509] 2 Corinthians 12:9

[510] Romans 8:29

But more importantly, this is what you are calling me to do, and I trust you I will be far better off for obeying you in this."

Motive

The next factor is motive. Why are we doing what we are doing? There are three basic motives. We can be like the Pharisees, who give and then blow a trumpet on the street corner to make sure everybody knows what they are doing?[511] Aren't I a great guy? They were doing it for glory.

We can do it for fear of judgment. That's what John addressed when he said there is no fear in love.[512] That's what Paul addressed to the Corinthian church when he talked about godly sorrow and worldly sorrow.[513] Worldly sorrow is when we feel bad because we got caught. We don't want to do something because we feel bad about what might happen to us. But given no consequences, we would continue to do what we are doing. Paul said, "For Christ's love compels us."[514] The word "compel" means to drive forward.[515] It's a word conveying control, movement, motivation, energizing. It keeps us going. In context, Paul was discussing all the beating and shipwrecks and imprisonments, and the rejection he faced for the sake of the gospel.[516] What kept him going was the love of God. The love which belongs to God, which only comes from God dwelling inside of the believer.

Power

How are we doing what we are doing? It's not important to ask if we want to do it, and why we want to do it, but how are we doing it. It's easy to get caught up and think we have some success with something and say, "Look at the great things I have accomplished." Like Nebuchadnezzar out on his palace, saying, "Look at this Babylon

---

[511] Matthew 6:2

[512] 1 John 4:18

[513] 2 Corinthians 7:10

[514] 2 Corinthians 5:14

[515] συνέχω Strong's Greek Lexicon Blue Letter Bible www.blueletterbible.org//lang/lexicon/lexicon.cfm?Strongs=G4912&t=KJV

[516] 2 Corinthians 11:23-28

that I created. Aren't I a great guy?"[517] And God drove him mad.[518] Getting into that same pattern is easy. We are dependent upon God until God does something through us, and then we look back and say, "Look what I did." But the truth of the matter is Jesus said, "Apart from me you can do nothing."[519]

Paul gives us a key verse for understanding the dynamics of the power of the Holy Spirit within us.[520] I love this verse because it is such a gem. There is so much packed into this one verse. When we read Ephesians 6, and it's talking about the armor of God, we want to jump through verse 10 and get on to the armor and shield and sword.

Here's what verse 10 says:

Finally, my brethren, be strong in the Lord, and in the power of his might. (Ephesians 6:10)

This verse can be compared to what happens when one turns on a light. They flip the light switch, and the light goes on. They flip it back, and the light goes off. Paul is making a similar analogy. Of course, they didn't have electricity back then, but God knows what he is doing.

The first Greek word in this verse is ἐνδυναμόω, which is where we get the English word dynamite.[521] Picture a battery or a generator. It's the source of power. Ultimately, we get our power from an electric power plant, or nuclear power plant, or water, solar, or wind energy. As a Christian, when Jesus said, "Apart from me you can do nothing,"[522] he was saying, "I am the vine you are the branches. Plug into me, abide in me, and you will bear much fruit."

The next Greek word we see in this verse is κράτος, and that's translated "in the power of."[523] That's the control switch. That's the light switch on the wall. The thing

---

[517] Daniel 4:29-30

[518] Daniel 4:33

[519] John 15:5

[520] Acts 1:8

[521] ἐνδυναμόω Strong's Greek Lexicon Blue Letter Bible www.blueletterbible.org//lang/lexicon/lexicon.cfm?Strongs=G1743&t=KJV

[522] John 15:5

[523] κράτος Strong's Greek Lexicon Blue Letter Bible www.blueletterbible.org//lang/lexicon/lexicon.cfm?Strongs=G2904&t=KJV

you flip on and off, and that's what this word means. To reign in, to take control over the emotion of the moment and what's in front of us. The Christian feels themselves being drawn in, and all of the sudden they say, "No!" It's an authority word, and Jesus through the power of his Holy Spirit, said, "That conflict you feel in the flesh between your desires and my desires, I gave you the switch. I gave you the power to say, 'No! I'm going to choose God's way. I'm going to do it God's way. I'm going to do the right thing. I'm not going to do the wrong thing right now. I'm going to do what God calls me to do. I'm not going to give into fear. I'm not going to give into worry. I'm going to do what God has called me to do. Here I stand. I can do no other.'" That's the switch.

Further, he said, "be strong in the power ... of his might." And that's the Greek word ἰσχύς.[524] In our analogy, compare this to the light bulb. One can have a source of power and flip the light switch on, but if there is no bulb, there is no light. It means empowerment. It's the strength, the physical ability to carry out the idea, desire and motive God has called the Christian to. If God has called a person to teach, he can give them the power to teach. If he's called them to encourage, he can give them the power to encourage. If he's called them to come alongside a friend who is going through cancer, or struggling from some physical illness in their life, they can, even if they're not articulate or emotionally intelligent, carry out what God has called them to do. At the moment, or long-term, the gifting God has given the Christian,[525] or the manifestation he is moving through them at the moment,[526] he can do it through them.

That's what Paul is saying here. Believers have every single tool at their disposal and in their arsenal, to combat the wiles of the enemy, and to resist the fiery darts of temptation he throws at them.[527] The Christian can carry out every good work God has given to them.[528] And that means Christians have the ability, through God's word and God's Spirit, to say, "Yes," and to receive the fullness of the gift of God he wants

---

[524] ἰσχύς "Strong's Greek Lexicon Blue Letter Bible www.blueletterbible.org//lang/lexicon/lexicon. cfm?Strongs=G2479&t=KJV

[525] Romans 12:6-8

[526] 1 Corinthians 12:7-11

[527] Ephesians 6:16

[528] 2 Timothy 3:17

to give us. By God's grace, we can see as little stunted grace as possible, and one day have the privilege of standing before the throne of God and hear him say, "Well done, good and faithful servant. You've been faithful with a few things. Now be ruler over many things. Enter the joy of the Lord."[529]

---

[529] Matthew 25:21

CHAPTER 36

That Nobody Can Boast

I've never seen a branch produce fruit through self-effort. Picture a vineyard. One hears a faint noise, they don't know where it's coming from, so they say to their companion, "Did you hear that?" "Yes, I heard that. What was that?" They get a little closer to the branch and hear the noise of straining. Have you ever heard that? I haven't either.

How do branches bear fruit? They're connected to the vine, they're connected to the roots. The question is, "Do we believe what the Bible says?" This passage says, "Apart from me, you can do nothing." Paul said a few different things. He said, "There is none who does good."[530] He said, "In my flesh dwells no good thing."[531] And he also said we are saved by grace through faith, not of works, lest anyone may boast.[532]

When I talk to believers, most of the time, when it comes to the salvation experience and accepting Jesus, they have no problems with the idea God operates by grace so nobody can boast. But the question, and as I dive deeper and deeper into this idea of grace, becomes whether we still believe this about ourselves after we have accepted Jesus as our Savior. What I'm finding is the only thing that changed about us when we accepted Jesus Christ is Jesus Christ came to dwell inside of us. Yes, we

---

[530] Psalm 14:3; 53:3; Romans 3:12

[531] Romans 7:18

[532] Ephesians 2:8-9

have his righteousness.[533] Yes, we are forgiven.[534] Yes, we have eternal life.[535] Yes, we have a new Spirit,[536] a new mind[537] and a new heart. And we are sealed with the Holy Spirit.[538] But we, in terms of what is still us, are still prone to wander.[539] And the only good thing true about us as believers is Jesus dwells on the inside of us.[540]

So it comes down to this question. Whose fruit is it? Paul discusses the fruit "of" the Spirit in Galatians 5, meaning it's his possession. It's his fruit. It belongs to him. In that passage, Paul contrasts works vs. fruit.

Works	**Fruit**
Works of the flesh	Fruit of the Spirit
Bring death	Bring life
Produced by the flesh	Produced by the Spirit

When I studied the items listed as the fruit of the Spirit, I found every one of these fruits is attributed to God's possession.[541] They belong to him. He simply uses us as a willing vessel to live his life out through us to bless others with his fruits.[542]

Who's Fruit is It?

1. My peace - John 14:27
2. My joy - John 15:11
3. My love - John 15:9-10
4. Longsuffering - Romans 2:4; Colossians 1:11
5. Gentleness - Romans 2:4; 11:22
6. Goodness - 2 Thessalonians 1:11

---

[533] Philippians 3:9

[534] Ephesians 4:32

[535] 1 John 5:13

[536] Ezekiel 11:19

[537] 1 Corinthians 2:16

[538] Ephesians 1:13

[539] Isaiah 53:6

[540] Colossians 1:27

[541] Galatians 5:19-23

[542] Colossians 3:4

7. Faith - Galatians 2:20; Romans 3:3, 22

8. Meekness - 2 Corinthians 10:1

9. Temperance - Galatians 5:22

When we love, it's not us loving. From beginning to end, Jesus is the author and finisher of our faith.[543] When we're honest about who we are, what happens, and I can testify to this from my own life, is we become more honest with God. I found before I started realizing how sinful I still am and how dependent I still am on Jesus, and apart from him I can do nothing, I found a tendency in myself to diminish sin. To not be honest about the sins I was committing and were a part of me. As soon as I embraced my identity as a sinner saved by grace, my prayer life became real. It stopped being focused on what I need and want and what needs to happen in this and that person's life. Yes, I still pray about those things because there is no trivial matter before God. But when I started reading in the Bible about who we are and should be in Christ, I started praying those things over my life and the life of those I love. I started praying for his desires to become my desires and his motives to become my motives.[544] The more real his word becomes to us, the more amazing Jesus and his grace will become in our lives.

---

[543] Hebrews 12:2

[544] Psalm 37:4

TACTIC #4

The Reliability of the Bible

CHAPTER 37

"Why Should I Trust the Bible?"

The topic we're going to tackle is this chapter is Why Should I Trust the Bible? How do we know the Bible has not been messed with, or retranslated, so we have what we should have?

The Claim of the Bible

All scripture [is] given by inspiration of God, and [is] profitable for doctrine, for reproof, for correction, for instruction in righteousness: That the man of God may be perfect, throughly furnished unto all good works. (2 Timothy 3:16-17)

That word "adequate" means complete, or perfect.[545] The word "inspired" means "God-breathed."[546] We're told other places men were carried along by the Holy Spirit as they used their intellect, own experiences, own language, background, culture, but

---

[545] ἄρτιος Strong's Greek Lexicon Blue Letter Bible www.blueletterbible.org//lang/lexicon/lexicon.cfm?Strongs=G739&t=KJV

[546] θεόπνευστος Strong's Greek Lexicon Blue Letter Bible www.blueletterbible.org//lang/lexicon/lexicon.cfm?Strongs=G2315&t=KJV

in doing so, God was speaking through them to us. [547]That's how he uses us. We have his Spirit in us.[548] We simply are a vessel through which he lives out his life.[549]

As a pastor, I found Christians assume people believe this, understand this, and comprehend it. We start sharing our faith by quoting Scripture and the watching, waiting and unbelieving world says, "Time out. Why are you using that Bible? I don't believe that's the Word of God, so can we start there? Why do you believe the Bible is the Word of God? Why should I believe that?" That's the question we're going to tackle in this chapter.

We need to thank the various groups addressed in this book for reminding us of this truth. They are calling time out as well, but claiming ancient scribes removed plain and precious truths from the Bible and the Book of Mormon, or their particular Scripture or writings of their founder, are more accurate than the Bible. Then there is the Islamic person who says they believe the Koran is the word of God. Or the Jewish person who believes the Torah, but not the New Testament.

We need to realize the Bible is not the only book claiming to come from God.

Other Scriptures that Claim to be the Word of God

1. LDS - Book of Mormon, Doctrine & Covenants, Pearl of Great Price
2. Islam - Koran
3. Christian Science - Science and Health with Key to the Scriptures
4. Hindu - Upanishads
5. Taoism - Tao Te Ching
6. Buddhism - Sacred Writings of Buddhism
7. Zoroastrianism - Avesta
8. Bahai - Sacred Writings of the Bahai
9. Shinto - The Kojiki and the Nihongi

All of these groups have their holy books, so the question we need to answer for people is how do we know which one came from God. And we need not use circular reasoning like "because it says so."

---

[547] 2 Peter 1:21

[548] 1 Corinthians 6:19

[549] 2 Timothy 2:21

Unless all of these books taught the same things, they can't all be true. And they all say something different about God, how we get saved, how we got here, what happens after death, etc... These books hardly agree on anything. They can't all be true. They can all be false. Are we secure enough to test the Bible is the Word of God? Truth is never afraid of being questioned or tested. There is something wrong with any religion that teaches one cannot explore, read, talk to, question things they've been taught, things other people are asking them. If questions are bad, and thinking outside the box or traditions is bad, that is a sign of religion as opposed to a relationship with Jesus Christ. Don't be afraid of the truth. Don't be afraid the Bible is not going to be true. If it's not, then walk away. It's the same thing I would say to an LDS person about their Scriptures, or an Islamic person about the Koran. If it's not the Word of God, then toss it, or keep it on the shelf as a novelty, but one shouldn't base their life on it, and they shouldn't trust their eternal life to it.

What's the Test?

So what's the test? Mormons would tell you, from Moroni 10:4, you should read the Book of Mormon, pray about it, and if it's true, then God will manifest himself by a burning in the bosom. But if that's true, then what about all the other groups that say they have had an experience that testifies their book is true? What about all of the other splinter groups of the LDS church that believe they have a testimony of their prophet and their Scriptures?

What Would You Expect from a Book that Claimed to be from God?

Here's the million dollar question. What would you expect from a book that claimed to come from God? I had to ask myself this question because people would come into my church and say, "That was a great message. Who's Moses?" They would ask basic questions, or they would ask me why they should believe certain things in the Bible. And I had to come up with an answer besides, "Because I said so."

So I had to ask myself, "What would prove to me this book came from God?"

Here's the list I came up with:

1. What it says happened historically actually happened
2. No scientific errors
3. Logical and consistent in the worldview it creates
4. It would have no need to change over time
5. It would demonstrate its origin was from outside our realm of existence

Here's the wager, and I challenge the Christians reading this book to put their money where their mouth is. To anyone reading this, I challenge them to look at what the evidence is and make a decision for themselves. Also, realize what I am going to present is not all of the evidence, but only a small fraction of the evidence. To the one coming from another religion, whether they are LDS, Islam, Buddhist, etc. they were probably given this by somebody who loves them and cares for them. My prayer for that person is they would prayerfully examine what the evidence is for the Bible and ask if it's true. I would also ask them to go to their holy books and put them to the same test. To the one who disagrees with one of my criteria, then I challenge them to come up with their list. Be reasonable, but challenge God. If this is the truth, the Word of God, then he will come out on top.

To the one who concludes the Bible is true, my challenge is for them to submit, confess their sins, and come into a relationship with Jesus Christ. That person should tell God they don't want religion. They want a relationship with him.

CHAPTER 38

Criteria #1 - What it Says Happened Historically Actually Happened

The first topic we're going to talk about is the Bible and history. As I said, what the Bible says happened better have happened. So how does the Bible compare to other historical sources?

How Do We Know Something Happened?

In order to take an objective look at the Bible from a historical perspective, we need to ask the question "How do we know something happened?" To do this, we'll use the analogy of a court of law.

There are two types of information: first-hand information or second-hand information. We know something firsthand if we see it, feel it, hear it, or experience it ourselves. Everything else is second-hand information. An example of a firsthand historical event for my generation would be the attack on the Twin Towers in New York on September 11th, 2001. However, even that was second-hand for those who did not watch it happen in front of them with their own eyes because it was filtered through cameras, news media, etc. In fact, I saw the plane in the Twin Towers on the television, thought it was a show, and didn't know it had happened until I went to school and people were in mourning. Some people even knew individuals who had died in the incident. That is firsthand information.

Second-hand experiences include at least everything that happened before you were born. Now, since we have televisions, we can watch stuff that happened before we were born, but there is still a level of trust, as I mentioned before. Anything one isn't physically present to experience with their senses is second-hand information.

How does one verify second-hand information? The analogy of a courtroom shows us how we can reasonably do this. The courtroom scenario is based on evidence and trying to get to the truth. The best testimony is eyewitness testimony, the person who says he/she possesses firsthand experience of the event. A good lawyer will secure as many eyewitnesses as possible, and get them to share truth from their perspective, which means they are not going to say the same words. If several separate eyewitnesses use the same words and phrasing, that is known as collusion. We don't trust their testimony. But if different people share their perspective of what happened, though different, we can put their stories together and conclude the event probably happened, and we can reasonably know what happened.

Think about the authors of the Bible. Think about who wrote the gospels. Matthew was a Roman tax collector, so he would have known shorthand, and possibly could have taken verbatim of the Sermon on the Mount as it took place. This could be why Matthew includes more of Jesus' teaching than any of the gospels. Next is Mark, and church history tells us Mark's account came from Peter's sermons, and Peter was an apostle and eyewitness of Jesus. Mark was in the book of Acts and an early believer and member of the church. The third gospel was written by Luke, who was not a disciple of Jesus, but he said he interviewed as many eyewitnesses of the events of Jesus' life as possible and put together the most accurate, chronological report of what happened in Jesus' life and the early church as possible.[550] He was a personal physician for Paul the apostle as is evidenced by the "we" descriptions of Paul's missionary journeys.[551] The last gospel was written by John, who was the disciple who Jesus loved.[552] He was the closest of all the disciples. So those are the types of guys who wrote the Bible and told the story of Jesus, what he did, his death and resurrection.

In a court of law, after eyewitness testimony has been heard, we would hear from multiple outside sources. In regard to the Bible, some historians testify to things that happened in the Bible. They testify to the reality of cities, people, things, miracles,

---

[550] Luke 1:1-4

[551] Acts 16:10

[552] John 19:26

etc. And there are non-believing, non-Christian sources such as Josephus and Philo, etc.[553] We do know Jesus existed because of historical testimony.

Circumstantial evidence is evidence relying on an inference to connect it to a conclusion of fact, like a fingerprint at the scene of a crime. Circumstantial evidence, in reference to the Bible, includes things like archaeology. Pontius Pilate,[554] the Hittites,[555] Nineveh.[556] Those three people and places are examples of things mentioned in the Bible people used to mock because no evidence had been found. Since then, evidence has been found, and now we know quite a bit about all three of those items and many more. They say every time a shovel goes into the ground, a skeptic is silenced. Archaeology cannot prove the Bible, but it's circumstantial evidence building up to make a case for the truth of what happened.

Maps. Ever stop to think about the fact there are maps in the back of many Bibles? Many Bibles have several maps to show the difference between what the land looked like in the times of Abraham, Moses, David, Jesus, Paul, etc. Ever thought about the fact we know where the places in the Bible were, that they existed? In fact, many of them are still around today. One can hop on a boat or a plane and go on tours of all of these places. One can visit the cities that Paul visited.

In court, the goal is to prove one's case beyond a reasonable doubt. Our next bit of evidence for the Bible is it hasn't been proven wrong. In a court of law, they try to create reasonable doubt. If there is reasonable doubt, then the prosecution can't prove the defendant is guilty, and the jury is required by law to declare the defendant not guilty. We need to give the Bible the same benefit of the doubt.

There have been several people throughout history who have tried to prove the Bible wrong. Inevitably what happens is these men come back believing in Jesus and the Bible, and many of them become the strongest apologists for the Christian

---

[553] Gleghorn, Michael, Ancient Evidence for Jesus from Non-Christian Sources http://www.bethinking.org/jesus/ancient-evidence-for-jesus-from-non-christian-sources

[554] Pontius Pilate http://www.allaboutarchaeology.org/pontius-pilate-faq.htm

[555] Hittite http://www.allaboutarchaeology.org/hittite-faq.htm

[556] McLerran, Dan, Saving Ancient Nineveh http://popular-archaeology.com/issue/june-2011/article/saving-ancient-nineveh

faith.[557] One of these men was Sir William Ramsay.[558] He thought the Apostle Paul and Luke were full of it and didn't know what they were talking about. So he tried to prove them wrong. He went on a journey following in Luke's footsteps, having only the Bible as his guide. He found every city, fact, government official and everything he experienced was the way Luke reported it. Sir William Ramsay called Luke a historian after the first rank. There were things in the book of Acts so accurate he had to have personally been there to have known it was that way, or that person was where they were.

C.S. Lewis is another great story.[559] He tried to disprove Christianity and ended up proving it. Josh McDowell, while in college, told his classmates he was going to disprove the Bible.[560] He ended up writing books like More Than a Carpenter, Evidence that Demands a Verdict, A Reasonable Defense, etc. Lee Strobel was a similar story.[561] His wife started believing and attending a church, and he didn't like it. He was a news journalist for the Chicago Tribune, so he drilled the experts with the most difficult questions he could ask. He ended up writing books like Case for Christ, Case for Faith, Case for a Creator, etc. What these attempts to disprove the Bible gave us was more evidence defending the trustworthiness of the Bible.

Consider the resurrection of Jesus. Who wrote about it? Eyewitnesses. Consider the facts. Jesus died.[562] We know this because it's verified by a Roman spear.[563] The Romans were breaking the legs of those on the cross to get them to die earlier because it was Passover. When they came to Jesus, he was already dead. To confirm it, the Roman soldier ran a spear through Jesus' side. Blood and water came out. Medical

---

[557] Graham, Jim, 5 Skeptics Who Tried to Disprove Christianity (and got saved)! http://askawiseman.com/skeptics/

[558] Archaeology Verifies the Bible as God's Word http://christiantrumpetsounding.com/Archaeology/Archaeology%20Bklt/Archaeology%20Verifies%20Bible%20Ch2.htm

[559] C.S. Lewis http://www.christianitytoday.com/history/people/musiciansartistsandwriters/cs-lewis.html

[560] McDowell, Josh, My Story: Josh McDowell https://www.cru.org/how-to-know-god/my-story-a-life-changed/my-story-josh-mcdowell.html

[561] Video: Former Atheist Lee Strobel's Powerful Conversion Testimony Proves God's Not Dead http://godsnotdead.com/blog/lee-strobels-testimony-atheist-believer/

[562] 1 Corinthians 15:3

[563] John 19:34

doctors, looking at the Bible, have confirmed and explained Jesus' cause of death.[564] Jesus was buried.[565] This was verified by the Pharisees.[566] It was the enemies of Jesus that did more to provide evidence for us in the New Testament than any other group. They made up a story, and they told the Roman guards they were to say Jesus' disciples stole the body during the night. Normally, a Roman guard that let a prisoner go free would be put to death.[567] The Pharisees offered them protection if they perpetuated the lie the disciples stole the body. The Pharisees, by making up their story, confirmed two things: 1) Jesus was buried in a tomb 2) It was empty.[568] The Pharisees provided their alternative story to explain away these facts. Over 500 separate eyewitnesses to the risen Christ on separate occasions saw Jesus risen from the dead. It's not an apparition. It's not a mass hallucination. It is an eyewitness account. Then there is the historical evidence backing this all up, and a pretty tight case exists Jesus did rise from the dead.[569] At least one knows many people believed Jesus rose from the dead. And all of these things were preached in the town where they happened days after it happened, and nobody contradicted their story.[570]

---

[564] Terasaka, David, Medical Aspects of the Crucifixion of Jesus Christ, Blue Letter Bible www.blueletterbible.org/Comm/terasaka david/misc/crucify.cfm

[565] 1 Corinthians 15:4

[566] Matthew 28:13

[567] Matthew 27 - Jesus' Trial, Death, and Burial http://biblehub.com/commentaries/guzik/commentaries/4027.htm

[568] Luke 24:12

[569] 1 Corinthians 15:6

[570] Acts 2:23-32

CHAPTER 39

Criteria #2 - No Scientific Errors

Many would teach science and the Bible are at total odds with one another. That is what I was always told growing up and in biology classes. I have a question for those who come from this point of view. How would they respond if their kid came home from school with a science textbook from 1970? 1970 is not that long ago. It was not even fifty years ago. But science has changed so much in the last fifty years a science class using a 1970 textbook would be a joke. There would be no sense wasting the kids' time or money on a textbook from 1970. They are probably free on Amazon if one can even find them.

Below are some examples of how science and the Bible interact with one another. The Bible is not a science textbook. It would be ridiculously long and would waste a lot of time addressing issues not ultimately important to a relationship with God. But when the Bible speaks to science, I do believe, if the Bible came from God, it should be without error.

Hygiene Practices

How does the Bible address issues of hygiene currently acknowledged by all scientific fields? We are told this about Moses in Acts 7:22.

> **And Moses was learned in all the wisdom of the Egyptians, and was mighty in words and in deeds. (Acts 7:22)**

Pharaoh was trying to kill off all the Hebrew baby boys born, so Moses' parents put him in a reed basket and sent him down the Nile river. He ends up being picked up by Pharaoh's daughter and brought up in Pharaoh's house.[571] This is where he was educated. This was the culture he was brought up in and influenced by. So one would expect Moses would have gotten his medical and hygiene practices from Egypt. But that's not what we find. We find in the law of Moses teachings radically different from his Egyptian background.

This is an example from an Egyptian medical text of Moses' day. "To prevent the hair from turning gray, anoint it with the blood of a black calf which has been boiled in oil, with the fat of a rattlesnake."[572] [573]

In Egyptian medical texts from Moses' day, we find suggestions like putting feces on a raw wound and other things are going to turn out bad. We may laugh or cringe at that, but here's another example from the 1840's. A Viennese doctor, Ignaz Semmelweis implemented a new practice of washing after autopsies and before doing pelvic exams of other patients.[574] It was greeted with sharp ridicule even though the death toll dropped. His license was not renewed, the washings stopped, and the death toll went back up.

What medical science was struggling to grasp in the 1840's AD, Moses had written as he was lead by the Holy Spirit somewhere around the 13th century BC.[575]

> **He that toucheth the dead body of any man shall be unclean seven days. He shall purify himself with it on the third day, and on the seventh day he shall be clean: but if he purify not himself the third day, then the seventh day he shall not be clean. Whosoever toucheth the dead body of any man that is dead, and purifieth not himself, defileth the tabernacle of the LORD; and that soul shall be cut off from Israel: because the water of separation was**

---

[571] Exodus 2:3-6

[572] Papyrus Ebers

[573] Scientific Facts and Insights in the Bible http://www.seekgodsword.com/articles/bible-science.asp

[574] Dr. Semmelweis' Biography http://semmelweis.org/about/dr-semmelweis-biography/

[575] Malick, David, An Introduction to the Book of Numbers https://bible.org/article/introduction- book-numbers

not sprinkled upon him, he shall be unclean; his uncleanness [is]
yet upon him. (Numbers 19:11-13)

There are several other examples we can talk about. I won't take the time in this book to cover all of them. Many other resources cover this in great detail.[576]

Nature of the Universe

What does the Bible teach about the nature of the universe? That's a pretty scientific topic. How did the universe come to be? Einstein first proposed time is a physical property that had a beginning in the same manner as mass and space with his Theory of Relativity in 1916.[577] E=mc (squared). Everyone knows the equation, but not many people know what it means. It means time, matter and space all had a beginning. They are measurable. They have value to them. They can be altered if one alters the other components. 1916 was one hundred years ago. This is one verse, of many, that teaches this truth in the Bible.

> ... who has saved us and called us with a holy calling, not
> according to our works, but according to His own purpose and
> grace which was given to us in Christ Jesus before time began, ...
> (2 Timothy 1:9)

Time has a beginning according to the Bible. According to Genesis 1:1, so does mass and space.

Origin of the Universe

In the beginning God created the heaven and the earth.
(Genesis 1:1)

---

[576] Video & Book list that give supporting evidence of young earth creation http://www.bible.ca/tracks/b-booklist.htm

[577] Relativity: The Special and General Theory https://reformation.edu/scripture-science-stott/aarch/pages/11-einstein-theory-relativity.htm

Did you know evolution is contrary to the scientific laws of entropy, which say everything is going from order to disorder?[578] Evolution, at least the Big Bang Model of Evolution, teaches there was a bang when nothing exploded, but it built the intricate fabric of our universe.[579] How intricate is it? There is a principle scientists refer to as the Anthropic Principle.[580] ἄνθρωπος is the Greek word for man.[581] It is as if scientists are acknowledging the earth is fine tuned that it was designed specifically for humanity to be able to live on it. What the Anthropic Principle teaches is the calculations of the earth in relation to the rest of the universe: how fast it's spinning, the distance of its orbit, the distance from the sun, distance from other planets, gravity, oxygen, etc. are so specific that if any of them were altered in the minutest sense, life would not be possible on earth. And it takes all of these factors together to make life possible on earth. Scientists would refer to this concept as Irreducible Complexity.[582] This is why life is not possible in other places. Did that happen by accident? Did it happen by nothing exploding and becoming an intricate universe? Or did it happen by an intentional designer who cares for his creation?[583] Christianity teaches one, and Evolutionary Science teaches another.

The Founding of Oceanography

One man who believed the Bible to be true scientifically was Matthew Fontaine Maury.[584] In 1855, he read Isaiah 43:16 and Psalm 8:8, both of which refer to the

---

[578] Morris, Henry, Does Entropy Contradict Evolution? http://www.icr.org/article/does-entropy-contradict-evolution/

[579] Lisle, Jason, Does the Big Bang Fit with the Bible? https://answersingenesis.org/big-bang/does-the-big-bang-fit-with-the-bible/

[580] Ross, Hugh, Anthropic Principle: A Precise Plan for Humanity http://www.reasons.org/articles/anthropic-principle-a-precise-plan-for-humanity

[581] ἄνθρωπος, Strong's Greek Lexicon Blue Letter Bible www.blueletterbible.org//lang/lexicon/lexicon.cfm?Strongs=G444&t=KJV

[582] Springer, Jim, Irreducible Complexity https://lifehopeandtruth.com/god/is-there-a-god/intelligent-design/irreducible-complexity/

[583] Jahns, Bill, Evidence for Intelligent Design https://lifehopeandtruth.com/god/is-there-a-god/intelligent-design/evidence-for-intelligent-design/

[584] Rudd, Steve, Matthew Fontaine Maury: "Pathfinder Of Sea" Psalms 8 http://www.bible.ca/tracks/matthew-fontaine-maury-pathfinder-of-sea-ps8.htm

"pathways in the seas." He believed it to be literal and as a result, spent most of his life mapping ocean currents for sailors to use. The result is the field of science we now know as oceanography.

When Finding Dory came out in theaters, I took my kids to see it. There Marlin and Dory were again, like in the original, riding along with Crush the Turtle in the pathways of the seas. God uses many different metaphors that talk about the universe and earth, the water cycles and all those types of things.[585] The Bible is amazingly accurate when it comes to science. In comparison to what was known 2,000 years ago (most recently written biblical book), Scripture reads more like a modern science textbook.

---

[585] Neller, Ron, Do you know the laws of the heavens?— the Bible and the hydrologic cycle http://creation.com/the-bible-and-the-hydrologic-cycle

CHAPTER 40

Mr. and Mrs. Flat and Horton
Explain the Mysteries of God

Let's talk about some friends of mine, Mr. and Mrs. Flat.[586] They have a severe disability. And that disability is they only exist in two dimensions, which has certain limitations to it. As you can see if I turn them on their side, they almost disappear.

Picture a parade. We as human beings are on the ground, and we're watching the floats go by, and it doesn't matter how good a seat one has, they can only see a certain amount of floats go by at one time. But at most parades, they are covering it on television, so a blimp, or some other aircraft, is live on the scene with a television camera, and they can see all the floats at one time. They are above the realm of existence of the parade.[587] They are not bound by being in a certain location.[588]

The second thing Mr. and Mrs. Flat teach us is God knows us better than we can know ourselves. And why? Because he is our creator.[589] He is our designer.[590] I can assemble Mr. and Mrs. Flat by cutting out stick figures on a piece of paper and putting them on a popsicle stick. As their designer, I know more about them than

---

[586] Flatland: A Project of Many Dimensions https://godandmath.com/tag/flatland/

[587] Isaiah 57:15

[588] Psalm 139:7-12

[589] Colossians 1:16

[590] Psalm 139:14

they know about themselves.[591] They, for instance, might not know they are attached to a popsicle stick. If somebody has a question about a machine, who are they going to come to? They are going to go to the one who made it. They aren't going to ask the machine. And if they're smart, they aren't going to ask somebody else. They are going to go to the maker if they can get to him, and ask him what is wrong with the machine.

Next, we find God can get closer to us than we can ever get to each other.[592] I enjoy an extra dimension Mr. and Mrs. Flat cannot. If they were trying to touch each other, or get close to each other, they have a certain boundary that limits them from getting any closer. But I enjoy an extra dimension, so I can get closer to them than they can get to each other.[593]

And here's the amazing thing about what God enjoys. He can get closer to us than we can ever get to each other without us even knowing he is there.[594]

The next thing we learn from Mr. and Mrs. Flat is God is able, because he is outside of our existence, to insert himself into our world.[595]

The following is a scene from the movie Horton Hears a Who:

Mayor: "Okay Horton, fake name, where are you?

Horton: Well, from where you're standing, I guess I'm in the sky. Compared to you I'm enormous, which is saying something because I've slimmed down a bit. I swim. Your whole world fits on a flower in my world.

Mayor: Oh man, this is pushing it even for you Bert.

Horton: Don't believe me? Watch what happens when I put you into the shade.

Mayor: This is impossible.

---

[591] Psalm 139:1-6
[592] Acts 17:27
[593] Proverbs 18:24
[594] 1 Timothy 1:17
[595] John 1:14

Horton: Light, dark, light, dark, light, dark.

Mayor: Whoa!

Horton: Don't you see? We're in the middle of some kind of cosmic convergence. Two vastly different worlds, miraculously crossing paths. Mine colossal, your's minuscule. Yet somehow we managed to make contact. If you think about it, it's pretty amazing."

When God interferes or gets involved, with our world, we experience some abnormalities. It's his way of telling us he's there. And when he inserts himself partially, we call that a miracle or manifestation.[596] In the Bible, we read of such events as the storm calming down on the sea[597] or a blind man receiving his sight again.[598] Because there is power being manifested, otherworldly, from the designer, the God who is transcendent and who dwells in eternity.[599]

But God can also do something even more remarkable, is his ability to insert himself, if he so chooses, into our existence.[600] And we call that, when it did happen, the Incarnation.[601]

The last thing Mr. and Mrs. Flat teach us is God, because he's outside the realm of existence, has a choice to reveal himself however he so chooses. He can reveal himself as either one or three, however he so chooses.[602] And essentially what we are bound by in our realm of existence is we see God interfering as we saw in the example from Horton. Sometimes God is manifested in one location. Sometimes he is manifested in several places and in several different ways. God is infinite. He is not bound by location. He is not bound by space or time. He is not bound by any of the physical limitations by which we are bound. Because he is our Creator, these are the

---

[596] Exodus 7:9

[597] Luke 8:24

[598] John 9:7

[599] Isaiah 57:15

[600] John 1:14

[601] Philippians 2:5-8

[602] Matthew 3:16-17

things he can enjoy as he interacts with us. But the amazing reality is this God, who is transcendent, above our realm of existence, has chosen to insert himself into our world. He desires to have a relationship so intimate he would come and dwell inside of us.[603] He desires to live out this miraculous and all-powerful life through us.[604]

---

[603] Romans 8:9

[604] Galatians 2:20

CHAPTER 41

Criteria #3 - Logical and Consistent in the Worldview it Creates

What about the unity of the Bible? Does it present a unified worldview, or does it contradict itself? As I said before, there are 66 books in the Bible, written by about 40 different authors. They lived in different time periods ranging from about 2500 BC to 100 AD. They lived in different locations, including Egypt, Israel, Babylon, Persia, Rome, etc. They came from different backgrounds. Some were priests while others were shepherds. Some were fishermen while others were tax collectors, court officials, etc. They wrote in different genres. And even in different languages.

Unity in the Main Subject

Search the scriptures; for in them ye think ye have eternal life: and they are they which testify of me. (John 5:39)

And beginning at Moses and all the prophets, he expounded unto them in all the scriptures the things concerning himself. (Luke 24:27)

The main subject of the Bible is clear. It's Jesus. From Genesis to Revelation it's Jesus. Everything points to him. The Old Testament points forward to him, and the New Testament points back to him.

Composite Unity

The New Testament is in the Old Testament concealed. The Old Testament is in the New Testament revealed.[605]

That quote, originally from Augustine, is communicating the Old Testament could be compared to a huge picture book God created to show us truths that would be coming. There are New Testament truths found in the Old Testament through picture, drama, prophets, law, all of which point to Jesus Christ.

The New Testament explains the pictures in the Old Testament and shows how they point to Jesus.

Unity is Topical

The Bible discusses the following and so much more:

1. History
2. Genealogy
3. Ethnology
4. Law
5. Ethics
6. Prophecy
7. Poetry
8. Eloquence
9. Medicine
10. Sanitary science
11. Politics
12. Economy
13. Origin of the universe
14. Meaning of life
15. Character of God
16. Perfect rules for life and conduct

... And yet not one contradiction can be found.

Remember, forty different men over thousands of years writing on these topics. Here's my challenge. Get four friends together, and have all five people sit down in a room and share their views on abortion, euthanasia, death penalty, war and the

---

[605] Sproul, R.C., Ancient Promises http://www.ligonier.org/learn/articles/ancient-promises/

meaning of life and see how much agreement there is amongst the five. Probably not much agreement. If one watches the news on four different channels in one day, they will get four different viewpoints on what happened, and they aren't even talking about the meaning of those events.

Unity in the Words Used

The unity goes further than this. And this is where we start getting into criteria #5 we listed for a book claiming to come from God. Showing the book came from extraterrestrial origin. Giving the benefit of the doubt, I can imagine one author who writes a book 200 pages long and uses metaphors consistently throughout the book. But I cannot give the benefit of the doubt to a book written over the span of 2000 years by 40 different guys and is describing real history. It's not telling stories or spreading myths. It's not free to make up the story as it goes. But it's able to communicate truth reliably and accurately, and yet every number, place name, color, metal, metaphor, type, etc. is there by design and used in a specific way.

Let me explain what I mean. Have you ever heard somebody say something like five is the number of grace, or six is the number of man or seven is the number of completeness, or forty is the number of testing, twelve is the number of government? Or speaking of color, purple is the color of royalty? Do you know where they're getting that? They're getting it from the Bible. How does one come to these conclusions? A concordance. A great internet site for this purpose is www.blueletterbible.com. A window will pop up allowing the user to type in a word or phrase and it will show every time that word or phrase is used in the Bible. Now keep in mind the Bible was originally written in Greek, Hebrew and Aramaic, which one can also access on that site by going one step further. Type in frog, donkey, serpent, shoes (sandals), etc. Have fun. Type in whatever word or phrase. One will find the Holy Spirit has found a way to use those metaphors and items consistently and yet not harm the narrative of real history and God's working through a people group called Israelites to bring about the salvation of the world.

Let me give an example. There's a story in the book of Numbers.[606] When Israel was wandering through the wilderness, times were tough, and they were complaining

---

[606] Numbers 21:4-9

a lot. One time they were complaining, and God sent them serpents, which started attacking the people. Some became sick, and some started dying. The people asked Moses to go before God on their behalf to see if God would listen to him and make the serpent attacks stop. Moses prayed, and God told Moses to form a fiery bronze serpent and lift it up on a pole. Anybody who looked at the serpent would be healed.

When one reads a passage like this, they might be thinking this is a strange thing for God to ask Moses to do. They might recall serpents are spoken of as evil or representative of Satan in the Bible.[607] A thought like this is a good clue. Take it a step further. Bronze and fire were symbols of judgment.[608] Putting these metaphors together presents a fiery bronze serpent, which would be a symbol of sin being judged. And everybody who looks at this symbol would be healed.

Fast forward to the New Testament, and Jesus alluded to this event in John 3 and said the Son of Man must be lifted up in the same way as the fiery bronze serpent in the wilderness.[609] Everyone who believes in Jesus' death and resurrection will be saved from their sins.

The Bible paints pictures like this over and over again. As I said earlier, if one digs below the surface, they will find everything in the Bible points to Jesus.[610]

What about Contradictions?

Webster defines a contradiction as "two statements which make propositions related in such a way it is impossible for both to be true or both to be false."[611] The key word in that definition is impossible. One needs to understand most of the contradictions people claim about the Bible are propositions slightly different, but reconcilable, and do not fit the definition of a contradiction.[612]

---

[607] Revelation 12:9

[608] Daniel 10:6

[609] John 3:14-15

[610] Proverbs 25:2

[611] Contradiction https://www.merriam-webster.com/dictionary/contradiction

[612] Geisler, Norman, Are There Any Errors in the Bible? http://normangeisler.com/are-there-any-errors-in-the-bible/

We need to ask the following questions:

1. Is it impossible for the propositions to both be true?
2. Is it impossible for the propositions in question to both be false?
3. Is the original language misunderstood? Does it allow latitude?
4. Are there other possible explanations for the alleged inconsistency?

CHAPTER 42

Criteria #4 - It Would Have No Need to Change Over Time

Has the Bible Changed Over Time? The answer is no! Here's where the rubber meets the road, particularly when one is dialoguing with somebody from The Church of Jesus Christ of Latter-day Saints. When they claim the church went apostate and plain and precious truths were taken out of the Bible by well-meaning or malicious scribes, they have no idea what they are claiming. None. The Bible has not changed over time.

Here's another thought-provoking question. How many of Shakespeare's original plays are still in existence? The answer is a big fat zero. Do you believe Shakespeare wrote his plays? Well, some don't, but most do. And that wasn't that long ago.

Now imagine a world without email or printing press. If one is going to copy something, they're going to copy it by hand. And they're going to be copying it on papyrus or leather. This is fragile material. And they're dealing with poor storage, weather, time, intentional destruction, fear of copying, persecution, etc.

A couple of things are obvious by acknowledging this. If one took the time to copy the Scriptures, they would pay careful attention to make sure they're doing it right. Malicious people who are enemies of the Scripture wouldn't waste their time or threaten their lives with copying the Scriptures. The second thing is the copies would be treasured. The Bible was a treasured possession for anybody who had it, and every Christian wanted their own. Wherever the Christians went in persecution, they took their copies of the Scriptures. The persecution itself is a great way to show the Bible wasn't changed over time because it's impossible to change something over time in that capacity. Because the persecution drove people underground and away. Every time they went, they took their Scriptures, and every time they went, they copied their Scriptures. And to change the Scriptures would have meant changing every single manuscript, or at least changing enough where we would find some drastically different and have things in it none of our Bibles have today. Somewhere along the line, something would surface.

A question can be asked concerning this. "What would it take for somebody to eliminate the memory of your existence from the face of the earth?" Even if the person managed to kill you and destroy all of your possessions, it would be next to impossible for them to destroy all items associated with you and every person who had a memory of you. The same would be true for anybody who desired to successfully remove the teachings of Jesus from the face of the earth. Besides this, Jesus promised nobody would be able to do this.[613]

The Mormons were hoping so badly when the Dead Sea Scrolls came out, their copies of the Old Testament would have teachings in it not in our previous manuscripts of the Old Testament. However, the Dead Sea Scrolls were almost identical to the Old Testament manuscripts previously used to translate the Old Testament.

There was a man named Voltaire in the 1700s who said, "In 100 years, Christianity will disappear, and my writings will be ever more popular."[614] Not many have heard of Voltaire? The Bible is still the number one best seller of all time.

The Number of Manuscripts

How about the number of manuscripts? Something the LDS church does a good job of doing is misinforming their people, or not informing their people, concerning this topic. Because if the average LDS person, or skeptic, knew this information, they would stop saying the Bible cannot be trustworthy and they would start answering the propositions and principles it teaches. There are presently 5,686 Greek manuscripts in existence today for the New Testament.[615] In addition, there are over 19,000

---

[613] Matthew 24:35

[614] Aikman, David, Atheist Apostle http://www.christianitytoday.com/ct/2007/march/28.80.html

[615] Geisler, Norman & Bocchino, Peter, Unshakeable Foundations, p. 256.

copies in the Syriac, Latin, Coptic, and Aramaic languages. The total manuscripts supporting New Testament manuscript base is over 24,000. This isn't copies of the entire New Testament. It's not even copies of an entire book. It's ranging from little pieces that have a few letters or one verse to whole manuscripts that have the entire New Testament. They include translations, manuscripts from early centuries to the printing press.

Homer's Iliad places second with only 643 copies. Why the drastic difference? Because the Bible is the Bible, and Homer's Iliad is a story. It might be a great story, but it's still a story. When people believe the Bible is the Word of God, they make lots of copies. When they believe something is history or a cute story, then once in while they copy it for some rich guy. By the way, Gallic Wars by Julius Caesar places third with only ten copies.

The Earliest Copy

The earliest copy we have of the New Testament is within 25 years of the event.[616] Remember we're discussing a culture when writing was scarce and oral tradition abounded. Oral tradition had several cultural rules.[617] They don't embellish the stories. They don't mess with the stories. The stories are almost sacred in a sense. In the case of the New Testament, they were sacred. They were stories of Jesus before they had the gospels in their hands.

A modern-day story, for example, is the assassination of John F. Kennedy. Let's say somebody said, "Did you know JFK was killed by a bow and arrow?" What would you say to them? It's been more than 25 years since JFK's death, and anybody would know that's absurd. Many people saw his death with their own eyes, and those who didn't see it have seen video footage or the movie made about it. It's common knowledge JFK was shot. We might argue over who shot him, but we know he was shot. So somebody cannot convince us he was killed by a bow and arrow. Why? Because the event is not far enough removed.

---

[616] The Bible's Manuscript Evidence http://www.debate.org.uk/debate-topics/historical/the-bible-and-the-quran/the-bibles-manuscript-evidence/

[617] InspiringPhilosophy, The Reliability of the New Testament (Oral Tradition) https://youtu.be/vCp-ayAp7fE

The Holocaust is another example. People are running around today trying to say the Holocaust never happened.[618] That's nonsense, but they hope as time goes on that story will gain more weight and credibility. But it's simply not true.

When dealing with the earliest copies of ancient texts, the next closest to the New Testament is Homer's Iliad, which is 500 years after it was written. Third is Gallic wars by Julius Caesar, which is 1000 years after it was written. Fourth is Herodotus, who is called the father of modern history, which was 1300 years after it was written. Much can happen in 1300 years, yet this is the source called the father of modern history.

I challenged the tour guide at the LDS Church History Museum. There was a copy of the Joseph Smith Translation under glass. It was a Bible with many scribbles through it where he changed, edited, and added to Scriptures to create the Joseph Smith Translation. I asked the tour guide, "Do you enjoy history?" He said yes, so I asked him, "Do you believe we can know stuff about the Roman Empire, or the Greeks, Egyptians, etc.?" He said yes. So I asked him why he doesn't believe the Bible is reliable. "Why don't you believe the Bible can tell us what happened and who it happened to, and how it relates to us?" He gave me circular reasoning. He said, "Because the Bible has been corrupted." "How do you know the Bible has been corrupted? Do we have any manuscripts that show something different?" No. "Do we have any manuscripts that support the Joseph Smith Translation?" "No. Joseph Smith had to translate it by revelation." So I challenged him with this thought. "If you don't believe the Bible is trustworthy, you don't have the right logically to trust any other historical source telling us about ancient history."

The Book of Mormon itself has changed thousands of times since the original edition was released in 1830.[619] And this is in spite of the fact these changes were made into English copies of the Book of Mormon without any manuscript evidence explaining the changes.

If one believes we can know things about history, then they should give the Bible the benefit of the doubt. It has not been proven historically wrong, and it has more weight in terms of its accuracy than any ancient document that has ever existed.

---

[618] Heretics claim: "the Holocaust Never Happened" http://vho.org/Intro/GB/Brochure.pdf

[619] Introduction: 3,913 Changes in the Book of Mormon http://www.utlm.org/onlinebooks/3913intro.htm

Internal Consistency

The internal consistency of the New Testament documents is about 99.5% textually pure.[620] The difference of 0.5% means if there were 200 problems on a math test, the student missed one. That is amazing accuracy. And that 0.5% difference is not hidden by any stretch of the imagination. It's not something being covered up. It's well documented. One can purchase a Hebrew copy of the Old Testament and a Greek copy of the New Testament? And in the Greek version of the New Testament, they can look at the bottom of the page and find footnotes that show alternate readings and where they can be found. The Greek New Testament will also give a grade for how certain they are that what they included in the main text is the original rendering. In addition to this, one can purchase a copy of the translator's guide, which goes through each of those gradings, and it gives the exact reason why they chose that rendering over another.

Many of the variant readings are slight misspellings of words, different punctuations, etc. There are times when it takes away something, but never theological truths dependent upon a translational issue. There are no doctrines of Christianity dependent upon a textual variant, and there are no doctrines removed as the LDS church claims.

What if the New Testament vanished from the face of the earth? Sir David Dalrymple is often cited as saying in the writings of the church fathers from 100 - 300 AD the entire New Testament quoted except for 11 verses. While this might be a misquote or exaggeration, the early church fathers do indeed attest to the New Testament as it is written, the Jesus it presents, and the theological beliefs that go along with these truths.[621] Keep in mind this is before the Council of Nicaea, which cults point to as the point when Constantine manipulated the creation of the canon of the Bible, which is false. That wasn't even a discussion point at the Council of Nicaea. This was not a time of apostasy. This is a time when the Bible was taught and Jesus was worshipped.

---

[620] Slick, Matt, Manuscript evidence for superior New Testament reliability https://carm.org/manuscript-evidence

[621] Wallace, J. Warner, Can We Construct The Entire New Testament From the Writings of the Church Fathers? http://coldcasechristianity.com/2016/can-we-construct-the-entire-new-testament- from-the-writings-of-the-church-fathers/

CHAPTER 43

Criteria #5 - It Would Demonstrate its Origin Was From Outside Our Realm of Existence

Prophecy is the trump card if there ever was one. When I talk about criteria #5, evidence the Bible came from outside our human origins, prophecy is that evidence. God says so himself. Here's what God said in Isaiah.

Remember the former things of old: for I [am] God, and [there is] none else; [I am] God, and [there is] none like me, Declaring the end from the beginning, and from ancient times [the things] that are not [yet] done, saying, My counsel shall stand, and I will do all my pleasure: (Isaiah 46:9-10)

God throws down a challenge to all the other pagan gods saying, "Just once tell me something before it happens. Can any of you do it? No. Okay. My turn. This is what I do. I inhabit eternity. I see the end from the beginning. I declare it as if it already happened."

Did you know in Hebrew much of prophecy is written in past tense?[622] God declares prophecy as if it has already happened, but it's in a tense and context which makes it clear it is prophecy.

---

[622] Ballinger, Tom L., Prophecy: Past Or Present Tense? http://www.plainerwords.com/artman2/publish/2007/Prophecy Past Or Present Tense.shtml

But here's God's standard of prophecy in case one thinks we're talking about Nostradamus or Sir Edgar Casey or Joseph Smith or somebody else who claimed to be a prophet. People read their writings, quote them whenever there is a natural disaster, and call them prophecy. But what one finds in those other prophecies is they are vague, poetic, and have little to do with what happened.[623] This is God's standard.

> **And if thou say in thine heart, How shall we know the word which the LORD hath not spoken? When a prophet speaketh in the name of the LORD, if the thing follow not, nor come to pass, that [is] the thing which the LORD hath not spoken, [but] the prophet hath spoken it presumptuously: thou shalt not be afraid of him. (Deuteronomy 18:21-22)**

God goes on in Deuteronomy 13 to say even if a prophecy does come true, but the prophet is leading you astray to follow other gods, then you should put that prophet to death. He is not speaking for God, and we should not be afraid of that prophet.

The Statistics of Prophecy

There was a professor named Peter Stoner[624] who taught statistics and experimented with his class going through the Old Testament prophecies of Jesus and calculating the statistical odds of one man fulfilling these by random chance. They examined Messianic prophecies similar to those contained below:

1. He would be a son and kinsman of Adam, but also the Son of God. (Genesis 3:15; Isaiah 9:6)
2. His origins would be from everlasting. His family line would get narrowed from son of Adam to Seth, Noah, Shem, Abraham, Isaac, Jacob, Judah, Boaz,

---

[623] Sathya Sai Baba's Historical Significance: Bogus Claims about Edgar Cayce and Nostradamus http://www.saibaba-x.org.uk/2/Edgar Cayce and Sai Baba.htm

[624] Reagan, David R., Applying the Science of Probability to the Scriptures: Do statistics prove the Bible's supernatural origin? http://christinprophecy.org/articles/applying-the-science-of-probability- to-the-scriptures/

Jesse, David, etc… (Micah 5:2; Genesis 4:25; 9:26; 12; 17:19; 27; 49:10; Ruth; Isaiah 11:1; 2 Samuel 7:8-16)

3. He would be born in Bethlehem Ephrathah (Micah 5:2)

4. He would be born of a virgin, the seed of a woman (Genesis 3:15; Isaiah 7:14)

5. He would be from the line of David through Joseph being adopted by Mary's father through the "daughters of Zelophehad" exception and therefore avoiding the bloodline curse on the royal line through Jehoiachin. (2 Samuel 7:8-16; Jeremiah 22:30; Numbers 27)

6. A star would precede him and foretell the birth of the one born King of the Jews who was also to be a prophet, priest and king. (Numbers 24:17; Genesis 49:10; Psalm 110:4)

7. He would present himself as Messiah the King, riding on a donkey, while crowds sing the lyrics of Psalm 118. (Daniel 9:25; Zechariah 9:9; Psalm 118)

8. He would be rejected by the religious leaders because he didn't physically save them from their oppressors. (Psalm 118)

9. Number 7 & 8 would happen 173,880 days "to the day" from the decree to restore and rebuild the city of Jerusalem following the Babylonian captivity (which we can verify to the day from history, and document the timing to the day). (Daniel 9:25)

10. His death would be presented as a Father offering up his only Son, whom he loves. (Genesis 22)

11. He would be offered as a sacrifice on the peak of Mount Moriah, also known as Calvary, the place of the skull. (Genesis 22)

12. By his death, God's wrath would pass-over us as we apply his blood as the wrath of God is poured out on him as a propitiation of our sins. (Exodus 12)

13. By his death, our sins are both poured out on him and carried away by him. (Leviticus 16)

14. He would be the High Priest, the sacrifice, the temple where the sacrifice was offered, and the embodiment of each piece of furniture in that temple. (Psalm 110:4; Exodus 12; Jeremiah 31:31-34)

15. Everybody who has been poisoned by sin that looks at this sacrifice will be healed. (Numbers 21)

16. He would be innocent himself, say nothing in his defense, be killed for a capital crime and die on behalf of others. (Daniel 9:26; Isaiah 53)

17. He would have his hands and feet pierced (spoken before crucifixion was even invented), yet none of his bones would be broken. (Psalm 22; Zechariah 12:10; Exodus 12)

18. His first and last words during his death were foretold, as well as the words of those who taunted him while he died. (Psalm 22)

19. People would cast lots for his clothes while he died. (Psalm 22:18)

20. He would die with criminals but be buried with the rich. (Isaiah 53:9)

21. He would be betrayed by a close friend for 30 pieces of silver that would be given to a potter, but be associated with the house of the Lord. (Zechariah 11)

22. Messiah would be the first fruits of the resurrection on the Passover Sabbath. (Exodus 23; 34; Leviticus 2; 23)

23. Messiah would be raised from the dead after three days, like Jonah and Isaac. (Genesis 22-24; Isaiah 53:10; Jonah)

24. Though he would die, he would prolong his days. Though he would die, Sheol had no hold over him. (Isaiah 53:10; Psalm 16:10)

Here's what Peter Stoner's class discovered:

The odds of one person randomly fulfilling eight prophecies by random chance is one chance in 1,000,000,000,000,000,000. (18 zeros) This would be like filling the state of Texas two feet deep with silver dollars, marking one, and sending a blindfolded man to find it randomly.

The odds of one person randomly fulfilling 16 prophecies by random chance is one chance in 10,000,000,000,000,000,000,000,000,000,000,000,000,000,000,000. (46 zeros) That would be like creating a ball of silver dollars with a radius 30 times the distance from the earth to the sun, marking one, and sending a blindfolded man to find it randomly.

The odds of one person randomly fulfilling 48 prophecies by random chance is one chance in 100,000,000,000,000,000,000,000,000,000,000,000,000,000,000,000,000,000,000,000,000,000,000,000,000,000,000,000,000,000,000,000,000,000,000,000,000,000,000,000,000,000,000,000,000,000,000 (158 zeros) That would be like creating a ball with every atom in the galaxy, and doing this for each atom in the universe, and doing this every second for 16 billion years, and do this 100,000,000 times, marking one, and sending a blindfolded man to randomly find it.

I should mention a few things at this point. First, Jesus fulfilled over 300 prophecies, and while some of those prophecies are rather common and not statistical oddities, others are more complex, as we have seen, and connected with multiple other prophecies. Second, these calculations were conservative, meaning they could have considered the odds more unlikely to be fulfilled than they did. The results are still statistically ridiculous to believe Jesus controlled, contrived or fulfilled these prophecies by random chance. Third, there are a few prophecies so specific that if Jesus is not the Messiah, then these prophecies will never be fulfilled. One of these prophecies involved the day Jesus would present himself as Messiah the King to the leaders in Jerusalem while riding on a donkey while other things were going on 173,880 days in advance. And remember, the Old Testament was in black and white in both Hebrew and Greek before Jesus was born.[625] [626] These copies are known as the Dead Sea Scrolls and Septuagint. This is not something one can write off as a statistical oddity. They must examine this evidence and come to their conclusion as to who Jesus is.

---

[625] Discovery and Publication http://www.deadseascrolls.org.il/learn-about-the-scrolls/discovery- and-publication?locale=en US

[626] Septuagint https://www.britannica.com/topic/Septuagint

TACTIC #5

Explaining the Trinity

CHAPTER 44

"What is the Trinity?"

I n this chapter we are going to tackle one of the trickiest topics when it comes to reaching out to one of these cults, or for that matter, even other religious groups who are monotheistic in nature, atheists, skeptics, etc. And that is the concept of the Trinity.

Many of the groups mentioned in this book teach early Christians made up this idea of the Trinity, and they have made God into a monster with three heads.[627] And they teach this happened at the Council of Nicaea in 325 AD.[628]

Our approach is going to be threefold. We're first going to deal with what the Bible says. I have a colleague in ministry named Andy Poland who used to be LDS and now works with a group called Concerned Christians in Mesa, Arizona.[629] And when he came out of the LDS church, one of the biggest things he had trouble with was this idea of the Trinity. But when he would talk with Christians, he would only be told analogies like eggs, water, etc. So he would ask them to show him where it says God is like an egg, water, etc. in the Bible, but of course, the Bible doesn't say that.

---

[627] Watson, Andy, The Trinity: Mormonism's Rejection of God's Highest Revelation (Part 4 of 4) http://blog.mrm.org/2012/12/the-trinity-mormonisms-rejection-of-gods-highest-revelation-part-4-of-4/

[628] Oaks, Dallin H., Apostasy and Restoration https://www.lds.org/general-conference/1995/04/apostasy-and-restoration?lang=eng

[629] Part 5: Explaining the Trinity http://oldwp.concernedchristians.com/training-videos/

Andy ultimately came upon Josh McDowell's book Evidence that Demands a Verdict[630] which gives biblical evidence for things like the Trinity and the trustworthiness of the Bible, and many other topics, and came to understand why Christians believe and teach concepts like the Trinity. The Bible teaches the Trinity. Early Christians didn't create it. They aren't heresies or deviations from the truth, or mutations of original Christianity or what Jesus taught.

The second area this section will cover is what happened at the Council of Nicaea. Forget all the myths. Forget about what you've been told. What happened at the Council of Nicaea?

Third, we're going to address the Trinity from the standpoint of logic. What does logic have to say about this idea of the Trinity? Is the Trinity logical?

What Does the Bible Say?

What are the passages one can point people to help others understand the concept of the Trinity? First of all, we are talking about one God who exists in three persons. We are not talking about the Father being the Son or the Father becoming the Son. That is a heresy called Modalism, which is taught by some of these false groups. We are talking about one God who exists in three persons.

There is One God

The Bible is clear in it's teaching there is one God.[631] And it doesn't teach one God "for us" as the LDS teach. There is one God. Perhaps the most famous verse that teaches this concept is what is called the Shema. This passage is recited a few times a day by faithful Jewish people. The verse after the Shema is familiar to Christians. That verse teaches what Jesus identified as the greatest commandment: "You shall love the Lord your God with all your heart, soul, mind and strength."[632]

---

[630] McDowell, Josh, The New Evidence That Demands A Verdict Fully Updated To Answer The Questions Challenging Christians Today
[631] Isaiah 44:6
[632] Matthew 22:37-38

Hear, O Israel: The LORD our God [is] one LORD: (Deuteronomy 6:4)

The Hebrew word שָׁמַע means "hear," referring to the first word in this verse.[633] Below are several other verses, from one section of the book of Isaiah, that teach there is only one God:

Thus saith the LORD the King of Israel, and his redeemer the LORD of hosts; I [am] the first, and I [am] the last; and beside me [there is] no God. (Isaiah 44:6)

Ye [are] my witnesses, saith the LORD, and my servant whom I have chosen: that ye may know and believe me, and understand that I [am] he: before me there was no God formed, neither shall there be after me. I, [even] I, [am] the LORD; and beside me [there is] no saviour. (Isaiah 43:10-11)

I [am] the LORD, and [there is] none else, [there is] no God beside me: I girded thee, though thou hast not known me: (Isaiah 45:5)

Remember the former things of old: for I [am] God, and [there is] none else; [I am] God, and [there is] none like me, (Isaiah 46:9)

For thou hast trusted in thy wickedness: thou hast said, None seeth me. Thy wisdom and thy knowledge, it hath perverted thee; and thou hast said in thine heart, I [am], and none else beside me. (Isaiah 47:10)

Now stop and think rationally about the LDS view of God.[634] If God is God, Jesus is God and the Holy Ghost is God, yet they are three separate and distinct beings, though united in purpose, this teaching would not be consistent with the verses above. Heavenly Father knew about Jesus and the Holy Ghost, as well as the God he worships

---

[633] שָׁמַע

Strong's Hebrew Lexicon www.blueletterbible.org//lang/lexicon/lexicon.cfm?StrongsH8085&t=KJV

[634] Godhead https://www.lds.org/topics/godhead?lang=eng&old=true

as his Heavenly Father. So, he could not "I know of no other" in a logical way. Don't let these groups dance around this idea by saying God is the only God "for us."

One - אֶחָד

Look at the word echad meaning one. There are two different words for "one" in Hebrew. This particular one is interesting because it doesn't mean a static one, but rather one with the idea of complexity.[635] It implies it is one within a series. Here's how it is used.

> **Therefore shall a man leave his father and his mother, and shall cleave unto his wife: and they shall be one flesh. (Genesis 2:24)**

Here we have one flesh made up of multiple persons.

> **And God called the light Day, and the darkness he called Night. And the evening and the morning were the first day. (Genesis 1:5)**

Here we have first in a series.

If a person meant the word one meaning an absolute and static one, they would use a different word.[636] God used אֶחָד to describe himself which allowed him to state emphatically there is one God while allowing for that one God to have multiplicity within his nature.

God - אֱלֹהִים

The LDS teach Elohim is the proper name of Heavenly Father. But this creates problems when we look at the Hebrew behind these verses.

There are tons of grammatical errors in the Bible. Let me explain what I mean. I'm not saying the Bible is not inerrant or inspired. Quite the contrary. We have already covered this topic in-depth in Tactic #4 - The Reliability of the Bible. But there are

---

[635] אֶחָד Strong's Hebrew Lexicon www.blueletterbible.org//lang/lexicon/lexicon.cfm?Strongs=H259 .

[636] Trinity: Oneness in unity not in number: Yachid vs. Echad http://www.bible.ca/trinity/trinity-oneness-unity-yachid-vs-echad.htm

grammatical errors in reference to the Hebrew word אֱלֹהִים.[637] "Im" is a plural ending for Hebrew words. It's a suffix one would throw on the end of a word to make it plural in Hebrew. The word for God in its pure sense is El in Hebrew, which is attached to many names like Daniel, Ezekiel, or if you are taking a compound name of God like El Elyon, meaning Most High God.

But the Bible often refers to God as אֱלֹהִים, which would be a plural word in Hebrew. Another example of this plural suffix would be cherubim or seraphim, or shamaim, the Hebrew word for "the heavens." The difference between when the Bible refers to God as Elohim and these other words is it will use this plural noun with a singular verb.[638] This is technically a grammatical error because one wouldn't under normal circumstances be able to pair this singular verb with a plural noun, but it does so every time in the Hebrew Bible when Elohim is referring to God. Interestingly enough, there are times when Elohim refers to other beings, even humans at times, but when it does so, it uses plural verbs with Elohim as a plural noun.[639]

So neither the word for one or for God are singular in a technical sense, yet it is communicated and translated into a singular reality. This implies there is one God with some multiplicity or an expansion on that idea.

The problem goes deeper for your LDS friend. The LDS church teaches Elohim is God's name and Yahweh or Jehovah is Jesus' name in the Old Testament.[640]

I will also show how one can use these verses with Jehovah's Witnesses who teach Jehovah is the one and only God.

Hear, O Israel: The LORD our God [is] one LORD: (Deuteronomy 6:4)

The Hebrew people would not say the name of God. The name of God would be יְהֹוָה (YHWH) to the Hebrews, not אֱלֹהִים (Elohim). [641]When the Jewish people added the vowel markings in the Hebrew Bible, they used vowel markings for אֲדֹנָי (Adonai)

---

[637] א הים Strong's Hebrew Lexicon www.blueletterbible.org//lang/lexicon/lexicon.cfm?Strongs

[638] Zecharia Sitchin's Errors on "Elohim" http://www.sitchiniswrong.com/Elohim/Elohim.htm

[639] Oakes, Jason, Why I Don't Believe Psalm 82:6 And John 10:34 Teach The LDS View Of Exaltation https://drive.google.com/file/d/0ByFtvrDqTG6JUTE4QWdXU0NXMEk/view?usp=sharing

[640] Wilson, Luke P. & Hansen, Roger P., Are Jehovah and Elohim Different Gods? http://mit.irr.org/are-jehovah-and-elohim-different-gods

[641] Exodus 3:14

whenever יְהֹוָה (YHWH) appeared to make sure they would not accidentally say the name of God when reading their Bible.

Here's what this verse would say in Hebrew. "Hear, O Israel: The יְהֹוָה (YHWH) our אֱלֹהִים (Elohim) is one יְהֹוָה (YHWH)." One can see if a person comes from a mindset that believes יְהֹוָה (YHWH) is the name of Jesus and אֱלֹהִים (Elohim) is the name of Heavenly Father this would be confusing. If one asked an LDS person if Heavenly Father is יְהֹוָה (YHWH), they would say no, but the two are intertwined in this verse.

> **Thus saith the LORD the King of Israel, and his redeemer the LORD of hosts; I [am] the first, and I [am] the last; and beside me [there is] no God. (Isaiah 44:6)**

Here it is in Hebrew. "Thus saith the יְהֹוָה (YHWH) the King of Israel, and his redeemer the יְהֹוָה (YHWH) of hosts; I am the first, and I am the last; and beside me, there is no אֱלֹהִים (Elohim)." Is it Jehovah or is it Elohim? Who's talking here? It's both. Elohim is the word for God and YHWH is the word translated Lord in our Bibles, but it comes from Exodus 3, where Moses asks God what his name is at the burning bush. God answers, "I am who I am," which is where the name YHWH comes from.

So this idea the LDS church teaches Elohim and Yahweh are specific people and differentiated from each other and are both gods is not valid. Neither is the Jehovah Witness idea YHWH is the one and only God. Neither is the rendering of this word in Hebrew as Jehovah.

The Father, Son and Holy Spirit are All Called God

God the Father is called God. We've already looked at several verses that teach this. Jehovah's Witnesses would say Jehovah is the only God. LDS would say Elohim is the only God "for us." Jehovah's Witnesses and LDS would both say Jesus is a created being who they would identify as "a god," but deny his co-eternality and co-equality with God.

Jesus is Called God

Several verses and passages have already been addressed in this book that teach Jesus is God in the Tactic #1 section of this book: "I'm a Christian Too." Here are a few verses to reinforce that point.

> **For unto us a child is born, unto us a son is given: and the government shall be upon his shoulder: and his name shall be called Wonderful, Counsellor, The mighty God, The everlasting Father, The Prince of Peace. (Isaiah 9:6)**

From our perspective, a child is born. From God's perspective, a Son was given. This speaks to the dual identity of Jesus while he was on this earth as one of us, the Messiah. He was both God and man.

We also see the Messiah, who we know as Jesus, would be the Mighty God and called the Everlasting Father.

> **But unto the Son [he saith], Thy throne, O God, [is] for ever and ever: a sceptre of righteousness [is] the sceptre of thy kingdom. (Hebrews 1:8)**

This is a quotation from the Old Testament[642] where God the Father calls God the Son, Jesus, God.

> **Saying, What think ye of Christ? whose son is he? They say unto him, [The Son] of David. He saith unto them, How then doth David in spirit call him Lord, saying, The LORD said unto my Lord, Sit thou on my right hand, till I make thine enemies thy footstool? If David then call him Lord, how is he his son? (Matthew 22:42-45)**

The religious leaders were asking Jesus several questions trying to trick him, and Jesus kept maneuvering perfectly through these questions, and finally, Jesus asks a question of his own. "If the Messiah is David's son, how does he refer to him as Lord

---

[642] Psalm 45:6-7

in the Spirit?"[643] The passage then says from that time on, they didn't ask Jesus any questions.[644] Jesus both descended from the line of David in his humanity and was David's Lord in his divinity.

Also, don't be thrown by the terminology "Son of God." The Pharisees understood this was a claim to equality with God and tried to kill Jesus for blasphemy because of this.[645] Even "Son of Man" comes from Daniel 7 and implies divinity.[646]

The Holy Spirit is Called God

But Peter said, Ananias, why hath Satan filled thine heart to lie to the Holy Ghost, and to keep back [part] of the price of the land? Whiles it remained, was it not thine own? and after it was sold, was it not in thine own power? why hast thou conceived this thing in thine heart? thou hast not lied unto men, but unto God. (Acts 5:3-4)

This is an enigma story. We don't know why this happened, but we're told people were selling their goods, giving the money to the apostles and they were distributing as people had need. This is an example of something descriptive, but not prescriptive. Even in the text this was something people wanted to do, not something they were commanded to do. This couple, Ananias and Sapphira, sold their property, claimed they were giving all of the money, but only gave a portion. Peter is clear they didn't have to give all of the money. The problem is they were lying about the amount. The problem goes deeper because they weren't lying to men, but to God.

Peter said they lied to the Holy Ghost. Then he said they lied to God. He also clarified they did not lie to man.

A = lie

B = Holy Ghost

C = God

---

[643] Matthew 22:43-45; Psalm 110:1

[644] Matthew 22:46

[645] John 10:33

[646] Daniel 7:13

D = man

From this verse we can conclude the following:

A = B (you have lied unto the Holy Ghost)

A = C (you have lied unto God)

So, B must = C (The Holy Ghost is God)

Also ...

A does not = D (you have not lied unto man)

So ...

B must not = D (Holy Ghost is not a man)

C must not = D (God is not a man)

When you communicate logic like this to cult members, they will say it's not talking about whether the Holy Ghost is God or not. They are under the mindset only those topics announced in the passage description contained in their church's version of the Bible are the only topics one can form doctrine. One has to communicate to them God does not communicate that way. He doesn't say things are true in one passage, but not true in another passage. One can take truths and principles from one end of Scripture and apply it to another area of Scripture, and it's still true. It still applies. In other words, Peter doesn't have to announce to Ananias he's going to discuss the divinity of the Holy Ghost before he declares the Holy Ghost is God.

Without explaining this principle, it will lead to many frustrating arguments. God explains through the prophet Isaiah he gives us Scripture line upon line, precept upon precept, here a little, there a little.[647] One of the principles of cryptology is to spread one's message throughout the entire bandwidth of the message if they anticipate hostile jamming from an enemy.[648] And that's what God has done. For those who would remove theological truths from God's word, it's like trying to fix a sweater by pulling on the one strand that is loose. What one will end up with is a bunch of thread on the floor. When one does this with God's word is a jumbled mess of gibberish that doesn't make any coherent sense in trying to keep a narrative flowing.

---

[647] Isaiah 28:13

[648] Missler, Chuck, Cosmic Codes - A Series: The Bible Codes https://www.khouse.org/articles/1998/145/print/

> **Now the Lord is that Spirit: and where the Spirit of the Lord [is], there [is] liberty. But we all, with open face beholding as in a glass the glory of the Lord, are changed into the same image from glory to glory, [even] as by the Spirit of the Lord. (2 Corinthians 3:17-18)**

The Lord is that Spirit. The Spirit of the Lord changes us into the image of God.

When discussing this passage, one may end up discussing the topic of exaltation or becoming gods. It is important to stay on topic, so one can ask the cult member to hold off talking about multiple topics and save those other questions or topics for another time.

The Father is Not the Son is Not the Holy Spirit

It is true the Father is God, the Son is God, the Holy Spirit is God.

It is not true the Father is the Son, the Son is the Spirit, the Spirit is the Father.

That second statement represents a false teaching called modalism.[649] The teaching of the Trinity is there is one God who manifests himself in three persons.

Let's look at some verses that talk about distinctions between the Father, Son and Holy Spirit.

> **And I will pray the Father, and he shall give you another Comforter, that he may abide with you for ever; (John 14:16)**

> **But the Comforter, [which is] the Holy Ghost, whom the Father will send in my name, he shall teach you all things, and bring all things to your remembrance, whatsoever I have said unto you. (John 14:26)**

God Became Man

In the Tactic #1 - "I'm a Christian Too" portion of this book, we took a look at several verses throughout the gospels where Jesus said he is less than the Father. If we don't

---

[649] Modalism: As taught by the United Pentecostal Church (UPCI) http://www.bible.ca/trinity/trinity-modalism.htm

understand the dual nature of Jesus, fully human and fully divine, and the concept of the incarnation, that God became man, the doctrine of the Trinity can become confusing.

> **Let this mind be in you, which was also in Christ Jesus: Who, being in the form of God, thought it not robbery to be equal with God: But made himself of no reputation, and took upon him the form of a servant, and was made in the likeness of men: (Philippians 2:5-7)**

Jesus didn't think equality with God was something he should cling on to or hold on to. So he was made in the likeness of men. The idea Jesus was a man who became God is the complete reverse of this passage. In the LDS mindset, if Jesus were God, then he would have already had a human body in heaven. But that's not what this passage says. Jesus had to take on himself the form of a servant. This is called the kenosis, Jesus emptying himself.[650] Jesus did amazing things, but he didn't do them as God. He did everything in the will of God and the power of the Holy Spirit. Jesus was filled with the Holy Spirit, and these are the types of things he said in his humanity.

> **Ye have heard how I said unto you, I go away, and come [again] unto you. If ye loved me, ye would rejoice, because I said, I go unto the Father: for my Father is greater than I. (John 14:28)**

This is a verse cults will point to show Jesus was not equal with God because he said the Father is greater than him. That must mean, they say, he is a lesser being. This is the time when one can ask, "When did Jesus say this?" From there they can help the cult member understand the difference between Jesus' identity as God before the incarnation and his becoming human while on this earth, and how he did everything by the will of God and through the power of the Holy Spirit. Part of that was submitting to the Father as one of us, truly human.

> **Then answered Jesus and said unto them, Verily, verily, I say unto you, The Son can do nothing of himself, but what he seeth the**

---

[650] Stewart, Don, In What Sense did Jesus Empty Himself? (Kenosis, Condescension of Christ) https://www.blueletterbible.org/faq/don stewart/don stewart 795.cfm

> **Father do: for what things soever he doeth, these also doeth the Son likewise. (John 5:19)**

Again, this is in the context of Jesus, as a man, being dependent upon God, so he can truly stand in our place, be tempted in all ways, yet without sin, and he can die as a substitutionary atonement. So our sins can go upon him, and his righteousness can be imputed to us.

So what does the Bible teach? The Bible teaches there is one God, who exists in multiplicity. The Father is called God. The Son is called God. The Holy Spirit is called God. Yet, they are three distinct beings. Jesus who always has been God became a man, so he was wholly dependent upon the Father and Holy Spirit to perform his ministry as a substitutionary atonement.

CHAPTER 45

What Happened at the Council of Nicaea?

Before[651] the Council of Nicaea occurred, there were several competing branches of Christianity. Then the emperor Constantine assembled them together to decide on one view of Jesus. They met for days, fighting and bickering until the current view of Christianity won, and the divinity of Christ was declared. Then the orthodox view used its power to erase and stamp out all competing views of Christianity ... or so we're told.

This story is told by atheists, cults, Muslims and several other non-Christian groups. They always give this false story to show the Council of Nicaea made up the divinity of Jesus, decided on which books would be in the Bible and created a new version of Christianity. However, when one studies the details of what happened before, during and after the council meeting, this fable is easily debunked, and we see that very little of this story is true.

Let's start with the events that preceded the council. On February 24, 303 AD, the worst persecution of Christians began under Emperor Diocletian and lasted until Emperor Galerius issued a general Edict of Tolerance in 311 AD.[652] Two years later in 313 AD, with the Edict of Milan, Emperor Constantine finally allowed Christianity

---

[651] InspiringPhilosophy, The Truth about the Council of Nicaea https://youtu.be/WSKBGdv07nQ

[652] The Tenth Persecution, Under Diocletian, A.D. 303 https://www.biblestudytools.com/history/foxs-book-of-martyrs/the-tenth-persecution-under-diocletian-a-d-303.html

and its practice.[653] Constantine did not make Christianity the official religion of the empire. He issued a decree of official tolerance of Christianity. He did outlaw Jews from stoning Christians in gladiator shows, although they did persist until the 5th century.[654]

It wasn't until 380 AD under Emperor Theodosius that Christianity was left as the only legal religion.[655] Shortly after Christianity was made legal, a pastor from Alexandria named Arius began preaching the idea Jesus was not God, but a created being. He gained a following and started disputing with Alexander, the Bishop of Alexandria. So in 321 AD, a local council declared Arius a heretic. However, Arius moved to Palestine, where he gained a larger following, and over the course of the next few years, the debate became so intense, he gained the attention of Emperor Constantine.[656]

Constantine, who had unified the empire, didn't want anything that would threaten division. He saw the debate between the Christians and Arians as a threat to the civility of the empire. So he resolved to settle the dispute. He officially called the council in 325 AD. There were no Gnostics involved, no Ebionites involved, or other groups. The council was called to settle the dispute between Christians and Arians only. Most other heretical views of Christianity, like Gnosticism, had mostly died out by this point. And the majority of Christians at that time were orthodox Christians. So there were not a wide variety of different views at the council.[657]

Although Constantine invited over 1800 bishops from across the empire, only around 300 were able to attend. Most of them were from the east, with only about a dozen from the west. Most of the men who participated in this council suffered through one of the greatest Christian persecutions of all time. Many of them faced brutal torture and imprisonment for their faith. So despite the modern view about the participants at the council, they were not men who were compromising their beliefs. A few years ago, they were willing to die for them. These men met at Nicaea to confirm what they already believed, and deal with Arius' teachings.[658]

---

[653] Edict of Milan https://www.britannica.com/topic/Edict-of-Milan

[654] Dowley, Tim, Eerdmans' Handbook to the History of Christianity

[655] Theodosius I http://www.christianitytoday.com/history/people/rulers/theodosius-i.html

[656] Jurgens, William A., Faith of the Early Fathers, Vol. 1

[657] Norris, Richard A., The Christological Controversy

[658] Stark, Rodney, The Rise of Christianity

There were three groups at the Council. The first was Arius and those who agreed with him. They taught the Father and Jesus were of different substance, or heteroousious. The larger group was the orthodox group, led by Hosius of Corduba and Alexander of Alexandria. Also in this group was a young deacon named Athanasius. This group held the long standing belief of the church Jesus was truly God and had existed eternally with the Father. They said Jesus was of the same substance, or homoousious.[659]

Then there was a third group, roughly equal in size to the Orthodox group, called the Eusebian group, led by Eusebius of Caesarea. However, this group didn't differ on theology from the Orthodox group. They also taught Jesus was truly God and had existed eternally with the Father. They only disagreed on the word homoousious. The only reason being, in previous centuries, modalists had used the word to teach the Father and Jesus were one person and not co-existing persons of the same being. So in actuality, the Orthodox group and Eusebian group didn't differ on theology or the deity of Christ. They only differed on terminology.[660]

A modern myth is Emperor Constantine forced Trinitarian views on the church. This is not historically supported. Although he presided over the council, he did not push any particular view. He was no theologian. All he wanted was both sides coming to an agreement, and there would be unity in the church. The orthodox group listened to the views of Arius, and they overwhelmingly rejected his views as being new and distant from the view of the church. Eusebius wrote some of the bishops tore up letters containing some of Arius' teachings. He then wrote they interrogated Arius, but found he had a new way of interpreting every piece of Scripture. He then pointed out Arius' views had to be wrong because his views were new and weren't taught in early church history. Athanasius rhetorically asked, "How many fathers can you cite for your phrases?"[661]

They then formed the Nicene Creed, which is a clear condemnation of Arius' teachings, and a confirmation of the orthodox view. In the end, all but Arius and two bishops signed the creed, showing there were no major divisions in church theology. The council then moved to solve other issues, such as which day to formally celebrate

---

[659] Eusebius, The Church History

[660] St. Jerome, Dialogus Adversus Luciferianos

[661] SAINT ATHANASIUS AND THE ARIAN CONTROVERSY http://orthodoxyinfo.org/StAthanasius.html

Easter. They formally denounced Gnosticism and other minor sects and dealt with other minor issues.[662]

The council did not decide on the biblical canon. The canon had evolved on its own over time. However, according to the Muratorian Fragment, the canon was nearly complete by the end of the second century. The council did not decide on the terminology of Trinity. It dealt primarily with the divinity of Christ. The word Trinity can be found in early church history as early church fathers used it. Acceptance of a divine three can also be found in early Christian writings.[663]

The results of the council did not please Constantine. In fact, he was angry with the Christians. He wanted unity and compromise, not for one side to denounce the other. He took pity on the Arians. Arius was exiled and fled to Illyricum for a short time, while his heresy spread and began to gain political power. Constantine's sister urged Constantine to support Arius, and he did. Arius found a new crafty way of interpreting the Nicene Creed in his favor, and Constantine invited him back so he could force the church to readmit him. However, Arius died before this could happen. A follower of Arius, Eusebius of Nicomedia, was able to sway Constantine more in favor of the Arian view. Before his death, Eusebius of Nicomedia, baptized Constantine, effectively symbolizing his siding with the Arians.[664]

After Constantine's death, the Arians continued to gain more ground against the Orthodox view. The Arian bishops Constantine had favored used their political power to fight against Christianity. Constantine was succeeded by two Arian Emperors in the east, who worked with Arian bishops in an attempt to override Nicaea and write a new creed. Although Arians were still in the minority, they were given more political power, which they used to stamp out Christianity. Many Christian leaders were forced to sign creeds that did not favor either side. Jerome later described this period as when the whole world groaned and was astonished to find itself Arian.[665]

However, despite the power of the Arians, one bishop fought back, almost by himself. Athanasius continued to argue from Scripture and stand against the might of the Arian heresy. Even when he was banished and removed from his position five

---

[662] Nicene Creed https://www.britannica.com/topic/Nicene-Creed

[663] The Muratorian Fragment http://www.bible-researcher.com/muratorian.html

[664] Life of Constantine (Book IV) http://www.newadvent.org/fathers/25024.htm

[665] Hall, Christopher A., How Arianism Almost Won http://www.christianitytoday.com/history/issues/issue-85/how-arianism-almost-won.html

times, he never swayed and stood for the truth against the Arians. The Arians turned to gaining more political power, but before the Arians consolidated their hold over the Empire, they turned to internal fighting and destroyed themselves. It wasn't long before all their political power was lost, and the Christians were able to meet in 381 AD at the Council of Constantinople, and reaffirm the Nicene faith.[666]

The battle between the Christians and the Arians did not end there. After the Council of Nicaea, many Arian bishops headed north and began converting the Germanic tribes to Arianism. They then eventually conquered the western Roman Empire, and the Christians had to deal with Arianism again. However, Arianism eventually died out, and Christianity is still going strong and growing.[667]

Christian bishops did not inherit absolute political power and use it to stomp out other competing sects. On the contrary, it was the Arians who gained the political power and tried to stomp out the true church. So there is no evidence the council created Christianity, the concept of the Trinity, the divinity of Jesus, or used political power to erase competing sects. This myth about the council is a complete fairy tale. It is amazing how many non-Christians use the council of Nicaea to try to claim Christianity was made up in 325 AD. Historically, there is no evidence for it.[668]

Why the Council of Nicaea is Not the Issue

The word Trinity is not in English Bibles because it is a Latin word. And it was a word invented to describe what the Bible is communicating about the nature of God. Here's what was said many years before the Council of Nicaea by the early church fathers.

Polycarp - 70-155 AD - "... I praise you for all things. I bless you, I glorify you, along with the everlasting and heavenly Jesus Christ, your beloved Son, with whom, to you, and the Holy Ghost, be glory both now and to all coming ages. Amen."[669] Does Polycarp not realize God said he would not share his glory with another? Polycarp was a disciple of the Apostle John, who did not die until around 100 AD. He was the only Apostle who was not martyred and died a natural death.

---

[666] Council of Constantinople https://www.britannica.com/event/Council-of-Constantinople-AD-381
[667] History of Arianism http://www.historyworld.net/wrldhis/PlainTextHistories.asp?historyid=ac61
[668] Marie, Andre, Arianism and the Council of Nicea http://catholicism.org/arianism-and-the-council-of-nicea.html
[669] Polycarp, The Martyrdom of Polycarp, chapter 14

Tertullian - 100 - 215 AD - "We define there are two, the Father and the Son, and three with the Holy Spirit, and this number is made by the patter of salvation ... which brings about unity in Trinity, interrelating the three, the Father, the Son, and the Holy Spirit. They are three, not in dignity, but in degree, not in substance but in form, not in power, but in kind. They are of one substance and power because there is one God from whom those degrees, forms and kinds devolve in the name of Father, Son and Holy Spirit."[670] If you want to blame anybody for the term Trinity, blame Tertullian, because he was the man who declared this .

Origen - 185 - 254 AD - "For if (the Holy Spirit were not eternally as he is, and had received knowledge at some time and then became the Holy Spirit), this were the case, the Holy Spirit would never be reckoned in the unity of the Trinity, i.e., along with the unchangeable Father and his Son, unless he had always been the Holy Spirit."[671]

That is what the church fathers were saying about the subject. And where did they get that language from? The Bible. They didn't make it up. It wasn't twisting that somehow made its way into the text and scribes had something to do with it. It's biblical. One God. Three persons.

---

[670] Tertullian, Adv. Prax. 23; PL 2, p. 156-157

[671] Alexander Roberts and James Donaldson, eds., The Anti-Nicene Fathers, Vol. 4, p. 253, de Principiis, 1.111.4

CHAPTER 46

Is the Trinity a Pagan Doctrine?

I s the Trinity a pagan deity? Unitarians and Christ-mythers often claim this. The evil bishops added the concept of the Trinity much later by blending Christianity with paganism. It doesn't reflect what the Bible teaches. Of course, they never provide any data that demonstrates Christians stole the Trinity from paganism. If Unitarians wish to show the Trinity is a stolen pagan deity, they must show the doctrine of the Trinity is taught explicitly in pagan literature prior to Christ, and Christians stole this idea.[672]

Trinity-pagan theorists pair a number of pagan legends with Christianity to show a connection. Some teach the Trinity is nothing more than the ancient Babylonian deity Nimrod and his wife Semiramis.[673] They were worshipped as god and goddess. When Nimrod died, his wife miraculously gave birth to him as her son, thus Nimrod was both the Father and the Son. Therefore the Trinity is pagan. That is all the evidence given, and no connection from Nimrod to the Trinity is given.

Nimrod, and himself, as his son, are not one being. They are two beings according to this legend. Neither is he three co-existing persons. He is the father and later becomes the son. This would be heresy if Christians taught this about God. This legend, if anything, is more akin to the heresy of Modalism, which says God is not three co-existing persons, but one person who changes form between the Father, Son

---

[672] Inspiring Philosophy, Is the Trinity Pagan? https://youtu.be/xAcDV270D_0
[673] King, Robert, The Jesus-is-God deception https://youtu.be/Svs5qxhZ1mQ

and Holy Spirit. The only similarity is in this legend there are three players, and there are three persons of the Trinity.[674]

This legend of Nimrod isn't even true. No scholar says Nimrod and Semiramis were married. Historians give us an actual explanation of who Semiramis was, and it has no connection to Nimrod.[675] Our best information on her comes from Diodorus, who records she married the king of Assyria, Ninus.[676] If she did exist, she would have been a queen from around 800 BC, whereas Nimrod was said to have lived 1200 years before that. The ironic fact is all of this comes from Alexander Hislop.[677] His Nimrod story, from his book "The Two Babylons," has been criticized by real historians as not being established fact.

Another attempt is to claim the Trinity came from Hinduism.[678] The Trinity is a copy of the Hindu Trimurti, which is the belief creator god has three forms as Brahma, Vishnu and Shiva. The Trimurti was never a set doctrine within Hinduism. A.L. Basham said, "Early western students of Hinduism were impressed by the parallelism of the Trinity and the Hindu Trimurti. In fact, the parallel is not close. In the Hindu Trinity, unlike the Trinity of Christianity, never caught on. All Hindu Trinitarianism tended to favor one god of the three."[679] From the context, it is clear Kalidasa's hymn to the Trimurti, is addressed to Brahma, here looked on as the High God.[680] The Trimurti was an artificial growth and never had any real influence within Hinduism. The Trimurti can be three forms. This is not three co-existing eternal persons. The only real similarity is the Trimurti has three forms, and there are three persons of the Trinity.

---

[674] The Origin of Sun Worship, Trinity, Babylon and Sunday Worship http://www.the-ten-commandments.org/origin_of_babylon_sun_worship.html

[675] Roux, Georges, "Semiramis: The Builder of Babylon, in Jean Botterfo, Everyday Life in Ancient Mesopotamia p. 141-61

[676] Siculus, Diodorus — Book II Chapters 1-34 http://penelope.uchicago.edu/Thayer/e/roman/texts/diodorus siculus/2a*.html

[677] Woodrow, Ralph, The Two Babylons http://www.equip.org/article/the-two-babylons/

[678] Restored COG, The Trinity - Does the Bible Teach It? (part 1) https://youtu.be/BjUeTctkSPY

[679] The Hindu Trinity https://www.wayoflife.org/reports/the hindu trinity.html

[680] Classical Hindu Thought: An Introduction, p. 73

Another claim is that Plato believed in a divine Triad of God, the Demiurge and the World Spirit.[681] However, Plato never harmonized a set doctrine on this. It was later Neo-Platonists that taught this, like Plotinus, who came long after Christianity. There is no evidence Plato's view of the creator was anything like the triune belief of three co-existing persons of one God. The Demiurge was said to create the world, but he was also created, finite, not omniscient, omnipotent and only semi-divine. This is more like the ancient heresy of Arianism, or modern-day Jehovah's Witnesses, who believe Jesus was only semi-divine and a created being.[682] The only connection is the number three. Early historians like Eusebius and philosophers like Justin Martyr argued the teachings of Moses influenced Plato.[683]

Another attempt involving Nimrod and Semiramis claims Nimrod is also the Assyrian King Ninus, escaped to Egypt, where they were worshipped as gods Osiris and Isis.[684] Then Osiris died and was born again as Horus, through Isis. This research isn't based on real scholarship, but on the same 18th-century fables used for the previous theory. No real historian say Osiris and Isis were Nimrod and Semiramis, or Nimrod was another name for Assyrian King Ninus or Osiris was reborn as Horus. Again, the only connection to the Trinity is the number three.

The pattern among Trinity-pagan conspiracy theorists is the number three. They claim all pagan religions had triad deities. One can find many triad patterns, as well as patterns of fours and twos. These attempts are misunderstanding the concept of the Trinity, which is not the same as a triad.

These conspiracy theories are more like the religions the conspiracy theories come from. Robert King is a Jehovah Witness, who believes Jesus is a creator god who is to be worshipped. Pagans also believe in created gods.[685] Plato's view and many other ancient religions believed in created deities who created the world. Did Jehovah's Witnesses steal their ideas from pagans? David C. Pack believes the Scripture teaches

---

[681] Platonism and the Trinity https://deeperwaters.wordpress.com/2011/02/23/platonism-and-the- trinity/

[682] Trinity: Arius and the Nicene Creed http://www.bible.ca/trinity/trinity-history-arius.htm

[683] St. Justin Martyr http://www.newadvent.org/cathen/08580c.htm

[684] Veith, Professor Walter J., Ph.D., Paganism and Catholicism: The Mother Son Sun Worship System http://amazingdiscoveries.org/S-deception paganism Catholic Nimrod Mary

[685] King, Robert, The Jesus-is-God deception https://youtu.be/Svs5qxhZ1mQ

the Father and the Son are separate gods.[686] Pagans also believe in separate gods. Did the Restored Church of God steal their theology from paganism?

Modern modalists, such as Oneness Pentecostals, believe three persons of God are three forms of one God, like Hindu pagans, so that must be where they got their theology from. All of these supposed parallels resemble the theology of the groups that espouse the connections, not the Trinity of orthodox Christianity. No pagans ever worshipped one God as three co-existing eternal persons. They talk of created gods, and gods taking on different forms, which all of these anti-Trinitarian groups hold to.

The next time one of the groups discussed in this book come to the door and talk about how the Trinity comes from pagan gods, ask them why their beliefs resemble the beliefs in those pagan gods more than the Trinity. My guess is that it will cause some interesting discussion.

---

[686] Pack, David C., The Trinity—Does the Bible Teach It? (Part 1) https://rcg.org/worldtocome/the-trinity-does-the-bible-teach-it-part-1

CHAPTER 47

What Does Logic Have to Say?

I throw this in because the idea of the Trinity is talked about as if it's crazy man's talk. This idea God can be one God and three persons. Here's what modern physics has to say about it. I'm going to re-introduce Mr. and Mrs. Flat from Tactic #4 - Why Should I Trust the Bible in a second, but here is what God said about himself.

> **For thus saith the high and lofty One that inhabiteth eternity, whose name [is] Holy; I dwell in the high and holy [place], with him also [that is] of a contrite and humble spirit, to revive the spirit of the humble, and to revive the heart of the contrite ones. (Isaiah 57:15)**

My favorite quote of Einstein is "Those of us who believe in physics understand the distinction between past, present and future is only a stubbornly persistent illusion."[687] What he was saying with his E=mc(squared) is time, matter and space are all physical properties that had a beginning and will have an ending as well.

Mr. and Mrs. Flat are not like normal three-dimensional human beings. They have a unique difference that handicaps them quite a bit, and that is they enjoy only two dimensions. All people live in a three-dimensional world, four if one counts time

---

[687] Albert Einstein and the Fabric of Time http://everythingforever.com/einstein.htm

as a physical dimension. So we enjoy things like spheres and cubes, and we have no problem even acknowledging there are even more dimensions even though we have problems understanding what that may look like. We have theories of superstrings and things of that nature. Mr. and Mrs. Flat cannot enjoy three-dimensional objects the way we do. What would happen if Mr. and Mrs. Flat were to experience the wonders and the joys of the Rubik's Cube?

Mr. and Mrs. Flat are not going to see what we see when we look at a Rubik's Cube. Let's say one of us in the three-dimensional world was going to show Mr. and Mrs. Flat a Rubik's Cube. They would see a two-dimensional representation of a three-dimensional reality. So if we showed them a side, they would see a one colored square. If we tried to show part of two sides, they would see a rectangle that splits into two different colors. If we spun the Rubik's Cube to show them all sides, the square would change colors, and they would wonder what is happening.

What if somebody spun the Rubik's Cube fast. Or maybe they grab three cubes and show Mr. and Mrs. Flat the different sides and tell them those are all part of the same object. What they see is three different colored squares laying on top of each other or appearing rapid fire.

The Baptism of Jesus

One of the passages those who are LDS or Jehovah's Witnesses love to discuss is the baptism of Jesus. What's going on at the baptism of Jesus? Jesus came to John the Baptist who said, "I have need to be baptized by you." John reluctantly agreed and baptized Jesus. When he came out of the water, the Holy Spirit descended in the form of a dove and rested upon Jesus. And then a voice came from heaven, "This is my beloved Son, in whom I am well pleased." The cultists love this passage because they think they have found a passage that contradicts the teaching of the Trinity. They will say, "If there is one God in three persons, and Jesus is on earth, then who is in heaven? Where's this voice coming from? And what's this thing coming in the form of a dove? Are all of them God? Then that's three gods."

What's going on here? We have experienced what life is like for Mr. and Mrs. Flat. What John the Baptist, Jesus' disciples, those waiting to be baptized and those witnessing have seen is God manifesting himself in three distinct ways at the same time. God inhabits eternity. He is infinite in his dimensionality, and he can interact with the world he created as he pleases. Sometimes this takes the shape of miracles. Sometimes it takes the shape of God manifesting himself in something like a burning bush, or pillar of fire by day and smoke and cloud by night. God manifests himself however and whenever he wants to, and he can manifest himself in multiple ways at the same time. So what they were experiencing at the baptism of Jesus was God in surround sound. God was manifesting himself first and foremost in the Son. He became a man and entered into our world, and to do so, he took upon himself the image of a man, and he was limited as a man is. He could only be in one location at a time. He could only do things in the will of God and by the power of the Holy Spirit if he was fully going to stand in our place to die for our sins. But after Jesus came out of the water, the Holy Spirit descended and rested on his shoulder in the form of a dove. And then the heavens opened, and a voice came out of the sky and said, "This is my Son, in whom I am well pleased." God manifested himself in three different ways at the same time. It's one of the most amazing events in all of Scripture. It's one of the most amazing moments in history. We saw and experienced God in surround sound. We, Mr. and Mrs. Flat, got to experience more of the fullness of God at that moment than any have. And yes, we only experienced it through the words on the page, but it is incredible.

Was God Speaking to Himself?

Another question cult members like to ask is "Was God speaking to himself?" Jesus prays to the Father, and particularly when he cries out on the cross, "My God, my God, why have you forsaken me?" or when he prays "Our Father, who is in heaven." They love to ask if God was talking to himself.

The answer is yes. I know they are trying to put us on the spot and make us seem silly, but the answer is yes. God loves to talk to himself. He does it all the time.

Have you ever talked to yourself? If anybody's says no, they are lying. One may not physically talk to themselves, but they have conversations within themselves. The reason why they do is because the Bible says all human beings are spirit, soul and body.

And the very God of peace sanctify you wholly; and [I pray God] your whole spirit and soul and body be preserved blameless unto the coming of our Lord Jesus Christ. (1 Thessalonians 5:23)

All humans are three in one. We are one person who is spirit, soul and body. And those parts of us interact in such a way sometimes they don't always agree. Sometimes one has to talk themselves into things. Sometimes our soul wants to do something our physical body says, "I'm tired. I don't want to." Or sometimes our physical body says, "I'm ready to go," and our emotions are scared to death. One finds themselves looking up at that roller coaster thinking "That looks like fun," but our soul is saying, "I don't know about that."

Here's what Paul said, especially for the Christian who's spirit has been made alive in Christ.

> **For the flesh lusteth against the Spirit, and the Spirit against the flesh: and these are contrary the one to the other: so that ye cannot do the things that ye would. (Galatians 5:17)**

What Paul is saying is Christians have been made alive in Christ. Their spirit is no longer dead and now wants to live for Christ. But their soul and their flesh fight against the things of the spirit.

Whether talking about temptation, or an important decision one has to make, or the rush of adrenaline that comes with fear attached to it, and mixed emotions one feels at times. We talk to ourselves. It may not be audible, but we talk to ourselves all of the time. And the reason we do is because we are one person who is spirit, soul and body.

And the same thing is true of God.

> **And God said, Let us make man in our image, after our likeness: and let them have dominion over the fish of the sea, and over the fowl of the air, and over the cattle, and over all the earth, and over every creeping thing that creepeth upon the earth. (Genesis 1:26)**

Who is God talking to? Is he talking to angels? No, because he's talking about making man in his image. Is he talking to a council of gods? No, because he has emphatically and repeatedly said he is one God.

> **Also I heard the voice of the Lord, saying, Whom shall I send, and who will go for us? Then said I, Here [am] I; send me. (Isaiah 6:8)**

This is when Isaiah saw the glory of the Lord when he was called into his ministry as a prophet. God first said, "I," and then said "us," referring to himself.

Psalm 2 is amazing. You may not agree with my divisions, but I believe it's a trialogue going on in Scripture written down for us in Scripture.

Holy Spirit: **"Why do the heathen rage, and the people imagine a vain thing? The kings of the earth set themselves, and the rulers take counsel together, against the Lord, and against his anointed, saying, 'Let us break their bands asunder, and cast away their cords from us.' He that sitteth in the heavens shall laugh. The Lord shall have them in derision. Then shall he speak unto them in his wrath, and vex them in his sore displeasure."**

Father: **"Yet have I set my king upon my holy hill of Zion. I will declare the decree."**

Son: **"The Lord has said unto me, 'You are my Son. This day have I begotten thee. Ask of me, and I shall give thee the heathen for thy possession. Thou shalt break them with a rod of iron. Thou shalt dash them in pieces like a potter's vessel.'"**

Holy Spirit: **"Be wise now therefore, O ye kings. Be instructed, ye judges of the earth. Serve the Lord with fear, and rejoice with trembling. Kiss the Son, lest he be angry, and ye perish from the way, when his wrath is kindled but a little. Blessed are they that put their trust in him."**

So What's the Difference?

What difference does believing in the Trinity make over believing there is only one God, or believing in modalism? The Bible says God is love.[688] And if one believes there was a time when only God existed, as we do, before he created the heavens and the earth. Then before creation, all that existed was himself. Then how can God be love unless there was an outlet for that love? The Trinity teaches God has always existed in plurality. He's always existed in a relational context. The Father, Son and Holy Spirit in a love relationship with each other. That's the difference. Our God is love. And because he loved, we can love one another.

---

[688] 1 John 4:16

CHAPTER 48

Case Study: Trinity in the Resurrection

One can help others understand the Trinity by showing them the names, titles, attributes and actions of God are attributed to the Father, Son and Holy Spirit as if each of them lay exclusive claim to them. This can be used to help them understand while the Father, Son, and Holy Spirit are distinct and separate persons, they are all equally and truly God.

In the resurrection of Jesus Christ, we can see the full Godhead, Father, Son and Holy Spirit, were involved.

> **That if thou shalt confess with thy mouth the Lord Jesus, and shalt believe in thine heart that God hath raised him from the dead, thou shalt be saved. (Romans 10:9)**

Here we see a popular gospel message verse Christians use today. But look at that last line. "If you believe in your heart God has raised Jesus from the dead." Which member raised Jesus from the grave? Certainly the Jehovah's Witnesses teach only the Father raised Jesus from the grave. But that's not the case.

> **Paul, an apostle, (not of men, neither by man, but by Jesus Christ, and God the Father, who raised him from the dead;) (Galatians 1:1)**

Here we can see it was God the Father that raised Jesus from the dead. But it doesn't stop there. It goes on.

> **But if the Spirit of him that raised up Jesus from the dead dwell in you, he that raised up Christ from the dead shall also quicken your mortal bodies by his Spirit that dwelleth in you. (Romans 8:11)**

Here we can see it was the Spirit that raised Jesus from the dead. Whenever one is born again, whenever they received Jesus as their Savior, the Bible tells us the Holy Spirit came to dwell within them.

> **Jesus answered and said unto them, Destroy this temple, and in three days I will raise it up. Then said the Jews, Forty and six years was this temple in building, and wilt thou rear it up in three days? But he spake of the temple of his body. When therefore he was risen from the dead, his disciples remembered that he had said this unto them; and they believed the scripture, and the word which Jesus had said. (John 2:19-22)**

Here we see when the disciples saw Jesus after he was raised from the dead, they remembered the word which Jesus said when he was still alive he would raise himself from the dead.

The Father was involved, the Spirit was involved, and the Lord Jesus Christ was involved. These passages show all three members of the Godhead Deity were involved in the resurrection of the Lord Jesus.

CHAPTER 49

Trinity Explained for Jehovah's Witnesses

The Jehovah's Witnesses do not understand who God is. The Jehovah Witnesses do not understand the Trinity. They think Christians are teaching Jesus Christ and the Father are the same person. Whenever one says to them God is in three persons, they ask how the Father can be in three persons.

Who is the God of the Watchtower organization? They teach God is one person, and his name is Jehovah. They teach only the Father is Almighty. In reference to Jesus Christ, they teach he is a mighty God, a second God as well.[689] They teach he is the word of God. They teach Jesus is a God besides God.

Let's look at some Scriptures to see how this view of God is false.

Contradiction #1 - Is There a God Beside Jehovah?

In the beginning was the Word, and the Word was with God, and the Word was a God. (John 1:1 New World Translation)

By comparing verses with verses throughout Scripture, we can see the idea Jesus is a separate God besides Jehovah (YHWH) does not make any sense.

---

[689] Mighty (El Gibbor) or Almighty (El Shaddai) http://www.letusreason.org/JW7.htm

**I [am] the LORD, and [there is] none else, [there is] no God beside
me: I girded thee, though thou hast not known me: (Isaiah 45:5)**

God is saying there is no God besides him. Whenever you speak to a Jehovah's
Witness on the streets, they will say God in Isaiah 45:5 is a big G God whereas Jesus
is a small g God.

**[There is] none holy as the LORD: for [there is] none beside thee:
neither [is there] any rock like our God. (1 Samuel 2:2)**

This verse tells us there is nobody else besides God. But John 1:1 in the New World
Translation says Jesus is a god besides God. This is the first contradiction.

The second question to ask them is who is the Savior of the world. The Jehovah's
Witness will say Jesus is the Savior of the world.

Contradiction #2 - Is Jesus or Jehovah the Savior?

**Yet I [am] the LORD thy God from the land of Egypt, and thou
shalt know no God but me: for [there is] no saviour beside me.
(Hosea 13:4)**

The Bible says in 1 John 4:14 God sent his Son to be the Savior of the world. But
God said in Hosea he expects us to know no other God. Then Hosea tells us there
is no Savior besides God. So according to Hosea from a Jehovah's Witness point of
view, God sent his Son to be a Savior but expects us not to know him. This is the
second contradiction.

Contradiction #3 - Is Jesus a True or False God?

The third contradiction is this. Is Jesus a true God or a false God? The Bible says there
is one true living God. If there is one true living God, then God the Father must be
the one true living God. So the question remains if Jesus is a true God or false God.
If the Bible says there is only one true living God, then Jesus must be a false God.
The Jehovah's Witness cannot answer this question. If they say Jesus is a true God,
then they are saying Jesus is a second true God. The Lord Jesus Christ said, "I am

the way, the truth and the life" in John 14:6. He didn't say his Father was the way, the truth and the life. So if the Bible says there is only one true living God, and Jesus said he is the truth, then either Jesus must be that one true God or he is a liar. The Bible says Jesus is God, but if Jehovah's Witnesses teach he is a God, then he is either a true God or a false God. This is the third contradiction.

Contradiction #4 - Did Jesus Share Glory with Jehovah?

> **I [am] the LORD: that [is] my name: and my glory will I not give to another, neither my praise to graven images. (Isaiah 42:8)**

God said he gives his glory to nobody else. Let's see what the Lord Jesus Christ said in John 17. In John 17, Jesus is praying to the Father.

> **And now, O Father, glorify thou me with thine own self with the glory which I had with thee before the world was. (John 17:5)**

Here Jesus is claiming he shared glory with his Father, but we saw in Isaiah 42:8 God gives his glory to nobody else. Is God a liar? No. The Bible says God cannot lie.[690] This makes Jesus a blasphemer because he cannot have something belonging to God if God said he gives it to no other. Jesus is a liar and blasphemer. This is the fourth contradiction.

Contradiction #5 - Is Jesus the Almighty?

Who is coming back again? The Jehovah's Witnesses teach Jesus Christ is coming back again. But what does the Bible say in reference to his second coming?

> **I am Alpha and Omega, the beginning and the ending, saith the Lord, which is, and which was, and which is to come, the Almighty. (Revelation 1:8)**

---

[690] Numbers 23:19

Who is coming back again? Jesus is but calls himself the Almighty. But according to Jehovah's Witnesses, they teach only God is the Almighty. They teach Jesus is only Mighty.

> **And they sing the song of Moses the servant of God, and the song of the Lamb, saying, Great and marvellous [are] thy works, Lord God Almighty; just and true [are] thy ways, thou King of saints. (Revelation 15:3)**

Who is King of Kings and Lord of Lords? Who is the Lamb of God? Jesus Christ. In this passage, those in heaven were singing about the Lamb, and they said, "Great and marvelous are thy works, Lord God Almighty." According to Jehovah's Witness beliefs, this would be a blasphemous song in reference to Jesus because only Jehovah is Almighty. This is the fifth contradiction.

In review:

1st contradiction - The Jehovah's Witnesses teach Jesus is a God besides God, but the Bible says there is no God besides God.

2nd contradiction - The Jehovah's Witnesses teach Jesus is the Savior of the world, but the Bible says there is no Savior besides God.

3rd contradiction - The Jehovah's Witnesses teach Jesus is a God, but also teach Jehovah is God. The Bible says there is only one true and living God. So Jesus must be a false God.

4th contradiction - The Jehovah's Witnesses teach only Jehovah is God, but Jesus prayed to share God's glory, which God said he doesn't share with anybody.

Who is the God of the Bible?

For there are three that bear record in heaven, the Father, the Word, and the Holy Ghost: and these three are one. (1 John 5:7)

There are not three gods. There is one God. They are not one person. They are three persons. The Father is not the Son. The Son is not the Holy Spirit. The Spirit is not the Father.

In the beginning was the Word, and the Word was with God, and the Word was God. (John 1:1 KJV)

This verse now makes perfect sense. Isaiah 45:5 says there is no other God besides God, which is correct according to the Trinitarian view, teaching there is only one God. It's not the Father in three persons. It's God in three persons. And there is no other God besides God.

In 1 Samuel 2:2, we learned there is no other God besides God. This is also true in the Trinitarian view.

Who is the Savior of the world? The Lord Jesus Christ. And as the Savior of the world, he came to save us from our sins. The Bible says the Father sent the Son to be the Savior of the world. What does Hosea 13:4 say? We should know no other God. This is still true in the Trinitarian view. It also says there is no Savior besides God, which is still true in the Trinitarian view.

The last point was whether Jesus was a true God or false God. In the Trinitarian view, Jesus is the one true living God. He is not the Father, but he is God.

We also read God gives his glory to nobody else. Yet Jesus said he had this glory with the Father before creation. In the Trinitarian view, Jesus has the glory of God but is not another God, but the same God with the Father and the Holy Spirit. Therefore, they can share the same glory, be separate persons, yet still be one God.

Who is coming back again? The Lord Jesus Christ. Revelation 1:8 says Jesus is the Almighty. In the Trinitarian view, God is the Almighty, which means Jesus is Almighty because he is God. In Revelation 15:3 we saw they were singing the song of the Lamb. Who is the Lamb? Jesus. They said, "Great and marvelous are thy works, Lord God Almighty?" In the Trinitarian view, this is a true song, not a blasphemous one. Because he is Lord God Almighty. He is not the Father. But he is Lord God Almighty.

Who is it that died on the cross for our sins? The Lord Jesus Christ. The Jehovah's Witnesses don't teach Jesus died on a cross but on a stake. The common ground is Jesus died for our sins. Which Jesus? Paul tells us in 2 Corinthians 11:4 there will be groups teaching a false Jesus. If one believes the Jesus of the Jehovah's Witnesses died for their sins, then they are still in their sins. If he died on a cross, he would have to suffer for his sins. He was a liar, a false God and a blasphemer, and therefore, he couldn't have paid the price for the sins of anybody else.

The Bible says in 1 John 3:5 Jesus had no sin of his own, so the Jehovah's Witness Jesus cannot be the true Jesus Christ.

The God of the Watchtower is a different God than the God of the Bible. The Jesus of the Watchtower is a different Jesus than that of the Bible.

TACTIC #6

Jesus is Better

CHAPTER 50

The "Jesus is Better" Approach

This is a tactic I started to develop a couple of years ago. It's in response to something I noticed was a pattern. I try to focus on the conversations I have all the time with these groups, so that's why this book focuses on what Jesus taught, what the various Scriptures represented by these groups teach, Grace, Why Should I Trust the Bible and the Trinity. This tactic is based on the conversation regarding the claim of all of these groups to have something more to offer Christians. Most of these groups have missionaries, and when one tells them they are a Christian, the response isn't, "Praise God. That's great. Maybe sometime we can get together and fellowship or study God's word on a whole different level." It's always the cult members trying to get their foot in the door. They still want to have their missionary conversations because being a follower of Jesus isn't enough for them. They will continue selling the Christ follower on why their church is better, why their Scripture is better, why their Jesus is better, and the "more" they have to offer the Christian than what they have in Christ. I started thinking about that, and how one can respond to those claims.

There was somebody who challenged me on one of the discussion groups on Facebook I'm a part of. They were challenging me with some passages in Hebrews that insinuate one can lose their salvation, or works come into play in some way, shape or form. Hebrews 6 and 10 are the two classic go-to passages for these groups.

As I was trying to respond to that person, I read the book of Hebrews, which was something I hadn't done in a while. And what I found is when I read the book of

Hebrews as a whole, a different scenario popped out at me as to what was going on in that book and what was going on in the early church at that time. As I preached through this book, taking the same approach as I'm teaching, I found if I put myself in the scenario of the author of Hebrews, what he was dealing with was Jewish people who were either checking out Christianity, perhaps even attending the church, and they were trying to make a transition from what they thought to be true in Judaism, which was steeped in many traditions. So much so one had to peel back several layers to find what God said in the Old Testament. They were trying to make the transition to believing the Messiah had come in Jesus. To do so, they had to place their whole faith and trust in him and him alone. So people were in various places on that journey, and they were facing persecution on top of that as Christians, and it was coming from the Jewish world, and starting to come from the Roman world. Many decisions had to be made. Were they going to be the fence sitters? Were they fully going to go over into Jesus' camp? For those who were trusting in their works, were they going to trust fully in Jesus' death and resurrection as a payment for their sins? Were they going to put on a mask and check out this Christianity thing and not let anybody who is close to them know because they were afraid of losing their social status or make other sacrifices?

When I realized this scenario as the backdrop to the book of Hebrews, I asked myself what I would say to somebody who used to be Mormon, Jehovah's Witness, etc. If they started to doubt what they were taught in the Mormon church, the Mormon Scriptures, the Mormon prophets. Started believing what they were reading in the Bible, the biblical Jesus, and made that journey of being born again. If this person was tempted to go back to the LDS ward or maybe even use their temple recommend every once in a while, take on a calling, so they could put on a good face. They could go to the ward in the morning and then hurry over to the Christian church in the afternoon so they could have their feet in both worlds. What would I say to them?

I realized what I would say to them is what the author of Hebrews said to his audience, and that is, "What are you thinking you're going to find over there? You left for a reason. You came toward Jesus for a reason. And I'm going to list every reason why you made the decision Jesus is better. Or in some cases why you should make that decision. And I'm going to show there is nothing left back there. You shouldn't go back because if you go back, what are you going to have more than what you already have in Jesus?"

This was an example of the false coming to the rescue of the true. Thinking about the LDS helped me understand the book of Hebrews, and it helped me to see we can take that same approach when these groups come to our door and start talking about all the things they have to offer that are better than what we have in Christ.

The case of Hebrews is Jesus is better:

1. Better Prophet
2. Better than the Angels
3. Better Salvation
4. Better Rest
5. Better High Priest
6. Better Sacrifice
7. Better Hope
8. Better Faith
9. Better God
10. Better Life

Following the Spirit's leading, this is what we can say to members of these groups. And certain of these are going to apply more directly to each specific group we've discussed in this book.

"Jesus is my ...

1. Prophet
2. Apostle
3. High Priest
4. Savior
5. God
6. Authority"

"Jesus spoke and gave me authority, and that is my authority for everything I do."

"I know ... I have eternal life"

"The Bible is ... everything I need"

"Now, tell me, what is it you think you have to offer me better than what I have right now in Jesus?"

That's the approach. Now we're going to walk through Hebrews, as well as some other Scriptures, to flesh this out and how it worked in the book of Hebrews.

Jesus is All You Need

Here are some verses that would be great to memorize and have handy when one has encounters with members of the groups discussed in this book.

> **And all things, whatsoever ye shall ask in prayer, believing, ye shall receive. (Matthew 21:22)**

> **But the Comforter, which is the Holy Ghost, whom the Father will send in my name, he shall teach you all things, and bring all things to your remembrance, whatsoever I have said unto you. (John 14:26)**

> **He that spared not his own Son, but delivered him up for us all, how shall he not with him also freely give us all things? (Romans 8:32)**

> **As sorrowful, yet alway rejoicing; as poor, yet making many rich; as having nothing, and yet possessing all things. (2 Corinthians 6:10)**

> **And God is able to make all grace abound toward you; that ye, always having all sufficiency in all things, may abound to every good work: (2 Corinthians 9:8)**

> **Blessed be the God and Father of our Lord Jesus Christ, who hath blessed us with all spiritual blessings in heavenly places in Christ: (Ephesians 1:3)**

> **And ye are complete in him, which is the head of all principality and power: (Colossians 2:10)**

Charge them that are rich in this world, that they be not highminded, nor trust in uncertain riches, but in the living God, who giveth us richly all things to enjoy; (1 Timothy 6:17)

All scripture is given by inspiration of God, and is profitable for doctrine, for reproof, for correction, for instruction in righteousness: That the man of God may be perfect, thoroughly furnished unto all good works. (2 Timothy 3:16-17)

Grace and peace be multiplied unto you through the knowledge of God, and of Jesus our Lord, According as his divine power hath given unto us all things that pertain unto life and godliness, through the knowledge of him that hath called us to glory and virtue: Whereby are given unto us exceeding great and precious promises: that by these ye might be partakers of the divine nature, having escaped the corruption that is in the world through lust. (2 Peter 1:2-4)

Better Prophet

With the LDS, Jesus is a better prophet than Thomas Monson, Joseph Smith. With the Jehovah's Witnesses, he is better than Charles Taze Russell and the Watchtower Society. With the other groups, he is better than Mary Baker Eddy, Ellen G. White, L. Ron Hubbard, and all the others.

Hebrews says prophecy must be tested.

Be not carried about with divers and strange doctrines. For [it is] a good thing that the heart be established with grace; not with meats, which have not profited them that have been occupied therein. (Hebrews 13:9)

Go back to Deuteronomy 13 & 18 and investigate the criteria. A video I would recommend on YouTube is the Bible vs. the Book of Mormon.[691] It was done by a pastor

---

[691] Kramer, Joel, The Bible vs. the Book of Mormon, https://youtu.be/G1mFdO1wB08

who used to be in Brigham City, Utah and has gone on to Israel to do archaeology and other video projects. His name is Joel Kramer, and I highly encourage you to watch his videos contrasting different areas of Christianity with the LDS faith. In this video, he sits down with an LDS person and starts walking through their Scriptures and their prophets and showing him they are false prophets. Then he contrasts that with the Bible and showing how it is reliable, much the same way we did in Tactic #4 - Why Should I Trust the Bible?

The other concept to point out with this idea of Jesus being a better prophet is that he is our prophet. We saw earlier how Jesus made this clear through several things he taught.

> **God, who at sundry times and in divers manners spake in time past unto the fathers by the prophets, Hath in these last days spoken unto us by [his] Son, whom he hath appointed heir of all things, by whom also he made the worlds; (Hebrews 1:1-2)**

The author said in times past, God spoke through prophets, and he spoke many different ways through the prophets, but in these last days, he has spoken to us through his Son.

Here's a challenge one can throw out to these groups. I call it the "Living Prophet" challenge. Ask them the following questions:

1. Do you believe the church should have a "living" prophet?
2. Who's your church's "living" prophet?
3. Is Jesus alive or dead right now?
4. So who did you say your church's "living" prophet was again?

With the Jehovah's Witnesses, one might need to use different language than prophet but get to the point all these groups teach there should be some central leader able to speak for God today. After they have acknowledged this, by asking them if Jesus is dead or alive right now, they will begin to process the fact if Jesus is alive and he is a prophet, then their church's "living" prophet is not necessary because Jesus is still alive and is a prophet.

Every cult I've ever seen …

A.Teaches a different view of God than the Bible

1. No Trinity
2. Multiple gods
3. God wasn't always God
4. God has a body of flesh and bones
5. We are or can become gods

B. Has false prophecies in their past if they dare to prophesy at all

C. Has an evolving doctrine where God changes his mind

D. Diminishes the role of Jesus

1. Jesus is not God
2. Jesus is "a" God
3. Jesus didn't die for all our sins
4. Removal of the cross as a symbol or means of atonement

Better than the Angels

This point is important to drive home when talking with the Jehovah's Witnesses and Seventh Day Adventists who teach Jesus is Michael the Archangel. This issue is talked about in Hebrews immediately for a chapter and a half.

> **God, who at sundry times and in divers manners spake in time past unto the fathers by the prophets, Hath in these last days spoken unto us by [his] Son, whom he hath appointed heir of all things, by whom also he made the worlds; Who being the brightness of [his] glory, and the express image of his person, and upholding all things by the word of his power, when he had by himself purged our sins, sat down on the right hand of the Majesty on high; Being made so much better than the angels, as**

he hath by inheritance obtained a more excellent name than they. (Hebrews 1:1-4)

Let's walk through this. First, Jesus created the angels. Jesus can't be an angel because he created them. Second, angels are commanded to worship Jesus.

But when he again brings his Firstborn into the inhabited earth, he says: "And let all of God's angels do obeisance to him." (Hebrews 1:6 New World Translation)

And again, when he bringeth in the firstbegotten into the world, he saith, And let all the angels of God worship him. (Hebrews 1:6 King James Version)

Obeisance is a word for honor or reverence. The word in Greek is προσκυνέω, which means to fall down before another.[692] It is the classic word for worship.

Here are some more questions you can ask in reference to this:

1. Is Jesus a created being?
2. How did he create all "things" then?[693]

If Jesus is an angel, he couldn't have created all angels. If Jesus is a created being, he couldn't have created himself or the one who created him.

Another great question:

Do you worship Jesus?

1. The 1961 edition of the NWT said "let all God's angels worship him."
2. The 1971 edition of the NWT changed it to "do obeisance" - honor, respect
3. The Greek word used here is προσκυνέω
4. Take them to the following verse to show this:

---

[692] προσκυνέω Strong's Greek Lexicon www.blueletterbible.org//lang/lexicon/lexicon.cfm?Strongs=G4352&t=KJV

[693] Colossians 1:16

> **And I John saw these things, and heard [them]. And when I had heard and seen, I fell down to worship before the feet of the angel which shewed me these things. Then saith he unto me, See [thou do it] not: for I am thy fellowservant, and of thy brethren the prophets, and of them which keep the sayings of this book: worship God. (Revelation 22:8-9)**

If God commanded the angels to worship Jesus, then it only makes sense he is God. If there was any doubt, two verses later in Hebrews, it says God called Jesus God in the Old Testament. Here we have an angel saying, "Don't worship me. Worship God." That word is προσκυνέω. It's the same word we have discovered all throughout the gospels when people are worshipping Jesus in Tactic #1 - I'm a Christian Too!

Better Scripture

Hebrews 1:1-3 talks about how God has spoken through the prophets and spoken through his Son.

We don't need more Scripture.

> **All scripture [is] given by inspiration of God, and [is] profitable for doctrine, for reproof, for correction, for instruction in righteousness: That the man of God may be perfect, throughly furnished unto all good works. (2 Timothy 3:16-17)**

So when the groups discussed in this book start talking to you about the Book of Mormon, New World Translation, Mary Baker Eddy, Ellen G. White, or all of the other Scriptures these groups have, one can take them to this verse and tell them, "God has said in his word I have everything I need to be thoroughly furnished to do every good work. So why do I need those books?"

At this point, they might start to talk about an apostasy and plain and precious truths being removed. At this point, take them to the following verses:

> **The grass withereth, the flower fadeth: but the word of our God shall stand for ever. (Isaiah 40:8)**

> **The words of the LORD [are] pure words: [as] silver tried in a furnace of earth, purified seven times. Thou shalt keep them, O LORD, thou shalt preserve them from this generation for ever. (Psalm 12:6-7)**

So how did malicious scribes manage to taint the word of God when God said and pledged back in the book of Psalms he was going to make sure he preserves his word forever to every generation?

Every cult I've ever seen:

1. Diminishes the authority of the Bible
2. Elevates their Scripture and/or the writings of their founder or current leader

Better Salvation

If one is playing the role of Savior, then they are saving somebody. If one is on the receiving end of salvation, that means they are being saved. If we consider this from an earthly perspective, I liken it to going it to the beach, and a lifeguard is sitting in his tower to make sure everybody is safe. Now tell me what lifeguard one typically wants. Would they want a lifeguard, who if somebody they love is drowning, they swim out to them, and then give them instructions on how they can get themselves back to shore? Would they want a lifeguard who swims halfway out to them, cheering them on and giving them instructions and says, "If you get out to me, I can take you the rest of the way?" Or would they like a lifeguard who swims out to them, throws them on his back, and gets them back to shore quickly and safely?

I would go for lifeguard #3. Biblical Christianity teaches option #3. Jesus does the saving. We're helpless.[694] Jesus comes and saves us and gets us where we need to go. End of story. Every other group discussed in this book teaching works-righteousness chooses either option #1 or option #2. Either Jesus is our example and teaches us some good stuff, and if we follow what he says and do what he did, then he can get us back to God safely. Or, they teach, like the Book of Mormon does, we are saved by grace after all we can do. So it's up to us to do all we can do on our end. Which the Book

---

[694] Psalm 14:3, 53:3; Romans 3:12

of Mormon makes it super clear we are capable to do everything God asks us to do, and repent of all of our sins.[695] Jesus, in these other groups, is not a Savior. He's not saving anybody. This is where one can play up that they know for a fact they have eternal life, that they have been forgiven.[696] One can even talk about Christianity in light of the fact being a Christian can be defined as somebody who knows they have been forgiven. Because they teach Jesus is their Savior, and a Savior saves. And that's all there is to it.

> **And they truly were many priests, because they were not suffered to continue by reason of death: But this [man], because he continueth ever, hath an unchangeable priesthood. Wherefore he is able also to save them to the uttermost that come unto God by him, seeing he ever liveth to make intercession for them. (Hebrews 7:23-25)**

You can liken salvation to humanity all lined up on a pier on the California coast. All of humanity runs off the pier one at a time and tries to jump to the island of Catalina, which is a couple of hours by boat away from the shore, but one can see it on a clear day. There might be some people who can jump considerably further than others, but when one compares the distance to Catalina, nobody gets even close to Catalina. So the amount of goodness or the things we do, in comparison with each other, look impressive. But in comparison with the goal, which is the glory of God, we all fall incredibly short. Christianity isn't about trying to jump as far as one can and get as close the island as they can, and beat everybody else in terms of how far they jumped. It's about waiting on the pier for their Savior to come pick them up and take them to Catalina Island.

Christianity is the only salvation that is really salvation. Everything else is do, do, do. Christianity is done, it's finished.

---

[695] 1 Nephi 3:7
[696] 1 John 5:13

Better Rest

A question one can ask is "Have you entered into his rest?" This is the question the writer of Hebrews asks.

For he that is entered into his rest, he also hath ceased from his own works, as God [did] from his. (Hebrews 4:10)

All of these cults want to push the idea of works, and the importance of works or one can't be saved without works, or can't go to the highest heaven without works. The writer of Hebrews hits it on the head. By the way, this is almost a quote, if you look at the original Greek, in Matthew 11 when Jesus said, "Come unto me, all you who are heavy laden, and I will give you rest." What he is saying in Greek is, "I will cause you to cease from your labors."

Another question:

"Do you know you have eternal life?"

These things have I written unto you that believe on the name of the Son of God; that ye may know that ye have eternal life, and that ye may believe on the name of the Son of God. (1 John 5:13)

Once a month at every LDS ward they have a fast and testimony Sunday. Everybody in the church is supposed to fast. They don't have any set service planned. But as people are lead, they are supposed to go up to the microphone and share their testimony. Good idea, but an LDS testimony is different than a Christian testimony. An LDS testimony contains this formula, "I know the Book of Mormon is true. I know Joseph Smith is a true prophet. I know the LDS church is the one true church, etc." Occasionally, they might say, "I know Jesus is 'the' Savior." Notice they say "the" Savior, not "my" Savior. It's a role Jesus was assigned in the pre-existence. They are not affirming they know Jesus is their Savior. Jesus doesn't save them, as we discussed. But one will never hear them say, "I know I have eternal life."

When asking this question, be prepared for heartbreak. I have never heard an LDS person answer this question with the affirmative, saying, "Yes, absolutely I know I'm forgiven. I know I have eternal life. I know if I were to die right now, I would get the best my God has to offer me." Never have I heard that. They will always say things like, "I'm trying," or "I hope so." It breaks my heart. I couldn't imagine living like that. Doing all they do, and never knowing where they stand before God.

Even from a human standpoint, our heart goes out to those children who grow up in homes where no matter how good they are, how much they accomplish, how many degrees they have, how much money they earn, how famous they are, it's never good enough for their parents. How much worse is it to believe this about God? This isn't the same God as Christianity. This isn't the same God who loved us so much he became one of us and died for us, bearing his wrath upon himself, so he might come to live inside of us, and we might live with him for eternity.

> **There is no fear in love; but perfect love casteth out fear: because fear hath torment. He that feareth is not made perfect in love. (1 John 4:18)**

1. Loving God and fearing his torment are mutually exclusive
2. The word torment means "everlasting punishment"
3. If one fears God's torment, it's because they fear God's eternal punishment
4. If one fears eternal punishment, then they can't love God
5. Put another way, if one doesn't know they have eternal life, then they can't love God
6. If one can't love God, then they can't obey God since the greatest commandment is to love God
7. If one can't obey God, and they are trusting in their works to save them, then they'll never know if they have eternal life
8. If one doesn't know they have eternal life, then they can't love God

And round and round and round it goes. This is a perfect way to help somebody who is coming from a cycle of works-righteousness to understand why grace is important. Why it must be salvation by grace through faith. Because one will never, ever get there on the treadmill of works.

Better High Priest

The writer of Hebrews almost seems like he was anticipating Joseph Smith because he spends three chapters talking about how Jesus is a priest after the order of Melchizedek.

This strange character who appears in the middle of the book of Genesis.[697] He disappears into oblivion except for one Psalm that said of the Messiah, "You are priest forever after the order of Melchizedek." [698]He disappears again until the writer of Hebrews uses it to establish why Jesus is a better High Priest than Aaron and the Aaronic Priesthood.

I'm going to walk through what I call the Melchizedek Priesthood Challenge. Why I'm doing this is because in 1829 Joseph Smith claimed Peter, James and John, the apostles of Jesus, returned and laid hands on him and Oliver Cowdery with him and gave them the Melchizedek Priesthood they had received from Jesus.[699] This is the same priesthood the Mormon church would teach is why the church went into apostasy. The apostles were killed, and they hadn't passed on their priesthood authority. Without this authority, one can't baptize, one can't heal, one can't do all of LDS requirements to go to the highest level of heaven according to Mormonism. This is also the priesthood Mormon missionaries claim to have, which is why their name tag says "Elder" on it.

"So you think you're a holder of the Melchizedek priesthood …"

Without father, without mother, without descent, having neither beginning of days, nor end of life; but made like unto the Son of God; abideth a priest continually. (Hebrews 7:3)

What the author of Hebrews is doing is comparing Melchizedek with Jesus. He's not saying he was Jesus. He said he was like Jesus. He's talking about the Holy Spirit edits in the book of Genesis. What I mean by that is there is a way the Holy Spirit communicates narrative accounts so they can be used for portraits and types of the Messiah later on. And he does it intentionally. In Genesis, it never discusses where Melchizedek comes from or what happens to him (i.e. birth and death). So the author of Hebrews compares him to Jesus not having a beginning or ending. Sorry Arius. Sorry LDS. Sorry Jehovah's Witnesses. Jesus doesn't have a beginning.

---

[697] Genesis 14:18

[698] Psalm 110:4

[699] Porter, Larry C., The Restoration of the Aaronic and Melchizedek Priesthoods https://www.lds.org/ensign/1996/12/the-restoration-of-the-aaronic-and-melchizedek-priesthoods?lang=eng

First criteria - "Do you have a mom and a dad? If you have a mom and dad, you don't fit the criteria for the Melchizedek Priesthood." If one is talking to an LDS person, they might say they existed as an intelligence before they existed as spirit children in the pre-existence, which was before they came to this earth. They might go there, but that's not what this is talking about. The writer of Hebrews is arguing Jesus is self-existent. He is eternal. Anybody still playing? I didn't think so. But let's go on.

> **But this [man], because he continueth ever, hath an unchangeable priesthood. (Hebrews 7:24)**

That word unchangeable, in Greek, means untransferable.[700] Why is it untransferable? Because the High Priest was High Priest until he died.[701] If he doesn't die, no need for a new High Priest. If Jesus is our High Priest, and he never dies, then he's our High Priest forever. That means he didn't pass the priesthood on to Peter, James and John, and they didn't pass it on to Joseph Smith, and Joseph Smith didn't pass it on and on and on to the 18-year-old at your door with a name tag.

> **Wherefore he is able also to save them to the uttermost that come unto God by him, seeing he ever liveth to make intercession for them. (Hebrews 7:25)**

Going back to that last question. "Do you know you are forgiven?" No? How is one who does not know they are forgiven going to offer forgiveness? Going a step further, many of the groups discussed in this book don't even teach Jesus can save to the uttermost.

> **For such an high priest became us, [who is] holy, harmless, undefiled, separate from sinners, and made higher than the heavens; (Hebrews 7:26)**

---

[700] ἀπαράβατος Strong's Greek Lexicon www.blueletterbible.org//lang/lexicon/lexicon.cfm?Strongs= G531&t=KJV

[701] Hebrews 7:23

Anybody still playing? No. Jesus is holy, harmless, undefiled, separate from sinners and made higher than the heavens. And Jesus alone is our High Priest after the order of Melchizedek.

What did he do as our High Priest?

> **Wherefore in all things it behoved him to be made like unto [his] brethren, that he might be a merciful and faithful high priest in things [pertaining] to God, to make reconciliation for the sins of the people. For in that he himself hath suffered being tempted, he is able to succour them that are tempted. (Hebrews 2:17-18)**

> **Seeing then that we have a great high priest, that is passed into the heavens, Jesus the Son of God, let us hold fast [our] profession. For we have not an high priest which cannot be touched with the feeling of our infirmities; but was in all points tempted like as [we are, yet] without sin. Let us therefore come boldly unto the throne of grace, that we may obtain mercy, and find grace to help in time of need. (Hebrews 4:14-16)**

Jesus became sin and felt separation from God.[702] But because Jesus was perfect, he canceled out the sin because death couldn't hold him.[703] At that moment, in the holy of holies, the veil separated the Sanctuary from the Holy of Holies was torn in two. [704]So we have direct access to the throne of God.[705] In the Holy of Holies was the mercy seat and the ark of the Covenant. That mercy seat in the book of Hebrews is also called the propitiation. Jesus, because of his death, tore the veil and the mercy seat became our propitiation and became the throne of grace. So we can come boldly to the throne of grace. Direct access. We do not need any intermediaries. Jesus is our High Priest. He is our Apostle. He is our everything. There is one mediator between God and man, the man Christ Jesus.[706] We don't need any other mediators. Nobody

---

[702] Matthew 27:46

[703] Acts 2:24

[704] Matthew 27:51

[705] Hebrews 4:16

[706] 1 Timothy 2:5

telling us what we have to do. Nobody we have to pray to, confess to, nobody. Jesus does all of that for us.

Better Sacrifice

> **For the law having a shadow of good things to come, [and] not the very image of the things, can never with those sacrifices which they offered year by year continually make the comers thereunto perfect. For then would they not have ceased to be offered? because that the worshippers once purged should have had no more conscience of sins. (Hebrews 10:1-2)**

Every religious, legalistic, works based system has something more for their followers to do. They've never done enough. They've never done their part. There's always more dead people to be baptized for in the temple. There are more callings. There are more doors for you to knock on. There's more stuff to do. The writer of Hebrews said of the sacrifices in the Old Testament, "If they would have been able to forgive sins, then people would have had a clear conscience before God." They would have had peace with God. They would have known they were forgiven. They would have never had a thought they had to offer another sacrifice. But lo and behold, the next time they sinned, they felt like they had fallen out of favor with God. They offered another sacrifice to clear their conscience.

That's what grace does. It clears the conscience. It gives true peace with God.

Better Faith

Here's a working definition I've come up with in reference to faith.

Faith is ... believing who God has revealed himself to be .... and allowing him to do ... through us ... what he has said he will do ... and by doing so proclaiming the truth of God to our watching friends and family.

> **Looking unto Jesus the author and finisher of [our] faith; who for the joy that was set before him endured the cross, despising the shame, and is set down at the right hand of the throne of God. (Hebrews 12:2)**

Is Jesus the author and finisher of our faith?[707] Did our faith originate with a gift of God?[708] Is he the reason why we will take our last breath in faith? Is he the one who gives our desires?[709] Motives?[710] Power?[711]

> **Make you perfect in every good work to do his will, working in you that which is wellpleasing in his sight, through Jesus Christ; to whom [be] glory for ever and ever. Amen. (Hebrews 13:21)**

Who makes us perfect? Jesus. Who makes us perfect to do every good work? Jesus. Who makes us perfect to do his will? Jesus. Who is working in Christians that which is well pleasing in his sight? Jesus. From start to finish. It's Jesus. We can't take credit for any of it. So tell me again, "What is it that you said I have to do to gain God's favor or get into a higher level of heaven?"

> **Now faith is the substance of things hoped for, the evidence of things not seen. (Hebrews 11:1)**

It's all in the word one emphasizes. Now faith "is" the foundation of things hoped for, the proof of things not seen. Faith is the foundation. Faith is the proof of things not seen. Faith always shows itself in action, as we see in the Hall of Faith in Hebrews 11. Faith always shows itself in action, but Jesus is the author and finisher of our faith. From start to finish, he's the one who is doing it.

Better God

Is God holy or sinner?

When we talk about God, we need to be clear who we are talking about. When we talk about God, are we talking about a God who has always been God? Or are we talking about somebody who progressed to be God? Are we talking about somebody

---

[707] Hebrews 12:2

[708] Ephesians 2:8-9

[709] Psalm 37:4

[710] 2 Corinthians 5:14

[711] Ephesians 6:10

who used to be like us, who needed to repent of his sins to receive eternal life from his God?

A colleague of mine who witnesses at Temple Square in Salt Lake City every week took a video on YouTube at General Conference where he interviewed LDS people asking if they believe God was perhaps once a sinner and how they felt about that.[712] The response he got was far different from Christianity's definition because we define holiness the way the Bible defines holiness. God has always been holy. He is light and there is absolutely no darkness in him.[713]

Here are some of the responses my friend received:

"I do. I think that making mistakes is an essential part of the learning process. So, if you follow logic and reason, then I think that is a distinct possibility. It doesn't make him any less powerful.... It makes me more comfortable, in the sense we have hope to overcome. If he could overcome and become as great as he is, then certainly we have hope to overcome all of our trials and sinful natures as well."

"Absolutely yes. He went through all the same things we did. He knows what we're going through. He lived his life right because he became our heavenly Father. One of the greatest fathers who ever lived."

> **For they verily for a few days chastened [us] after their own pleasure; but he for [our] profit, that [we] might be partakers of his holiness. (Hebrews 12:10)**

> **Follow peace with all [men], and holiness, without which no man shall see the Lord: (Hebrews 12:14)**

Here are some more questions to ask:

"Is your God holy, or is he a sinner?"
"If your God self-sufficient?"

> **Who being the brightness of [his] glory, and the express image of his person, and upholding all things by the word of his power,**

---

[712] Shafovaloff, Aaron, God Never Sinned: Do Mormons Agree? https://youtu.be/WyH61ybnPBE

[713] 1 John 1:5

when he had by himself purged our sins, sat down on the right hand of the Majesty on high; (Hebrews 1:3)

If one can imagine the sun without its rays, or the rays of the sun without the sun, then they can imagine the Father without the Son. [714]There has never been a time when he was not there. Father, Son, and Holy Spirit. We call it the Trinity. Jesus is the brightness, or radiance, of the glory of God. God is glory. We see the radiance of that glory in Jesus. There's no way to separate those two.

The Bible says God is love.[715] There is no other God on the face of the earth it could be said before creation, he is love. Because Father, Son and Holy Spirit have always loved each other with a perfect love from eternity past.

And they have need of nothing. They didn't create us because they were bored, or they needed us. Some of the other gods out there, like Allah, are capricious and unknowable. And Joseph Smith's God is not even God. He's not even the Most High God.

God is love, and God is judge. In the Old Testament, God established by the mouth of two or three witnesses, a fact shall be established.[716] So much so that in the Ten Commandments he said we should not bear false witness.[717] I believe the law is a reflection of the glory of God. So, if God limited himself to a standard by which only by two or three witnesses can a fact be established, then he must not be a static one. If so, he could not judge us. But because he is one God in three persons, God can establish truth and be judge of all.[718]

So one can walk members of these groups through these truths and ask them: "What is it you think you have to offer me?"

1. That's better than Jesus
2. That's better than assurance of salvation
3. That's better than the Bible

---

[714] Athanasius of Alexandria, Against the Arians, 3:3

[715] 1 John 4:16

[716] Deuteronomy 19:15

[717] Exodus 20:16

[718] Hebrews 12:23

I've shared this with some of them, and I said, "Listen, what you are asking me to do is to go from knowing for a fact I have been forgiven, and I have eternal life, give that up, so I will never know, until I stand before God, I've done enough. You're asking me to go from having a full confidence God has preserved his word in the Scriptures, and it's everything I need for life and godliness, to constantly changing Scriptures I'll be dependent upon every October and every Spring, going into General Conference to hear the new thing God has revealed to the prophet, and never know what is official doctrine, and then have the rug pulled out from underneath me when things I've believed for years are suddenly changed. You're asking me to go from believing Jesus is my prophet, my High Priest, my direct access to God, I can go before the throne of grace and get what I need from a God who sympathizes with me and was tempted in every way, yet without sin, to trusting in a God who may have been a more vile sinner at some point than I am, a God who hasn't always been God and who is worshipping a God of his own, and if at some point is not deemed worthy can be removed from his place as God. What would that even mean for me?"

I think you get the point. There is nothing these groups have to offer us. Absolutely nothing. So I pray for boldness to reach out to people in these groups and equip the people in our congregations to do the same. I pray believers would have absolute confidence in their Savior, in their standing and identity in Christ, and absolute confidence in the word of God and the gospel of Jesus Christ.

EPILOGUE

How LDS View Joseph Smith

Jayson Kunzler gave a speech at BYU Idaho called "Millions Shall See Brother Joseph Again."[719] It was a talk given in their chapel about Joseph Smith and the LDS member's relationship to Joseph Smith. I think this is an important message for Christians and LDS to be exposed to. In this final chapter, I wanted to share some quotes from this speech from various LDS leaders and writers of the past in reference to Joseph Smith. I hope it causes a passion for LDS people, as well as members of all of the groups we have discussed in this book, and a burden to share the gospel with them.

Joseph Fielding Smith said, "We link the names of Jesus Christ and Joseph Smith."[720]

Brigham Young taught, 'What I have received from the Lord, I have received by Joseph Smith. If I drop him, I must drop these principles. No man on the earth can say Jesus lives, and deny at the same time the Prophet Joseph. This is my testimony."[721]

Bruce McConkie believed the measure of a person's spiritual maturity is found in his or her loyalty to the Prophet Joseph Smith. How loyal are we to him?[722]

---

[719] Kunzler, Jayson, Millions Shall Know Brother Joseph Again http://www2.byui.edu/Presentations/Transcripts/Devotionals/2015 10 20 Kunzler.htm

[720] Smith, Joseph Fielding, Teachings of the Presidents of the Church: Joseph Fielding Smith, p. 107

[721] Young, Brigham, Teachings of the Presidents of the Church: Brigham Young, p. 345-346

[722] McConkie, Joseph Fielding, The Bruce R. McConkie Story: Reflections of a Son, p. 256

Brigham Young testified, "No man or woman in this dispensation will ever enter into the Celestial Kingdom of God without the consent of Joseph Smith. From the day the priesthood was taken from the earth to the winding up scene of all things, every man and woman must have the certificate of Joseph Smith Jr. as a passport to their entrance into the mansion where God and Christ are. I with you and you with me. I cannot go there without his consent. He holds the keys of that kingdom for the last dispensation."[723]

"Cursed are all those that shall lift up the heel against mine anointed, saith the Lord, and cry they have sinned when they have not sinned before me, saith the Lord, but have done that which was meet in mine eyes, and which I commanded them."[724]

"And they who do charge thee with transgression, their hope shall be blasted, and their prospects shall melt away as the hoar frost melteth before the burning rays of the rising sun."[725]

Joseph Smith declared, "I have a conscience void of offense toward God and toward all men. I shall die innocent."[726]

Joseph Smith said, "I do not the wrongs that I am charged with doing."[727]

Brigham Young said, "Who can justly say aught [or anything] against Joseph Smith? I was as well acquainted with him, as any man. I do not believe his father and mother knew him any better than I did. I do not think that a man lives on the earth that knew him any better than I did; and I am bold to say, Jesus Christ excepted, no better man ever lived or does live upon this earth. I am his witness."[728]

Brigham Young said, 'Who can justly say anything against Joseph Smith. I was as well acquainted with him as any man. I don't believe his father and mother knew him any better than I did. I don't think a man lives on the earth that knows him any better than I did. And I am bold to say Jesus Christ accepted no better man who ever lived or does now live upon this earth. I am his witness.'[729]

---

[723] Young, Brigham, Journal of Discourses, 7:289.

[724] Doctrine & Covenants 121:16

[725] Doctrine & Covenants 121:11

[726] Doctrine & Covenants 135:4

[727] Smith, Joseph, Teachings of the Presidents of the Church: Joseph Smith (2011), p. 522.

[728] Young, Brigham, Journal of Discourses, 9:332

[729] Young, Brigham, Journal of Discourses, 9:332. See also Joseph Smith, Teachings of the Presidents of the Church: Joseph Smith, p. 24; also quoted in Gordon B. Hinckley, "The Lengthened Shadow of the Hand of God," Ensign, May 1987, p. 53-54.

"Joseph Smith, the Prophet and Seer of the Lord, has done more, save Jesus only, for the salvation of men in this world, than any other man that ever lived in it."[730]

Boyd K. Packer said, "I know Joseph Smith was a mighty prophet, seer and revelator, with the exception of Jesus Christ, he is the greatest being who ever walked the face of this earth."[731]

Joseph Smith taught, "Prophets, priests and kings have looked forward with joyful anticipation to the day in which we live, and fired with heavenly and joyful anticipations, they have sung and written and prophesied of this our day."[732]

Joseph Smith said, "All saints! Profit by this important key, that in all your trials, troubles, temptations, afflictions, bonds, imprisonments and death, see to it that you do not betray Jesus Christ, that you do not betray the brethren, that you do not betray the revelations of God, whether in the Bible, the Book of Mormon or Doctrine & Covenants. In all your kicking and floundering, see to it that you do not this thing, lest innocent blood be found on your skirts and you go down to hell."[733]

Joseph Smith said, "'You don't know me. You never knew my heart. No man knows my history. I cannot tell it. I shall never undertake it. I never did harm any man since I was born in the world. I never think any evil, nor do anything to the harm of my fellow men. When I am called by the trump of the archangel and weighed in the balance, you will all know me then. I add no more. God bless you all."[734]

Brigham Young said, "Joseph Smith Jr. will again be on this earth, dictating plans and calling forth his brethren, and he will never cease his operations under the directions of the Son of God, until the last ones of the children of men are saved that can be, from Adam until now."[735]

"Come on! ye prosecutors! ye false swearers! All hell, boil over! Ye burning mountains, roll down your lava! for I will come out on the top at last. I have more to boast of than ever any man had. I am the only man that has ever been able to keep a whole church together since the days of Adam. A large majority of the whole have stood by me. Neither Paul, John, Peter, nor Jesus ever did it. I boast that no man ever

---

[730] Doctrine & Covenants 135:3

[731] Packer, Boyd K., Mine Errand From the Lord, p. 387.

[732] Smith, Joseph, Teachings of the Presidents of the Church: Joseph Smith, p. 513

[733] Smith, Joseph, Teachings of the Prophet Joseph Smith, comp. by Joseph Fielding Smith, p. 156.

[734] Smith, Joseph, Teachings of the Presidents of the Church: Joseph Smith, p. 525.

[735] Young, Brigham, Journal of Discourses, 7:289-290.

did such a work as I. The followers of Jesus ran away from Him; but the Latter-day Saints never ran away from me yet."[736]

In case one thinks that this is a teaching of the distant past, let me share a conversation I had with two local LDS missionaries. I asked them toward the end of our discussion what they believed will happen to a person like me, who believes everything Jesus said, has put my faith in his death and resurrection for my salvation but doesn't believe what Joseph Smith taught, on the day of judgment. The missionaries answered, "It is a package. If you don't believe in Joseph Smith, you can't fully benefit from the atonement of Jesus."

This mindset of complete and total loyalty toward a central leader or founder is not unique to Mormons. One will find this same mindset among most, if not all, of the groups we have discussed in this book. My prayer is that all those who read these words will join me in prayerfully discerning those who God has brought into our lives specifically to share the gospel with them, and inviting them into the most wonderful relationship and adventure this life, and eternity has to offer.

---

[736] History of the Church, vol. 6, p. 408-409

TOPICAL INDEX

Scripture Index

Science and Health

Made in the USA
Lexington, KY
12 June 2018